Topics in Applied Physics   Volume 41

Topics in Applied Physics Founded by Helmut K. V. Lotsch

The Computer
in Optical Research

Methods and Applications

Edited by B. R. Frieden

With Contributions by
R. Barakat   W. J. Dallas   B. R. Frieden   L. Mertz
R. J. Pegis   A. K. Rigler

With 92 Figures

Springer-Verlag Berlin Heidelberg New York 1980

Professor *B. Roy Frieden*, PhD

Optical Sciences Center, University of Arizona, Tucson, AZ 85721, USA

ISBN 3-540-10119-5 Springer-Verlag Berlin Heidelberg New York
ISBN 0-387-10119-5 Springer-Verlag New York Heidelberg Berlin

Library of Congress Cataloging in Publication Data. Main entry under title: The Computer in optical research methods and application. (Topics in applied physics; v. 41) Bibliography: p. Includes index. 1. Optics–Data processing. I. Frieden, B. Roy, 1936–. II. Barakat, Richard, 1931–. QC355.2.C65   535.028′54   80-15930

© by Springer-Verlag Berlin Heidelberg 1980
Printed in Germany

The use of registered names, trademarks, etc. in this publication does not imply, even in the absence of a specific statement, that such names are exempt from the relevant protective laws and regulations and therefore free for general use.

Monophoto typesetting, offset printing and bookbinding: Brühlsche Universitätsdruckerei, Giessen
2153/3130-543210

Preface

The ability to measure, and to *compute* with speed and accuracy, are hallmark requirements of the physical or exact sciences. Since its introduction in the late 1950 s, the digital computer has furthered the latter ability beyond man's wildest dreams. Today, the computer has uses ranging from mildly useful, to vital, in just about every field of research in optics. Any institution that calls itself a research facility in optics must have a large computer available.

The fields of optics that have particularly profited from the computer's existence are lens and thin film design, image processing and evaluation, and atmospheric optics including remote sensing. The general approaches to problem solving upon a computer fall into three overall areas: *deterministic* or direct calculation methods, as in the evaluation of diffraction integrals; *statistical* methods, as in the Monte Carlo calculation of photographic emulsion characteristics; and *iterative* methods, as in recursive image processing or in optimization problems of lens design. It is remarkable that all these methods stem from the computer's single, only real ability: to add very rapidly.

Of course, as is known to long-term "cybernauts", the machine does have its drawbacks. Computer terminal rooms are notoriously dull places, monopolized by the chatter of the high-speed printer and the visual blight of old Fortran manuals. Worse yet, the computer is the ultimate in harsh taskmasters, requiring a perfect program, with its own, sometimes unpredictable meaning of the word "perfect". Computer programmers often suffer the effects of years of interaction with a rigid and demanding machine. Nevertheless, computer based research has some definite advantages, a not insignificant one being *non*-reliance upon the purchase, delivery, and correct operation of expensive and complicated laboratory equipment. Many a research project and Ph. D. dissertation have foundered on the long time delays caused by these problems.

The aim of this volume is to bring together as wide and representative a scope of problem-solving techniques as can fit within the confines of a modest-sized text. Applications of the techniques to important problems in optics have been emphasized as well. We hope, in this way, to introduce use of "the machine" to newcomers in optics, and to encourage its wider use among even experienced cybernauts.

The following general areas of research techniques are covered. Chapter 1 is an overall survey of computer developments in optics, somewhat from a historical viewpoint, and with a survey of the other chapters. Chapter 2 treats modern methods of computing diffraction integrals. Chapter 3 introduces and develops probabilistic and statistical methods of analysis. Chapter 4 covers optimization techniques, and especially as they apply to lens and thin film design. Chapter 5 offers an introduction to computer uses in optical astronomy. And Chapter 6 surveys the field of computer-generated holograms.

I would like to thank Dr. Robert E. Hopkins of the University of Rochester for first introducing me to computer based research, and guiding my early career when it so acutely needed guidance.

I would also like to thank Dr. Helmut Lotsch for first suggesting the need for this kind of text. Many thanks are due the authors of the different chapters for their kindness in agreeing to contribute to the book, for their extreme kindness in actually carrying through with the promise, and finally, for their perseverence in meeting the various deadlines and revising and updating where these were necessary.

Tucson, Arizona
August, 1980
B. Roy Frieden

Contents

Contributors

Barakat, Richard
Aiken Computation Laboratory, Division of Applied Sciences,
Harvard University, Cambridge, MA 02138, USA

Dallas, William John
Philips GmbH, Forschungslaboratorium Hamburg, Vogt-Kölln-Str. 30,
D-2000 Hamburg 54

Frieden, B. Roy
Optical Sciences Center, University of Arizona,
Tucson, AZ 85721, USA

Mertz, Lawrence
Lockheed Palo Alto Research Laboratories, 3251 Hanover Street,
Palo Alto, CA 94304, USA

Pegis, Richard John
34 Argyle Street, Rochester, NY 14607, USA

Rigler, A. Kellam
Mathematics Computer Science Building, University of Missouri – Rolla,
Rolla, MO 65401, USA

1. Introduction

B. R. Frieden

With 15 Figures

The digital computer is today the most widely used tool of research in optics. It is no longer true that optics, the study of light, actually requires *observation* of light. In many areas of research, it is sufficient to observe *numbers* instead, particularly those that stream out of the high-speed digital printers at such a stupefying rate [1].

The impact of the computer has effected many important changes in optical research. First, we might consider the impact on personnel, i.e., specifically *who* does the research. Optics has become a haven for applied mathematicians, occupationally displaced physicists, and computer programmers. The ability to program numerically sound algorithms for computing optical effects has largely replaced the need for an extensive background in optics, per se. These people can literally start doing research in optics the week they are employed at an optical research facility (more on this later).

Second, the computer has revitalized certain fields of research, such as lens design, optical testing, and medical optics, and has created new fields of its own, such as Monte Carlo (and other statistical) techniques in optics, computational optics, digital image processing, and computer-generated holography. The result has been a distinct contribution to the prodigious growth that optics has been enjoying. Graduating students with advanced degrees in the subject do not have trouble finding good jobs, even nowadays.

Third, we might consider the feedback effect of optics, and the other hard sciences, on computer manufacturers. The demand for ever-faster and larger-memoried computers has spurred the manufacturers onward at a dizzying pace. A generation ago, an engineer could be recognized by an ever-ready slide rule hanging from his belt (a phallic symbol if there ever was one). Today, you are likely to see a pocket-sized electronic calculator in exactly the same place. Moreover, the three digits of accuracy in the slide rule have been replaced by eight or more in today's calculator, and, further, at no real increase in cost, when dollar depreciation is taken into account.

Digital computers range in size from the pocket calculator to the desk-top "mini" computer, to the full-sized computer found at computer centers, to computers linked in a network. It is upon the full-sized computers that most optical programming and research have been performed although the advent of

---

1 This leads one to speculate on a) the fraction of these numbers that are actually looked at, and b) whether such research would continue even if photons went out of existence.

cheap storage media, such as the "floppy disc", is making the minicomputer more competitive. What the future holds for this explosively developing field is anybody's guess, but the present trend seems to be toward greater use of minicomputers, which, in fact, are being bought and used *at home* by many scientists.

The aims of this volume are twofold: a) to introduce the reader to *digital methods*, of both a basic and advanced nature, which are today being used in optical research; and b) to bring the reader up to date on computer *applications* in many areas of optics. Aim a) might be considered as basically didactic, while b) corresponds to a survey of research in the various fields. For these purposes, we have sought contributions from some of the foremost researchers in the fields of numerical analysis, statistical analysis, lens and thin-film design algorithms, computer-generated holography, and astronomical optics. Although it would be natural to include medical optics as well, this has not been done because an entire volume needs to be prepared on this subject. Instead, we have prepared below some *introductory* material on medical optics.

Which brings us to the aim of this chapter – to supplement the later chapters with introductory and/or advanced material, and to provide a synopsis where one would appear useful. A personal perspective will be taken, so that the coverage will be uneven; such are the liberties permitted editors. The anecdotes and comments cited below are vignettes that made an impression on this author while he was "growing up" in the field, largely at the Institute of Optics of the University of Rochester. We hope these anecdotes will be taken in the same spirit of good-natured nostalgia that we feel for them.

1.1 Lens Design

All fields of optics have been advanced by computer-based research, but probably the one field which has been most profoundly affected is that of lens design. Today's lens designer spends most of his creative time interacting with a computer. Probably no other field of optics is so dependent upon the machine. This is no coincidence.

Practically from the outset, when digital computers became commercially available in the early 1950s, lens designers with foresight (see, e.g., [1.1]) were trying to automate the calculation of the basic aberrations. Such automated calculation replaced hours of ray-trace drudgery using manual desk-top calculators and, before that, the even more primitive logarithmic tables.

Progress, however, was not simple and straightforward. The human element came into play in the form of jealousy of the capabilities of the machine, with accompanying feelings of job insecurity, etc. (One might term this the "John Henry" complex, because the symptoms are similar to those found in the folk song about railroad man John Henry versus the automatic stake driver.) This situation was assayed by *Hopkins* and *Spencer* [1.2]:

"When computing machines came into being after the war, they caused quite a stir among optical people. By and large, we underestimated the great potential in machines and what they could do for us. We felt jealous of the tricks of our trade and resented the thought of simple-minded machines doing what we could do.

On the other side of the fence, the computer people went overboard and claimed the machine could do everything, and that we might as well discard all the old methods and tackle the problem from a completely new approach."

The latter remark probably refers to attitudes and statements made by more computer-oriented people of the day, who envisioned (in the extreme) a *complete takeover* of the design problem by the machine, for example, by merely telling the computer what first- and third-order requirements to make and what number and indices of optical surfaces to assume. The *input* design would be pure optical flats! Hence, only a primitive knowledge of optical design would be needed. The following answer to *Hopkins* and *Spencer*, by *Feder* [1.3], seems to typify this attitude:

"The removal of drudgery and the stimulation of creative thinking in optical design has been stressed by Hopkins and Spencer. Naturally I am in agreement with them on the desirability of stimulating thinking among lens designers, and only would suggest going a little further and, by making the lens design problem a numerical exercise for the computer, *freeing these valuable individuals* [italics by editor] for even more important problems."

The worst fears of the John Henry complex were being realized, or so it seemed. The lens design problem would be reduced to a mere machine exercise in seeking the minimum in a merit function.

This view contrasted with that of *Hopkins* who felt that the new computers should be used in an *interactive* way, by trained optical designers who would judge each step of the design process and bring into play their past experience and design talents.

Since those days, a marriage of the two views has taken place. The computer has cranked out new and unexpected designs, even with its simplistic goal of minimizing a merit function. However, it is safe to say that the *best* designs do not typically arise out of an initial assumption of optical flats. A basic knowledge of optical design is a real advantage, if a truly optimum design is being sought.

Chapter 4, by *Rigler* and *Pegis*, is a comprehensive review of the more effective optimization procedures taken by computers, given a set of performance requirements and an initial design input. An interesting historical view of developments is also given.

1.2 Thin Films

I used to work with *R. J. Pegis* at Bausch and Lomb, and can relate an interesting tale of computer versus man that runs counter to usual developments: this time the man won. The thin film multilayer design problem was being computer automated concurrent with the lens design problem, when a famous English opticist (who shall remain nameless) published the following statement:

"There is, *of course* [italics by editor], no synthetic design model which will enable a multilayer to be designed with specified properties. However, trial and error methods are used and also some devices for particular cases are known."

This statement was taken by many American workers to mean that *in principle* no exact synthesis approach was possible and that, therefore, the computer would have to be used in the same kind of trial-and-error mode of operation as in lens design. What a triumph it was, then, when an exact synthesis approach was later invented, *in the face of these attitudes*, by *Pegis* [1.4a].

Unfortunately, this exact approach has an important drawback: the refractive indices of the film multilayers are output *variables* and may not be fixed by the user to realistic values. Values such as 6, 18, 36, etc., are commonly required as a result. Hence, most of the output designs from the Pegis synthesis algorithm are physically unrealizable. On the other hand, they do provide the designer with physical insight into what his required transmittance curve demands of a multilayer stack and, perhaps, the extent to which his demands are unrealistic. Also, synthesis designs can be used to suggest *initial* designs for input into a "relaxation" design program, such as one described by *Baumeister* [1.4b].

Computer-oriented people who enjoy working with the fast Fourier transform (FFT) algorithm (see Chaps. 2 and 3) would appreciate particularly the design approach of *Delano* [1.4c]. For a required reflectance versus wave number curve $\varrho(\mu)$, the approximate multilayer design expressed as continuous refractive index U versus optical thickness p (at normal incidence) obeys

$$U(p) = \exp\left[-2\int_0^p dp' \int_{-\infty}^{\infty} d\mu \varrho(\mu) e^{2\pi i \mu p'} \right].$$

This relation is true in the limit of weak reflectance from each multilayer, and hence may be used directly to attack problems requiring antireflection coatings. Alternatively, it may be viewed as a first cut at a design, which is to be refined by a relaxation program [1.4b].

The most recent use of FFT methods to effect thin film design is by *Dobrowolski* and *Lowe* [1.4d]. This method is closely related to Delano's.

1.3 Image Analysis

Historically, the second significant use of the computer in optics seems to be that of image analysis, i.e., calculation of image structure due to diffraction and aberrations, both on-axis and off-axis. Prior to the computer work of *Barakat* (see [1.5–7] for example) not much was known quantitatively about image structure. Various expansions *existed* for its evaluation, but not many people bothered to use them; it was too tedious.

By the use of advanced methods of numerical integration, many of which are treated in Chap. 2, *Barakat* established computer programs for actually computing diffraction images. A synopsis of Chap. 2 follows.

1.3.1 Synopsis of Chapter 2

Chapter 2 is an introduction to computer methods for the evaluation of optical image structure. Here we come face to face with the problem of numerical evaluation of *oscillatory* integrals, a direct outcome of the wave nature of diffraction. As the author notes, although the utilization of a computer is necessary for the evaluation of such integrals, it is by no means sufficient. Knowledge of what algorithms fit a particular problem is an absolute necessity.

Among the algorithms studied are the trapezoidal and Simpson's rules, which are surprisingly useful given their simplicity; Romberg's quadrature, which is becoming a widely used tool despite its controversy; Gauss quadrature, with its error advantage; Euler's method of speeding the convergence of alternating series; application of Euler's method to the evaluation of Fourier and Hankel transforms, which may be cast as an alternating series; a transformation which simplifies evaluation of the Hilbert transform by making the singularity and its neighborhood contribute negligibly to the integral; and a general approach to the problem of evaluating diffraction integrals at large argument, followed by many specific examples.

The author then briefly reviews the basics of diffraction image formation, including definition of point amplitude and point spread functions, optical transfer function, and the essential relation between optical transfer function and pupil function. The basic polynomial aberrations are defined through fifth order, and the Zernicke method of defining aberrations is also addressed briefly. This review of image formation is basically addressed to people with a background in image theory, so as to identify the author's notation and terminology. The underlying aim is to identify those integrals which will later be evaluated by numerical quadrature formulas described above.

The first formula so considered is the expression for the optical transfer function as the autocorrelation of an input pupil function. This is evaluated by a double Gauss-quadrature formula, i.e., a Gauss quadrature separately for each of the x and y coordinate directions. This result is central to all that follows, since the author's orientation is to express all other quality factors as integrals over the transfer function.

The encircled energy function, for a given radius within the point spread function, is considered next. This is an important merit function for optical quality. The author analytically shows how the encircled energy function may be expressed as a finite Hankel transform of the angle-averaged optical transfer function. This expression lends itself to evaluation because a) it has a finite domain of integration, for any input radius, and because b) the optical transfer function may be regarded as already evaluated by methods described above, in a stepwise computer program for computing quality criteria in sequence.

An alternative approach to computing the encircled energy function is to directly express it in terms of the pupil function. This is conveniently done when the aperture is circular and the aberrations rotationally symmetric. The result is a double integral over the pupil times itself, which again may be evaluated by double Gauss-quadrature formula. Analogous expressions for a slit pupil are also developed. Asymptotic formulas for small and large argument are developed, for both the circular pupil and slit pupil cases.

The author next turns to evaluating the images of extended non-coherent objects. Convolution and transfer theorems are derived for general objects. These general results are applied to evaluation of the images of the most widely used test objects for measuring image quality: the slit, edge, sinusoid, square wave, and disc. We highlight some of his findings here.

A handy expression is derived relating the line spread function to an integral over the transfer function. An asymptotic expansion for large argument shows that the *line spread falls off quadratically with argument for all optical systems.*

The "edge spread function" (or image of an edge object) is defined and related to the transfer function. An interesting result is that at the geometrical edge position the image value is one-half maximum, *only if the imaginary part of the transfer function is zero.*

Finitely extended sinusoidal objects are considered. The author discusses the arbitrary nature of the meaning of "image quality" in such an image. Square-wave objects have to be considered because of their more frequent use than the difficult-to-manufacture sinusoids. Expressions relating square-wave images to integrals over the transfer function are developed and discussed. Finite-extended square-wave objects are also analyzed. The author shows precisely why truncated sinusoids and square waves are imaged nearly identically in the medium- and high-frequency regions.

The final object under consideration is the uniform disc. Again, its image is expressed as an integral involving the transfer function. For small argument this expression shows that a small uniform disc has an image that is indistinguishable from that of a point source, a well-known effect. Also, at large argument this expression shows that the intensity drops off as the inverse *third* power of argument (recall, by comparison, that the line spread function falls off inversely as the second power of argument).

Although he had already considered methods of numerical integration, the author sets aside a new section for remarks on the most widely used numerical integration scheme used in optics: the FFT algorithm. His remarks devolve from the fact that the FFT method is used in optics to approximate a continuous Fourier integral, and that the degree of approximation is as crude as is possible for an integral: a zeroth order, or rectangular rule, quadrature formula. The question arises as to whether a series of weights might be used to modify the (implied) unit weights ordinarily used in FFT. For example, Simpson's rule weights could be used. As a restriction on such weighting schemes, the phase part of the FFT operation cannot be weighted because it has the *fixed form* $2\pi imn/N$ (in one dimension).

The author applies an integration method of Filon to obtain an optimum set of weights. Filon's method consists in fitting parabolic arcs to the function to be transformed, but *not* to the cosine or sine part of the integrand (the latter satisfies the restriction mentioned above). This results in a useful set of weights for the input function to the FFT.

A class of rectangular-rule quadrature formulas which are perfect(!) approximations of their corresponding integrals are the sampling theorems. These are integrals of *band-limited functions*, which are common in optics and which have the special property of being *exactly* representable as a weighted sum of discrete values of the functions themselves. Aside from computational significance, this also has experimental significance. The functions are often experimental observables (e.g., the line spread function). This allows quality factors for existing optical systems to be accurately measured.

The author takes up this subject, deriving first the Whittaker-Shannon sampling theorem, then showing how to represent the Fourier integral transform of the line spread function (which is the transfer function) by a discrete Fourier series whose coefficients are point samples of the line spread function. Similar expressions are developed for the encircled energy function, and for the edge spread function. Sampled values of the line spread are inputs to these expressions as well. We emphasize that these expressions have no computational error whatsoever. The only real source of error, in their use, is possible experimental error in the input line spread function values.

The case of two dimensions is a direct carryover, except for the special case of rotational symmetry. The author shows that a band-limited, rotationally symmetric function may be expressed in terms of sampled values of itself, but the samples are not equally spaced as in one dimension. In this manner, for a rotationally symmetric pupil of unit radius, the optical transfer function is expressed as a discrete Hankel series (in place of the integral) defined by samples of the point spread function. The samples are at radius values equal to the zeros of the zero-order Bessel function.

The method is extended to the evaluation of integrals involving the transfer function. For example, Linfoot's quality factor F is shown representable as a series of weighted sampled values of the *square* of the line spread function.

The extensive numerical work of *Barakat* led to a better understanding of what optical images really are, how seriously they are affected by various aberrations, how the various quality criteria (point, line, and edge spread; encircled energy; transfer function F) interrelate, how to correctly sample an image, etc. This work is also the forerunner of today's image processing work, which uses sampling and filtering principles that trace back to it.

Finally, his work set two important precedents. It is among the first publishable optical research done entirely on the digital computer, and it showed that an instrument existed (the computer) that allows people with little or no optical training to do publishable research in optics.

The last point is particularly important from the standpoint of encouraging new people to enter the field. What better impetus is there for a research-oriented person than the potential to do research almost as soon as he enters a new field? This author, for one, profited from the effect, as do many of today's new students at the Optical Sciences Center. Of course, optics is not alone in benefitting in this way from the computer's existence.

1.4 Computer Simulation

Perhaps the most widely used property of the computer is its ability to simulate experimental conditions. The motivation behind simulation work is usually one or more of the following: a) to *predict* a physical effect on the basis of a reasonable (and usually simple) model; b) the converse, to test out a theory or model of why such and such a physical effect is *observed*; c) to test an *estimation technique*; d) to extend a *gedanken experiment* to its ultimate limit where it yields quantitative, not merely theoretical, results; and e) to *avoid buying* costly optical equipment simply for the purpose of testing out a proposed optical configuration or test procedure.

Simulation can be of either a deterministic or a probabilistic form. (The latter is called a "Monte Carlo" calculation; see Chap. 3.) In the deterministic form, every physical effect from start to finish (or, input to output) is known precisely, usually by some formula. An example of *deterministic* simulation is the work done by *Fox* and *Li* [1.8a] in simulating the lasing effect within an optical resonator. This was accomplished by repeated use of Fresnel's diffraction

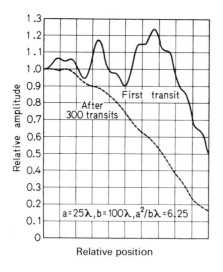

Fig. 1.1. Relative amplitude distribution of field intensity for infinite strip mirrors. The initially launched wave has a uniform distribution [1.8a]

formula at each endplate reflection of the laser wave. The results clearly showed convergence toward the theoretical, *functional* form for the mode shapes, which derive from an equilibrium condition for the wave. Hence, the theoretical equilibrium model was verified. Figure 1.1 shows the transition in wave amplitude from the first transit of the wave to the 300th. The amplitude is approaching the theoretical Gaussian shape that well approximates the zero-order mode (in the limit of an infinitely large Fresnel number [1.8b]). This actually is a demonstration of the "central limit theorem" of statistics as well (see Chap. 3).

1.5 Computer-Generated Holograms

Another, and famous, deterministic simulation is the computer-generated hologram. This technique produces an artificial, binary hologram by ingenious use of a computer plotter, followed by (extreme) photo reduction. The plotter paper is subdivided into cells, each cell representing a pixel in the hologram. Both intensity and phase have to be coded into each cell. Intensity can be established by the *height* of a constant-width black line within the cell. Phase is defined by the position within the cell of the line. When photographically reduced to a transparency and illuminated with coherent light, an off-axis hologram image is produced. Figure 1.2a shows a hologram that produces the image ICO in Fig. 1.2b; see *Lohmann* and *Paris* [1.9a].

Naturally the procedure is not limited to producing letters of the alphabet. In principle, any desired image can be artificially constructed, even three-dimensional ones. A new art form, based on computer-generated holography, is

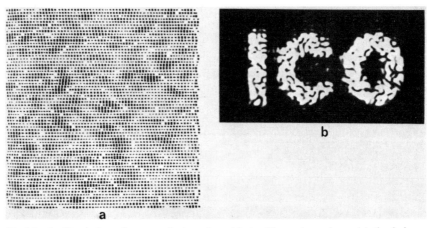

Fig 1.2.a, b. Simulation of a ground glass, i.e., object with random phase: (**a**) the hologram; (**b**) the image [1.9 a]

an intriguing possibility. So is the possibility of a new form of three-dimensional display. The state of the art in producing computer-generated holograms is described in Chap. 6 by Dallas.

1.6 Monte Carlo Simulations

The other kind of simulation, the Monte Carlo or probabilistic approach, is of more recent vintage in optics. This technique was widely used in nuclear physics and dates back to atom bomb development in 1944. It supposes every possible event that can take place during the experiment to be describable by a *known probability* law (rather than a known deterministic law). Typical events are then constructed on the computer, by random sampling from the probability laws, and in this way a histogram of "experimental" outputs is constructed. This histogram can then be compared with the *observed* histogram of events for the actual experiment, to decide whether the assumed probability laws are correct. Or, alternatively, the laws can be assumed correct and the histogram used to *predict* outcomes of the experiment. Specific examples best clarify these points, and these are given in Sect. 3.4.3. There, the Monte Carlo calculation is more fully discussed and developed, using probability theory.

1.7 Statistical Methods

The Monte Carlo approach is but one among many potential statistical techniques for solving statistical problems in optics. Many of these techniques, e.g., linear regression, are typically applied to large data sets, and so depend heavily upon the digital computer for their application. Some fields of research which have recently undergone statistical investigation are photographic theory, atmospheric turbulence [1.36, 37], laser speckle [1.19], image detection, and image restoration. We believe this is but the tip of the iceberg regarding potential applications of statistical methods, since a) at this time, most optical workers simply do not know the methods, b) the methods have been successfully applied in many other, nonoptical fields with great success (notably psychology and sociology, where the great number of unknown phenomena make ideal candidates for statistical methods), c) first applications in optics have been highly successful, and d) to remedy the lack of knowledge about methods, optical workers are finally being educated and exposed to the methods (viz., this book).

Regarding point d), we have tried to further the process by devoting a section of the book, Chap. 3, to methods of probability and statistics. The subject is developed from its basis in Kolmogoroff's three axioms, through the various statistical tests (chi square, t, and F test). The digital computer is often needed for actual application of these tests to real data, and we often discuss this aspect of the problem. To help in understanding the theory, numerous examples and applications to problem solving are given, all of which are from fields of optics. These applications are also meant to show the reader where important statistical research in optics has already been done, and the novel *kinds of answers* it provides. Phrases such as "confidence at the 5% level", "significant experimental parameters", and "significant data" are not the kinds of answers people in the hard sciences are used to hearing (but ought to be). To our knowledge, Chap. 3 is the first exposition on probability and statistics written specifically from the optical perspective and for the optical community.

1.8 Optical Testing

This field is one of the more recent to benefit from the computer. Until recently, optical surfaces could be tested for deformation errors no smaller than about rms $\lambda/8$, except in special cases. However, the advent of the large storage computer coupled with the high-speed microdensitometer, some of which can collect interferometric data with 1 or 2 μm accuracy at speeds of about 4000 μm/s, now permits rms errors of between $\lambda/20$ and $\lambda/50$ to be rather routinely tested for. Hence, a gain in sensitivity of about 4 : 1 has been realized. Even geometrical tests, such as the Hartmann ray-trace procedure, have been made enormously more effective by these computer-microdensitometer developments. Progress in the field of optical testing has been summarized rather recently [1.9b], and the subject will not be further elaborated upon here.

1.9 Medical Optics

The computer has had a strong impact on the field of medical picture diagnostics. It has enabled physicians to obtain views of the body never before possible, as in reconstruction tomography and in coded-source imagery. These methods require a computer to unscramble a coded image into a recognizable picture.

The computer also allows enhancement of the features of conventional pictures, such as x-ray images and thermographs. Digital filtering and pattern recognition methods are used for these purposes.

For a survey of the state of the art of reconstruction tomography, see *Ter-Pogossian* et al. [1.10a] and *Herman* [1.10b]; also see *Barrett* et al. [1.11] for an introduction to coded-source imagery and *Kruger* et al. [1.12] for a method of enhancing chest x-ray images for the detection of lung disease.

Reconstruction tomography, in particular, is an explosively developing subject. Because tomographic images can now be made of portions of the body that were formerly inaccessible to live viewing, such as the brain interior, they have caused great excitement in the medical community. The machines that

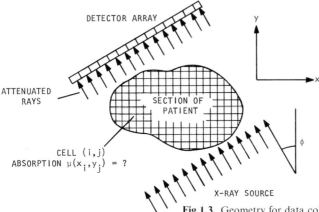

DETECTOR ARRAY

y

x

ATTENUATED
RAYS

SECTION OF
PATIENT

CELL (i,j)
ABSORPTION $\mu(x_i, y_j)$ = ?

ϕ

X-RAY SOURCE

Fig 1.3. Geometry for data collection at one azimuth ϕ

perform this task, the so-called "computerized tomographic (C.T.) scanners", cost up to $\$10^6$, are decidedly big business, and have become somewhat controversial because they have contributed significantly to rising hospital costs. The scanners also use x-rays as the physical means of picking up image data from the patient, and this is of growing concern because of the potential for causing cencer. The reader may be interested, then, in an introduction to the subject of reconstruction tomography. We use one approach and the notation from [1.13].

As shown in Fig. 1.3, a patient is irradiated by a large number of parallel x-ray beams (on the order of 100) in a plane. The energy in each of these is known both at the sources and at the receivers. The logarithm of the ratio of output energy to input energy for each ray gives the total integrated absorption loss, along the path of the ray, due to the subject. The aim is to display the point-by-point absorption loss $\mu(x_i, y_j)$ throughout the plane section defined by the rays within the subject. These numbers would form a picture of the different tissues within the plane, based on their absorptivity to x-rays; luckily, different tissues have significantly different absorptivities.

How can this be done when only the *integrated* absorptances are known? There are (by now) many methods of accomplishing this trick; e.g., see the summary in *Barrett* and *Swindell* [1.13].

These are based on the data collected when the direction common to the rays in Fig. 1.3 is altered stepwise by amounts $\Delta\phi$ in azimuthal angle, until the subject has been irradiated from all directions. At each azimuthal step, a new set of integrated absorptances is measured. Obviously, each change in direction of the rays causes the individual absorptances $\mu(x, y)$ to contribute to each data set in a slightly different way (specifically, each contributes to a different ray sum); this implies that they contribute in a linearly independent way to the data set made up of all the ray sums, and hence stand a chance of being solved for in a system of linear equations. One such method of solution is outlined next. It is

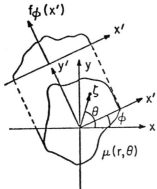

Fig 1.4. Relation between fixed and rotated coordinate systems [1.13]

called the "filtered back-projection" method. This approach is particularly wellsuited to computer use because it is based upon Fourier transform operations, which are very rapidly taken by use of the FFT algorithm; see Chaps. 2 and 3, and also *Cooley* and *Tukey* [1.14].

As shown in Fig. 1.4, regard XY as the coordinate system for a fixed patient and $X'Y'$ as the rotated coordinate system for any azimuth ϕ taken by the parallel rays. These point in the Y' direction. At any fixed ϕ, the absorptance data is therefore one-dimensional in X'; call it $f_\phi(x')$. As we had before,

$$f_\phi(x') = \int_{-\infty}^{\infty} dy'\, \mu(x', y') \tag{1.1}$$

is the total integrated absorptance along the ray at coordinate x' when the common ray direction is ϕ. Let (r, θ) be the polar coordinates corresponding to a point (x, y) in the subject. From Fig. 1.4

$$x' = r \cos(\theta - \phi). \tag{1.2}$$

Now at fixed ϕ the data $f_\phi(x')$ represent only one-dimensional information. However, from these data a highly redundant *two*-dimensional picture $b(x', y')$ may be formed,

$$b(x', y') \equiv f_\phi(x'). \tag{1.3}$$

Obviously at any x', the picture b has the same intensity regardless of y'. Hence, it is merely a smeared-out-in-y' version of the one-dimensional signal $f_\phi(x')$. We alternatively can express b in the XY frame, as

$$b(x, y) = b(r, \theta) = f_\phi[r \cos(\theta - \phi)]. \tag{1.4}$$

This entity b is called the "back-projection" image, at angle ϕ. Although b lacks *any* information in the y' direction, we may look for some simple combination of b curves from different ϕ directions that might work to effect *real* structure in the y' direction. The first and simplest thought to come to mind is direct averaging over ϕ. This is called the "summation image",

$$g(x, y) - g(r, \theta) = \pi^{-1} \int_0^\pi d\phi \, b(x', y')$$

$$= \pi^{-1} \int_0^\pi d\phi \, f_\phi[r \cos(\theta - \phi)] \tag{1.5}$$

by virtue of (1.3, 4). [Note: The range of ϕ integration is limited to 0 and π since any value of ϕ beyond π will cause rays to pass through identical (x, y) values, and hence produce the same data, as for an azimuth of $\phi - \pi$.]

The amazing thing is that $g(x, y)$ actually forms a picture of the object absorptance image $\mu(x, y)$. This may be shown as follows. Suppose the object $\mu(x, y)$ is purely a point absorber located at the origin,

$$\mu(x, y) = \delta(x)\,\delta(y) = \delta(x')\,\delta(y'). \tag{1.6}$$

The resulting summation image $g(x, y)$ will now represent the point spread function for this image reconstruction procedure. Call it $s_{rec}(x, y)$. Using (1.1, 5, 6),

$$s_{rec}(x, y) = \pi^{-1} \int_0^\pi d\phi \int_{-\infty}^\infty dy' \, \delta(y')\,\delta[r \cos(\theta - \phi)]$$

$$= \pi^{-1} \int_0^\pi d\phi \, \delta[r \cos(\theta - \phi)] \tag{1.7}$$

after integrating dy', or

$$s_{rec}(x, y) = (\pi r)^{-1} \int_0^\pi d\phi \, \delta[\cos(\theta - \phi)] \tag{1.8}$$

by the identity $\delta(ax) = |a|^{-1}\,\delta(x)$. Finally

$$s_{rec}(x, y) = (\pi r)^{-1} \tag{1.9}$$

since for any fixed θ there is one and only one azimuth ϕ within interval $(0, \pi)$ for which the argument of the delta function in (1.8) is zero. (That value is $\phi = \theta + \pi/2$ if $-\pi/2 < \theta < +\pi/2$; or $\phi = \theta - \pi/2$ if $+\pi/2 < \theta < +3\pi/2$.)

Next we note that the operation (1.5) upon data $f_\phi(x')$ is *linear*. This means that if the operation results in an image s_{rec} for one point object located at the

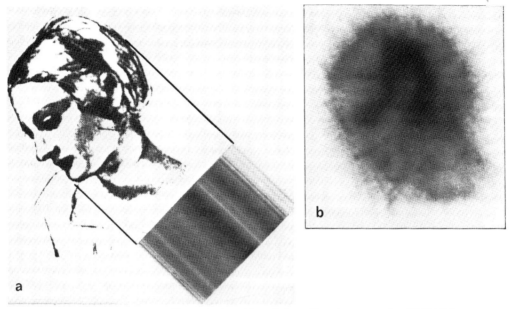

Fig. 1.5. An object and one of its projections (**a**), and the unfiltered reconstuction (**b**) [1.15b]

origin, it will result in a *superposition of displaced* images s_{rec} for an object which is a superposition of points; see, e.g., [1.15a]. The result is that the summation image $g(x, y)$ relates back to the object $\mu(x, y)$ through a convolution

$$g(x, y) = \mu(x, y) \otimes s_{rec}(x, y). \tag{1.10}$$

This shows that a) the summation image really is an image of the object μ, but that b) it suffers from $1/r$ type blur. The extreme steepness and narrowness of $1/r$ near the origin means that g will be a sharp version of μ. However, the extremely slow falloff of $1/r$ with r acts like a dc, or background haze, effect. The net effect is a sharp, but low-contrast picture. Figure 1.5a shows a biological object and one of its projections $b(x, y)$. Figure 1.5b shows the summation image g for this object.

Finally, it is possible to go one step further and improve the summation image g. Since, by (1.10) it suffers from a known, linear source of blur, that blur may be lessened by any number of restoring methods; see, e.g., the survey in *Frieden* [1.16]. The simplest approach is direct filtering of the $g(x, y)$ image with a filter whose response is linear with frequency. This follows from (1.10) whose Fourier transform (FT) yields

$$G(\omega_1, \omega_2) = M(\omega_1, \omega_2) \cdot 1/\pi\omega, \quad \omega \equiv (\omega_1^2 + \omega_2^2)^{1/2}. \tag{1.11}$$

G is the FT of g, M is the FT of μ, and $1/\pi\omega$ is the FT of s_{rec}. (ω_1, ω_2) are the $X - Y$ coordinates of spatial frequency. From (1.11), application of the filter $\pi\omega$ to the data G yields an estimate of the object M. This technique is called "filtered back-projection". Filtering methods of this type are discussed extensively and compared in [1.10].

1.10 Optical Astronomy

Optical astronomy is another field which has been strongly affected by computer developments. Even more so has been the field of *radio* astronomy, which practically owes its existence to the digital computer; see the review given in [1.17]. (We consider radio astronomy to lie outside the scope of this optical volume.) The field of digital optical astronomy is surveyed in Chap. 5 by Mertz, and we supplement his thoughts in greater detail here.

The overall area we address is image improvement by digital methods. Specifically, we shall describe methods of reducing the blurring effects of random atmospheric turbulence, i.e., "seeing" for both short-term exposure images and long-term ones. This includes recent work by *Labeyrie* and others [1.18–22]).

1.10.1 Short-Term Turbulence Methods

Anyone who has viewed a distant object through a telescope, especially if such viewing is over land and in the daytime, has seen the shimmering effect of atmospheric turbulence at work. This random effect is basically due to the breakup of an initially smooth and laminar flow of air into ever smaller-scale eddy currents. The breakup is usually initiated by rising heat. The random eddy currents cause correspondingly random fluctuations in local temperature. This, in turn, causes local fluctuations in the index of refraction of the air. The net effect is that an optical ray that enters the medium is randomly bent from side to side, causing the shimmering effect we see. This is alternatively described as a random optical phase, when a *wave* analysis is in use.

The time constant for random turbulence is usually on the order of 0.001 s. Hence, during time exposures of this duration (which can be effected by use of a fast motion picture camera) the random optical phase across a pupil is effectively "frozen", or unchanging. Pictures of this duration are called "short-term" exposure images. A typical short-term image of a single star is shown in Fig. 1.6. Turbulence has broken up the star image into randomly placed "speckles".

At the other extreme are time exposures on the order of 0.01 s or longer where the random phase in the pupil has changed so many times that it has effectively gone through all fluctuations typical of its distribution. The result is a well-defined point spread function smear. Since a major part of the pupil

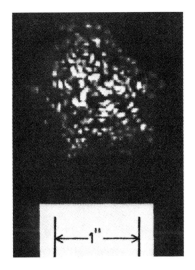

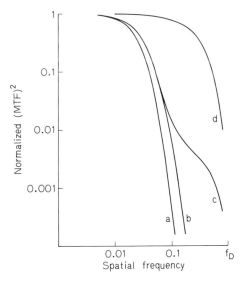

Fig. 1.6. Typical short-term image of a single star; turbulence has broken up the star image into random "speckles" [1.19]

Fig. 1.7. Theoretical system response functions for various data processing techniques: *a* is long-exposure imaging; *b*, short-exposure imaging; *c*, speckle interferometry; and *d*, ideal lens (no atmosphere). [1.26]

fluctuations is pure tilt (by one measure, 90%; see [1.23]), the long-term point spread function suffers from a great amount of image motion blur, and is much broader (on the order of 10 : 1 is common) than any of its short-term spread functions.

Hence, short-term images taken through the atmosphere are much sharper, albeit a lot more random, than are long-term images. It is not surprising, then, that the modulation transfer function (MTF) for short-term images is much broader than the MTF for long-term images. Hence, short-term images have the potential for carrying more information about the object scene than do long-term images.

In fact, the situation is even more extreme: the MTF for the long-term image falls off with frequency as nearly a Gaussian (see [1.24]), with usually a standard deviation much less than diffraction cutoff, whereas the average of the *short-term* modulus-*squared* MTF behaves at high frequencies as the diffraction-limited pupil! (see [1.25]).

The situation is shown graphically in Fig. 1.7 [1.26]. All curves are the modulus squared of an MTF, computed on the basis of assuming a Gaussian bivariate frequency distribution for phase within the optical pupil. Curve *a* is the modulus squared of the *long*-term average MTF; this cuts off the quickest. Curve *b* is the modulus squared of the *short*-term average MTF; this cuts off further out than the former curve, but is still not diffraction limited. Curve *c* is the average of the modulus squared short-term exposure MTF, the averaging going over many short exposures. *That curve c crosses over to meet with d at high frequencies is the diffraction-limited behavior mentioned above.* This is an unexpected and serendipitous effect. It suggests that an image processing method should be fashioned which takes the modulus squared of the image spectrum for many short-term images, and then averages them. Such an output image would contain object spatial frequencies (albeit strongly attenuated; see Fig. 1.7) right out to *diffraction-limited* cutoff!

This was, in fact, the approach taken by Labeyrie and co-workers; see [1.18]. Let the image spectrum due to a fixed object and any one short-term spread function be denoted as $I(\omega)$, ω the spatial frequency (we use one-dimensional notation for simplicity). Denote the object's spectrum as $O(\omega)$ and that short-term instantaneous transfer function as $S(\omega)$. Then for this single image

$$I(\omega) = S(\omega)O(\omega). \tag{1.12}$$

Let many such images (on the order of 100) of the one object be formed and Fourier transformed. Take the modulus squared of each, and then average over the set of images. The result is an experimental quantity $\langle |I(\omega)|^2 \rangle$ obeying

$$\langle |I(\omega)|^2 \rangle = \langle |S(\omega)|^2 \rangle |O(\omega)|^2. \tag{1.13}$$

Note that the *unaveraged* quantity $|O(\omega)|^2$ is present, since only one object is assumed present during the imagery. The averaged quantity on the right-hand side is the diffraction-limited curve *c* in Fig. 1.7. Since $\langle |S(\omega)|^2 \rangle$ cuts off at the diffraction limit, so does experimental quantity $\langle |I(\omega)|^2 \rangle$. In this way, diffraction-limited information is obtained about the unknown object $O(\omega)$.

In practice, the Fourier transforms may be taken either by the use of a standard coherent processor setup, or by digital use of the FFT (fast Fourier transform) algorithm. The coherent processor also allows the modulus-squared operation to be taken in analog fashion, by judicious choice of the photographic gamma in the (Fraunhofer) image plane.

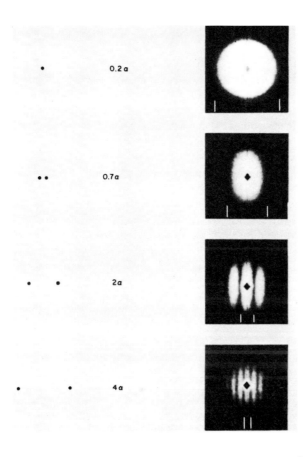

0.2 a

0.7 a

2 a

4 a

Fig. 1.8. A sequence of simulated binary-star measurements. The tick marks for the point object locate the diffraction limit, and for the binaries show the predicted location of the fringe zeros [1.27]

We can go one step further, noting that $\langle |S(\omega)|^2 \rangle$ is itself an experimental quantity; it is, in fact, the output $\langle |I(\omega)|^2 \rangle$ of the experiment when the object is a single star. Therefore, (1.13) may be directly solved for $|O(\omega)|^2$ through the inverse filtering operation

$$|O(\omega)|^2 = \langle |I(\omega)|^2 \rangle / \langle |S(\omega)|^2 \rangle . \qquad (1.14)$$

But, what does it mean to know $|O(\omega)|^2$? We really want to know the object $o(x)$. Now by the Wiener-Khintchine theorem

$$\int_{-\infty}^{\infty} d\omega |O(\omega)|^2 e^{-i\omega x} = \int_{-\infty}^{\infty} dx'\, o(x') o(x + x') . \qquad (1.15)$$

This says that knowledge of the modulus-squared spectrum $|O(\omega)|^2$ is equivalent to knowledge of the autocorrelation of the object. This leads us to ask whether knowledge of the autocorrelation can imply in some way knowledge of $o(x)$. This question is currently being worked on by various people, and we shall return to it below. It uses the capabilities of the large digital computers to their fullest.

The technique of forming the averages in (1.13) is called "speckle interferometry". The reason for the term "interferometry" will become apparent now. Suppose the unknown object is known to be a double star, of unknown separation $2a$. Then its spectrum $O(\omega) = K\cos(a\omega)$, K being a constant, and so $|O(\omega)|^2 = K^2\cos^2(a\omega)$. These are fringes of spacing π/a, resembling interference fringes. Then by (1.13) the experimental quantity $\langle|I(\omega)|^2\rangle$ will be a blurred version of this fringe system. However, the fringe period will remain π/a. Thus, *observation of the experimental image $\langle|I(\omega)|^2\rangle$ will enable the double star separation $2a$ to be determined.* Figure 1.8 (from [1.27]) shows laboratory simulations of these effects. Row D in this figure shows the output images $\langle|I(\omega)|^2\rangle$ due to averaging over 200 speckle images.

Note that for this problem, and for a whole class involving unknown objects which can be defined by a single parameter, it is not necessary to know $|O(\omega)|^2$. Direct observation of $\langle|I(\omega)|^2\rangle$ suffices. This is an advantage since, then, a) $\langle|S(\omega)|^2\rangle$ does not have to be estimated; and b) experimental data $\langle|I(\omega)|^2\rangle$ need not be inverse filtered in (1.14) to form $|O(\omega)|^2$. Inverse filtering is a hazardous operation at the high frequencies that define the fringe period.

1.10.2 Inverting the Autocorrelation Equation: Fienup's Approach

However, inverse filtering will have to be attempted if recent work of *Fienup* [1.21] is to be allowed to reach fruition. He attacked the problem, mentioned before, of attempting to estimate $o(x)$ from knowledge of the *modulus* of its Fourier transform $|O(\omega)|$. This is equivalent to estimating the phase $\phi(\omega)$ of $O(\omega)$. By the Wiener-Khintchine formula, (1.15), this problem is also equivalent to inverting the autocorrelation equation (1.15) for its unknown $o(x)$. Unfortunately, the problem is known to have a high multiplicity of solutions. Specifically, if the autocorrelation integral in (1.15) is replaced by an approximating sum consisting of N points, there are 2^{N-1} possible solutions $\hat{o}(x)$ consistent with N given autocorrelation values.

Nevertheless, there are a few effects that counter the multiplicity problem. First of all, if the spectrum $O(\omega)$ with ω replaced by a general complex variable z has only real zeros, then there is a unique $o(x)$ consistent with the given $|O(\omega)|$; see [1.28]. This is true for some simple objects such as the double star $o(x) = \delta(x-a) + \delta(x+a)$ or the rectangle $o(x) = \text{Rect}(x/a)$. Sometimes the user knows the object to be of such a type.

Second, the solution is unique if the object has azimuthal symmetry, and if the user knows it. Then the phase $\phi(\omega) = 0$ everywhere, and $O(\omega) = |O(\omega)|$, so that $|O(\omega)|$ need only be Fourier inverted to obtain $o(x)$.

Third, as we are dealing with intensity objects, any candidate $o(x)$ for solution must obey a positivity constraint

$$\hat{o}(x) \geqq 0. \tag{1.16}$$

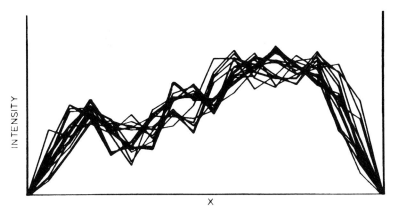

Fig. 1.9. Reconstruction results: test object (thick curve) and 15 other solutions [1.21]

This constraint will rule out those of the 2^{N-1} possibilities which have *any* negatives among them.

Fourth, as found by *Frieden* and *Currie* [1.21a], even with an autocorrelation that *has* a multiplicity of solutions, if the initial guess at the solution is fairly close to the true object, an iterative algorithm will "home in" on the true solution. The algorithm in use was the conventional Newton-Raphson "relaxation" one, with autocorrelation data as target values.

Fifth, of the candidate solutions that both have the given $|O(\omega)|$ and obey (1.16), the vast majority are often very close together in their details. Therefore, it *often does not matter* which one is converged upon. Uniqueness becomes a moot question. For example, see Fig. 1.9, due to *Fienup* [1.21]. Note that the general trend of the object is followed by most of the solutions. This effect becomes stronger for impulse-type objects. The effect also becomes much stronger for two-dimensional imagery, even if the object is not impulsive; see below.

Fienup used an ingeniously simple algorithm to attack the two-dimensional problem. This is an iterative technique which takes advantage of the speed of the FFT. It starts with an initial, random guess at $o(x)$, call it $o^{(0)}(x)$. (Note: x is now a two-dimensional point.) This is Fourier transformed to yield $O^{(0)}(\omega) \equiv |O^{(0)}(\omega)| \exp[i\phi^{(0)}(\omega)]$. The modulus part is replaced by the known modulus $|O(\omega)|$, but the phase function is retained. This is inverse transformed to yield the first iterated object estimate $o^{(1)}(x)$.

Now $o^{(1)}(x)$ must obey the positivity constraint, (1.16), and perhaps others peculiar to the user's particular problem. Designate x values for which the constraints are obeyed as falling within domain OK. Then one possible way to define an $o^{(2)}(x)$, which obeys the constraints everywhere, is to set

$$o^{(2)}(x) = \begin{cases} o^{(1)}(x) & \text{for} \quad x \in OK \\ 0 & \text{for} \quad x \notin OK \end{cases}$$

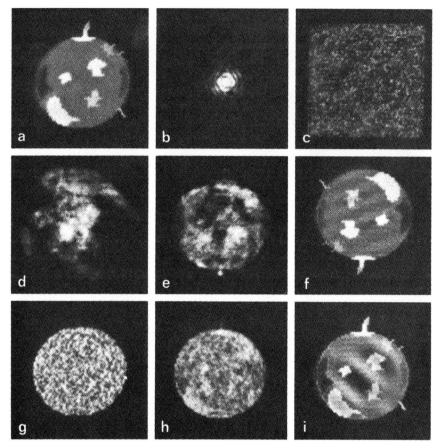

Fig. 1.10. (a) Test object; (b) modulus of its Fourier transform; (c) initial estimate of the object (first test); (d) (f) reconstruction results – number of iterations: (d) 20, (e) 230, (f) 600; (g) initial estimate of the object (second test); (h), (i) reconstruction result – number of iterations (h) 2, (i) 215 [1.21]

or in general for the kth iteration

$$o^{(k+1)}(x) = \begin{cases} o^{(k)}(x) & \text{for} \quad x \in OK \\ 0 & \text{for} \quad x \notin OK \end{cases} \tag{1.17}$$

The philosophy here is that if $o^{(1)}(x)$ goes negative at some x, which is unphysical for a true solution, it may mean that $o(x)$ really is 0 there. Thus (1.17) tries to force the tendency toward zeros in regions of x that appear to need it.

If now a spectrum $O^{(2)}(\omega)$ is formed from $o^{(2)}(x)$, and the cycle repeated, the method is simply that due to *Gerchberg* and *Saxton* [1.29]. In this case it can be shown that the integrated square error in an estimate $o^{(k)}(x)$ from the true $o(x)$

must decrease monotonically with iteration k. However, in practice this "error-reduction" approach decreases rapidly only for the first few iterations, and then decreases extremely slowly for later iterations. An impractically large number of iterations would be required for convergence.

Instead of using the tactic (1.17) alone, then, the author found it necessary to alternate its use with another, called the "input-output" approach. This tactic is to replace

$$o^{(k+1)}(x) = \begin{cases} o^{(k-1)}(x) & \text{for} \quad x \in OK \\ o^{(k-1)}(x) - \beta o^{(k)}(x) & \text{for} \quad x \notin OK \end{cases} \qquad (1.18)$$

Here β is some preassigned constant > 0, $o^{(k)}(x)$ is the output of the given FT operation, and $o^{(k-1)}(x)$ is the previous estimate that was forced to obey the constraints by either (1.17) or (1.18).

A one-dimensional test of the method was shown above in Fig. 1.9. A two-dimensional test is shown in Fig. 1.10. The object was contrived to resemble a sun, of diameter 52 pixels, within a field of 128×128 pixels. The figure pretty well speaks for itself. Results are very good.

The high number of iterations indicated for Fig. 1.10 indicates that a great amount of computer time is needed for images of this size; 1200 Fourier transforms had to be taken to produce the image. Nevertheless, this is quite an accomplishment for a problem which seemed *in principle* impossible a few years ago. *Fienup* also showed that the technique is not overly sensitive to the presence of noise added to the $|O(\omega)|$ data.

This work is a good example of a phenomenon which may be called "computer replacement". Where vital experimental data is lacking – in this case, all the phase values $\phi(\omega)$ – sometimes the computer can make up for the missing data. However, as illustrated here, the time/cost factor is liable to be enormous. Sometimes, however, such a tradeoff is worthwhile.

1.10.3 Use of Augmented Speckle Data: Knox's Approach

An alternative approach to the "phase problem" of speckle interferometry has been provided by *Knox* [1.20]. Rather than using "computer replacement", his approach is to provide *supplemental data* to the problem. This avoids the phase-retrieval problem described above. In effect, a heavy load is lifted from the computer and placed back upon the experimenter.

As before, each short-term image is Fourier transformed to form $I(\omega)$. But from this quantity, now all possible products $I(\omega)I^*(\omega + \Delta\omega)$ are formed over the two-dimensional domain of ω. Vector $\Delta\omega$ typically takes on two coordinate displacements, $(0, \Delta\omega)$ and $(\Delta\omega, 0)$. Then the average value of $\langle I(\omega)I^*(\omega + \Delta\omega) \rangle$ over all the short-term images is formed. This forms *autocorrelation data*. In addition, the displacement $\Delta\omega = (0, 0)$ is used, once again, to form speckle interferometry data. Hence, the latter are a subset of the Knox data set.

In terms of the unknown object, this more general data set obeys

$$\langle I(\omega)I^*(\omega+\Delta\omega)\rangle = \langle S(\omega)S^*(\omega+\Delta\omega)\rangle O^*(\omega)O(\omega+\Delta\omega) \qquad (1.19)$$

by (1.12). Then if $\phi(\omega)$ is the unknown phase of $O(\omega)$,

Phase

$$[\langle I(\omega)I^*(\omega+\Delta\omega)\rangle] = \phi(\omega+\Delta\omega) - \phi(\omega) + \text{Phase}[\langle S(\omega)S^*(\omega+\Delta\omega)\rangle], \ (1.20)$$

where notation Phase[·] means the phase of the function in the bracket. Now the left-hand phase is known from the data. Also, the right-hand Phase[$\langle S(\omega)S^*(\omega+\Delta\omega)\rangle$] can be known by forming the image autocorrelation in the presence of a single point object. Alternatively, it may be assumed to be negligible compared to the object phase difference. Therefore, the unknown object phase difference $\phi(\omega+\Delta\omega) - \phi(\omega)$ may be solved for in (1.20)! This is the touchstone of Knox's method.

The actual phase $\phi(\omega)$ is then found by summing the known phase differences $\phi(\omega+\Delta\omega) - \phi(\omega)$ outward from the origin. Note for this purpose that $\phi(0,0)$ is known and is, in fact, zero since $o(x)$ is a real function. In fact, being a two-dimensional problem, there are *any number* of paths in frequency space that can be taken to produce ϕ at a required ω point. Each path should give rise to the correct $\phi(\omega)$ value. Therefore, in the case of noisy data, the different path values may be averaged to effect some gain in accuracy.

In a computer simulation, Knox used two independent paths to estimate each $\phi(\omega) \equiv \phi(\omega_1, \omega_2)$. Path 1 was outward from the origin along the X direction until value ω_1 is attained, then along Y until value ω_2 is attained. Path 2 was the complement to path 1. Use of these paths requires two values of $\Delta\omega$ in forming autocorrelation data: $(0, \Delta\omega)$ and $(\Delta\omega, 0)$.

The object distribution used in the simulation is shown in Fig. 1.11. This was meant to model a moon of Jupiter. Forty images of this object were generated in the computer, by convolution with 40 random point spread functions. The latter resemble the speckle pattern in Fig. 1.6 and wipe out all recognizable object details from the image (see Fig. 1.12). These image data sets were then Fourier transformed, and autocorrelated, to provide inputs to (1.20). The $\phi(\omega)$ were estimated as described above. Next the unknown modulus function $|O(\omega)|$ was estimated via (1.14), i.e., the standard speckle interferometry approach [using the autocorrelation data for $\Delta\omega = (0,0)$]. This permits the full object spectrum $|O(\omega)| \exp i\phi(\omega)$ to be estimated and, hence, $o(x)$ by a Fourier transform.

Results are shown in Fig. 1.13. Comparison with a typical speckle image in Fig. 1.12 shows a vast improvement in image quality. The geometric shapes of the round details are seen to be well restored, although the absolute intensity levels are not.

These simulations were done using noiseless data. However, other authors have carried through Knox's procedure in the presence of a significant amount of image noise (see, e.g., [1.30]). Results indicate that the method does not

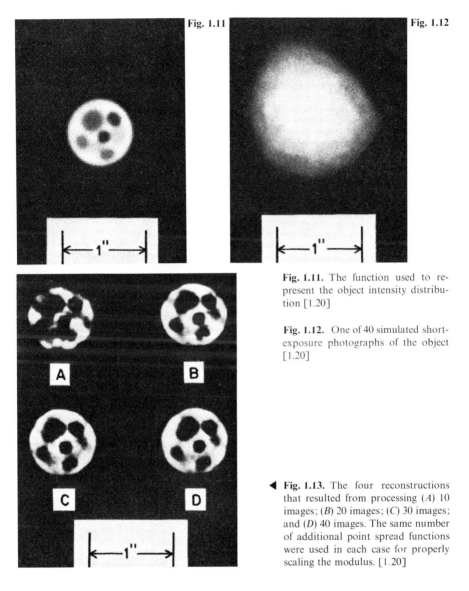

Fig. 1.11

Fig. 1.12

Fig. 1.11. The function used to represent the object intensity distribution [1.20]

Fig. 1.12. One of 40 simulated short-exposure photographs of the object [1.20]

◄ **Fig. 1.13.** The four reconstructions that resulted from processing (*A*) 10 images; (*B*) 20 images; (*C*) 30 images; and (*D*) 40 images. The same number of additional point spread functions were used in each case for properly scaling the modulus. [1.20]

seriously deteriorate in the presence of significant noise. Work on this problem is continuing.

1.10.4 Long-Term Exposure Methods: Digital Restoration

The degree to which these short-exposure methods of *Labeyrie, Fienup,* and *Knox* are sensitive to noise will ultimately limit their range of astronomical (and other) applications. This is because the objects of interest to astronomers are, almost by definition, distant and weak sources. Such weak sources of light are statistically Poisson sources, and hence are received as very noisy data. [Recall that the signal-to-noise S/N=(average signal level)$^{1/2}$ for a Poisson source.] To combat this effect, time exposures on the order of an hour are typically used; then enough photons are received to produce a relatively high S/N image. The trouble is that such images then suffer the effects of *long*-term exposure imagery. Such imagery is characterized by curve *a* in Fig. 1.7, the worst of the lot! Thus, these images are severely blurred by the random atmosphere.

In this situation, *image restoration* methods are of use. Their aim is to invert the imaging equation

$$i(x) = \int_{-\infty}^{\infty} dx' \, o(x') s(x - x') + n(x) \tag{1.21}$$

for the object distribution $o(x')$, in the presence of random noise $n(x)$, given image data $i(x)$ and an estimate of the point spread function $s(x)$. Analog and digital methods have been used. The field of *digital* image restoration, up to 1974, was surveyed by *Frieden* [1.16]. Extensive lists of references are also provided in [1.31, 32].

Decomposition of Images into Foregrounds and Backgrounds

For the given problem, $n(x)$ is Poisson noise and $s(x)$ is a long-term exposure point spread function. Many astronomical problems also have a smoothly varying background term $B(x)$ additive to the right-hand side of the imaging equation (1.21). Use of such a term, which may represent, e.g., the night sky airglow plus interstellar dust, separates out "foreground" details $o(x)$, which are *intrinsically high frequency* and therefore want restoration, from "background" details which are *intrinsically smooth* and therefore do not require restoration.

Aside from this philosophical viewpoint, there is a tactical reason for not restoring the additive background. It is often rather bright relative to the foreground details, and its restoration will induce inevitable Gibbsian oscillations which will swamp the restored foreground details. One of the classical problems of restoration has been, in fact, to restore with high resolution a narrow spike sitting atop a pedestal function. (This has astronomical application to the case of a quasar located within the nuclear region of a galaxy.) No method, including even positive-constrained ones, has been able to accomplish such resolution, again, because of the induced Gibbsian oscillations caused by the restored pedestal.

Convinced of the necessity for estimating the background, how may this be done? We summarize here some recent progress on this problem, and show the restorations that result.

A simple and direct approach is to simply blur the entire image by convolution with, say, a Gaussian whose halfwidth is a good multiple of that of the spread function. Such a convolution will leave the slowly varying back-

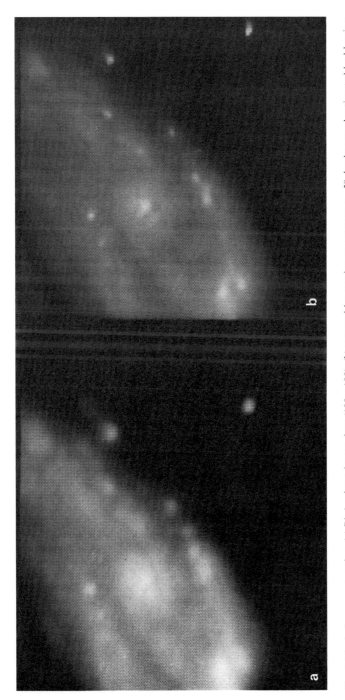

Fig. 1.14a, b. Image restoration. (**a**) Bird galaxy, image data (100×100); (**b**) restored by maximum entropy $\varrho = 50$, background estimated by blurring image

ground almost the same, except for a slight decrease in dc level caused by blur leakage to the sides. On the other hand, it will flatten all the foreground spread function details to nearly zero, so that the total output of the convolution operation will be very nearly the background *alone*. This is then the background estimate.

An example of the use of this method is shown in Fig. 1.14. Image (a) was taken through long-term turbulence by Dr. R. Lynds of Kitt Peak National Observatory. It is a part of the "Bird" galaxy, a newly discovered and very weak source. Note the white puffs, which are point spread functions, due to individual stars. These form the foreground image that is to be restored. The smooth background behind these puffs is assumed to be additive background $B(x)$.

In order to estimate $B(x)$, we convolved the entire image with a Gaussian kernel function whose standard deviation is 2.5 times that of the estimated spread function in the image (the latter obtained from the lower right-hand puff, which appears to be an isolated star). The resulting background estimate $\hat{B}(x)$ was stored for later display, and also was used during restoration of the foreground as a presumed Poisson source of noise. The precise method of restoration was the *maximum entropy* technique, as described in *Frieden* and *Wells* [1.22b].

The restored foreground image is shown superimposed upon the estimated background in Fig. 1.14b. The former are the apparent point and line sources in the image, while the latter is everything else. Note in particular the complete absence of Gibbsian oscillation, which was one aim of the technique. The resolution increase is significant as well.

A defect in this method of estimating the background becomes evident now. Surrounding many of the restored foreground structures is an apparent halo of a faint gray shade; see, e.g., the bright pointlike source in Fig. 1.14b in the upper right-hand region. These halos are an artifact of the background-estimation procedure, resulting from an incomplete flattening toward zero of the image spread functions after purposeful blurring with the Gaussian kernel. A circular area of residual flux remains in place of each former spread function, and in this way the "halo" is incorporated into the estimate of the background.

In order to avoid this artificial halo effect, a different background estimation procedure was sought. Such a procedure would have to recognize that if an image segment is *monotonically* either increasing or decreasing over a sufficiently large distance, then that image segment is a segment of the background.

Use of the Median Window

A digital technique that accomplishes this trick very well is the *median window* operation. This is defined in one dimension as a window of length L points which is centered on L successive points of a one-dimensional image, and which outputs the median [the $(L+1)/2$ largest number] of the image values within

Table 1.1. (a) Operation of median window upon monotonic image. Monotonic region is exactly reproduced. (b) Operation of median window upon spread function against background. Only background comes through.

		Low plateau + noise	Monotonic region	High plateau + noise
a	Image	← 1 2 2 3 1 2 1 3 1 2 1 →	← 3 5 8 8 9 10 10 10 11 12 14 14 15 15 →	← 14 15 16 14 15 17 15 →
	Median window outputs $L=15$ points		2 2 3 3 3 5 8 8 9 10 10 10 11 12 14 14 14 14 ← Region of exact reproduction →	

		Background	Spread function	Background
b	Image	← 1 2 2 3 1 2 1 3 1 2 1 →	← 3 5 8 9 4 →	← 1 3 3 2 1 2 3 1 1 2 3 2 1 2 1 1 →
	Median window outputs, $L=15$ points		2 2 2 3 3 3 3 3 3 3 3 3 3 3 2 2 2 2 2 ← Spread function passed over →	

the window. The window is centered in sequence upon *each* point of the image, and its outputs form a new image. To judge how this nonlinear operator works, the reader is referred to Table 1.1. In (a), the numbers across the top row represent a possible edge type of image. There is a low plateau region on the left, plus superposed oscillations due, say, to noise; a transitional, monotonic region in the middle; and a higher plateau region on the right, again, with superposed oscillations. The bottom row of numbers is the result of median windowing the top row, using a window length of 15 points. As can be seen, and easily verified, the monotonic region is *exactly* duplicated in the median window output, except for its end points. In fact, *this duplication effect will occur for any image segment which is monotonic over distance L or more.*

Suppose, then, we choose to define the background as a median windowing of the image. From the preceding, if the user prescribes a value for L, he really is defining what he *means* by the "background" image. This comprises all segments of the image data which are monotonic over distance L *or longer*. Those segments that are monotonic over *smaller* distances than L will, in fact, be smoothed out (see below). Thus, the larger we make L, the more restrictive we are in permitting background regions to fluctuate as rapidly as the image data. That is, the slower we are demanding the background to vary.

We saw above the effect of median windowing upon a fluctuation whose length equals L. Now we examine the effect of median windowing upon fluctuations whose length is *less than* $L/2$. This is seen in part (b) of Table 1.1. A spread function of length 7 is centered upon a noisy background. Hence the fluctuation length is 7. A median windowing operator for $L=15$ is performed.

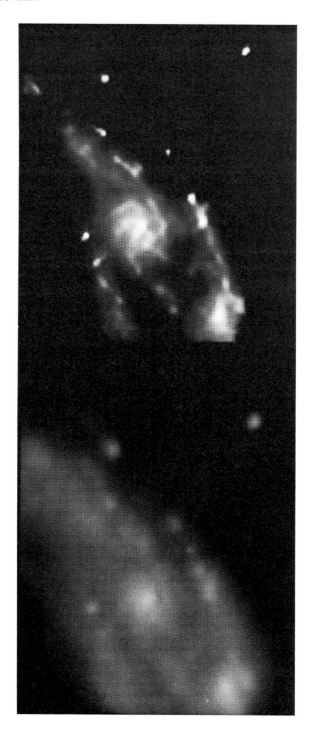

Fig. 1.15a, b. Image restoration. (a) Bird galaxy, image data (100 × 100); (b) restored by maximum entropy $\varrho = 200$. median window background

We see that the output *completely ignores* the spread function, substituting for it a kind of average local background value (of 3 in this case).

The implications of these effects are that a) foreground details will be correctly ignored, and replaced by local background values, as long as a window length L is used that exceeds twice the spread function width; and b) all image details that vary slower than L, i.e., have a fluctuation length *exceeding L*, will be considered as background values.

In this way, the median windowing operation allows us to define, and easily compute, an estimate of a variable background. We emphasize the nonlinear nature of this background estimate. For example, no convolution operation could *both* reproduce monotonic regions exactly, as in Table 1.1a, and yet completely obliterate (severely blur) quick oscillations such as the spread function detail in Table 1.1b.

Restoration of the galaxy image in Fig. 1.14a was redone, now using the median windowing algorithm to estimate the background. Here a *circular* window was used because of the two-dimensional nature of the problem. The window diameter (corresponding to L in the preceding) was made twice the effective spread function width. The new estimate $\hat{B}(x)$ of background was used in a restoring step, as before. The result is shown in Fig. 1.15b. We see that the artifact "halo" effect no longer surrounds the restored individual stars. (Note: The extra resolution in Fig. 1.15b as compared with Fig. 1.14b is mainly due to the use of a much higher sharpness parameter ϱ; see [1.22 b] for details.)

Conventional calculation of the median for these purposes is too slow. Typical point spread functions are about 15 pixels wide. For the latter to be obliterated, in a median windowing operation to estimate background, would require a window diameter L of at least 31 pixels. This encompasses 675 pixels, and the median would be the 338th maximum. The conventional approach would be to find the maximum among the 675 values, set this to zero, find the second maximum, set that to zero, etc., until the 338th is found.

The trouble with this approach is that it requires 338 searches through 675 numbers, or $2(338^2)DO$ loop executions to test each candidate for the maximum property. And this is for only one placement of the window! Thus, if the point spread extent is α, an $N \times N$ image would require about $5N^2\alpha^4$ comparison operations to establish the background $\hat{B}(x)$. This would amount to about 5 min of central processor time on a Cyber 175 computer, for a 100×100 image where the spread function width is 15 pixels.

Fast Median Window Algorithms

In practice, a saving of about 5:1 in computer time was accomplished by the following reasoning. Since the background is by hypothesis smooth, the median window outputs should hardly (if at all) change from one pixel to the next. Therefore, a median window search algorithm should be contrived which can *test* a given number (namely, the *preceding* median output) to see if it is the median at the given window position. In this way the output of one median evaluation is used as input to the next. Since the outputs hardly change from one window position to the next, at most one or two median tests would be needed for determining each new output.

In fact, *there is* a procedure for testing a given number P for the median property. Suppose the median is to be the Qth highest maximum. *Then there should be* $Q - 1$ *numbers that are either greater than or equal to P.* Suppose the $2Q$ numbers in the set are compared with P, and Q' numbers are found greater than or equal to P. If $Q' = Q$, then P is accepted as the median value. If instead, $Q' < Q$, this means that P is too high (there are fewer numbers above it than are below it). Therefore, search through the number set and find the closest number to P that is *smaller than P*. Call this P'. Again, test if this P' has Q numbers greater than or equal to to it, etc. If, on the other hand, a $Q' > Q$, this means that the current candidate P is too low. Therefore, search through the number set and find the closest number to P that is *larger than P*.

After each closest number search to establish a new candidate P, test P for the property that $Q - 1$ numbers exceed it. In this way, the median is converged upon stepwise through numbers in the set. We call this a fast median window algorithm.

The number of *DO* loop executions required to establish a background image is now about $12N^2\alpha^2$. This assumes an average of two nearest number searches to establish a new median at a given image position. For a general m searches required, the answer would be $6mN^2\alpha^2$.

This number cannot, however, be directly compared with the $5N^2\alpha^4$ *DO* loop executions required of the conventional approach, since different operations are carried through in the *DO* loops by the two approaches. We found empirically that for a comparison that is in line with execution *time*, a better estimate for the fast approach is $100\,mN^2\alpha^2$. Therefore, a time-saving factor of $20\,m/\alpha^2$ results. With $m = 2$, as is usual, for a 15 pixel-wide spread function the time-saving factor is about one-fifth by use of the fast method.

Another fast median window algorithm was recently proposed by *Huang* et al. [1.33].

The median window has been used to digitally process images in other ways as well. Early uses of the idea seem to have been directed toward rejecting noisy, isolated lines of data, in the same way that the spread function in Table 1.1b was obliterated; see, e.g., [1.34]. It may be used in the frequency domain to smooth out unwanted high-frequency spikes. Also, it may be used as the nonlinear step in a two-step algorithm that restores step like objects (edges, ramps, staircases, etc.) beyond the diffraction limit; see [1.35]. A limitation to the latter approach is immediately evident, however: since the median window operation rejects spread functions, it will reject isolated point sources in the object as well, and will bridge groups of point sources with an approximating ramp. Hence the scope of application of the algorithm is limited to objects which *are known* to consist of step like objects. In this sense it is complementary to the positive-constrained restoring algorithms (for summary, see [1.16]), which are strongly beneficial only for *pointlike* objects such as star fields or spiral arms. A restoring method that exceeds the diffraction limit for both edge-type and impulse-type objects has yet to be found.

References

1.1   R.E.Hopkins, C.A.McCarthy, R.Walters: J. Opt. Soc. Am. **45**, 363 (1955)

1.2   R.E.Hopkins, G.Spencer: J. Opt. Soc. Am. **52**, 172 (1962)

1.3   D.P.Feder: J. Opt. Soc. Am. **52**, 177 (1962)

1.4   a) R.J.Pegis: J. Opt. Soc. Am. **51**, 1255 (1961)
      b) P.Baumeister: J. Opt. Soc. Am. **52**, 1149 (1962)
      c) E.Delano: J. Opt. Soc. Am. **57**, 1529 (1967)
      d) J.A.Dobrowolski, D.Lowe: Appl. Opt. **17**, 3039 (1978)

1.5   R.Barakat: J. Opt. Soc. Am. **51**, 152 (1961)

1.6   R.Barakat: J. Opt. Soc. Am. **52**, 985 (1962)

1.7   R.Barakat, D.Lev: J. Opt. Soc. Am. **53**, 324 (1963)

1.8   a) A.G.Fox, T.Li: Bell Syst. Tech. J. **40**, 453 (1961)
      b) H.K.V.Lotsch: Optik **28**, 65, 328, 555 (1968/69) and **29**, 130, 622 (1969)

1.9   a) A.W.Lohmann, D.P.Paris: Appl. Opt. **6**, 1739 (1967)
      b) D.Malacara (ed.): *Optical Shop Testing* (John Wiley, New York 1978)

1.10 a) M.M.Ter-Pogossian, M.Phelps, G.Brownell, J.Cox, D.Davis, R.Evens (eds.): *Reconstruction Tomography in Diagnostic Radiology and Nuclear Medicine* (University Park Press, Baltimore 1977)
      b) G.T.Herman (ed.): *Image Reconstruction from Projections*. Topics in Applied Physics, Vol. 32 (Springer, Berlin, Heidelberg, New York 1979)

1.11 H.Barrett, K.Garewall, D.T.Wilson: Radiology **104**, 429 (1972)

1.12 R.P.Kruger, G.L.Hall, A.F.Turner: Appl. Opt. **16**, 2637 (1977)

1.13 H.Barrett, W.Swindell: Proc. IEEE **65**, 89 (1977)

1.14 J.W.Cooley, J.W.Tukey: Math. Comput. **19**, 297 (1965)

1.15 a) R.M.Bracewell: *The Fourier Transform and Its Applications* (McGraw-Hill, New York 1965)
      b) B.K.Vainshtein: Sov. Phys. Crystallogr. **15**, 781 (1971)

1.16 B.R.Frieden: "Image Enhancement and Restoration", in *Picture Processing and Digital Filtering*, 2nd ed., ed. by T.S.Huang, Topics in Applied Physics, Vol. 6 (Springer, Berlin, Heidelberg, New York 1979)

1.17 G.W.Swenson, N.C.Mathur: Proc. IEEE **56**, 2114 (1968)

1.18 D.Y.Gezari, A.Labeyrie, L.V.Stachnik: Astrophys. J. **173**, L1 (1972)

1.19 J.C.Dainty (ed.): *Laser Speckle and Related Phenomena*. Topics in Applied Physics, Vol. 9 (Springer, Berlin, Heidelberg, New York 1975)

1.20 K.T.Knox: J. Opt. Soc. Am. **66**, 1236 (1976)

1.21 J.R.Fienup: Opt. Lett. **3**, 27 (1978)

1.22 a) B.R.Frieden, D.G.Currie: J. Opt. Soc. Am. **66**, 1111A (1976)
      b) B.R.Frieden, D.G.Wells: J. Opt. Soc. Am. **68**, 93 (1978)

1.23 D.L.Fried: J. Opt. Soc. Am. **55**, 1427 (1965)

1.24 R.E.Hufnagel, N.R.Stanley: J. Opt. Soc. Am. **54**, 52 (1964)

1.25 D.Korff: Opt. Commun. **5**, 188 (1972)

1.26 M.G.Miller, A.M.Schneiderman, P.F.Kellen: Astrophys. J. **186**, L91 (1973)

1.27 A.M.Schneiderman, P.F.Kellen, M.G.Miller: J. Opt. Soc. Am. **65**, 1287 (1975)

1.28 A.Walther: Opt. Acta **11**, 41 (1963)

1.29 R.W.Gerchberg, W.O.Saxton: Optik **35**, 236 (1972)

1.30 P.Nisenson: In Proceedings of the SPIE/SPSE Symposium on Imaging through the Atmosphere, Vol. 25 (1976)

1.31 W. K. Pratt (ed.): "Bibliography on Digital Imaging Procedures and Related Topics"; USCGG Report 453, University of Southern California, Los Angeles (1973)

1.32 T. S. Huang, W. F. Tretiak, O. I. Schreiber: Proc. IEEE **59**, 1568 (1971)

1.33 T. S. Huang, G. Yang, G. Tang: "A Fast Two-Dimensional Median Filtering Algorithm", paper presented at IEEE Conference on Pattern Recognition and Image Processing, Chicago (1978)

1.34 G. W. Wecksung, K. Campbell: Comput. Mag. **7**, 63 (1974)

1.35 B. R. Frieden: J. Opt. Soc. Am. **66**, 280 (1976)

1.36 J. W. Strohbehn (ed.): *Laser Beam Propagation in the Atmosphere*, Topics in Applied Physics, Vol. 25 (Springer, Berlin, Heidelberg, New York 1978)

1.37 G. I. Marchuk, G. A. Mikhailov, M. A. Nazaraliev, R. A. Durbinjan, B. A. Kargin, B. S. Elepov: *The Monte Carlo Methods in Atmospheric Optics*, Springer Series in Optical Sciences, Vol. 12 (Springer, Berlin, Heidelberg, New York 1980)

2. The Calculation of Integrals Encountered in Optical Diffraction Theory

R. Barakat

The purpose of this treatment is basically pedagogic. Although, paradoxically, many investigators working in various aspects of optical diffraction theory are expert in analytical manipulations of Fourier integrals, special functions, etc., they seem to know very little about established numerical procedures. The editor has suggested to the contributor that a presentation describing various numerical techniques of evaluating optical diffraction type integrals would be useful; the present chapter is the final result of our discussions.

2.1 Historical Background

It is useful to start with a historical example. Fresnel, in his pioneering work on diffraction of light by a straight edge, encountered the integrals (now termed the Fresnel integrals)

$$C(v_0) = \int_0^{v_0} \cos(\pi v^2/2) dv, \quad S(v_0) = \int_0^{v_0} \sin(\pi v^2/2) dv. \tag{2.1}$$

In order to evaluate them, Fresnel used an ingenious approach; he considered the integral

$$\int_l^{l+u} \cos(\pi v^2/2) dv, \tag{2.2}$$

where l is given and u is small enough so that its square can be neglected. Now let $v = l + u'$; then

$$\cos(\pi v^2/2) \approx \cos[\pi(l^2 + 2lu')/2]. \tag{2.3}$$

Consequently,

$$\int_l^{l+u} \cos(\pi v^2/2) dv \approx \int_0^u \cos[\tfrac{\pi}{2}(l^2 + 2lu')] du'$$

$$= \cos(\pi l^2/2) \int_0^u \cos(\pi l u') du' - \sin(\pi l^2/2) \int_0^u \sin(\pi l u') du'$$

$$= (\pi l)^{-1} \{ \sin[\tfrac{\pi}{2}(l^2 + 2lu)] - \sin(\tfrac{\pi}{2} l^2) \}. \tag{2.4}$$

In like fashion,

$$\int_l^{l+u} \sin(\pi v^2/2)\,dv \approx (\pi l)^{-1}\{-\cos[\tfrac{\pi}{2}(l^2+2lu)]+\cos(\tfrac{\pi}{2}l^2)\}\,. \tag{2.5}$$

Using these expressions, Fresnel evaluated the C and S integrals in stepwise fashion starting with $v_0 \approx 0$. He most likely used logarithm tables in the actual evaluation!

After Fresnel published his results, a number of mathematicians (Cauchy, Gilbert, etc.) took up the challenge of producing series expansions, asymptotic expansions, etc. The main point here is that in the very first work on the wave theory of diffraction it was necessary to face up to the numerical evaluation of oscillatory integrals.

The development of algorithms (both practical and impractical) for the numerical evaluation of integrals has been a continuing activity since the beginning of calculus. The last century was particularly rich in this regard. The appearance of the electronic computer in the 1950s has had a profound influence on quadrature methods. It is ironical that the electronic computer has cut a wide swatch through these algorithms, leaving only the simplest (trapezoidal, Simpson, etc.) and the most sophisticated (Gauss) as useful candidates for computer use.

The integrals that generally occur in optical diffraction theory are such that the integrand is highly oscillatory, and the interval of integration often quite large. Sometimes these integrals can be evaluated in terms of known functions, but the vast majority must be handled numerically. The availability of an electronic computer is a *necessary* but not a *sufficient* condition for extracting numerical information from the integrals. Suitable quadrature schemes are also required.

The outline of this chapter is as follows. Section 2 contains a description of some quadrature schemes that are useful in evaluating optical diffraction integrals as well as an asymptotic method which complements the numerical schemes. I have tried to include enough relevant detail so that the reader will not view the matter as a series of dogmatic statement. The next section is devoted to the problem of optical imagery in the presence of incoherent light so that methods discussed in Sect. 2 will take on a more concrete meaning. Section 4 returns to the question of quadrature in the context of the fast Fourier transform (FFT), while Sect. 5 is devoted to sampling expansions as computational tools.

Rather than cluttering up the text with detailed references to the literature, I have collected all the references at the end of the chapter. References for each section are collected together and commented upon. It is hoped that this approach will allow the reader to concentrate upon the main ideas; there is nothing quite as devastating as trying to learn a subject when every sentence in the text is pregnant with references.

2.2 Quadrature and Associated Formulae

The analysis to follow is developed in the context of one-dimensional integrals, even though many of the quadrature problems encountered in diffraction optics are two dimensional. A knowledge of the one-dimensional case is generally fundamental in that the evaluation of two-dimensional integrals can be cast into the repeated evaluation of one-dimensional integrals.

There are an almost unbelievable number of quadrature schemes in the literature, the vast majority of interest only to the specialist. The methods that are described are ones that have been employed by the author at various time on diffraction integrals.

2.2.1 Trapezoidal and Simpson's Rules

The trapezoidal and Simpson's rules are two special cases of an approach (Newton-Cotes formulae) that seek to approximate an integral

$$I = \int_a^b f(p)\,dp \tag{2.6}$$

by integrating a polynomial $R_n(p)$ of degree n whose coefficients are chosen such that

$$R_n(p) = f(p_l), \quad l = 0, 1, \ldots, N \tag{2.7}$$

with the requirement that the quadrature points (or nodes) p_l are equidistant. Furthermore, we shall include the end points b and a as quadrature points (formulae that include both end points are termed *closed*); thus

$$p_l = a + lh, \quad l = 0, 1, \ldots, N; \quad h = (b-a)/N. \tag{2.8}$$

The trapezoidal rule is based on the polynomial being a linear function

$$R_1(p) = c_1 p + c_2, \tag{2.9}$$

where c_1 and c_2 are numerical constants to be determined. It can be shown that

$$\int_a^b f(p)\,dp = \frac{h}{2}[f(b) + f(a)] + \text{error}. \tag{2.10}$$

Simpson's rule follows by making the approximating polynomial a quadratic, i.e., $R_2(p) = c_2 p^2 + c_1 p + c_0$. The final result is

$$\int_b^a f(p)\,dp = \frac{h}{3}\left[f(b) + 4f\left(\frac{b-a}{2}\right) + f(a) \right] + \text{error}. \tag{2.11}$$

One can continue to use higher degree approximating polynomials, but attractive as this may appear there are serious impediments to the use of such a scheme. First, the function $f(p)$ may not be approximated adequately by a polynomial, resulting in the fact that the error term can become unacceptably large; second, these high-order quadrature formulae may be subject to excessive rounding error in the calculation of the coefficients of the approximating polynomial. In the derivation of these formulae, including trapezoidal and Simpson's rules, the error term is shown to be dependent on a derivative of the function to be integrated. These high-order derivatives can become very large, even for simple functions; consequently the use of high-order Newton-Cotes formulae generally lead to a large error term.

One way to reduce the error to an acceptable level is to divide the integration interval (b, a) into subintervals and use a low-order formula (trapezoidal or Simpson). The error term in each subinterval now depends on a low-order derovative, so the problem of dealing with the concatenations of high-order derivatives is avoided. The price paid is that, although h is reduced, several subintervals must be summed. The corresponding error terms must also be summed. Quite frankly, this is a small price to pay! When a quadrature formula is used over several intervals, it is termed a composite formula. The composite trapezoidal rule with $h = (b-a)/N$ and N equal to the number of subintervals is

$$\int_a^b f(p)\,dp = \sum_{l=0}^N H_l f(p_l) + \text{error} \tag{2.12}$$

with

$$H_0 = H_N = \frac{h}{2},$$

$$H_l = h, \quad \text{for} \quad l \neq 0, N. \tag{2.13}$$

The composite Simpson's rule is (N must now be an even integer)

$$H_0 = H_N = \frac{h}{2}$$

$$H_l = \tfrac{4}{3}h, \quad \text{for} \quad l = 1, 3, \ldots$$

$$\quad = \tfrac{2}{3}h, \quad \text{for} \quad l = 2, 4, \ldots. \tag{2.14}$$

Note that the weight coefficients H_l are positive and all of the same order of magnitude.

The accuracy of these rules can be ascertained by evaluating the error term. If we set

$$M_2 \equiv \max_{a \leq p \leq b} f^{(2)}(p), \quad M_4 \equiv \max_{a \leq p \leq b} f^{(4)}(p), \tag{2.15}$$

then the absolute value of the error can be shown to be given by

$$|\text{error}| \leqq \frac{Nh^3}{12} M_2 = \frac{(b-a)^3}{12N^2} M_2 \quad \text{(trapezoidal)} \tag{2.16}$$

and

$$|\text{error}| \leqq \frac{Nh^5}{90} M_4 = \frac{(b-a)^5}{90N^4} M_4 \quad \text{(Simpson)}. \tag{2.17}$$

Consequently, we require the boundedness of the second and fourth derivatives of the function in the interval of integration for the convergence of these quadrature schemes as N is made to increase. The evaluation of the upper limit of these derivatives can be a forbidding task. The inherent error for Simpson's rule vanishes for a function whose fourth derivative is zero, but a polynomial of third degree has a zero fourth derivative. This means that Simpson's rule, which is based on second-degree approximating polynomials, is also exact for third-degree approximating polynomials! *It is this bonus in accuracy which accounts for its popularity.*

In principle, we can turn these expressions around and ask for the number of intervals N required for a given maximum absolute error. Thus, for Simpson's rule, we have

$$N \geqq \left[\frac{(b-a)^5 M_4}{90|\text{error}|} \right]^{1/4}, \tag{2.18}$$

but the difficulty in evaluating M_4 is probably the same order of magnitude as that in evaluating the original integral.

2.2.2 Romberg Quadrature

We have already seen that the composite trapezoidal rule is simple to use; we now describe a modification which can lead to high accuracy and which is convenient to use on computers. This method is termed Romberg quadrature. For our purposes we can approach the method by the well-known Euler-Maclaurin formula of classical analysis which is

$$T_0(h) = \int_a^b f(p)dp + a_2 h^2 + a_4 h^4 + a_6 h^6 + \dots, \tag{2.19}$$

where

$$T_0(h) \equiv \sum_{l=0}^{N} H_l f(p_l) \tag{2.20}$$

and the H_l and p_l are those appropriate for the trapezoidal rule. The a coefficients are expressed in terms of the derivatives of $f(p)$ at the end points b and a; the first few are

$$a_2 = \frac{1}{12} [f^{(1)}(b) - f^{(1)}(a)]$$

$$a_4 = -\frac{1}{720} [f^{(3)}(b) - f^{(3)}(a)] \tag{2.21}$$

$$a_6 = \frac{1}{30240} [f^{(5)}(b) - f^{(5)}(a)].$$

Usually the Euler-Maclaurin formula is encountered when we wish to estimate sums by converting them into integrals plus correction terms. Our purpose here is just the opposite.

Before proceeding let us detour momentarily to point out an amazing property of the trapezoidal rule. Suppose that $f^{(n)}(b) = f^{(n)}(a)$ for $n = 1, 3, 5, \ldots 4$; then the correction terms vanish identically and the trapezoidal rule becomes

$$T(h) = \int_a^b f(p)dp \tag{2.22}$$

with no error!

We now return to the main development and suppose that we have calculated the integral using a specified value of h; the approximation to the integral is now calculated with the interval halved, giving

$$T_0\left(\frac{h}{2}\right) = \int_a^b f(p)dp + a_2\left(\frac{h}{2}\right)^2 + a_4\left(\frac{h}{2}\right)^4 + a_6\left(\frac{h}{2}\right)^6 + \ldots. \tag{2.23}$$

The first term in the error series (i.e., $a_2 h^2$) can be eliminated between (2.19) and (2.23) by taking a suitable combination of the two equations; the final result is

$$T_1(h) \equiv \frac{4}{3} T_0\left(\frac{h}{2}\right) - \frac{1}{3} T_0(h)$$

$$= \int_a^b f(p)dp + a_4^{(1)} h^4 + a_6^{(1)} h^6 + \ldots, \tag{2.24}$$

where $a_4^{(1)} = -a_4/4$, $a_6^{(1)} = -5a_6/16$, $\ldots$. This equation says that $T_1(h)$ should be a better approximation to the integral than either $T_0(h)$ or $T_0(h/2)$ because the error goes as h^4 rather than h^2.

The process which led to this improvement can be carried farther. We have

$$T_1\left(\frac{h}{2}\right) = \int_a^b f(p)dp + a_4^{(1)}\left(\frac{h}{2}\right)^4 + a_6^{(1)}\left(\frac{h}{2}\right)^6 + \ldots. \tag{2.25}$$

We can combine these last two equations to eliminate the $a_4^{(1)}h^4$ error terms

$$T_2(h) \equiv \frac{16}{15} T_1\left(\frac{h}{2}\right) - \frac{1}{15} T_1(h)$$

$$= \int_a^b f(p)dp + a_6^{(2)}h^6 + \dots \tag{2.26}$$

where $a_6^{(2)} = -a_6^{(1)}/20, \dots$. Now $T_2(h)$ is an even better possible approximation because the error term is now proportional to h^6. In an obvious fashion, we can show that

$$T_3(h) \equiv \frac{64}{63} T_2\left(\frac{h}{2}\right) - \frac{1}{63} T_2(h)$$

$$= \int_a^b f(p)dp + a_8^{(2)}h^8 + \dots, \tag{2.27}$$

further improving the accuracy of the approximation. By induction, we have

$$T_k(h) = \frac{2^k}{(2^{2k}-1)} T_{k-1}\left(\frac{h}{2}\right) - \frac{1}{(2^{2k}-1)} T_{k-1}(h)$$

$$= \int_a^b f(p)dp + a_{2k+2}^{(k-1)}h^{2k+2} + \dots. \tag{2.28}$$

This procedure (which is nothing but a straightforward application of Richardson's deferred approach to the limit) can be continued to form a sequence of columns with error terms of increasing order. Thus we pick an h and compute $T_0(h)$, $T_0(h/2)$, ..., $T_0(h/2^l)$ where l is some positive integer. We then construct a table, which for $l=3$ is

h^2	h^4	h^6	h^8
$T_0(h)$			
$T_0(h/2)$	$T_1(h)$		
$T_0(h/4)$	$T_1(h/2)$	$T_2(h)$	
$T_0(h/8)$	$T_1(h/4)$	$T_2(h/2)$	$T_3(h)$.

The method is especially suitable for computer use because successive values can be compared to check when the process has converged. It is not necessary to store quadrature points or quadrature weights since only the trapezoidal rule is used.

Because Romberg quadrature is so attractive we illustrate it by two examples. The first example is

$$\int_1^2 \frac{dp}{p} \approx 0.693147.$$ (2.29)

The evaluation of the integral using $l=3$ is set out below.

h^2	h^4	h^6	h^8
0.750000			
0.708333	0.694444		
0.697024	0.693254	0.693175	
0.694122	0.693155	0.693175	0.693147

The results speak for themselves.

As we have already seen, if the function to be integrated is periodic *and* if the interval of integration is a complete period of that function, then the trapezoidal rule gives high accuracy. In this case there is no advantage to using Romberg integration because the convergence of $T_0(h)$ to the desired integral is already more rapid than any power of h. Even if the interval of integration is not a full period of the function, we must expect that the Romberg integration scheme will converge very slowly. To illustrate this point, we take as our second example the integral

$$\int_0^{\pi/2} \sin p\,dp = 1$$ (2.30)

and let $l=6$ in the Romberg scheme. The results are summarized in Table 2.1 and show how slow the convergence of the method can be in these situations.

2.2.3 Gauss Quadrature

The previous techniques operate by first fixing the quadrature points (they are required to be equidistant) and then finding the corresponding weight factors

Table 2.1

h^2	h^4	h^6	h^8	h^{10}	h^{12}
0.785398					
0.948059	1.002279				
0.977049	0.986712	0.985674			
0.987116	0.990472	0.990723	0.990803		
0.991762	0.993311	0.993500	0.993544	0.993555	
0.994282	0.995122	0.995243	0.995271	0.995277	0.995279

H_n. A novel approach to the problem was initiated by Gauss who allowed both quadrature points and weight factors to be free parameters.

Consider the integral

$$\int_a^b f(p)w(p)dp, \quad w(p)>0, \tag{2.31}$$

where a, b are finite; $w(p)$ is a given function termed the weight function and such that the moments

$$\int_a^b w(p)p^k dp \equiv m_k, \quad k=0,1,2,\ldots \tag{2.32}$$

exist. We transform the integral in (2.31) to the standard Gauss interval $(-1,+1)$ by the general formula

$$\int_a^b f(p)w(p)dp = \frac{b-a}{2} \int_{-1}^{+1} f(x)w(x)dx, \tag{2.33}$$

where

$$p=\tfrac{1}{2}(b+a)-\tfrac{1}{2}(b-a)x. \tag{2.34}$$

We seek to write

$$\int_{-1}^{+1} f(x)w(x)dx = \sum_{n=1}^N H_n f(x_n) + \text{error term}. \tag{2.35}$$

Note that $w(x)$ does not explicitly appear on the right-hand side. If the N quadrature points are taken to be distinct, then we can always find weight factors H_n such that the error term is zero whenever $f(x)$ is a polynomial degree $\leq (N-1)$.

It was Gauss' achievement which showed that the error term in (2.35) also vanishes if $f(x)$ is a polynomial of degree $(2N-1)$, provided that both x_n and H_n are allowed to be determined. Furthermore this is the highest degree of polynomial that is possible for a formula with N points. As one can guess, the solution depends on the orthogonal polynomials generated by the weight factor $w(x)$. Gauss proved that the quadrature points $x_n (n=1, 2, \ldots, N)$ are the zeros of an orthogonal polynomial $\mathscr{P}_N(x)$ with respect to $w(x)$, i.e.,

$$\int_{-1}^{+1} \mathscr{P}_N(x)w(x)\mathscr{P}_M(x)dx = \delta_{NM}. \tag{2.36}$$

$\mathscr{P}_N(x)$ has N real, distinct, but *nonequidistant*, in $[-1, +1]$. The Gauss weight factors obey two conditions: $H_n = H_{-n}, H_n > 0$.

The previous methods do not generally guarantee any convergence to the true value of the integral as the number of quadrative points is made to increase. Gauss quadrature has the remarkable property that if $f(x)$ is continuous on $[-1, +1]$, then the Gauss quadrature sequence $N = 1, 2, 3, \dots$ converges to the true value of the integral. Gauss quadrature employing N nonequidistant quadrature points is *exact* for a function $f(x)$ of degree $(2N-1)$ or less. If we had used conventional equidistant quadrature formulae (e.g., Simpson's rule), we would have been required to use $2N$ quadrature points to obtain the exact answer. Thus, the Gauss approach effects a considerable reduction in computation at the expense of having to compute the function at irrational points [i.e., zeros of $\mathscr{P}_N(x)$].

Perhaps the most important case is when $w(x)$ is a constant; then the orthogonal polynomials are Legendre polynomials $P_N(x)$. Fortunately for us, the evaluation of the x_n and H_n have been extensively studied and numerical values are available for a wide variety of weight functions. See references at end of the chapter.

Most of the problems encountered in actual practice are such that $f(x)$ is *not* a polynomial. There is an expression for the error term in (2.35); it is

$$\text{error term} = \frac{1}{(2n)!} f^{(2n)}(\xi) \int_{-1}^{+1} [\mathscr{P}_N(x)]^2 w(x) dx, \qquad (2.37)$$

where ξ lies on $(-1, +1)$. This formula is not particularly useful for computations. However, do not make the mistake that so many users of Gauss quadrature have made; (2.37) does not have a continuous $2n$th derivative.

This brings us to another point of mythology: Gauss quadrature is unstable if N is taken to be large, i.e., $N > 25$. This is supposed to occur because x_n and H_n are irrational numbers and round-off will cause trouble. The author has never had any problems provided $N < 50$; of course, there will be trouble if $N = 500$ and care is not taken. However this can be alleviated by repeated use of low-order Gauss quadrature.

2.2.4 Finite Fourier Integrals

We now turn our attention to the numerical evaluation of finite Fourier integrals

$$a(x) = \int_{-1}^{+1} A(p) \exp(ixp) dp, \qquad (2.38)$$

where we allow $A(p)$ to be complex valued. For large values of $|x|$, the graph of the integrand consists of positive and negative areas of nearly equal size. The addition of these two areas results in substantial cancellations with loss of accuracy. Straightforward use of any of the previous integration schemes would require an extremely large number of quadrature points.

Filon conceived the idea of retaining Simpson's rule, but requiring that only $A(p)$ be fitted to a parabola between quadrature points instead of the entire integrand. In other words, he separated out the behavior of $A(p)$ and $\exp(ixp)$. The fact that $A(p)$ has to vary quadratically over the integration interval means that we can take the number of quadrature points to be relatively small in many cases of practical interest.

Upon carrying out the manipulations (which are extremely tedious), *Filon* showed that

$$\int_{-1}^{1} A(p)\cos(xp)dp = h\alpha(hx)[A(+1)+A(-1)]\sin(x)$$

$$+ h\beta(hx)C_{\text{even}}(x) + h\gamma(hx)C_{\text{odd}}(x), \tag{2.39}$$

where

$$C_{\text{even}} = \tfrac{1}{2}A(Nh)\cos(Nhx) + \sum_{n=1}^{N-1} Ah(N-2n)\cos[(N-2n)hx]$$

$$+ \tfrac{1}{2}A(-Nh)\cos(-Nhx), \tag{2.40}$$

$$C_{\text{odd}} = \sum_{n=0}^{N-1} Ah[N-(2n+1)]\cos\{[N-(2n+1)]hx\}. \tag{2.41}$$

The weight coefficients now depend upon the functions $\alpha(hx)$, $\beta(hx)$, and $\gamma(hx)$, which themselves depend upon x,

$$\alpha(hx) = [(hx)^2 + hx\sin(hx)\cos(hx) - 2\sin^2 hx](hx)^{-3}, \tag{2.42}$$

$$\beta(hx) = 2[(hx) + hx\cos^2 hx - 2\sin(hx)\cos(hx)](hx)^{-3}, \tag{2.43}$$

$$\gamma(hx) = 4[\sin(hx) - hx\cos(hx)](hx)^{-3}. \tag{2.44}$$

A similar expression holds for the sine-modulated integral

$$\int_{-1}^{+1} A(p)\sin(xp)dp = h\alpha(hx)[A(+1)-A(-1)]\cos x$$

$$+ h\beta(hx)S_{\text{even}}(x) + h\gamma(hx)S_{\text{odd}}(x), \tag{2.45}$$

where

$$S_{\text{even}}(x) = \tfrac{1}{2}A(nh)\sin Nhx + \sum_{n=1}^{N-1} A(Nh-2nh)\sin[(Nh-2nh)x]$$

$$+ \tfrac{1}{2}A(-nh)\sin(-Nhx), \tag{2.46}$$

$$S_{\text{odd}}(x) = \sum_{n=0}^{N-1} A[Nh-(2n+1)h]\sin[(Nh-2nh-h)x]. \tag{2.47}$$

The principal advantage of the Filon scheme is that it avoids the necessity of providing quadrature points which follow the rapid variations of the function $\exp(ixp)$ at large values of xp; all that is required is the use of enough quadrature points to follow the variations of $A(p)$.

When the product hx is small, the functions of α, β, and γ are best calculated from a power series in (hx). The reason is that there is strong cancellation among the trignometric terms. The power series are

$$\alpha = \frac{2\theta^3}{45} - \frac{2\theta^5}{315} + \frac{2\theta^7}{4725}, \tag{2.48}$$

$$\beta = \frac{2}{3} + \frac{2\theta^2}{15} - \frac{4\theta^4}{105} + \frac{2\theta^6}{567} - \frac{4\theta^8}{22275}, \tag{2.49}$$

$$\gamma = \frac{4}{3} - \frac{2\theta^2}{15} + \frac{\theta^4}{210} - \frac{\theta^6}{11340}, \tag{2.50}$$

where $\theta \equiv hx$; they should be used when $\theta \leq 1/6$.

A modification of Filon's original scheme is also of interest. Rather than approximating $A(p)$ by a quadratic function (i.e., parabola) between quadrature points, one can use a linear approximation (i.e., straight line) between quadrature points. The resultant formulae are now

$$\int_{-1}^{1} A(p) \sin xp\, dp = h\alpha_1(hx)[A(1) - A(-1)] \sin x$$
$$+ h\beta_1(hx) \sum_{n=1}^{2N-1} A[(N-n)h] \sin[(N-n)hx], \tag{2.51}$$

$$\int_{-1}^{1} A(p) \cos xp\, dp = \frac{h}{2}\beta_1(hx)[A(1) + A(-1)] \cos x$$
$$+ h\beta_1(hx) \sum_{n=1}^{2N-1} A[(N-n)h] \cos[(N-n)hx], \tag{2.52}$$

where

$$\alpha_1(hx) \equiv (hx - \sin hx)(hx)^{-2}, \tag{2.53}$$

$$\beta_1(hx) = [\sin(hx/2)]^2/(hx/2)^2. \tag{2.54}$$

Note that we recover the usual trapezoidal rule by making the interval very small,

$$\alpha_1(hx) \to 1/2, \quad \beta_1(hx) \to 1 \tag{2.55}$$

as $(hx) \to 0$.

These expressions are much simpler to evaluate than those of the original Filon scheme. The price we have to pay is that the number of quadrature points used will have to be larger in order to maintain the same accuracy.

2.2.5 Euler Transformation of Alternating Series

Consider the series

$$S = \sum_{n=0}^{\infty} (-1)^n a_n, \tag{2.56}$$

where a_n are numerical constants. This series need not be an alternating series in that all the a_n have the same sign. However there is an advantage in the formal manipulations in writing S as an alternating series. In many problems of interest, S converges slowly enough to cause serious problems in the summation.

Euler shows how to speed up the convergence. Let $\varDelta$ be the forward difference operator

$$\varDelta a_0 \equiv a_1 - a_0$$
$$\varDelta^2 a_0 = \varDelta(\varDelta a_0) = \varDelta a_1 - \varDelta a_0 = a_2 - 2a_1 + a_0$$
$$\varDelta^3 a_0 = \varDelta(\varDelta^2 a_0) = \varDelta^2 a_1 - \varDelta^2 a_0 = a_3 - 3a_2 + 3a_1 - a_0$$
$$\cdots\cdots\cdots\cdots\cdots\cdots\cdots\cdots\cdots\cdots\cdots\cdots \tag{2.57}$$

Also consider the operator E defined by

$$Ea_0 = a_1$$
$$E^2 a_0 = a_2 \tag{2.58}$$
$$E^k a_0 = a_k.$$

The relation between $\varDelta$ and E is $E = \varDelta + I$, where I is the unit operator.
Thus, we have

$$S = \sum_{n=0}^{\infty} (-1)^n a_n = \sum_{n=0}^{\infty} (-1)^n E^n a_0$$
$$= \left[\sum_{n=0}^{\infty} (-1)^n E^n \right] a_0 = (I+E)^{-1} a_0$$
$$= (2I + \varDelta)^{-1} a_0$$
$$= \sum_{n=0}^{\infty} \frac{1}{2^{n+1}} (-1)^n \varDelta^n a_0. \tag{2.59}$$

Mathematicians have shown that if the original series converges, then the transformed series also converges to the same value. The usefulness of the transformed series is that it generally converges more rapidly than the original series!

As a simple example, let $a_n = (n+1)^{-1}$. Simple computations yield

$$\Delta a_0 - \tfrac{1}{2}, \quad \Delta^2 a_0 = -\tfrac{1}{3}, \dots, \Delta^n a_0 = \frac{(-1)^n}{n+1} \tag{2.60}$$

so that

$$S = \sum_{n=0}^{\infty} \frac{(-1)^n}{n+1}$$
$$= \tfrac{1}{2} + \sum_{n=0}^{\infty} \frac{1}{2^{n+1}(2n+1)}. \tag{2.61}$$

The results speak for themselves!

In the problems we encounter in diffraction optics, the differences Δ, Δ^2, etc., must be obtained numerically. This is easily done by setting up a difference table in the usual fashion.

2.2.6 Computation of Hankel and Fourier Transforms

Given the background information on the Euler summation method, let us consider (for example) the transform

$$b(v) = \int_0^{\infty} H(\omega) J_0(v\omega) d\omega \tag{2.62}$$

which we rewrite as

$$b(v) = v^{-1} \int_0^{\infty} H(x/v) J_0(x) dx. \tag{2.63}$$

Let $\gamma_1^0, \gamma_2^0, \dots$ be the zeros of $J_0(x)$, i.e., $J(\gamma_l^0) = 0$ and write $b(v)$ as

$$v b(v) = \int_0^{\gamma_1^0} + \int_{\gamma_1^0}^{\gamma_2^0} + \int_{\gamma_2^0}^{\gamma_3^0} + \dots$$
$$= b_0 - b_1 + b_2 - b_3 + \dots. \tag{2.64}$$

The integral is thus given by an alternating series. Generally this series converges slowly but we can speed up the convergence by using the Euler summation method.

This approach involves performing the integration over each half cycle defined by two successive zeros, γ_l^0, γ_{l+1}^0. An alternate approach involves integration between two successive maxima of $J_0(x)$, that is, between two successive zeros of its derivative $J_1(x)$, γ_l', and γ_{l+1}'.

The same procedure can be employed if $J_0(x)$ is replaced by $J_1(x)$ or by $\sin x$ or $\cos x$. Probably the best method for evaluating the individual integrals is Gauss quadrature.

This method can also be adapted for use when the upper limit is finite, say ω_0. Then

$$vb(v) = b_0 - b_1 + b_2 - \int_{\gamma_1^0}^{\omega_0} H(x/v) J_0(x) dx \qquad (2.65)$$

if $\gamma_2^0 < \omega_0 < \gamma_3^0$. The remaining manipulations are obvious.

2.2.7 Hilbert Transforms

Hilbert transforms are of common occurrence in diffraction optics particularly with respect to coherent spatial filtering techniques. We have

$$\hat{f}(p_1) = \int_a^b \frac{f(p)dp}{(p - p_1)}, \qquad a < p_1 < b, \qquad (2.66)$$

where $f(p)$ is bounded in the interval of integration, although it can have discontinuities. For example, such integrals occur in the diffraction theory of the Foucault knife-edge test where $f(p)$ is the pupil function of the system under test. The integral is to be interpreted as a Cauchy principal value integral. Although many people pay lip service to this restriction, it is actually a nontrivial point and has led to some confusion.

By definition, an integral is Cauchy principal valued if the following limit exists:

$$\lim_{\varepsilon \to 0} \left(\int_a^{p_1 - \varepsilon} + \int_{p_1 + \varepsilon}^b \right) \frac{f(p)dp}{(p - p_1)} \qquad (2.67)$$

for $a < p_1 < b$. The integral is not even defined if $p_1 = a$ or b. This limit can be finite or infinite. The general value of this same integral is

$$\lim_{\varepsilon \to 0} \int_a^{p_1 - \varepsilon} \frac{f(p)dp}{p - p_1} + \lim_{\eta \to 0} \int_{p_1 + \eta}^b \frac{f(p)dp}{p - p_1} \qquad (2.68)$$

and can be finite, infinite, or even of undetermined value. The Cauchy principal value is the special case $\varepsilon = \eta$.

As a simple example consider

$$\int_{-a}^{b} \frac{dp}{p} = \log \left| \frac{b}{a} \right| + \log \left| \frac{\varepsilon}{\eta} \right|, \qquad a > 0. \tag{2.69}$$

The general value

$$\int_{-a}^{b} \frac{dp}{p} = \log \left| \frac{b}{a} \right| + \lim_{\substack{\varepsilon \to 0 \\ \eta \to 0}} \log \left| \frac{\varepsilon}{\eta} \right| \tag{2.70}$$

is perfectly arbitrary in that we can attain any value, depending upon how we take the limits. The principal value on the other hand is well defined

$$\int_{a}^{b} \frac{dp}{p} = \log \left| \frac{b}{a} \right|. \tag{2.71}$$

The numerical evaluation of Hilbert transforms can be carried out in several ways. One common technique is to subtract the singularity

$$\int_{a}^{b} \frac{f(p)dp}{p - p_1} = \int_{a}^{b} \frac{f(p) - f(p_1)}{p - p_1} dp + f(p_1) \int_{a}^{b} \frac{dp}{p - p_1} \tag{2.72}$$

and evaluate the first integral on the right-hand side by a standard quadrature formula.

A second way out of the difficulty is to split the interval of integration into two subintervals, one of which contains the singular point $p = p_1$ at its center. Thus,

$$\int_{a}^{b} \frac{f(p)dp}{(p - p_1)} = \int_{a}^{a + 2p_1} \frac{f(p)dp}{(p - p_1)} + \int_{a + 2p_1}^{b} \frac{f(p)dp}{(p - p_1)} \tag{2.73}$$

if $2p_1 < b - a$, with an obvious modification if $2p_1 > b - a$. The singular point $p = p_1$ in the second integral on the right-hand side is now outside the interval of integration. Consequently, the integrand is bounded and can be evaluated by any of the standard quadrature formulae we have studied. The first integral is still singular at $p = p_1$, but since the singular point now lies at the midpoint of the interval of integration we can employ an even-point Gauss quadrature formula. The use of the even-point scheme is such that the values of the integrand in the immediate vicinity of the singular point tend to cancel each other and thus the integral can be evaluated accurately.

2.2.8 Some Asymptotic Formulae

The integrals under discussion must usually be evaluated for large values of the parameters. Consider, for example, the integral in (2.38). When x is very large we are going to have a problem with it no matter how many quadrature points we use. Yet we would expect $a(x)$ to have a simple asymptotic behavior for very large values of x. This section is devoted to an ingenious approach (due to *Willis*) for handling such problems.

Let us consider the integral

$$I(\alpha) = \int\limits_0^\infty g(p)G(x, p)e^{-\alpha p}\, dp, \tag{2.74}$$

where $\alpha \geq 0$. Assume that $g(o)$ can be expanded in a Taylor series about $p=0$ and that the radius of convergence of this series covers the range of integration. Thus,

$$I(\alpha) = \sum\limits_{n=0}^\infty \frac{1}{n!} g^{(n)}(0) \int\limits_0^\infty G(x, p)p^n e^{-\alpha p}\, dp \tag{2.75}$$

upon interchange of summation and integration. Now set

$$\phi(\alpha) \equiv \int\limits_0^\infty G(x, p)e^{-\alpha p}\, dp \tag{2.76}$$

and also expand it in a Taylor series about $\alpha = 0$

$$\phi(\alpha) = \sum\limits_{n=0}^\infty \frac{1}{n!} \phi^{(n)}(0)\alpha^n, \tag{2.77}$$

where

$$(-1)^n \phi^{(n)}(\alpha) = \int\limits_0^\infty G(x, p)p^n e^{-\alpha p}\, dp. \tag{2.78}$$

Consequently, $I(\alpha)$ becomes

$$I(\alpha) = \sum\limits_{n=0}^\infty \frac{1}{n!}(-1)^n g^{(n)}(0)\phi^{(n)}(\alpha). \tag{2.79}$$

If we now let α approach zero, we obtain the following expansion for the original integral:

$$\int\limits_0^\infty g(p)G(x, p)dp = \sum\limits_{n=0}^\infty \frac{1}{n!}(-1)^n g^{(n)}(0)\phi^{(n)}(0). \tag{2.80}$$

Several special cases are of importance in diffraction optics. As our first example consider the integral

$$\int\limits_0^\infty g(p)p^{-1} \sin xp\, dp \tag{2.81}$$

so that $G(x,p)=p^{-1}\sin xp$. To obtain an expression for large x, we start with the integral

$$\phi(\alpha)= \int_0^\infty p^{-1}\sin xp\, e^{-\alpha p}\, dp$$

$$= \frac{\pi}{2} - \frac{1}{x}\alpha + \frac{1}{3x^3}\alpha^3 - \frac{1}{5x^5}\alpha^5 + \dots \tag{2.82}$$

so that

$$\phi(0)=\frac{\pi}{2}, \qquad \phi^{(3)}(0)=\frac{2!}{x^3}$$

$$\phi^{(1)}(0)=\frac{1}{x}, \qquad \phi^{(4)}(0)=0$$

$$\phi^{(2)}(0)=0, \qquad \phi^{(5)}(0)=\frac{4!}{x^5} \tag{2.83}$$

$$I(0)= \int_0^\infty g(p)p^{-1}\sin xp\, dp$$

$$\sim \frac{\pi}{2}g(0) + \frac{g^{(1)}(0)}{x} - \frac{g^{(3)}(0)}{3x^3} + \dots \tag{2.84}$$

is the appropriate asymptotic formula. Letting x approach infinity, we obtain the known result

$$\lim_{x\to\infty} \int_0^\infty g(p)p^{-1}\sin xp\, dp = \frac{\pi}{2}g(0). \tag{2.85}$$

As our second worked example, take $G(x,p)=J_0(xp)$. Then

$$\phi(\alpha)= \int_0^\infty J_0(xp)e^{-\alpha p}\, dp$$

$$=(\alpha^2+x^2)^{-1/2}$$

$$= \frac{1}{x} - \frac{1}{2x^3}\alpha^2 + \frac{3}{8x^5}\alpha^4 - \dots, \tag{2.86}$$

$$I(0)= \int_0^\infty g(p)J_0(xp)\, dp$$

$$\sim \frac{g(0)}{x} - \frac{g^{(2)}(0)}{2x^3} + \frac{g^{(4)}(0)}{8x^5} - \dots. \tag{2.87}$$

In like fashion one can derive numerous expansions of which the most useful (for diffraction optics) are

$$\int_0^\infty g(p)\sin xp\,dp \sim \frac{g(0)}{x} - \frac{g^{(2)}(0)}{x^3} + \frac{g^{(4)}(0)}{x^5} - \cdots, \tag{2.88}$$

$$\int_0^\infty g(p)\cos xp\,dp \sim -\frac{g^{(1)}(0)}{x^2} + \frac{g^{(3)}(0)}{x^4} - \frac{g^{(5)}(0)}{x^6} + \cdots, \tag{2.89}$$

$$\int_0^\infty g(p)J_1(xp)\,dp \sim \frac{g(0)}{x} + \frac{g^{(1)}(0)}{x^2} - \frac{g^{(3)}(0)}{2x^4} + \cdots. \tag{2.90}$$

Although $G(x, p)$ is generally oscillatory, this is not a requirement. Two important formulae which $G(x, p)$ is nonoscillatory are

$$\int_0^\infty g(p)e^{-xp}\,dp \sim \frac{g(0)}{x} + \frac{g^{(1)}(0)}{x^2} + \frac{g^{(3)}(0)}{x^3} + \cdots, \tag{2.91}$$

$$\int_0^\infty g(p)e^{-x^2p^2}\,dp \sim \left(\frac{\pi}{4}\right)^{1/2}\frac{g(0)}{x} + \frac{g^{(1)}(0)}{2x^2} + \left(\frac{\pi}{4}\right)^{1/2}\frac{g^{(2)}(0)}{4x^3} + \cdots. \tag{2.92}$$

For many diffraction problems, the upper limit will be finite rather than infinite but this causes no trouble. By the time the above expressions are numerically useful, the oscillations have caused the main contribution to the integral to be from the integrand evaluated at the origin.

Strictly speaking, these formulae are really not asymptotic formulae but Tauberian, since the behavior of the integral for large values of the parameter is determined by the behavior of the integrand at the origin.

2.3 Diffraction Integrals of Incoherent Imagery

Given the information of Sect. 2.2, let us now consider the various diffraction integrals of incoherent imagery.

2.3.1 Point Spread Function

We employ Luneberg's formulation of the Kirchhoff scalar diffraction theory. The complex diffracted amplitudes $a(x, y)$ at a point (x, y) in the Fraunhofer receiving plane due to a point source located at (x_0, y_0) in the object plane are given by

$$a(v_p', v_q') = \iint\limits_{\text{aperture}} A_0(p', q')\exp[ikW(x_0, y_0, p', q')$$

$$+ i(v_p'p' + v_q'q')]\,dp'\,dq'. \tag{2.93}$$

Here p', q' are the optical direction cosines of the normals to the converging wave front in the image space; also $v'_p = kx$, $v'_q = ky$.

$A_0(p', q')$ is the amplitude distribution over the wave front; more precisely

$$A_0(p', q') = \frac{\text{amplitude distribution over the exit pupil}}{\text{amplitude distribution over the entrance pupil}}. \tag{2.94}$$

Obviously,

$$-1 \leq A_0(p', q') \leq 1 \tag{2.95}$$

for the system to be physically realizable. In particular, if $A_0(p', q')$ is a constant, then one has the so-called Airy objective which is an excellent approximation to the usual types of low numerical aperture systems that occur in practice. The aberration function W is measured in wavelength units and is the Hamilton mixed characteristic.

We will find it convenient to convert dimensionless variables p, q, v_p, v_q defined through the relations

$$\begin{aligned}
p \equiv p'/p'_{max}, \qquad q \equiv q'/q'_{max} \\
v_p \equiv v'_p p'_{max}, \qquad v_q \equiv v'_q q'_{max}
\end{aligned} \tag{2.96}$$

where p'_{max} and q'_{max} are the maximum values of p' and q'.

Since only the absolute square of $a(v_p, v_q)$ is an observable quantity, we shall work only with the ratio

$$t(v_p, v_q) \equiv \left| \frac{a(v_p, v_q)}{a(0, 0)} \right|^2. \tag{2.97}$$

$t(v_p, v_q)$ is termed the point spread function. It is a nonnegative function bounded by the limits

$$0 \leq t(v_p, v_q) \leq 1. \tag{2.98}$$

Furthermore,

$$t(v_p, v_q) \to 0 \quad \text{as} \quad v_p^2 + v_q^2 \to \infty \tag{2.99}$$

such that

$$\int\int_{-\infty}^{\infty} t(v_p, v_q) dv_p dv_q = \int\int_{\text{aperture}} |A_0(p, q)|^2 dp dq. \tag{2.100}$$

Probably the two most important aperture configurations are the circle and the slit (very narrow rectangle). For the former,

$$a(v,\phi)= \int\limits_{0}^{1} \int\limits_{0}^{2\pi} A_0(\varrho,\theta)\exp[iv\varrho\cos(\theta-\phi)]\,d\theta\,\varrho\,d\varrho, \tag{2.101}$$

where we have converted to cylindrical coordinates in both the aperture and image plane. If A_0 depends only on ϱ, then

$$a(v)= \int\limits_{0}^{1} A_0(\varrho)J_0(v\varrho)\varrho\,d\varrho. \tag{2.102}$$

(Note that unessential numerical factors in front of integrals will be dropped because a normalization will almost always be imposed at the end of the analysis.) The corresponding expression for the slit aperture is

$$a(v_p)= \int\limits_{-1}^{+1} A_0(p)\exp[ikW(p)+v_p p]\,dp. \tag{2.103}$$

There are two general approaches to handling W. Following Hamilton (the traditional approach), we develop W into a series of the form

$$-W=W^{(0)}+W^{(1)}+W^{(2)}+W^{(3)}+W^{(4)}+\dots, \tag{2.104}$$

where $W^{(n)}$ is homogeneous and of degree n in x_0, y_0, p, q. When the optical system is rotationally symmetric, the appropriate combination of independent variables is

$$u_1 \equiv x_0^2+y_0^2$$
$$u_2 \equiv p^2+q^2$$
$$u_3 = x_0 p+y_0 q. \tag{2.105}$$

However, no loss of generality results from setting $y_0=0$, so that x_0^2, p^2+q^2, and xp are the independent variables. It can also be shown that $W^{(n)}\equiv 0$ when n is an odd integer. When the optical system is not rotationally symmetric, the analysis is more complicated. The three cases of importance are: 1) no symmetry of any kind, 2) one plane of symmetry, and 3) two planes of symmetry. The classification is now very tedious and reference is made to the literature for the details. We confine ourselves to rotationally symmetric optical systems.

The terms in $W^{(2)}$ are

$$W^{(2)}=W_{020}(p^2+q^2)+M(x_0 p+y_0 q), \tag{2.106}$$

where W_{020} is the defocusing parameter and M is the magnification ratio.

The third-order aberrations (i.e., terms in $W^{(4)}$) are

$$C_{311}x^3p = W_{311}p, \qquad \text{(distortion)}$$

$$C_{040}(p^2+q^2)^2 = W_{040}(p^2+q^2)^2, \qquad \text{(spherical aberration)}$$

$$C_{131}x_0p(p^2+q^2) = W_{131}p(p^2+q^2), \qquad \text{(coma)}$$

$$C_{222}x_0^2p^2 = W_{222}p^2 \qquad \text{(astigmatism)}$$

$$C_{220}x_0^2(p^2+q^2) = W_{222}(p^2+q^2), \qquad \text{(field curvature)}.$$

The fifth-order aberrations (i.e., terms in $W^{(6)}$) are

$$C_{420}x_0^4(p^2+q^2) = W_{420}(p^2+q^2), \qquad \text{(field curvature)}$$

$$C_{240}x_0^2(p^2+q^2)^2 = W_{240}(p^2+q^2)^2, \qquad \text{(spherical aberration)}$$

$$C_{060}(p^2+q^2)^3 = W_{060}(p^2+q^2)^3, \qquad \text{(spherical aberration)}$$

$$C_{511}x_0^5p = W_{511}p, \qquad \text{(distortion)}$$

$$C_{331}x_0^3p(p^2+q^2) = W_{311}p(p^2+q^2), \qquad \text{(coma)}$$

$$C_{151}x_0p(p^2+q^2)^2 = W_{151}p(p^2+q^2)^2, \qquad \text{(coma)}$$

$$C_{422}x_0p^2 = W_{422}p^2, \qquad \text{(astigmatism)}$$

$$C_{242}x_0^2p^2(p^2+q^2) = W_{242}p^2(p^2+q^2), \qquad \text{(astigmatism)}$$

$$C_{333}x_0^3p^3 = W_{333}p^3. \qquad \text{(trefoil)}$$

Some of the fifth-order aberrations differ by only a constant term (at *fixed* x_0) from some of the third-order aberrations. When we collect terms of the mixed characteristic, it collapses to

$$
\begin{aligned}
-W = {} & (W_{131}+W_{151})q + (W_{222}+W_{422})q^2 + W_{333}q^3 \\
& + (W_{220}+W_{420}+W_{020})(p^2+q^2) \\
& + (W_{040}+W_{240})(p^2+q^2)^2 + W_{060}(p^2+q^2)^3 \\
& + (W_{131}+W_{331})q(p^2+q^2) + W_{151}q(p^2+q^2)^2 \\
& + W_{242}q_2(p^2+q^2).
\end{aligned} \tag{2.107}
$$

A word of warning. The series expansion, (2.104), of W is purely formal and the question of the convergence of the expansion to W has never been answered. The class of aberration functions which admit these series expansions is limited. It is conceivable that practical systems exist for which the Hamilton expansion is inadequate, as for example any W which has a discontinuity such as in a Fresnel lens.

It is now convenient to employ slightly different variables in the basic diffraction integral. The terms of $W^{(2)}$ are combined with the linear terms

$$(v_p - Mx_0)p + (v_q - My_0)q \equiv xp + yq \tag{2.108}$$

so that $a(v_p, v_q) \to a(x, y)$.

The alternative approach to representing W is due to Zernike. In this approach, the aberration function is first expressed in terms of cylindrical coordinates ϱ and θ; then $W(\varrho, \theta)$ at a fixed object point is expanded in a double series over the angular and radial variables. The angular functions are $\cos m\theta$, $\sin m\theta$ while the radial functions are the Zernike circle polynomials $\mathscr{R}_n^{(m)}(\varrho)$. Reference is made to the standard literature for details.

2.3.2 Optical Transfer Function

Let us consider the two-dimensional Fourier transform of the point spread function

$$\mathscr{T}(\alpha, \beta) = \int\limits_{-\infty}^{\infty} \int t(x, y) \exp(i\alpha x + i\beta y) dx dy. \tag{2.109}$$

The integral exists since $t(x, y)$ is integrable. The normalized quantity

$$T(\alpha, \beta) = \mathscr{T}(\alpha, \beta)/\mathscr{T}(0, 0) \tag{2.110}$$

is termed the incoherent optical transfer function (or more often just the transfer function). It is generally a complex valued function of its arguments. The reasons for this nomenclature will be made clear shortly, but for the interim we can consider $T(\alpha, \beta)$ to be a useful ancillary function of the space^{-1} variables α, β.

The fact that

a) $t(x, y) \geq 0$ for $\forall x, y$

b) $\int\limits_{-\infty}^{\infty} \int t(x, y) dx dy = \text{constant}$

bestows upon $T(\alpha, \beta)$ many special properties. For those familiar with probability theory, t and T correspond to a bivariate probability density function and its corresponding bivariate characteristic function, respectively. It is not our intention to go into any great detail concerning these properties, except to quote two important ones

$$|T(\alpha, \beta)| \leq T(0, 0) = 1 \tag{2.111}$$

and

$$T^*(\alpha, \beta) = T(-\alpha, -\beta) \tag{2.112}$$

or

$$T_R(\alpha, \beta) = T_R(-\alpha, -\beta)$$
$$T_I(\alpha, \beta) = -T_I(-\alpha, -\beta). \tag{2.113}$$

In other words, the real part of the transfer function is an even function while the imaginary part is an odd function.

In some cases it is possible to evaluate $T(\alpha, \beta)$ directly from the two-dimensional Fourier transform by brute force integration (more on this shortly). However, an alternate expression for $T(\alpha, \beta)$ as a convolution integral over the pupil function $A(p, q)$ follows by noting that $t(x, y) = a(x, y)a^*(x, y)$ and recalling that the Fourier transform of the product of two functions is the convolution of their Fourier transforms. It is convenient to split the convolution-free variables α, β equally between A and A^*; hence,

$$T(\alpha, \beta) = \frac{\int\limits_{\infty}^{\infty} \int A(p + \tfrac{1}{2}\alpha, q + \tfrac{1}{2}\beta) A^*(p - \tfrac{1}{2}\alpha, q - \tfrac{1}{2}\beta) dp\, dq}{\int\limits_{-\infty}^{\infty} \int A(p, q) A^*(p, q) dp\, dq}. \tag{2.114}$$

If $A(p, q)$ is such that $A_0(p, q) = 1$, then the denominator is simply the area of the aperture. The infinite limits of integration are purely formal. The importance of the above expression lies in the fact that is expresses the transfer function directly in terms of the pupil function and, hence, the aberrations. Furthermore, $A(p, q)$ vanishes identically for value of p, q outside the aperture; therefore, the region of integration depends upon the shape of the aperture. This convolution operation is simply the product of the two displaced pupil functions integrated over their common area. At some point (α', β') the convolved area will vanish and $T(\alpha, \beta)$ remains zero for any values of α, β exceeding α', β'.

It is convenient, however, to reduce the problem to a single frequency variable $\omega \equiv (\alpha^2 + \beta^2)^{1/2}$ by transforming the aperture variables p, q to new variables s, t, by a rotation through an angle $\phi \equiv \arctan(s/t)$

$$s = p\cos\phi + q\sin\phi$$
$$t = q\cos\phi - p\sin\phi. \tag{2.115}$$

The optical transfer function is now given by

$$T(\omega, \phi) = T_R(\omega, \phi) + iT_I(\omega, \phi), \tag{2.116}$$

where

$$T_R(\omega, \phi) = \int\limits_{-a}^{a} \int\limits_{-b}^{b} A_0(s + \tfrac{1}{2}\omega, t) A_0(s - \tfrac{1}{2}\omega, t)$$

$$\cdot \cos[kW(s + \tfrac{1}{2}\omega, t) - kW(s - \tfrac{1}{2}\omega, t)] \, ds \, dt, \tag{2.117a}$$

$$T_I(\omega, \phi) = \int\limits_{-a}^{a} \int\limits_{-b}^{b} A_0(s + \tfrac{1}{2}\omega, t) A_0(s - \tfrac{1}{2}\omega, t)$$

$$\cdot \sin[kW(s + \tfrac{1}{2}\omega, t) - kW(s - \tfrac{1}{2}\omega, t)] \, ds \, dt. \tag{2.117b}$$

We now drop the normalization factor and assume that $T(0, \phi) = 1$ for all ϕ. A useful fact: $T_R(\omega, \phi)$ is an even function of ϕ; $T_I(\omega, \phi)$ is an odd function of ϕ.

In the important case of a circular aperture of unit normalized radius, the limits of integration are

$$\int\limits_{-a}^{a} \int\limits_{-b}^{b} (\cdot) \, ds \, dt, \tag{2.118}$$

where

$$a \equiv [1 - (\omega/2)^2]^{1/2}, \quad b \equiv (\omega - t^2)^{1/2} - \omega/2 \quad \text{for} \quad 0 \le \omega \le 2. \tag{2.119}$$

The problem thus reduces to evaluating these integrals as functions of the aberrations, spatial frequency ω, and azimuth ϕ.

The number of cases for which $T(\omega, \phi)$ can be evaluated in closed form is very small. For an aberration-free circular aperture its result is

$$T(\omega) = (2/\pi)[\arccos(\omega/2) - (\omega/2)\Omega], \quad 0 \le \omega \le 2$$

$$= 0 \qquad\qquad\qquad , \quad \omega > 2, \tag{2.120}$$

where $\Omega \equiv (1 - \omega^2/4)^{1/2}$.

We now outline a numerical integration scheme in enough detail so that anyone wishing to employ the method can easily fill in the details and adapt the method to available computers. One desirable feature is that in the convolution operation the same number of quadrature points is always available. Gauss quadrature, as previously discussed, is generally the most accurate. We have found that six-digit accuracy is desirable when using the transfer function to evaluate the images of extended objects. This accuracy is, of course, not required in lens design.

Consider the integration of (2.117a or b) over the inner integrals

$$\int\limits_{-b}^{b} A_{\cos}^{\sin}[\cdot] \, ds \equiv \int\limits_{-b}^{b} f(\omega, \phi, s, t) \, ds. \tag{2.121}$$

Change the interval of integration $(-b, b)$ to the standard Gauss quadrature interval $(-1, 1)$ by the formula

$$F \equiv \int_{-b}^{b} f(\omega, \phi, s, t) ds = b \int_{-1}^{1} f(\omega, \phi, s', t) ds', \qquad (2.122)$$

where $s = bs'$. Employing N point Gauss quadrature to evaluate this expression yields

$$F = b \sum_{n=1}^{N} H_n f(\omega, \phi, s'_n, t). \qquad (2.123)$$

The outer integral then becomes

$$\int_{-a}^{a} [(\omega - t^2)^{1/2} - \tfrac{1}{2}\omega] \sum_{n=1}^{N} H_n f(\omega, \phi, s'_n, t) dt . \qquad (2.124)$$

Repeat the same procedure with respect to t; call the integrand in (2.124) $G(\omega, \phi, t)$; then

$$\int_{-a}^{a} G(\omega, \phi, t) dt = a \int_{+1}^{-1} G(\omega, \phi, t') dt', \qquad (2.125)$$

where $t = at'$. Consequently,

$$T(\omega, \phi) = (1 - \omega^2/4)^{1/2} \sum_{n=1}^{N} H_m G(\omega, \phi, t_m). \qquad (2.126)$$

When the aperture is circular, the spatial frequency ω is limited to $(0, 2)$ because when $\omega > 2$, the convolution integral vanishes. The dimensionless spatial frequency ω is related to the physical parameters of the system by

$$\Omega = \omega/2\lambda F ,$$

where Ω is the dimensional spatial frequency expressed in cycles/length, λ is the wavelength of the light, and F is the f/number of the system. The physical cutoff of the system occurs at $\Omega = 1/\lambda F$.

The slit aperture configuration is much easier to handle. Here the transfer function $T(\alpha)$ can often be evaluated analytically by direct Fourier transformation of the point spread function $t(x)$. Failing this, one can employ one of the numerical integration schemes discussed in Sect. 1. The alternate procedure is to evaluate the convolution integral

$$T_R(\alpha) = \int_{-a}^{a} A_0(p + \tfrac{1}{2}\alpha) A_0(p - \tfrac{1}{2}\alpha)$$
$$\cdot \cos[kW(p + \tfrac{1}{2}\alpha) - kW(p - \tfrac{1}{2}\alpha)] dp$$

$$T_I(\alpha) = \int_{-a}^{a} A_0(p + \tfrac{1}{2}\alpha) A_0(p - \tfrac{1}{2}\alpha)$$
$$\cdot \sin[kW(p + \tfrac{1}{2}\alpha) - kW(p - \tfrac{1}{2}\alpha)] dp,$$

(2.127)

where $a \equiv 1 - |\alpha|$ and $|\alpha| \leq 2$. The procedure outlined at (2.122, 123) would apply, for example.

2.3.3 Cumulative Point Spread Function

The cumulative point spread function (also termed the total illuminance, encircled energy, etc.) is a quantity that serves as a useful index of the diffraction performance of an optical system. This function describes the integrated behavior of the point spread function and is thus a smooth function in comparison with the point spread function. We define the cumulative point spread function by

$$L(v_0) = M \int \int t(x, y) dx dy,$$

(2.128)

where the integration is taken over a circle of radius $v_0 = (x^2 + y^2)^{1/2}$ from the Gaussian image point. Since all the intensity must be contained in a large enough circle

$$\lim_{v_0 \to \infty} L(v_0) = 1,$$

(2.129)

M is the corresponding normalization constant. By virtue of the condition $t(x, y) \geq 0$, it obviously follows that $L(v_1) \geq L(v_2)$ if $v_1 \geq v_2$, so that $L(v_0)$ is a monotone nondecreasing positive function.

Although direct numerical evaluation of $L(v_0)$ is sometimes the only available approach, there are alternative representations that are useful. It seems reasonable to expect a functional relation between $L(v_0)$ and $T(\omega, \phi)$ in view of the fact that the point spread function and the transfer function are Fourier transform pairs. At this stage, it is convenient to change to cylindrical coordinates in the receiving plane $x = v \cos\theta$, $y = v \sin\theta$ (we now assume a circular aperture),

$$L(v_0) = M \int_0^{2\pi} \int_0^{v_0} t(v, \theta) v \, dv \, d\theta.$$

(2.130)

But also

$$t(v,0)= \int\limits_{-\pi}^{\pi} \int\limits_{0}^{2} T(\omega, \phi)\exp[iv\omega\cos(\phi-\theta)]\omega\,d\omega\,d\phi, \tag{2.131}$$

which is the expression that t is the inverse Fourier transform of T.

Substitution of this double integral into the previous double integral yields, upon changing the order of integration,

$$L(v_0)=M \int\limits_{0}^{2\pi} \int\limits_{0}^{2} T(\omega, \phi)\omega\,d\omega\,d\phi \int\limits_{0}^{v_0} v\,dv \int\limits_{0}^{2\pi}$$

$$\cdot \exp[iv\omega\cos(\phi-\theta)]\,d\theta. \tag{2.132}$$

However, the integral over θ is independent of ϕ and is expressible as a Bessel function. This leaves

$$L(v_0)=2\pi M v_0 \int\limits_{-\pi}^{\pi} \int\limits_{0}^{2} T(\omega, \phi)\omega\,d\omega\,d\phi \int\limits_{0}^{v_0} J_0(\omega v)v\,dv$$

$$=2\pi M v_0 \int\limits_{0}^{2} \int\limits_{-\pi}^{\pi} T(\omega, \phi)\,d\phi\,J_1(v_0\omega)\,d\omega. \tag{2.133}$$

This expression is advantageous because it allows us to evaluate $L(v_0)$ from a knowledge of the transfer function whose effective domain is finite, whereas a direct numerical evaluation of $L(v_0)$ requires a knowledge of $t(x,y)$ over the infinite plane.

In order to determine the normalizing constant M, we utilize (2.129). Consequently,

$$L(\infty) \sim 2\pi M \int\limits_{-\pi}^{\pi} T(0, \phi)\,d\phi \tag{2.134}$$

but $T(0, \phi)\equiv 1$ for all ϕ so that $M=(2\pi)^{-2}$.

The final result is best expressed in the form

$$L(v_0)=v_0 \int\limits_{0}^{2} \tilde{T}(\omega)J_1(v_0\omega)\,d\omega, \tag{2.135}$$

where

$$\tilde{T}(\omega)\equiv \frac{1}{2\pi} \int\limits_{-\pi}^{\pi} T(\omega, \phi)\,d\phi$$

$$=\frac{1}{2\pi} \int\limits_{-\pi}^{\pi} T_R(\omega, \phi)\,d\phi \tag{2.136}$$

is the angle-averaged transfer function. Note that only the real part of the transfer function enters into the evaluation of the cumulative point spread function. In the special case where the only aberrations are spherical aberration and defocusing,

$$T_R(\omega, \phi) = T(\omega), \quad \text{so that} \quad \tilde{T}(\omega) = T(\omega). \tag{2.137}$$

Before examining numerical schemes, we examine the qualitative behavior of $L(v_0)$.

For small values of v_0, we obtain the behavior of $L(v_0)$ in terms of the moments of the transfer function by expanding the Bessel function $J_1(v_0\omega)$ in a power series and integrating termwise

$$L(v_0) \approx \frac{v_0^2}{2} \int_0^2 \tilde{T}(\omega)\omega \, d\omega - \frac{v_0^4}{16} \int_0^2 \tilde{T}(\omega)\omega^3 \, d\omega + O(v_0^6). \tag{2.138}$$

The first integral is the volume under the transfer function [namely, the Strehl criterion $t(0, \theta)$], while the second integral is the second moment of the transfer function. In fact, the series in (2.138) is simply an expansion of $L(v_0)$ in terms of the even moments of $\tilde{T}(\omega)$.

For large values of v_0, $L(v_0)$ behaves as

$$L(v_0) \sim 1 + \frac{\tilde{T}^{(1)}(0)}{v_0} - \frac{\tilde{T}^{(3)}(0)}{2v_0^3} + \dots \tag{2.139}$$

by virtue of (2.90). Note that $\tilde{T}^{(1)}(0) < 0$. If $A(p, q) \equiv \text{constant}$, then $\tilde{T}^{(1)}(0) = -2/\pi$ independent of the aberrations. Thus, $L(v_0)$ ultimately behaves as

$$L(v_0) \sim 1 - (2/\pi v_0). \tag{2.140}$$

This result is not really surprising because the behavior of $L(v_0)$ for large v_0 is governed by the behavior of $T(\omega, \phi)$ in the vicinity of $\omega = 0$ where aberrations are not important. The approach to the limiting value of unity is slow, having only v_0^{-1}.

As an illustrative example, consider an aberration-free circular aperture. Lord Rayleigh showed, via direct integration of the point spread function, that

$$L(v_0) = 1 - J_0^2(v_0) - J_1^2(v_0). \tag{2.141}$$

Numerical values of $L(v_0)$ as evaluated by (2.140, 141) are compared in Table 2.2. The agreement is excellent even for values as small as $v_0 = 4$.

The main difficulty with the above approach is that a knowledge of the transfer function is required. An alternative representation of $L(v_0)$ which is useful when the aperture is circular and the aberrations rotationally symmetric can be developed directly in terms of the pupil function. Set $t = aa^*$ and

Table 2.2. Comparison of numerical values
of $L(v_0)$

v_0	L (exact)	L (Tauberian)
4	0.8379	0.8408
6	0.9008	0.8939
8	0.9155	0.9204
10	0.9376	0.9363
12	0.9478	0.9469
14	0.9530	0.9545
16	0.9612	0.9602

substitute the integral representations of a and a^* into (2.135). Upon changing the order of integration, the final result can be cast into the form

$$L(v_0) = M \int_0^1 \int_0^1 A_0(\varrho) A_0(\varrho') \cos[kW(\varrho) - kW(\varrho')]$$
$$\cdot Q(v_0, \varrho, \varrho') \varrho \varrho' \, d\varrho \, d\varrho', \tag{2.142}$$

where

$$Q(v_0, \varrho, \varrho') = \int_0^{v_0} J_0(\varrho v) J_0(\varrho' v) v \, dv$$
$$= (v_0^2/2) [J_0^2(v_0 \varrho) + J_0^2(v_0 \varrho')], \quad \varrho = \varrho'$$
$$= v_0^2 (\varrho^2 - \varrho'^2)^{-1} [\varrho J_0(v_0 \varrho) J_0(v_0 \varrho')$$
$$- \varrho' J_0(v_0 \varrho) J_0(v_0 \varrho')], \quad \varrho \neq \varrho'. \tag{2.143}$$

The normalization constant N can be determined by Parseval's theorem applied to the Fourier transform pair $a(v)$ and $A(\varrho)$

$$L(\infty) = \int_0^\infty t(v) v \, dv = \int_0^1 A_0^2(\varrho) \varrho \, d\varrho. \tag{2.144}$$

Consequently,

$$M^{-1} = \int_0^1 A_0^2(\varrho) \varrho \, d\varrho, \quad \text{(general case)}$$
$$= 1/2, \quad A_0 = 1. \tag{2.145}$$

Assuming that the aberration function is given, then the double integral can be evaluated by a quadrature scheme of the form

$$L(v_0) = M \sum_{n=1}^N \sum_{m=1}^N H_n H_n f(\varrho_n, \varrho_m', v_0), \tag{2.146}$$

where f is the integrand of (2.142). A further reduction in computing time follows from the fact that f is a symmetric function of the independent variables, allowing us to reduce the above expression to

$$L(v_0) = M \sum_{n=1}^{N} H_n^2 f(\varrho_n, \varrho_n, v_0)$$

$$+ (M/2) \sum_{n=1}^{N} \sum_{m=1}^{n-1} H_n H_m f(\varrho_n, \varrho_m, v_0). \tag{2.147}$$

A modification of the preceding analysis is necessary when a slit aperture is employed; now

$$L(x_0) = M \int_{-x_0}^{x_0} t(x) dx, \tag{2.148}$$

where M is a normalizing constant such that $L(\infty) = 1$.

A representation analogous to (2.135) is

$$L(x_0) = (1/\pi) \int_{-2}^{2} T(\omega) \omega^{-1} \sin x_0 \omega d\omega$$

while the representation corresponding to (2.142) is

$$L(x_0) = M \int_{-1}^{1} \int_{-1}^{1} A_0(p_1) A_0(p_2) \cos[kW(p_1) - kW(p_2)]$$

$$\cdot Q(p_1, p_2, x_0) dp_1 dp_2, \tag{2.149}$$

where

$$Q(p_1, p_2, x_0) = 2(p_1 - p_2)^{-1} \sin[x_0(p_1 - p_2)], \quad p_1 \neq p_2$$
$$= 2x_0, \quad p_1 = p_2 \tag{2.150}$$

and

$$M^{-1} = \int_{-1}^{1} A_0^2(p) dp. \tag{2.151}$$

2.3.4 Images of Extended Objects

Although the previous diffraction functions have important uses, the actual diffraction image of an (incoherently illuminated) object is often times the desired quantity.

The image $h(x, y)$ of an extended object $o(x, y)$ can be obtained by direct integration of the point spread function over the object intensity. Thus

$$h(x, y) = \int\int t(x, y'; y, y') o(x', y') dx' dy'. \tag{2.152}$$

In order to proceed further, we assume spatial invariance of the point spread function $t(x, x'; y, y') = t(x - x'; y - y')$ so that

$$h(x, y) = \int\int t(x - x'; y - y') o(x', y') dx' dy'. \tag{2.153}$$

Generally the validity of the spatial invariance assumption can only be justified on *an a posteriori* basis. Or putting it another way, if we don't make the assumption we won't proceed very far (!)

Equation (2.153) in the form of a convolution integral whose Fourier transforms obey the product relation

$$H(\alpha, \beta) = T(\alpha, \beta) O(\alpha, \beta), \tag{2.154}$$

where $O(\alpha, \beta)$ is the spatial frequency spectrum of the object intensity distribution and $H(\alpha, \beta)$ is the spatial frequency spectrum of the object intensity distribution. For example,

$$O(\alpha, \beta) = \int\int_{-\infty}^{\infty} o(x, y) \exp[-i(\alpha x + \beta y)] dx dy. \tag{2.155}$$

Having computed $O(\alpha, \beta)$ and already being in possession of $T(\alpha, \beta)$, either numerically or analytically, we simply invert (2.154) to obtain

$$h(x, y) = \int\int_{-\infty}^{\infty} T(\alpha, \beta) O(\alpha, \beta) \exp[i(x\alpha + y\beta)] d\alpha d\beta. \tag{2.156}$$

The actual limits of integration are finite.

One of the most important classes of objects (especially for test purposes) are line objects. If the object is a line object (edge, bar target, etc.) at an angle ϕ to the azimuth, then it is convenient to work in polar coordinates. It can be shown that (2.156) reduces to

$$h(v, \phi) = \int_{0}^{2} T(\omega, \phi) O(\omega) \exp(iv\omega) d\omega, \tag{2.157}$$

omitting constants.

There are a few line objects that have become standards; in view of their importance we shall treat them separately.

I) *Line spread function.* Here the object is an infinitely narrow incoherent line

$$o(v) = \delta(v) \tag{2.158}$$

whose spatial spectrum is a constant. Consequently,

$$h(v, \phi) = \int_0^2 T(\omega, \phi) \exp(iv\omega) d\omega. \tag{2.159}$$

We term the right-hand side $\tau(v, \phi)$, the line spread function. If there are two lines, say,

$$o(v) = o(v - v_0) + o(v + v_0) \tag{2.160}$$

then

$$h(v, \phi) = \tau(v - v_0, \phi) + \tau(v + v_0, \phi) \tag{2.161}$$

as the reader can easily prove.

Returning to (2.159), when v is large we can use (2.89) to prove that

$$\tau(v, \phi) \sim - T_R^{(1)}(0)/v^2$$
$$\sim (2/\pi v^2) \tag{2.162}$$

for all systems.

Note that there is no characteristic width of the object. A second object also devoid of a characteristic width is the edge.

II) *Edge spread function.* The object is now an edge

$$o(v) = 0 \quad v < 0$$
$$= 1 \quad v > 0. \tag{2.163}$$

The object spectrum $O(\omega)$ is

$$O(\omega) = \pi \delta(\omega) + (i\omega)^{-1}. \tag{2.164}$$

The image of the edge, normalized so that the intensity is as $v \to + \infty$, and zero as $v \to - \infty$, is

$$e(v, \phi) = \tfrac{1}{2} + \pi^{-1} \int_0^2 T_R(\omega, \phi) \omega^{-1} \sin v\omega \, d\omega$$
$$+ \pi^{-1} \int_0^2 T_I(\omega, \phi) \omega^{-1} \cos v\omega \, d\omega. \tag{2.165}$$

At the geometric edge $v=0$, this reduces to

$$e(0, \phi) = \tfrac{1}{2} + \pi^{-1} \int_0^2 T_{\mathrm{I}}(\omega, \phi) \omega^{-1} d\omega. \tag{2.166}$$

The value of the edge spread function is determined by the weighted integral of the imaginary part of the transfer function. If $T_{\mathrm{I}} \equiv 0$, then $e(0, \phi) = 1/2$ for all ϕ.

III) *Sinusoidal target*. The object is given by

$$o(v) = A_0 + B_0 \cos\omega_0 v, \quad 0 < B_0 \leq A_0. \tag{2.167}$$

The corresponding spectrum is

$$O(\omega) = A_0 \delta(\omega) + (B_0/2)\delta(\omega + \omega_0) + (B_0/2)\delta(\omega - \omega_0). \tag{2.168}$$

Upon substitution of this expression into (2.159) and use of the shift theorem for the Dirac delta function, we get

$$h(v, \phi) = A_0 + (B_0/2) T(\omega_0, \phi) \exp(i\omega_0 v) + (B_0/2) T(-\omega_0, \phi)$$
$$\cdot \exp(-i\omega_0 v) \tag{2.169}$$

or

$$h(v, \phi) = A_0 + B_0 |T(\omega, \phi)| \cos[\omega_0 v + \delta(\omega_0, \phi)]. \tag{2.170}$$

A comparison of this expression and that of the corresponding object reveals that $h(v, \phi)$ now has a phase term $\delta(\omega_0, \phi)$ which shifts the image relative to the object, thereby causing spurious resolution. Secondly, the term $|T(\omega, \phi)|$ must be less than or equal to unity, otherwise there would be more energy in the output than the input. The modulus of $T(\omega, \phi)$ governs the contrast reduction.

The difficulty with this analysis is that the input object is physically impossible; an infinite object has neither a beginning nor end. Thus, there arises the question of how many cycles of a truncated, periodic target (which is physically realizable) are required in order that it act effectively as an infinite, periodic target. This leads to the consideration of

IV) *Truncated sinusoidal target*. The object is now of the form

$$o(v) = (1/2)[1 + \cos(\pi v/2L)], \quad |v| \leq 2NL$$
$$= 0, \quad |v| > 2NL, \tag{2.171}$$

where N is taken to be an even integer. The object spectrum is

$$O(\omega) = (\pi/2\omega)\sin(2NL\omega)(\pi^2 - 4L^2\omega^2)^{-1} \tag{2.172}$$

Table 2.3. Modulation of truncated sine and square wave targets ($L=1$) for aberration-free system

Cycles	Sine	Square
5	0.119	0.152
7	0.118	0.151
9	0.118	0.150

so that the image is given by

$$h(v, \phi) = (1/\pi) \int_0^2 \omega^{-1}(\pi^2 4L^2\omega^2)^{-1} \cos v\omega \sin(2NL\omega)T(\omega, \phi)d\omega. \qquad (2.173)$$

The numerical evaluation of this integral is fraught with difficulties since the integrand is not only rapidly oscillating, but also has strong, narrow peaks at $\omega=0$, $\pm(\pi/2L)$. These peaks become higher and narrower as N increases. Any quadrature scheme must include a very large number of quadrature points in order to pick up the peaks.

Another complication arises. How does one compute the modulation of the image since the image maxima are at different levels? One approach starts with a five-cycle target, then one calculates the modulation by averaging the peaks and troughs separately but neglects the cycles at each end, in order to obtain

$$\text{modulation} = \frac{\tilde{h}_{max} - \tilde{h}_{min}}{\tilde{h}_{max} + \tilde{h}_{min}}, \qquad (2.174)$$

where $\tilde{h}_{max}$, $\tilde{h}_{min}$ represent the average values. Extension to seven, nine, etc., cycle targets is obvious.

Since we are interested in general results only, we confine our attention to an aberration-free system with a target having $L=1$. The modulation data are summarized in Table 2.3. By the time we have reached a seven-cycle target the modulation has settled down to its limiting value.

V) *Square wave targets.* These objects are of interest because they are relatively easy to manufacture; unfortunately, the manufacture of sine wave targets is still a matter of some delicacy and luck. For a single bar target of unit intensity, the object intensity distribution is

$$o(v) = 0, \quad -\infty < v < -v_0$$

$$= 1, \quad -v_0 < v < v_0$$

$$= 0, \quad v_0 < v < \infty. \qquad (2.175)$$

The corresponding spatial frequency spectrum is

$$O(\omega)=(2\sin v_0\omega)/\omega. \tag{2.176}$$

When the object is very narrow ($v_0 \ll 1$), then $O(\omega) \approx v_0$ and

$$h(v,\phi)\approx v_0\int_0^2 T(\omega,\phi)\exp(iv\omega)d\omega. \tag{2.177}$$

Thus the presence of a narrow bar is to multiply the line spread function, but not alter its shape.

The numerical evaluation of these integrals offers no particular problem.

If there are now $N(=$ even integer) square wave targets of period $4L$, just as in the truncated sine wave case, then the image is given by

$$h(v,\phi)=(1/\pi)\int_0^2 (\omega\cos L\omega)^{-1}\cos v\omega \sin(2NL\omega)\,T(\omega,\phi)d\omega. \tag{2.178}$$

The arguments concerning its numerical evaluation are the same as those pertaining to (2.173).

When $L \ll 2$ and the frequency ω such that $L\omega \ll 1$, then spectra of sine and square waves are essentially equal to

$$O(\omega)=(2\pi\omega)^{-1}\sin 2NL\omega. \tag{2.179}$$

Suppose that the targets are such that the frequency is high, but that we can approximate

$$(\cos L\omega)^{-1}\approx 1+(1/2)(L\omega)^2+\dots$$
$$(\pi^2-4L^2\omega^2)^{-1}\approx(1/\pi^2)[1+(4/\pi^2)(L\omega)^2+\dots]. \tag{2.180}$$

Then the image of the truncated square wave target is

$$h(v,\phi)|_{sq}\approx(1/\pi)\int_0^2 \cos v\omega \sin(2NL\omega)\omega^{-1}T(\omega,\phi)d\omega$$
$$+(L^2/2\pi)\int_0^2 \omega\cos v\omega \sin(2NL\omega)T(\omega,\phi)d\omega+\dots \tag{2.181}$$

while that of the truncated, sinusoidal target is

$$h(v,\phi)|_{si}\approx(1/\pi)\int_0^2 \cos v\omega \sin(2NL\omega)\omega^{-1}T(\omega,\phi)d\omega$$
$$+(4L^2/\pi^3)\int_0^2 \omega\cos v\omega \sin(2NL\omega)T(\omega,\phi)d\omega. \tag{2.182}$$

The difference between these two expressions

$$(h|_{eq} - h|_{si}) = (\pi^2 - 8)L^2/2\pi^3 \int_0^2 \omega \cos v\omega \sin(2NL\omega) T(\omega, \phi) d\omega \tag{2.183}$$

is numerically quite small. Thus, the difference between the images of truncated sinusoidal and square wave objects is small in the medium- and high-frequency regions.

2.3.5 Disc Target

Besides the various line objects just discussed, the other standard object is the uniform disc of radius v_0

$$o(v) = 1, \quad 0 < v < v_0$$
$$= 0, \quad v > v_0. \tag{2.184}$$

When the optical system has only rotationally symmetric aberrations, then it is convenient to carry out the analysis using zero-order Hankel transforms. The object spectrum is

$$O(\omega) = \int_0^\infty o(v) J_0(\omega v) v dv$$

$$= (v_0/\omega) J_1(v_0\omega) \tag{2.185}$$

and the image is

$$h(v) = v_0 \int_0^2 T(\omega) J_1(v_0\omega) J_0(v\omega) d\omega. \tag{2.186}$$

For small values of v

$$h(v) \approx (v_0^2/2) \int_0^2 T(\omega) J_0(v\omega) d\omega + \dots$$

$$\approx (v_0^2/2) t(v). \tag{2.187}$$

Thus the image of a small uniformly illuminated disc is essentially that due to a point source multiplied by a constant factor. In fact, it is simple to prove that (2.187) is true irrespective of the exact shape of the object spectrum, namely,

$$h(v) \approx O(0) t(v). \tag{2.188}$$

In other words a small pinhole, whether uniformly illuminated or not, acts essentially as a point source, a fact well known to anyone who has engaged in experimental work.

At large distances from the edge of the disc, the intensity drops off as the inverse third power of v. To prove this, we use (2.87) and take $g(\omega) = T(\omega)J_1(v_0\omega)$. Now

$$g(0) = 0, \quad g^{(2)}(0) = v_0 T^{(1)}(0) ; \tag{2.189}$$

hence,

$$h(v) \sim -v_0^2 T^{(1)}(0)/2v^3$$
$$\sim v_0^2/\pi v^3 . \tag{2.190}$$

2.4 Fast Fourier Transform and Quadrature

Undoubtedly the reader has encountered the fast Fourier transform (FFT) in discussions in optics as well as in other areas. The FFT has revolutionized the calculation of *finite* Fourier series (the finite Fourier transform in optical usage) because of the extreme rapidly of the algorithm. (See also Chap. 3.)

2.4.1 Naive FFT Quadrature

Let us consider the integral

$$a(v) = \int_0^{2\pi} A(p)\exp(ivp)dp, \tag{2.191}$$

where we have scaled the variables so that the interval of integration is now $(0, 2\pi)$. The integral can be crudely approximated by the series (it is a rectangular rule approximation, not even a trapezoidal rule approximation)

$$a(v) = (2\pi/N) \sum_{j=0}^{N-1} A(p_j)\exp(ivp_j), \tag{2.192}$$

where $p_j = j\Delta p = 2\pi j/N$ and N is taken to be an integral power of 2 (i.e., $N = 2^l$ where l is an integer). If we also force $v = n (= 0, 1, ..., N-1)$, then (2.192) is in the form of a discrete Fourier transform. Finally, since upper limit $N-1$ is finite, the ground rules are met for using the fast Fourier transform (FFT) algorithm. Finally, since upper limit $N-1$ is finite, the ground rules are met for using the fast Fourier transform (FFT) algorithm.

Direct evaluation of (2.192) by the FFT algorithm is now a standard technique. The FFT is an algorithm for computing the discrete Fourier transform using relatively few operations so that the computation of (2.192) can be evaluated very rapidly. However, the numerical integration scheme represented by (2.192) is crude; in fact, the error is generally proportional to $1/N$. Consequently, we are faced with Hobson's choice: use the FFT to compute very rapidly but with low accuracy or use more points so that the accuracy is increased but at the loss of computing speed. Of course, in some cases in diffraction optics this is not a serious problem because the final results are only used for graphical display.

2.4.2 FFT-Filon

The question naturally arises as to the marriage of the FFT with one of the classical quadrature formulas discussed in Sect. 2.2. The most obvious candidate is the Filon method. Rather than work directly with the final expressions for the Filon method, (2.39, 45) let us consider the basic expression derived by *Filon* for three equally spaced quadrature points, p_{l+2}, p_{l+1}, and p_l with step size h.

The expression for the sine integral is (where we have set $v = n = $ integer)

$$\int_{p_l}^{p_{l+2}} A(p)\sin np\,dp = -n^{-1}[A(p_{l+2})\cos(np_{l+2}) - A(p_l)\cos(np_l)]$$
$$+ (2n^2h)^{-1}\{[3A(p_{l+2}) - 4A(p_{l+1})$$
$$+ A(p_l)]\sin(np_{l+2}) + [A(p_{l+2}) - 4A(p_{l+1})$$
$$+ 3A(p_l)]\sin(np_l)\} + (n^3h^2)^{-1}[A(p_{l+2})$$
$$- 2A(p_{l+1}) + A(p_l)][\cos(np_{l+2})$$
$$- \cos(np_l)] \tag{2.193}$$

Now let the original interval $(0, 2\pi)$ be divided into $2^l \equiv N$ subintervals so that $p_0 = 0$ and $p_N = 2\pi$ where l is an integer. Upon adding up the individual contributions, we finally obtain

$$\int_0^{2\pi} A(p)\sin np\,dp = n^{-1}[A(p_0) - A(p_N)]$$
$$+ (n^3h^2)^{-1}[A(p_N) - 2A(p_{N-1}) + A(p_{N-2})]$$
$$+ (2n^2h)^{-1}\sum_{j=0}^{N-1} S_j\sin np_{2j}$$
$$+ (n^3h^2)\sum_{j=0}^{N-1} C_j\cos np_{2j}, \tag{2.194}$$

where

$$S_0 = 3A(p_0) - 4A(p_1) + A(p_2)$$
$$S_j = A(p_{2j-2}) - 4A(p_{2j-1}) + 6A(p_{2j}) - 4A(p_{2j+1}) + A(p_{2j+2})$$

and

$$C_0 = -A(p_0) + 2A(p_1) - A(p_2)$$
$$C_j = A(p_{2j-2}) - A(p_{2j-1}) + 2A(p_{2j+1}) - A(p_{2j+2}). \tag{2.195}$$

Before commenting on this expression, let us set down the analogous result for the cosine integral version. The Filon formula corresponding to (2.193) is

$$\int_{p_l}^{p_{l+2}} A(p)\cos(np\,dp = n^{-1}[A(p_{l+2})\sin(np_{l+2}) - A(p_l)\sin(np_l)]$$
$$+ (2n^2h)^{-1}\{[3A(p_{l+2}) - 4A(p_{l+1})$$
$$+ A(p_l)]\cos(np_{l+2}) + [A(p_{l+2}) - 4A(p_{l+1})$$
$$+ 3A(p_l)]\cos(np_l)\} - (n^3h^2)^{-1}[A(p_{l+2})$$
$$- 2A(p_{l+1}) + A(p_l)][\cos(np_{l+2}) - \sin(np_l)] \tag{2.196}$$

so that

$$\int_0^{2\pi} A(p)\cos(np\,dp = (2n^2h)^{-1}[3A(p_N) - 4A(p_{N-1}) - 4A(p_{N-1}) + A(p_{N-2})]$$
$$+ (2n^2h)^{-1}\sum_{j=0}^{N-1} S_j\cos np_{2j} - (n^3h^2)\sum_{j=0}^{N-1} C_j\sin np_{2j}. \tag{2.197}$$

The series in (2.194) and (2.197) are now in the form given by (2.191) and can be summed via FFT. We have to use the FFT twice on each integral, however. The number of quadrature points is now half the original number because we operate on p_{2j} not p_j.

This version of the FFT-Filon scheme does not contain the functions $\alpha(h)$, $\beta(h)$, and $\gamma(h)$ of the original Filon scheme as discussed in Sect. 2.2.

2.4.3 FFT for Fast Hankel Transform Evaluation

Let us consider an integral

$$a(v) = 2\pi \int_0^\infty pA(p)J_n(2\pi pv)dp \tag{2.198}$$

whose numerical evaluation is required. This is nothing like the basic form (2.191), and so appears incapable of evaluation by FFT. J_n is the nth-order Bessel function.

Siegman has shown how to cast (2.198) in the form of a one-dimensional *cross-correlation* integral

$$\hat{a}(y) = \int_{-\infty}^\infty \hat{A}(x)\hat{J}(x+y)dx. \tag{2.199}$$

This is a accomplished by the change of variables

$$p = p_0 e^{\alpha x}, \quad p_0 v = v_0 e^{\alpha y}, \tag{2.200}$$

where parameters p_0, v_0, and α are set by the user. The key relation here is that

$$pv = p_0 v_0 e^{\alpha(x+y)},$$

so that in (2.198)

$$J_n(2\pi pv) \rightarrow J_n(2\pi p_0 v_0 e^{\alpha(x+y)}),$$

or purely a function of $(x+y)$. The form (2.199) then immediately follows.

With the original integral (2.198) now cast as a cross correlation (2.199), the FFT may be introduced. Approximating the integral (2.199) by a sum, where $\{\hat{a}_m\}$ is the discrete version of $\hat{a}(y)$, etc., for $\hat{A}(x)$ and $\hat{J}(x)$, we have

$$\hat{a}_m = \mathrm{FFT}[\mathrm{FFT}(\hat{A}_m) \times \mathrm{FFT}^{-1}(\hat{J}_m)]. \tag{2.201}$$

Details on accuracy, etc., were taken up by *Siegman*.

2.5 Sampling Expansions

In some cases it is possible to use the band-limited properties of the point and line spread functions to develop sampling expansions that can be used for *computational* purposes. (See also Chap. 3.)

Consider a function $g(x)$ band limited to $(-a, +a)$; then

$$g(x) = \int_{-a}^{a} G(\alpha) \exp(-ix\alpha) d\alpha. \tag{2.202}$$

Since $G(\alpha)$ vanishes identically for $|\alpha| > 2$, let us expand it as a complex Fourier series in the interval $|\alpha| \leq 2$

$$G(\alpha) = \sum_{n=-\infty}^{\infty} G_n \exp(in\pi\alpha/a), \tag{2.203}$$

where

$$G_n = \frac{1}{2a} \int_{-a}^{a} G(\alpha) \exp(-in\pi\alpha/a) d\alpha$$

$$= \frac{1}{2a} g(n\pi/a). \tag{2.204}$$

The relation between G_n and $g(n\pi/a)$ follows by virtue of (2.202). Equation (2.203) expresses the function G directly in terms of g evaluated at the discrete points $(n\pi/a)$. Equation (2.203) is an orthogonal expansion and as such its Fourier coefficients G_n should generally depend on all values of $g(x)$ in the fundamental interval. One of the remarkable properties of band-limited functions is that each Fourier coefficient now depends only on $g(x)$ evaluated at a single point $x = n\pi/a$ in the fundamental interval.

Let us take $g(x) = t(x)$ and $G(\alpha) = T(\alpha)$ for the slit aperture situation with $a = 2$. Now $t(x)$ is a nonnegative real function and if we set $T(\alpha) = T_R(\alpha) + iT_I(\alpha)$, then

$$T_R(\alpha) = \tfrac{1}{2}t(0) + \tfrac{1}{2}\sum_{n=1}^{\infty}[t(n\pi/2) + t(-n\pi/2)]\cos(n\pi\alpha/2), \tag{2.205}$$

$$T_I(\alpha) = -\tfrac{1}{2}\sum_{n=1}^{\infty}[t(n\pi/2) - t(-n\pi/2)]\sin(n\pi\alpha/2). \tag{2.206}$$

These expressions are useful for computation because they express the transfer function directly in terms of the point spread function evaluated at the discrete points $x = n\pi/2$.

If we next set $g(x) = \tau(v, \phi)$ and $G(\alpha) = T(\alpha, \phi)$ (that is, the line spread function situation) we again obtain (2.205) and (2.206) with $t(n\pi/2)$ replaced by $\tau(n\pi/2, \phi)$.

Substitution of (2.203) into (2.202) yields the cardinal function

$$t(x) = \sum_{n=-\infty}^{\infty} t(n\pi/2)\operatorname{sinc}(2x - n\pi), \tag{2.207}$$

where $\operatorname{sinc} x \equiv (\sin x)/x$. A similar formula holds for the line spread function. If we know the slit aperture point spread function or circular aperture line spread function at its sampled points, then these two functions can be reconstructed from their sample values.

We can utilize the cardinal functions of $t(x)$ and $\tau(v, \phi)$ to obtain expressions for the cumulative point spread function with a slit aperture $L(x_0)$ and the edge spread function with a circular aperture $e(v, \phi)$. Substitution of (2.207) into (2.148) yields

$$L(x_0) = \frac{1}{2\pi}\sum_{n=-\infty}^{\infty} t(n\pi/2)\int_{-2x_0-n\pi}^{2x_0-n\pi}(\operatorname{sinc} x)dx$$

$$= \frac{1}{2\pi}\sum_{n=-\infty}^{\infty} t(n\pi/2)[\operatorname{Si}(2x_0 - n\pi) + \operatorname{Si}(2x_0 + n\pi)], \tag{2.208}$$

where $\operatorname{Si}(x)$ is the sine integral. Note that all the sampled values of $t(x)$ contribute to $L(x_0)$ even those points $x_n \equiv n\pi/2 > x_0$. The corresponding expression for the edge spread function is

$$e(v, \phi) = \tfrac{1}{2} + \tfrac{1}{2} \sum_{n=-\infty}^{\infty} \tau(n\pi/2, \phi) \, \mathrm{Si}(2v + n\pi). \tag{2.209}$$

There are various extensions to two dimensions; we shall concern ourselves only with the rotationally symmetric case. The expression corresponding to (2.203) is

$$g(r) = \int_0^a G(\varrho) J_0(r\varrho) \varrho \, d\varrho. \tag{2.210}$$

Expand $G(\varrho)$ in a zero-order Fourier Bessel series in the interval $0 \le \varrho \le a$

$$G(\varrho) = \sum_{n=1}^{\infty} G_n J_0(k_n \varrho), \tag{2.211}$$

where

$$G_n = \frac{1}{J_1^2(2ak_n)} \int_0^a G(\varrho) J_0(k_n \varrho) \varrho \, d\varrho$$

$$= \frac{1}{J_1^2(ak_n)} g(k_n). \tag{2.212}$$

But $J_0(ak_n) = J_0(\alpha_n) = 0$ where α_n are the positive roots of J_0. Hence, the sampling series for $G(\varrho)$ is

$$G(\varrho) = \sum_{n=1}^{\infty} [J_1(\alpha_n)]^{-2} g(\alpha_n/a) J_0(\alpha_n \varrho/2) \tag{2.213}$$

in the fundamental interval. The sampling points are not equidistant as in the previous case. The cardinal function of $g(r)$ is

$$g(r) = (2/a) J_0(ar) \sum_{n=1}^{\infty} \frac{(\alpha_n/a) g(\alpha_n/a)}{J_1(\alpha_n) [(\alpha_n/a)^2 - r^2]}. \tag{2.214}$$

If $g(r)$ is taken to be the point spread function $t(v)$ and $G(\varrho)$ the corresponding transfer function $T(\omega)$, then we have for the Strehl criterion $t(0)$ the series

$$t(0) = 4 \sum_{n=1}^{\infty} [\alpha_n J_1(\alpha_n)]^{-1} t(\alpha_n/2). \tag{2.215}$$

Now $t(0)$ was one of the sampled points for the slit aperture. The situation is different for the circular aperture in that $t(0)$ is not one of the sampled points. Thus, (2.215) expresses the intensity at the center of the diffraction pattern in terms of the sampled values of the intensity.

Table 2.4

ω	Exact	Series
0	1.0000	0.9618
0.1	0.9364	0.9368
0.2	0.8729	0.8765
0.4	0.7471	0.7459
0.8	0.5046	0.5045
1.2	0.2848	0.2850
1.6	0.1041	0.1046
1.8	0.0374	0.0366

The series for the transfer function is given by (2.213) with $G(\varrho) \to T(\omega)$ and $g(r) \to$ the radially symmetric point spread function. In order to give some indication of the usefulness of this expansion, we compute the transfer function of an aberration-free aperture using ten terms of the series. The results are listed in Table 2.4. The comparison is excellent except at the origin where there is a 4% error.

The cumulative point spread function $L(v_0)$ is also expressible by a sampling series, although we shall not quote the complicated formula.

Sampling expansions can also be used to provide computationally efficient schemes for the image quality factors developed by Linfoot. Consider, for example, the relative structural content for a circular aperture

$$F \propto \int_0^2 |T(\omega)|^2 \phi(\omega) d\omega, \tag{2.216}$$

where $\phi(\omega)$ is the power spectrum of the scene. When $\phi(\omega) =$ constant, F becomes

$$F \propto \sum_{n=1}^{\infty} [J_1(\alpha_n)]^{-2} [t(n\pi/2)]^2. \tag{2.217}$$

Bibliography

The following listing is arranged according to relevant sections.

Section 2.2

The number of texts and treatises on numerical analysis is extremely large. Most of the newer texts are not particularly useful because they emphasize the more modern problems associated with differential equations, sparse matrices, etc., rather than the numerical integration problem. For those readers who need an elementary and practical introduction to numerical methods, two no-nonsense texts are

Z. Kopal: *Numerical Analysis* (Wiley, New York 1961)
P. W. Williams: *Numerical Computation* (Harper and Row, New York 1972)

A scholarly, in-depth study of integration schemes is
P. J. Davis, P. Rabinowitz: *Methods of Numerical Integration* (Academic Press, New York 1975)

Also unseful are
V. I. Krylov: *Approximate Evaluation of Integrals* (Macmillan, New York 1962)
W. Squire: *Integration for Engineers and Scientists* (Elsevier, New York 1970)

Romberg quadrature has been the subject of controversy. For a critical review and assessment see
J. Oliver: The efficiency of extrapolation methods for numerical integration. Numer. Math. **17**, 17 (1971)

Two books which contain lucid pedagogic discussions of Gauss quadrature are
Z. Kopal: *Numerical Analysis* (Wiley, New York 1961)
A. H. Stroud: *Numerical Quadrature and the Solution of Ordinary Differential Equations* (Springer, Berlin, New York, Heidelberg 1973)

Extensive tables of the various Gauss quadrature schemes (as well as computer programs for generating them) are listed in
A. H. Stroud, D. Secrest: *Gaussian Quadrature Formulas* (Prentice-Hall, Englewood Cliffs 1966)

Although Filon's method is now extensively used, about the only place where the details are given is
L. Filon: On a quadrature formula for trigonometric integrals. Proc. Roy. Soc. Edinburgh **49**, 38 (1928)

The following reference is very valuable:
S. M. Chase, L. D. Fosdick: An algorithm for Filon quadrature. *Comm. ACM* **12**, 453 (1969)

There are a large number of modifications of Filon's scheme, most being of doubtful usefulness. The very recent method of Piessens and Poleunis, which uses a truncated Chebyschev series, appears to offer substantial accuracy over Filon's method. However, their method is much more involved.
R. Piessens, F. Poleunis: A numerical method for the integration of oscillatory functions. *BIT* **11**, 317 (1972)

The modification of Filon's original scheme whereby one uses linear approximations between quadrature points has been rediscovered many times by many people (including the author!), e.g.,
E. O. Tuck: A simple Filon-trapezoidal rule. *Math. Comp.* **21**, 239 (1967)

However, it goes back to a problem given in
C. J. Tranter: *Integral Transforms in Mathematical Physics* (Methuen, London 1956) p. 76

The computation of Hankel and Fourier transforms via the Euler summation method is due to
I. M. Longman: Note on a method for computing infinite integrals of oscillatory functions. *Proc. Camb. Phil. Soc.* **52**, 764 (1956)

A review of the method is
P. Cornille: Computation of Hankel transforms. *SIAM Rev.* **14**, 278 (1972)

The valuable asymptotic formulae due to Willis are outlined in
H. F. Willis: A formula for expanding an integral as a series. *Phil. Mag.* **39**, 455 (1948)

Optical diffraction applications are given in

R.Barakat, A.Houston: Reciprocity relations between the transfer function and total illuminance. *J. Opt. Soc. Am.* **53**, 1244 (1963)

R.Barakat, A.Houston: Line spread function and cumulative line spread function for systems with rotational symmetry. *J. Opt. Soc. Am.* **54**, 768 (1964)

B.Tatian: Asymptotic expansions for correcting truncation error in transfer function calculations. *J. Opt. Soc. Am.* **61**, 1214 (1971)

R. Barakat, E.Blackman: The expected value of the edge spread function in the presence of random wavefronts. *Opt. Comm.* **8**, 9 (1973)

V.Mahajan: Asymptotic behavior of diffraction images. *Opt. Acta* (submitted for publication)

Section 2.3

Most of the material in this section is taken from the author's papers in *J. Opt. Soc. Am.*, *Opt. Acta*, and *J. Appl. Opt.*, circa 1961–1969.

Section 2.4

An excellent introduction to the theory of the discrete Fourier transform along with a discussion of the fast Fourier transform is

E.O.Brigham: *The Fast Fourier Transform* (Prentice-Hall, Englewood Cliffs 1974)

See also

G.D.Bergland: A guided tour of the fast Fourier transform. *IEEE Spectrum* **6**, 41 (1969)
Bergland's article is especially useful in pointing out the pitfalls in using the discrete Fourier transform (with the FFT) as an approximation to the continuous Fourier transform.

The FFT-Filon quadrature scheme is based on an unpublished report of the author dating back to 1972. Abramovici has also developed a technique for using the FFT and Filon.
F.Abramovici: The accurate calculation of Fourier integrals by the Fast Fourier transform technique. *J. Compt. Phys.* **11**, 28 (1973)

For an ingenious application of the FFT to Hankel transforms see
A.E.Siegman: Quasi-fast Hankel transform. *Opt. Lett.* **1**, 13 (1977)

A marriage of the FFT and Gauss quadrature is given by
L.L.Hope: A fast Gaussian method for Fourier transform evaluation. *Proc. IEEE* **63**, 1353 (1975)
[Hope claims that his expression [Eq. (2)] is a trapezoidal rule, but it is only a rectangular rule approximation.]

Section 2.5

Application of sampling expansions as a computational tool in evaluating optical diffraction functions is outlines in
R.Barakat: Application of the sampling theorem to optical diffraction theory. *J. Opt. Soc. Am.* **54**, 920 (1964)

Sampling expressions for evaluating image quality measures are given in
B.R.Frieden: Image evaluation by use of the sampling theorem. J. Opt. Soc. Am. **56**, 1355 (1966)

3. Computational Methods of Probability and Statistics

B. R. Frieden

With 33 Figures

Optics is the study of light, in particular light that conveys information. Optical design, spectroscopy, laser design, etc., all have as their common goal an improvement in the ability to extract information, or to transport information, via light beams. The challenge to such improvement arises from the statistical nature of the little messenger bearing the information – the photon – which tries to be everywhere at once. Because of its quantum nature, the photon does not follow a predictable trajectory through a medium, but rather suffers a spread in trajectories, and does not even preserve a fixed wavelength; this quantity also suffers a spread, owing to Heisenberg's uncertainty principle.

These uncertainties give rise to the optical problems of "diffraction spread", which is in reality the probability density describing the photon's random trajectories, and Poisson image noise, which is the realization of but a finite number of photon trajectories. Both problem areas are basically statistical, then, although diffraction spread is traditionally regarded as deterministic. However, at low light levels, even this deterministic viewpoint must be abandoned; see Sect. 3.4.4.

Thus, randomness and uncertainty exist at the most basic level of optics, down at the photon level. But even if the photon were a *non*random or deterministic entity, other sources of uncertainty would creep in (recalling that the entropy and confusion of the Universe must always be increasing!).

It is the nature of instruments to be imperfect. Aside from the statistical nature of the photon, there is another basic statistical quantity that often intrudes into optical problems, and this is the villain called "noise". Any measurement of a real physical signal suffers random error. "Noise" is the name we give this error much as the word "weed" is used when describing an unwanted plant. The analysis of noise is a major problem taken up by statistics. Although any one measurement suffers an unpredictable amount of noise, i.e., individual noise values cannot be predicted, their long-term averages can. A histogram of noise values can be built out of many observations, and this can be used to improve future performance of the instrument.

A third source of uncertainty in optics is accurate, but *insufficient*, data. A direct example is an overly coarse sampling of an image. If the sampling were spaced at the Nyquist interval, the whole image lying continuously *between* sampling points could be reconstructed *uniquely* from the data. However, with coarser sampling there is an infinity of possible images consistent with the data, even if the data are noise free. Inadequate data drive one to seek a probabilistic answer, such as the "most likely" image. In general, the field of statistics called "estimation theory" addresses this problem.

Aside from addressing problems of uncertainty, the methods of probability and statistics we shall describe are also applicable to solving deterministic problems! The methods are so powerful that they carry over into the analysis of nonstatistical situations as well. An example is determination of a spot diagram, or intensity point spread function, in geometrical optics. For a given lens configuration, there is no uncertainty in this profile: it has a well-defined shape in principle. Hence, the problem does not appear to be statistical. However, it is one thing to know that the profile exists uniquely, and another matter to determine it in practice. An oft-used method of estimating the profile is to trace through the lens system many rays, and to build up a histogram of ray strikes in the image plane. The histogram approximates the unknown spot profile. However, such an estimated histogram suffers from strong error where not many rays strike the image. On the other hand, a better method of estimation exists, which arises out of probability theory, and has the remarkable property that each pair of rays (as designated) establishes *with arbitrary accuracy* one point on the theoretical spot profile curve. This method is described further on in the chapter.

So far we have been using the terms "probability" and "statistics" interchangeably. There is, in fact, a distinction between the two according to the problems they address. Probability theory addresses the problem of *analysis*, i.e., what the data distribution will be for a *given* set of inputs into a known physical situation. Statistics treats the reverse problem, where the data outputs of an experiment are known and from this, some properties of *the input* are required. An aim of statistics is to arrive at an answer without making any assumption about the nature of the physical system involved. This is called a "distribution-free" estimate. An example is where a set of measurements of c, the speed of light, is given, with no other information (as, for example, the experimental procedure which was used to arrive at these numbers). From these data a measure of their accuracy is required. We shall see how a remarkably simple test of the data, called the t-test, attempts to answer this problem.

Conventional methods of statistics such as the t-test and others, for example, the F-test and chi-square test, have been used successfully in many fields of research, such as psychology. However, they are by and large not used in optics. Neither are such useful modeling approaches as *linear regression*, which provides a first step toward analyzing an unknown physical phenomenon. It is a chief aim of this chapter to show how these methods arise from probability theory, and where they are potentially applicable to optics.

On the way, we shall develop probability theory from "scratch" using Kolmogoroff's beautiful and simple axiomatic approach. We shall show how probability theory is applicable to optics, through various examples taken from the theory of turbulence, laser speckle, and image formation. Emphasis will be placed upon the role of "statistical modeling", which aims to simplify problems to the extent that they are soluble; upon the almost separate computer discipline call the "Monte Carlo" calculation, which is playing an increasingly important role in the theory of remote sensing; and upon computational aspects of the various approaches. Sampling theorems, the fast Fourier transform technique, and other computational "shortcuts" will be discussed.

The methods of analysis which will be developed below may easily be viewed as a branch of linear theory, embodying convolutions, transfer theorems, Jacobian transformation, etc., all of which are usually familiar to people in optics. We have found, by teaching a probability course, that students with a one-term graduate course in linear theory can quite readily learn the material.

As promised, we begin at the beginning, with basic probability theory as it follows from Kolmogoroff's three axioms. The reader with limited time, or with an intuitive grasp of basic probability may, however, find it more fruitful to skip ahead to Sect. 3.2. There the important and intersting connection with linear theory is made.

3.1 Basic Concepts

In order to keep this section brief, we shall take a heuristic attitude and avoid a rigorous set-theory approach. Set theory merely bestows mathematical dignity upon the terms "or" and "and". We shall instead use these words in their intuitive sense. The reader interested in the rigorous approach might wish to read, for example, *Papoulis* [3.1].

3.1.1 Notion of an Experiment; Events

An "experiment" can be described abstractly as any fixed procedure for obtaining an outcome. Each repetition of the experiment is called a "trial". The procedure might be actual, as in the laboratory, or *gedanken*, but in any case is imagined to be repeated many times over. These trials result in a set of outcomes, which are direct, experimental observables. Associated in an arbitrary way with each outcome, is an "event".

For example, the experiment consists in the roll of a die[1]. The outcome of the experiment is a single number (it may in other experiments be many numbers), namely, the number on the upturned face of the die. The outcomes after four repetitions of the experiment might be the numbers 4, 2, 1, and 5. Each outcome is selected from the numbers 1 through 6. The events $\{A_n\}$ describing the experiments might, e.g., be chosen as "evenness" or "oddness" of the outcomes.

The "Space" Event. A set of N events which includes all possible events for an experiment defines the "space" event. For example, in the roll of a die, events $\{A_n\} = (1, 2, ..., 6)$ are elements of a space. The space event is event $C = (A_1$ or A_2 or ... or $A_N)$.

---

1 Note that this is a fitting experiment to start off our study of probability, because the concept of probability *historically arose* in the study of winning games of chance using dice (see [3.2]).

However, the elements of a space are not unique. The same experiment may be described by many different possible spaces. For example, in the roll of a die we might instead define as space elements

$\{A_n\} =$ (all rolls less than 4, the roll 4,

$n = 1, 2, 3$ all rolls greater than 4).   (3.1a)

The space to use depends on the probability it is desired to estimate (more on this later in Sect. 3.1.4).

Disjoint Events. This concept ultimately allows probabilities to be computed. Two events A and B are called mutually exclusive, or disjoint, if the occurrence of A rules out the occurrence of B. For example, if the die turns up two dots, this event rules out the event "five dots". Hence the events "two dots", "five dots" are disjoint.

Two *non*disjoint events would be "a roll less than 4", "a roll greater than 2". Obviously if the outcome is a "3" *both* these events occur simultaneously. There is no exclusion.

The Certain Event. Let us consider the event "any number from 1 to 6", when the experiment is the roll of a die. This event is *certain* to occur at each repetition of the experiment. It is consequently called the "certain" event. In general, every experiment has a "certain" event associated with it, namely, its entire event space (A_1 or A_2 or ... A_n).

3.1.2 Definition of Probability

Associated with each possible event A of an experiment is its "probability" of occurrence $P(A)$. This number, by definition, obeys the following axioms (see [3.3]).

Axiom I $P(A) \geq 0$. That is, the probability is never negative.

Axiom II $P(C) = 1$, where C is the certain event (see above). This ultimately fixes a scale of numbers for the probabilities to range over.

Axiom III   If events A and B are disjoint. $P(A$ or $B) = P(A) + P(B)$. For example, for the die experiment $P(\text{roll } 1$ or $\text{roll } 2) = P(\text{roll } 1) + P(\text{roll } 2)$. The word "or" is taken in the intuitive sense; point set theory (see [3.1]) defines it mathematically.

These three axioms, along with a generalization of III to include an infinity of disjoint events (see below), *imply all the rules of probability, and hence all the methods of statistics.* One of the aims of this chapter is to show that this rather startling statement is true.

3.1.3 Some Elementary Consequences

Building on these postulates, we note the following. Suppose $\bar{A}$ denotes "not A", the complementary event to A. Obviously, A and $\bar{A}$ are disjoint, by Sect. 3.1.1. Therefore, by Axiom III, $P(A$ or $\bar{A})=P(A)+P(\bar{A})$. Furthermore, the two events A, $\bar{A}$ together comprise the certain event, by Sect. 3.1.1. Therefore, by Axiom II, $P(A$ or $\bar{A})=P(A)+P(\bar{A})=1$. Combining the latter with Axiom I applied to $\bar{A}$, it must be that $P(A)\leq 1$. Hence combining this with Axiom I

$$0\leq P(A)\leq 1. \tag{3.1b}$$

All probabilities lie between 0 and 1. An event having zero probability is termed the "impossible" event. Hence all events lie somewhere between the certain and the impossible (a not very profound statement, but certainly necessary!).

Additivity Property. Consider disjoint events A_1 and A_2. Also, suppose that A_2 is disjoint with an event A_3. Temporarily let $B_1 =(A_2$ or $A_3)$. Then A_1 is disjoint with B_1 (heuristic assertion), and hence, by Axiom III, $P(A_1$ or $B_1)=P(A_1)+P(B_1)$. Then combining the last two relations

$$P(A_1 \text{ or } A_2 \text{ or } A_3)=P(A_1)+P(A_2+A_3),$$

and hence, by Axiom III, once again

$$P(A_1 \text{ or } A_2 \text{ or } A_3)=P(A_1)+P(A_2)+P(A_3).$$

This process may evidently be continued to n disjoint events. Hence, if the events $A_1, A_2, ..., A_n$ are disjoint,

$$P(A_1 \text{ or } A_2 \text{ or } ... \text{ or } A_n)=P(A_1)+P(A_2)+...+P(A_n). \tag{3.2}$$

This is called the "additivity" property for n disjoint events. Note that in the rigorous formulations of probability this result cannot be generalized to $n=\infty$. This property, for $n=\infty$, is regarded as Axiom IV.

Normalization Property. Suppose events $A_1, A_2, ..., A_N$ are disjoint and form an event space (see Sect. 3.1.1). Then

$$(A_1 \text{ or } A_2 \text{ or } ... \text{ or } A_N)=C,$$

the certain event. Then Axiom II may be combined with result (3.2) to produce

$$P(A_1)+P(A_2)+...+P(A_N)=1, \tag{3.3}$$

the normalization property for probabilities that form a space. We see, from the preceding, that (3.3) is really a statement that some one of the possible events $A_1, ..., A_N$ *must* occur at a given experiment.

Marginal Probability. Consider $P(A_m B_n)$, the probability of the joint event A_m and B_n, where the $\{B_n\}$ are disjoint and form a space. If $P(A_m B_n)$ is known, can $P(A_m)$ somehow be computed from it?

The event A_m is equivalent to the joint event A_m and $(B_1$ or B_2 or ... or $B_N)$, since the latter is the certain event. This joint event may also be expressed as $(A_m$ and $B_1)$ or $(A_m$ and $B_2)$ or ... or $(A_m$ and $B_N)$, where these are disjoint since the $\{B_n\}$ are disjoint. Then we may use identity (3.2), which yields

$$P(A_m) = \sum_{n=1}^{N} P(A_m B_n), \tag{3.3a}$$

called the "marginal" probability, in the sense of summing the mth row of elements across the page to the margin.

3.1.4 The "Traditional" Definition of Probability

Suppose further that all the probabilities $P(A_n)$, $n = 1, ..., N$ in (3.3) are equal. Then by (3.3) each $P(A_n) = 1/N$.

Suppose, next, that an event B is defined as a *subset* $(A_1$ or A_2 or ... or $A_n)$, $n \leq N$, of event space. Then by (3.2)

$$P(A_1 \text{ or } ... \text{ or } A_n) \equiv P(B) = n(1/N),$$

or

$$P(B) = n/N. \tag{3.4}$$

This was the traditional definition of probability taught in high school a generation ago. It has a simple interpretation. Recall that n is the number of disjoint events which may each imply the event B. Also, N is the total number of disjoint events possible. Then (3.4) states that $P(B)$ is *simply the ratio of the number of independent ways B can occur, divided by the total number of permissible events*. The exercise in high school consisted in counting up by permutations the unknowns n and N. (This thought still conjures up dreaded memories of red and white balls drawn from urns.)

Equation (3.4) is the first expression we have encountered that actually allows probability to be *computed*. Many common experiments permit n and N to be directly (if not easily) computed. An example illustrates this point.

Illustrative Problem. Two "fair" dice are rolled. By "fair" is meant *equal* probability for each of the six possible outcomes of a die roll. Find the probability of the event $B = $ (one die even, the other greater than 4).

The unknown probability is to be found by the use of identity (3.4). This means that B has to be enumerated as the occurrence of n equiprobable events. Also, to simplify the calculation, B ought to be one member of event space. This point will become clear below.

A frontal attack on the problem is to consider each possible experimental outcome with regard to its eveness or oddness (parity) and size relative to level four. Thus, let e represent the event "an even die value", o the event "odd die value", LE the event "die value less than or equal to 4", and G the event "die value greater than 4". Then the following event space may be constructed, where the first item in each couplet denotes parity, and the second denotes size relative to 4:

$$(e, LE), (e, G), (o, LE), (o, G). \tag{3.5}$$

There are no other possibilities as regards these joint possibilities. To simplify the approach, we have made B one event (the first) in the space.

Now, according to approach (3.4) we have to express event B in terms of equiprobable events. But directly B can only be formed as

$$B \equiv (e, G) = [2, 5] \text{ or } [2, 6] \text{ or } [4, 5] \text{ or } [4,6] \text{ or } [6,5] \text{ or } [6,6]$$

where each square-bracketed couplet describes the two dice values. Each of these number couplets *is* equally probable by the fairness of the dice; see preceding. Therefore we have but to count them and this defines n.

There are six such couplets shown above, and actually 12 in total since the dice may be interchanged to give rise to six more. By the same counting procedure we may compute N, the total number of possible dice combinations giving rise to the *space* of events (3.5). We find $N = 36$, and hence, by (3.4), $P(B) = 12/36 = 1/3$

This example has been given mainly for didactic reasons. Luckily, probability problems *in optics* are almost never of the permutation variety; they're easier.

3.1.5 Law of Large Numbers

We shall diverge temporarily from the axiomatic approach here and simply present the result. A proof is given in Sect. 3.11.1.

Suppose the experiment that gives rise to B in (3.4) is actually carried through a large number of times. What will be the relative number of times event B *will* occur? This is defined as the number m of times that B occurs divided by the number M of experiments performed, and is called the "frequency of occurrence" $f(B)$ for B. Hence, $f(B) = m/M$.

The "law of large numbers" states that $f(B)$ asymptotically approaches $P(B)$ as $M \to \infty$,

$$P(B) = \lim_{M \to \infty} (m/M). \tag{3.6}$$

This allows the theoretical $P(B)$ to be determined experimentally for the first time; see Sect. 3.11 for a discussion of the accuracy of this method.

The Law is actually the vehicle for many optical applications of probability theory. See, e.g., the illustrative problem on p. 89.

3.1.6 Conditional Probability

Suppose that the outcome of an experiment obeys property A. We may ask what the probability is that it also obeys property B. (Note: It is common to interchangeably use the phrases "is event" and "obeys property".) This is in fact defined as

$$P(B|A) = P(AB)/P(A), \tag{3.7}$$

where $P(B|A)$ denotes the conditional probability in question, of "B if A". Note that we have used notation AB to describe the event "A and B simultaneous".

Although (3.7) is a definition, it is also reasonable in that it complies with the corresponding expression for frequency of occurrence. [Given the law of large numbers (3.6) we would demand this correspondence.] Cross-multiplying (3.7) and substituting frequency f for probability P,

$$f(AB) = f(A) f(B|A).$$

This relation is commonly used. For example, in a certain student body, 60% are coeds and of these 72% smoke. What percentage of the student body is both coed and smokes? The answer is intuitively set up as the fraction of the student body that is female times the fraction of those females who smoke. That is, $0.60 \times 0.72 = 0.432$.

Statistical Independence. If $P(B|A) = P(B)$, then events A and B are termed "independent". This equality states that the probability of B given the property A is the same as the probability of B when it is *not known* whether property A holds. Hence, property A really has no affect upon the occurrence of B; they are independent effects. Note that in this case definition (3.7) becomes

$$P(AB) = P(A)P(B).$$

This is generalizable to the case where n events $A_1, \ldots, A_n$ are statistically independent. Then

$$P(A_1 A_2 \ldots A_n) = P(A_1) P(A_2) \ldots P(A_n). \tag{3.8}$$

A note of caution: the converse is not necessarily true. That is, *given* (3.8) for events $A_1, \ldots, A_n$, it is not necessarily true that these are statistically independent events. To prove their mutual independence from expressions such as (3.8) requires $2^n - (n+1)$ expressions

$$P(A_{k_1} A_{k_2} \ldots A_{k_m}) = P(A_{k_1}) P(A_{k_2}) \ldots P(A_{k_m}) \quad m = 2, 3, \ldots, n. \tag{3.9}$$

(see [Ref. 3.1, p. 41]).

3.1.7 Partition Law

Consider an event space $\{A_n\}$ of disjoint events, and an event B that *includes some of the* $\{A_n\}$. Then it is trivial to state that if B occurs, some one (or more) of the A_n *must* occur as well. For example, this is the case if the $\{A_n\}$ are the outcomes of rolling a die and B is any even outcome.

Now since the $\{A_n\}$ are mutually disjoint, so are the events $(B$ and $A_n)$, $n = 1, ..., N$. Also, B occurs if and only if some one of the events $(B$ and $A_n)$ occurs. Then, identically

$$P(B) = P[(B \text{ and } A_1) \text{ or } (B \text{ and } A_2) \text{ or } ... \text{ or } (B \text{ and } A_N)]$$

and by (3.2)

$$P(B) = P(B \text{ and } A_1) + P(B \text{ and } A_2) + ... + P(B \text{ and } A_N).$$

Finally, we use definition (3.7) repeatedly to find that

$$P(B) = P(A_1)P(B|A_1) + ... + P(A_N)P(B|A_N). \tag{3.10}$$

We call this a "partition" law because event B has been partitioned into all its possible component events A_1 through A_N.

Illustrative Problem. The partition law has some immediate optical use. Suppose, for example, a light beam composed of three primary colors impinges upon a film. The colors are C_1, C_2, and C_3 or red, blue, and green, respectively. The relative proportions of each color in the beam are $p_1 = 0.4$, $p_2 = 0.5$, and $p_3 = 0.1$ (the color is purple). Suppose the film energy transmittance for each color is $t_1 = 0.6$, $t_2 = 0.1$, and $t_3 = 0.3$. What is the net light transmittance for the film?

By the law of large numbers (3.6), *the net light transmittance for the film is actually the probability that a photon is transmitted through the film.* Let B describe this event. Further, the $\{p_n\}$ describe the probability of a photon being a certain color, while the $\{t_n\}$ define the probabilities of passage through the film, *conditional upon* color. Hence, $P(B) = p_1 t_1 + p_2 t_2 + p_3 t_3 = 0.32$ by direct substitution. (Note that once again in a practical problem recourse has been made to use of the law of large numbers. Physical quantities such as color ratio or energy transmittance are really expressions of frequency of occurrence, and hence probability, by the law of large numbers.)

3.1.8 Transition to the Continuum

A *random variable* (r.v.) x is defined as the outcome of an experiment which can have a *continuum* of possible values $-\infty \leq x \leq \infty$.

An example is the experiment where a ray of light is randomly bent by atmospheric turbulence as it travels from a geometrical point source to a receiving screen. If x is the coordinate of the ray as it strikes the screen, obviously x can have any *continuous* value, and at the same time x is *random* since the turbulence varies randomly from one experiment to the next.

For such an experiment it is true that a *probability density* function $p(x)$ exists, such that the probability of the event $A=(a\leq x\leq b)$ may be computed. The *defining relation* between $P(A)$ and $p(x)$ is

$$P(a\leq x\leq b)\equiv \int_a^b p(x)dx. \tag{3.11}$$

This is supposed to hold for all intervals (a,b) so long as $a\leq b$ (see Fig. 3.1).

Taking extreme values for the interval (a,b) unravels the significance of the new function $p(x)$. First, consider the case $a=-\infty$, $b=+\infty$. Then A is the event $(-\infty \leq x\leq \infty)$, which is of course the *certain* event (see Sect. 3.1.1). Then, by Axiom II,

$$P(-\infty \leq x\leq \infty)=P(C)=1=\int_{-\infty}^{\infty} dx\, p(x), \tag{3.12}$$

which is a normalization property analogous to (3.3).

Next consider the opposite extreme, where $b=a+dx$, $dx>0$. Then by (3.11)

$$P(a\leq x\leq a+dx)=p(a)dx=p(x)|_{x=a}dx. \tag{3.13}$$

This shows that $p(x)dx$ is *actually a probability*, and that therefore $p(x)$ is a probability *density*. The consequence of $p(x)dx$ being a probability is that *all the preceding laws from the axioms through (3.10) are also obeyed by a probability density* $p(x)$, with suitable modification (sums replaced by integrals, etc.). Key ones are listed.

$$0\leq p(x)\leq \infty, \tag{3.14a}$$

$$p(x|y)=p(x,y)/p(y) \tag{3.14b}$$

defines the conditional probability density $p(x|y)$ where (x,y) means x *and* y,

$$p(x|y)=p(x) \tag{3.14c}$$

if x and y are *statistically independent*,

$$p(x)=\int_{-\infty}^{\infty} dy\, p(x|y)p(y) \tag{3.14d}$$

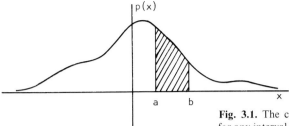

Fig. 3.1. The curve $p(x)$ is so constructed that for any interval (a, b) the probability $P(a \leq x \leq b)$ is simply the area (shaded) under the curve

is a *continuous partition law*,

$$p(x) = \int_{-\infty}^{\infty} dy\, p(x, y) \tag{3.14e}$$

for the *marginal* probability density $p(x)$.

An alternative to (3.11) for defining $p(x)$ is to regard the real line $-\infty \leq x \leq \infty$ of event space to consist of *disjoint* events $x_n \equiv n\,dx,\ -\infty \leq n \leq \infty$, and to *define* $p(x)$ to obey $P(x_n) \equiv p(x_n)dx$. Then note that the event $A \equiv (a \leq x \leq b)$ may be expressed as $x = (a$ or $a + dx$ or $a + 2dx$ or $\ldots$ or $b - dx$ or $b)$. As each of these alternatives is disjoint, by (3.2) $P(a \leq x \leq b) = P(a)$ $+ P(a + dx) + \ldots + P(b) = \sum_{x_n = a}^{b} p(x_n)dx$, which is the previous definition (3.11).

3.1.9 Expected Value, Moments

Suppose that the outcome of each experiment is operated upon by a fixed function f. That is an outcome A_n gives rise to a quantity $f(A_n)$. Then the mean or expected value of f is defined by

$$\langle f \rangle \equiv \sum_{n=1}^{N} f(A_n) P(A_n). \tag{3.15a}$$

Likewise there is the continuous mean,

$$\langle f \rangle \equiv \int_{-\infty}^{\infty} dx\, f(x) p(x). \tag{3.15b}$$

The function f may be any well-defined function. In the special case where $f(x) = x^k$, $k =$ an integer, the expected value is the kth moment m_k,

$$m_k \equiv \int_{-\infty}^{\infty} dx\, x^k p(x), \quad k = 1, 2, 3, \ldots. \tag{3.16a}$$

The particular number $m_1 \equiv \langle x \rangle$ is usually called the "mean value of x" or the "mean" of the probability density $p(x)$.

The *central* moments μ_k are defined as

$$\mu_k \equiv \int_{-\infty}^{\infty} dx(x - \langle x \rangle)^k p(x), \tag{3.16b}$$

that is, they are the moments of $p(x)$ about axes located at the mean of $p(x)$. The particular moment μ_2 is termed the "variance" and is denoted as σ^2. The square root of this quantity, σ, is called the "standard deviation".

Direct use of (3.16b) for $k = 2$ establishes the important relation

$$\sigma^2 = \langle x^2 \rangle - \langle x \rangle^2. \tag{3.16c}$$

σ^2 is usually computed from this relation, rather than from (3.16b).

For *jointly distributed* random variables, specified by a density function $p(x_1, x_2, ..., x_n)$, the expectation of a general function $f(x_1, x_2, ..., x_n)$ is the n-dimensional analog to (3.15b),

$$\langle f \rangle \equiv \int_{-\infty}^{\infty} \int_{-\infty}^{\infty} ... \int dx_1 \, dx_2 ... dx_n f(x_1, x_2, ..., x_n) p(x_1, x_2, ..., x_n). \tag{3.16d}$$

Case of Statistical Independence. If the r.v.'s $\{x_n\}$ are statistically independent, then by separation effect (3.8)

$$\langle f \rangle = \int ... \int dx_1 ... dx_n f(x_1, ..., x_n) p(x_1) ... p(x_n).$$

Finally, if in addition f is itself a product function $f_1(x_1) ... f_n(x_n)$ we get complete separation of the integrals, so that

$$\langle f \rangle = \langle f(x_1) \rangle ... \langle f(x_n) \rangle. \tag{3.16e}$$

Deterministic Limit; Representation of the Dirac δ Function. If an r.v. x can take on only one value x_0, then $p(x)$ can still describe this situation by taking on a Dirac delta function form

$$p(x) = \delta(x - x_0). \tag{3.16f}$$

The Dirac $\delta(x)$ function is defined as obeying

$$\delta(x) = 0 \quad \text{for} \quad x \neq 0 \tag{3.16g}$$

and yet

$$\int_{-\infty}^{\infty} dx \, \delta(x) = 1. \tag{3.16h}$$

These almost conflicting properties can be satisfied only if $\delta(x)$ is imagined to have an infinitely narrow [in view of (3.16g)] spike centered on the origin, of infinite height [in order to yield unit area as required by (3.16h)].

The significance of representation (3.16f) for $p(x)$ is that $p(x)$ is then infinitely narrow and concentrated about the event $x = x_0$. Hence, no other event but x_0 can occur. This is, of course, what we mean by determinism.

Dirac $\delta(x)$ has a further "sifting" property,

$$\int_{-\infty}^{\infty} dx\, f(x)\delta(x-x_0) = f(x_0) \tag{3.16i}$$

which follows simply from definition (3.16g, h). Hence in the deterministic limit, by (3.15b)

$$\langle f \rangle = f(x_0),$$

as would be expected since $p(x)$ has no spread about the point x_0.

Use of the correspondence (3.16f) with $x_0 = 0$, in particular, allows us to form functional representations for $\delta(x)$. Every probability density $p(x)$ has as a free parameter its standard deviation σ. Then by (3.16f) *we may represent $\delta(x)$ as simply*

$$\delta(x) = \lim_{\sigma \to 0} p(x), \tag{3.16j}$$

where $p(x)$ is any probability density. Note further that because $p(x)$ has unit area under it regardless of σ, $\delta(x)$ formed from (3.16j) automatically obeys the necessary property (3.16h).

As an example of such use, we may choose the Gaussian distribution (see Sect. 3.1.12), so that

$$\delta(x) = \lim_{\sigma \to 0} \frac{1}{\sqrt{2\pi}\,\sigma} e^{-x^2/2\sigma^2}. \tag{3.16k}$$

An infinity of such representations exists.

3.1.10 Correspondence Between Discrete and Continuous Cases

A discrete law P_n may be regarded as an extremely spikey version of a corresponding continuous law

$$p(x) = \sum_{n=0}^{\infty} P_n \delta(x-n), \tag{3.17}$$

where $\delta(x)$ is the Dirac delta function. Notice that because of the Dirac delta functions, the right-hand sum is zero except at the yield points $x = n$.

This relation is very useful, since it allows any probabilistic relation involving probability *density* to be expressed in the proper form for a *discrete* probability case. One merely substitutes (3.17) into the relation in question and performs any necessary integration by use of the handy sifting property (3.16i) for $\delta(x)$. For example, the normalization property (3.12) for density becomes, after substitution of (3.17),

$$1 = \sum_{n=0}^{\infty} \int_{-\infty}^{\infty} P_n \delta(x-n) = \sum_{n=0}^{\infty} P_n,$$

which is, of course, the normalization property for the discrete case.

Hence, *we may now consider the continuous situation to be the general one; interested readers can take the discrete limit (3.17) of a continuous law as required.* Most of the development that follows therefore emphasizes the continuous situation.

3.1.11 Cumulative Probability

Directly from definition (3.11) of density,

$$P(-\infty < x' < x) = \int_{-\infty}^{x} dx' \, p(x'). \tag{3.18}$$

This is also simply denoted as $F(x)$ at times. Quantity $F(x)$ is commonly called the cumulative probability or distribution function for random variable x. Since $p(x') \geq 0$, F is a monotonically increasing function of x. By (3.18), it has the same mathematical form as an optical edge spread function. This correspondance has practical application: see, e.g., (3.58), which originated in optical image theory.

3.1.12 Examples of Probability Distributions

Poisson. The most well-known discrete probability curve $P(A_n) \equiv P_n$ is the Poisson, defined as

$$P_n \equiv e^{-a} a^n / n!, \quad n = 0, 1, 2, \ldots, \tag{3.19}$$

with $a > 0$. This curve is illustrated in Fig. 3.2 for particular values of a. The parameter a is the sole determinant of the curve shape. By the use of definition (3.15a) it can directly be shown that a is both the mean and the variance, and even the third central moment, of the curve.

Binomial. Another discrete probability curve that arises commonly in physical application is the binomial probability

$$P_n = \binom{N}{n} p^n q^{N-n}, \quad \binom{N}{n} \equiv \frac{N!}{n!(K-n)!}, \tag{3.20}$$

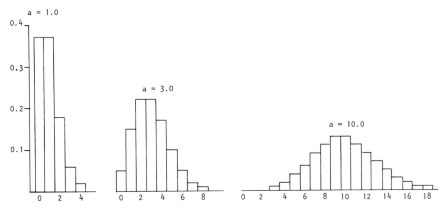

Fig. 3.2. Poisson curves, for various means *a*. Note skewness for $a=1.0$, 3.0

where $p+q=1$ and brackets denote the binomial coefficient. Direct use of definition (3.15a) shows that $\langle n\rangle = Np$ and $\sigma^2 = Npq$.

Uniform. The most elementary *probability density* is the uniform law

$$p(x)= \begin{cases} 1/(b-a) & \text{for} \quad a\leq x\leq b \\ 0 & \text{for} \quad x<a \quad \text{or} \quad x>b. \end{cases} \tag{3.21}$$

Use of definition (3.16) shows that $\langle x\rangle = (b-a)/2$, and $\sigma^2 = (b-a)^2/12$.

For the particular case $a=0$, $b=1$ the RANF($\cdot$) computer function generates a random variable whose fluctuations follow the uniform law (3.21). This is the only probability law that may be directly accessed at many computer centers. Yet Monte Carlo calculations (Sect. 3.4.3) and other simulations usually require random variables that follow other probability laws. Luckily, a mere mathematical transformation on the outputs from the RANF($\cdot$) function will make these outputs fluctuate according to any prescribed law. This is one of the subjects we take up later in Sect. 3.4.

Normal (One-Dimensional). The most frequently used probability law, bar none, is the famous normal law

$$p(x)=(2\pi\sigma^2)^{-1/2}\exp[-(x-\langle x\rangle)^2/2\sigma^2]. \tag{3.22a}$$

The phrase, "*x* is a normal r.v. with mean $\langle x\rangle$ and variance σ^2" is repeated so often that it now has its own notation.

$$x=N(\langle x\rangle,\sigma^2). \tag{3.22b}$$

Particular values for $\langle x\rangle$ and σ^2 are usually inserted. In the particular case $\langle x\rangle=0$, the normal law is called the "Gaussian" probability law. This is illustrated in Fig. 3.3.

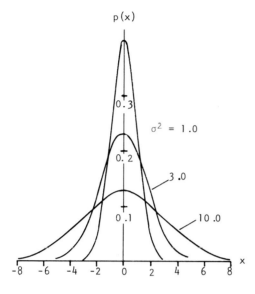

Fig. 3.3. Gaussian probability law for indicated values of variance σ^2. Compare with the three Poisson curves in Fig. 3.2

The reason for the popularity of the normal law is its common occurrence in physical problems, this due to the "central limit" theorem (see Sect. 3.2.5)[2].

Normal (Two-Dimensional). The most common *bivariate* law (i.e., describing *two* random variables x, y) is, by far, the normal bivariate one,

$$p(x,y) = \frac{1}{2\pi\sigma_1\sigma_2(1-\varrho^2)^{1/2}} \exp\left\{ -\frac{1}{2(1-\varrho^2)}\left[\frac{(x-m_{x1})^2}{\sigma_1^2} + \frac{(y-m_{y1})^2}{\sigma_2^2} \right.\right.$$

$$\left.\left. -\frac{2\varrho(x-m_{x1})(y-m_{y1})}{\sigma_1\sigma_2} \right]\right\}. \tag{3.23}$$

This law, for example, describes the joint fluctuation of pupil phase values x and y, at two points, caused by atmospheric turbulence (see Sect. 3.5.1).

Remarkably the *marginal* density $p(x)$, computed by use of identity (3.14e), is independent of parameters ϱ and σ_2^2, obeying

$$x = N(m_{x1}, \sigma_1^2). \tag{3.24}$$

A similar case exists for random variable y.

---

2 This theorem applies so extensively that an aura has developed about it. To "invoke" it (it is never merely "applied") as in "x must be normal because of the central limit theorem", is usually considered proof enough. Few have the temerity to question the statement, especially if it is said in an authoritative voice.

Since we have a *two*-dimensional probability law here, to find moments we use the generalized form (3.16d) with $n=2$,

$$\langle f \rangle \equiv \int\limits_{-\infty}^{\infty}\int dx\, dy\, f(x, y) p(x, y). \tag{3.25}$$

For example,

$$\langle (x - \langle x \rangle)(y - \langle y \rangle) \rangle \equiv \int\limits_{-\infty}^{\infty}\int dx\, dy (x - \langle x \rangle)(y - \langle y \rangle) p(x, y).$$

Substitution of (3.23) for $p(x, y)$ into this integral yields

$$\langle (x - \langle x \rangle)(y - \langle y \rangle) \rangle = \varrho \sigma_1 \sigma_2,$$

or

$$\varrho = \langle (x - \langle x \rangle)(y - \langle y \rangle) \rangle / \sigma_1 \sigma_2. \tag{3.26}$$

ϱ is called the "correlation coefficient" for fluctuations in x and y. If $\varrho = 0$, from (3.23) $p(x, y) = p(x) p(y)$, or x and y are statistically independent.

Regarding other means, from (3.25)

$$\langle x \rangle = \int\limits_{-\infty}^{\infty}\int dx\, dy\, x\, p(x, y)$$

$$= \int\limits_{-\infty}^{\infty} dx\, x\, p(x)$$

by the use of indentity (3.14e) for the *marginal density*,

$$= m_{x1}$$

by identity (3.24). Likewise $\langle y \rangle = m_{y1}$.

Normal (Multidimensional). As a direct generalization of the preceding, the n-dimensional normal density function is of the form

$$p(x_1, x_2, \ldots, x_n) \equiv p(\boldsymbol{x}) = \frac{|A|^{1/2}}{(2\pi)^{n/2}} e^{-2^{-1}(\boldsymbol{x} - \langle \boldsymbol{x} \rangle)^T [A](\boldsymbol{x} - \langle \boldsymbol{x} \rangle)}, \tag{3.27}$$

where vector

$$(\boldsymbol{x} - \langle \boldsymbol{x} \rangle) \equiv \begin{pmatrix} x_1 - \langle x_1 \rangle \\ \vdots \\ x_n - \langle x_n \rangle \end{pmatrix}.$$

Matrix $[A]$ is *positive definite*. The latter means that all its principal minors are positive

$$A_{11}>0, \begin{vmatrix} A_{11} & A_{12} \\ A_{21} & A_{22} \end{vmatrix} >0, ..., \det[A]>0. \tag{3.28}$$

The n-dimensional generalization to the correlation coefficient (3.26) is the *covariance coefficient*

$$\varrho_{jk} \equiv \frac{\langle (x_j - \langle x_j \rangle)(x_k - \langle x_k \rangle) \rangle}{\sigma_j \sigma_k}. \tag{3.29a}$$

Use of (3.27) in the n-dimensional average (3.16d) yields

$$\varrho_{jk} = \frac{\text{cofactor } A_{jk}}{(\text{cofactor } A_{jj} \text{cofactor } A_{kk})^{1/2}}, \quad j \neq k \tag{3.29b}$$

with

$$\sigma_j^2 = \frac{\text{cofactor } A_{jj}}{|A|}. \tag{3.29c}$$

In the special case where the $\{x_n\}$ are mutually independent, matrix $[A]$ is diagonal, so the exponent in (3.27) becomes purely a sum of squares over the $\{x_n\}$. The effect is to make $p(x_1, ..., x_n)$ a product of *one-dimensional* normal density functions (3.22a). Likewise with $[A]$ diagonal the cofactors $A_{jk}, j \neq k$, are zero so that by (3.29b) all covariances ϱ_{jk} are zero.

Skewed Gaussian Case; Gram-Charlier Expansion. A real probability law is often close to Gaussian, but significantly different to require a separate description. A very useful way to describe such a probability law is by the "Gram-Charlier" expansion

$$p(x) = p_0(x) \left[1 + \sum_{n=1}^{N} \frac{c_n}{n!} H_n(x) \right], \tag{3.30}$$

where $p_0(x)$ is the closest Gaussian to $p(x)$, obtained say by least-squares fit. Coefficients $\{c_n\}$ measure the departure from a pure Gaussian $p_0(x)$ case, and are to be determined. The $H_n(x)$ are Hermite polynomials. The latter obey an orthogonality relation

$$\int_{-\infty}^{\infty} dx \frac{1}{\sqrt{2\pi}} e^{-x^2/2} H_m(x) H_n(x) = n! \delta_{mn} \tag{3.31}$$

with respect to a Gaussian weight function. The first few are

$$H_0(x)=1, \quad H_1(x)=x, \quad H_2(x)=x^2-1, \quad H_3(x)=x^3-3x. \tag{3.32}$$

The size of coefficients $\{c_n\}$ determines closeness to the pure Gaussian $p_0(x)$ case. The odd coefficients c_1, c_3, etc., multiply odd polynomials $H_n(x)$ and hence describe a "skewness" property for the $p(x)$ curve. The even coefficients in the same way define an even contribution to the curve which is often called "peakedness", in that it causes $p(x)$ to be more peaked than a pure Gaussian. With $p(x)$ observed experimentally as histogram (frequency of occurrence) data, the unknown $\{c_n\}$ may be determined in the usual manner for a series of orthogonal functions. Combining (3.30) and (3.31),

$$c_n = (2\pi)^{-1/2} \int_{-\infty}^{\infty} dx [p(x)/p_0(x) - 1] e^{-x^2/2} H_n(x). \tag{3.33}$$

The observation of glitter patterns reflected from ocean waves has been proposed as a means of remotely determining wind velocity at the ocean surface (see [3.4]). Glitter patterns are formed by specular reflection of sunlight and depend for their interpretation on knowledge of the probability distribution for *wave slope* as a function of wind velocity.

In a classic study, *Cox* and *Monk* [3.5] established this distribution. They determined the joint probability $p(x, y)$ linking *wave slope x along* wind direction and slope y *transverse to* wind direction. We describe this work next.

First, note that $p(x)$ should differ from $p(y)$. Along the wind direction, i.e., along x, waves tend to build from one direction and hence statistically should have gentler slopes on the windward side than on the leeward side. This should cause the histogram $p(x)$ for such slopes to be skewed away from the origin (zero slope) toward steep leeward (negative on plots) slope. The histogram $p(y)$ for slope *transverse* to the wind *should not show such bias*, since waves in this direction are not directly formed by the wind, but rather by a leakage of energy from the longitudinal wave motion *per se*.

The latter also suggests that x and y are generally *dependent* variables, so that $p(x, y)$ should not separate into a simple product. *Cox* and *Monk* used a two-dimensional Gram-Charlier expansion of the type (3.30),

$$p(x, y) = p_0(x)p_0(y)\left[1 + \frac{c_1 d_2}{2!} H_1(x)H_2(y) + \frac{c_3}{3!} H_3(x) \right.$$

$$+ \frac{d_4}{4!} H_4(y) + \frac{c_2 d_2}{2!2!} H_2(x)H_2(y)$$

$$\left. + \frac{c_4}{4!} H_4(x)\right| \tag{3.34}$$

to model an experimentally observed histogram curve $p(x, y)$. This series is actually selected terms in the direct product $p(x)p(y)$, each of which is represented by a series (3.30). Since not all terms of the product are included, the expression is *not* factorable into $p(x) \cdot p(y)$, which is required by the above assumption of dependence between x and y.

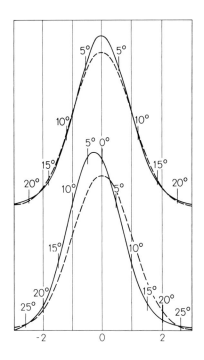

Fig. 3.4. Principal sections through the wave slope distribution. The upper curve is transverse to the wind direction. The dashed curves are the closest Gaussians in the two directions. Thin vertical scale lines show the slopes relative to the standard deviations for slope in the two directions. Angles indicated on the curves are the actual slope angles, in degrees, for a wind speed of 10 m/s. Note the skewness, from the closest Gaussian, in the bottom curve [3.5]

The coefficients in (3.34) were determined using linear regression (see Sect. 3.16) and least-square fits (see Sect. 3.16.3) to the experimental data. Results are shown in Fig. 3.4 for the two principal directions.

3.2 Fourier Methods in Probability

There is probably no aspect of probability theory that more delights the eye of a person versed in Fourier methods (*à la Bracewell* [3.6], for example) than its Fourier aspect. All of the linear theory involving convolutions, Dirac delta functions, transfer theorems, and even sampling theorems, have counterparts in probability theory. Moreover, as a practical matter, the calculation of probabilities often becomes a mere exercise in the use of the FFT (fast Fourier transform) algorithm. We take up these points below.

3.2.1 Characteristic Function

Consider the operation of taking the Fourier transform of the probability density function $p(x)$

$$\phi(\omega) \equiv \int_{-\infty}^{\infty} dx\, p(x) e^{i\omega x}. \tag{3.35}$$

Quantity $\phi(\omega)$ is called the "characteristic function" for the r.v. x. What significance does $\phi(\omega)$ have?

First of all, noting definition (3.15b) of the expectation, we see that in actuality

$$\phi(\omega) = \langle e^{i\omega x} \rangle. \tag{3.36}$$

That is, it represents the average response to a sinusoid, which is in the spirit of linear theory.

Use in Generating Moments. Secondly, by taking successive derivatives of (3.35) at $\omega = 0$ we see that

$$\phi^{(n)}(0) = i^n \int_{-\infty}^{\infty} dx\, x^n p(x)$$

$$= i^n \langle x^n \rangle, \quad n = 1, 2, \ldots \tag{3.37}$$

with the particular value $\phi^{(0)}(0) = \phi(0) = 1$.

Hence, the behavior of $\phi(\omega)$ at the origin defines all the moments of $p(x)$. This has practical use for *computing* the moments, since it is always easier to differentiate $\phi(\omega)$ than to integrate $x^m p(x)$ [provided that $\phi(\omega)$ is known analytically].

An Alternative to Describing r.v. x. This suggests that $\phi(\omega)$ offers an alternative to $p(x)$ for describing the random nature of x. Of course it does, since (3.35) may be inverted to give

$$p(x) = (2\pi)^{-1} \int_{-\infty}^{\infty} d\omega\, \phi(\omega)\, e^{-i\omega x}. \tag{3.38}$$

Hence, either of $p(x)$ or $\phi(\omega)$ suffice to describe r.v. x completely.

The final point worth noting about $\phi(\omega)$ is that *optical amplitude* is precisely of the form $e^{i\omega x}$, if x is regarded as optical phase. Hence by (3.36) $\phi(\omega)$ actually has a *physical* interpretation; namely, the average amplitude at a point in the field of a randomly fluctuating phase front. Much advantage has been taken of this correspondence in optical applications (see Sect. 3.5).

Shift Theorem. It is well known in optics that a linear phase term in the Fourier domain is equivalent to a shift in the linear domain. This has its counterpart here. Suppose r.v. x undergoes a linear shift, to form a new r.v.

$$y = ax + b, \quad a, b \text{ constants}.$$

What is $\phi_Y(\omega)$?

Using definition (3.36)

$$\phi_Y(\omega) = \langle e^{i\omega y} \rangle = \langle e^{i\omega(ax+b)} \rangle$$
$$= e^{i\omega b} \langle e^{i(a\omega)x} \rangle,$$

or

$$\phi_Y(\omega) = e^{i\omega b} \phi_X(a\omega). \tag{3.38a}$$

This is called the "shift" theorem.

Poisson Case. The Poisson probability law is a *discrete* one (3.19), whereas the definition (3.35) assumes a continuous $p(x)$ in use. Of course we may simply use the trick (3.17) to now define a characteristic function for the discrete case. Definition (3.35) becomes

$$\phi(\omega) = \int_{-\infty}^{\infty} dx\, e^{i\omega x} \sum_{n=1}^{\infty} P_n \delta(x-n)$$
$$= \sum_{n=0}^{\infty} P_n e^{i\omega n} \tag{3.39}$$

by the sifting property. Note that this is $\langle e^{i\omega n} \rangle$, which directly corresponds to the continuous version (3.36).

To evaluate $\phi(\omega)$ for the Poisson case we merely substitute (3.19) for P_n into definition (3.39),

$$\phi(\omega) = \sum_{n=0}^{\infty} (e^{-a} a^n / n!) e^{i\omega n}$$
$$= e^{-a} \sum_{n=0}^{\infty} (a e^{i\omega})^n / n!$$
$$= e^{-a} e^{a e^{i\omega}}, \tag{3.40}$$

having recognized the series for $\exp(\cdot)$. It is not often that we see a double exponential in actual use. By successively differentiating (3.40) we easily find the successive moments of the Poisson r.v., via identity (3.37). The mean, variance σ^2, and (remarkably) third central moment all equal a.

Normal Case (One-Dimensional). Here we have a continuous case, and so may use definition (3.35). Substitution into (3.35) of the normal law (3.22a) yields

$$\phi(\omega) = e^{i\omega\langle x \rangle - \sigma^2 \omega^2 / 2} \tag{3.41}$$

after completing the square and integrating.

Normal Case (Two-Dimensions). Substitution of probability law (3.23) into the two-dimensional generalization of (3.36)

$$\phi(\omega_1, \omega_2) = \langle e^{i(\omega_1 x + \omega_2 y)} \rangle \tag{3.42}$$

yields

$$\phi(\omega_1, \omega_2) = e^{i(\omega_1 \langle x \rangle + \omega_2 \langle y \rangle) - 2^{-1}(\sigma_1^2 \omega_1^2 + \sigma_2^2 \omega_2^2 + 2\sigma_1 \sigma_2 \varrho \omega_1 \omega_2)}. \tag{3.43}$$

This will have a direct application to the problem of finding the average *optical transfer function* in the presence of normal bivariate turbulence.

3.2.2 Convolution Theorem, Transfer Theorem

The probability density function $p(x)$ is conceptually quite similar to that of the point impulse response in linear systems theory. That is, $p(x)$ defines the "spread" permissible in x at a single event (impulse occurrence). Continuing the comparison, $\phi(\omega)$ is then analogous to the transfer function of the linear system since it is the Fourier transform of $p(x)$.

Will a convolution operation occur? In linear systems theory, a convolution occurs when the input to the system is an extended function of x, and the output function is sought. In probability theory, a convolution arises when the sum of two independent r.v.'s is sought. This is shown next.

Sum of Two Independent r.v.'s. Suppose random variables y and z are statistically independent. Define a new r.v.

$$x = y + z. \tag{3.44}$$

We seek the probability density for x. Call this $p_X(x)$.

Let us first try to find $\phi_X(\omega)$, the characteristic function for r.v. x. By definition

$$\phi_X(\omega) \equiv \langle e^{i\omega x} \rangle,$$
$$= \langle e^{i\omega(y+z)} \rangle$$

by (3.44),

$$= \langle e^{i\omega y} \rangle \langle e^{i\omega z} \rangle$$

by independence effect (3.16e)

$$= \phi_Y(\omega) \phi_Z(\omega) \tag{3.45}$$

by definition (3.36).

This may be considered as a transfer theorem for probabilities, when two independent r.v.'s add. We may now use the inverse transform (3.38) to find the required $p_X(x)$. The transform of product (3.45) yields a convolution

$$p_X(x) = \int_{-\infty}^{\infty} dx' \, p_Y(x') p_Z(x - x')$$

$$= p_Y(x) \otimes p_Z(x) \tag{3.46}$$

where $\otimes$ denotes convolution.

The result (3.46) makes sense intuitively. Since by (3.14a) both p_Y and p_Z are nonnegative, their convolution in (3.46) can only be a broader and smoother curve than either of them. That is, r.v. x must be more random than either y or z. As an example, consider the following problem.

Suppose y and z are both Gaussian r.v.'s with respective variances σ_Y^2 and σ_Z^2. What is the probability law for their sum? Although convolution expression (3.46) may be used, it is in fact easier to use the transfer theorem (3.45). Using this in conjunction with (3.41), we immediately find that

$$\phi_X(\omega) = e^{-(\sigma_Y^2 + \sigma_Z^2)\omega^2/2}. \tag{3.47}$$

This has the form of the characteristic function for a *Gaussian* $p(x)$ with net variance $\sigma_Y^2 + \sigma_Z^2 \equiv \sigma_X^2$. This again shows that $p_X(x)$ can only be a broader function than either of p_Y or p_Z.

Sum of n Independent r.v.'s. Suppose r.v.'s $y_1, ..., y_n$ are statistically independent. By the same methods as above, it can easily be shown that the new r.v.

$$x \equiv y_1 + ... + y_n \tag{3.47a}$$

has a characteristic function ϕ_X that is formed as a multiple product

$$\phi_X(x) = \phi_{Y_1}(\omega)...\phi_{Y_n}(\omega), \tag{3.48}$$

with a density function p_X formed as a multiple convolution

$$p_X(x) = p_{Y_1}(x) \otimes p_{Y_2}(x) \otimes ... \otimes p_{Y_n}(x). \tag{3.49}$$

Resulting Mean and Variance. In the special case where each of the $\{y_m\}$ is normal,

$$y_m = N(\langle y_m \rangle, \sigma_m^2),$$

it can be proven as above that p_X is also normal, and with a variance

$$\sigma_X^2 = \sum_{m=1}^{n} \sigma_m^2 \tag{3.50a}$$

and a mean

$$\langle x \rangle = \sum_{m=1}^{n} \langle y_m \rangle. \tag{3.50b}$$

These results (3.50a, b) also follow in the more general case of $\{y_m\}$ independent *and following any distribution*. This may be shown by squaring both sides of (3.47a) and taking the expectation termwise.

Finally, consider the special case where each of the $\{y_m\}$ is Poisson with mean and variance parameter a_m. Direct use of the Poisson characteristic function (3.40) in the product theorem (3.48) shows that the new r.v. x is also Poisson, and with a parameter

$$a_x = \sum_{m=1}^{N} a_m. \tag{3.51}$$

Hence, in either the Gaussian case or the Poisson case, the sum of r.v.'s is a r.v. whose variance is the sum of the constituent variances, and whose mean is the sum of the constituent means. This is not, however, true of random variables in general.

Sum of n Dependent r.v.'s. Suppose more generally r.v.'s $y_1, y_2, ..., y_n$ must be regarded as *dependent*, and the probability density for their sum x is required. Then the characteristic function for x is

$$\phi_x(\omega) \equiv \langle e^{i\omega x} \rangle = \langle e^{i(\omega y_1 + \omega y_2 + ... + \omega y_n)} \rangle \tag{3.51a}$$

$$\equiv \phi_Y(\boldsymbol{\omega}) \Big|_{\boldsymbol{\omega} = \omega} \tag{3.51b}$$

in obvious vector notation.

This is the n-dimensional characteristic function of $\phi_Y(\boldsymbol{\omega})$ evaluated where it intersects a hyperplane $\boldsymbol{\omega} = \omega$.

By definition the required density is

$$p_x(x) \equiv (2\pi)^{-1} \int_{-\infty}^{\infty} d\omega \, \phi_x(\omega) e^{-i\omega x}$$

$$= (2\pi)^{-1} \int_{-\infty}^{\infty} d\omega \, \phi_Y(\boldsymbol{\omega}) \Big|_{\boldsymbol{\omega} = \omega} e^{-i\omega x}$$

by (3.51b),

$$= (2\pi)^{-1} \int_{-\infty}^{\infty} d\omega \left[\int_{-\infty}^{\infty} ... \int dy \, p_Y(y) e^{i\boldsymbol{\omega} \cdot y} \right]_{\boldsymbol{\omega} = \omega} e^{-i\omega x}$$

by (3.51a),

$$= (2\pi)^{-1} \int_{-\infty}^{\infty} \ldots \int dy \, p_Y(y) \int_{-\infty}^{\infty} d\omega \, e^{i\omega(y_1 + \ldots + y_n) - i\omega x}$$

$$\underbrace{\qquad\qquad}_{2\pi\delta(y_1 + \ldots + y_n - x)}$$

$$= \int_{-\infty}^{\infty} \ldots \int dy_1 \ldots dy_{n-1} \, p_Y(y_1, \ldots, y_{n-1}, x - y_1 - \ldots - y_{n-1}) \qquad (3.51c)$$

by the sifting property of $\delta(x)$.

Hence Fourier methods have allowed us to solve the general problem as well.

Note that (3.51c) goes over into the convolution result (3.49), when the $\{y_n\}$ in (3.51c) are *independent*. This follows by the separation effect (3.8) for independent r.v.'s.

Case of Two Gaussian Bivariate r.v.'s. In actual calculations, it is often easier to use (3.51b), with later Fourier transformation, than to use the direct answer (3.51c). For example, consider the case where $x = y_1 + y_2$, with y_1, y_2 *jointly Gaussian bivariate*. To find $\phi_X(\omega)$, first the prescription (3.51b) says to merely take the characteristic function $\phi_{y_1 y_2}(\omega_1, \omega_2)$ and replace $\omega_1 = \omega_2 = \omega$. Hence by (3.43),

$$\phi_X(\omega) = e^{-2^{-1}\omega^2(\sigma_1^2 + \sigma_2^2 + 2\sigma_1\sigma_2\varrho)}.$$

This is simply the characteristic function for a Gaussian r.v. whose variance is

$$\sigma_X^2 = \sigma_1^2 + \sigma_2^2 + 2\sigma_2\sigma_2\varrho.$$

Hence $x = N(0, \sigma_1^2 + \sigma_2^2 + 2\sigma_1\sigma_2\varrho)$ in this case.

3.2.3 Sampling Theorems for Probability

A common way of finding the probability density $p(x)$ for a r.v. x is to use the product theorem (3.48) to first establish $\phi_X(\omega)$, and then to FT (Fourier transform) this to form $p(x)$. However, $\phi(\omega)$ is often too complicated a function for its Fourier transform to be analytically known. In this case the FT integral

$$p(x) = (2\pi)^{-1} \int_{-\infty}^{\infty} d\omega \, \phi(\omega) e^{-i\omega x} \qquad (3.52)$$

must be evaluated numerically. Of course, the digital computer can only evaluate this integral as a discrete sum, and this usually means a loss of precision. However, there is a situation where no precision is lost. This is the case where a "sampling theorem" holds true, as described next.

Case of Limited Range of x, Derivation. In some cases it is a priori known that r.v. x cannot take on values beyond a certain value, i.e., $|x| \leq x_0$. For example, x is a random phase angle, $-\pi \leq x \leq \pi$. Then by Fourier's basic theorem $p(x)$ may be represented within the limited interval as a series

$$p(x) = \sum_{n=-\infty}^{\infty} a_n e^{-in\pi x/x_0} \tag{3.53a}$$

for $|x| \leq x_0$,

with

$$p(x) = 0 \tag{3.53b}$$

for $|x| > x_0$.

The coefficients obey

$$a_n = (2x_0)^{-1} \int_{-x_0}^{x_0} dx\, p(x) e^{in\pi x/x_0}. \tag{3.54}$$

This expression may be compared with the one for $\phi(\omega)$,

$$\phi(\omega) = \int_{-x_0}^{x_0} dx\, p(x) e^{i\omega x} \tag{3.55}$$

because of (3.53b). These show that

$$a_n = (2x_0)^{-1} \phi(n\pi/x_0).$$

Substitution of this a_n back into (3.53a) shows that

$$p(x) = (2x_0)^{-1} \sum_{n=-\infty}^{\infty} \phi(n\pi/x_0) e^{-in\pi x/x_0} \tag{3.56}$$

for $|x| \leq x_0$.

This is one-half of the sampling theorem.

The other half is produced by substituting (3.56) back into (3.55), switching orders of summation and integration, and integrating termwise,

$$\phi(\omega) = \sum_{n=-\infty}^{\infty} \phi(n\pi/x_0) \operatorname{sinc}(x_0\omega - n\pi) \tag{3.57}$$

for all ω, where $\operatorname{sinc}(x) \equiv \sin(x)/x$.

Discussion. Recall that our original aim was to numerically integrate the right-hand side of (3.52). Compare this with the sampling theorem (3.56), which exactly equals (3.32). We see that the integral has been replaced by a summation over discrete samples of the known integrand and, furthermore, there is no error in making the replacement. This permits $p(x)$ to be evaluated with *arbitrary accuracy* on a digital computer.

The *proviso* has been, of course, that x be limited to a finite interval of values. This is not generally true, and depends on the case under study. Notice that the less this is true, i.e., the larger the interval size $2x_0$ is, by (3.56) the closer together the sampling of ϕ must be, in fact, to the limit where the sum *again becomes* the integral. *Barakat* [3.7] has used sampling theorem (3.56) to compute probability densities in the case of laser speckle.

The second sampling theorem, (3.57), is actually the Whittaker-Shannon interpolation formula; see [3.8] for a classic discussion of the analogous sampling theorem for optical imagery. This formula permits $\phi(\omega)$ to be perfectly computed anywhere in between the sampled values $\phi(n\pi/x_0)$, based on these sampled values as the sole data. Theoretically, this permits the infinity of values $\phi(\omega)$ over any finite interval of ω to be computed with arbitrary precision from a finite number of sampled values $\phi(n\pi/x_0)$. The greater the precision required, the higher the number of sampled values to be included in the sum.

Formulas such as these sampling theorems are ideal for the digital computer, since they allow continuous functions to be computed from a finite set of data, thus minimizing core storage needs.

Case of Limited Range of ω. Sampling theorems may also be established if, instead of x being limited in range, ω is. This would be the case if $p(x)$ is a band-limited function, such as $\mathrm{sinc}^2(ax)$, or $[\mathrm{sinc}^2(ax)] \otimes g(x)$ with $g(x)$ arbitrary, etc. In this event, ω is limited to a finite interval $|\omega| \leq \omega_0$, and sampling theorems of the form (3.56, 57) hold, where now the roles of ϕ and p are reversed, and similarly for x and ω, and x_0 and ω_0. These new formulas would have computational advantages similar to the preceding.

We also have a third sampling formula. Recall that corresponding to any $p(x)$ is a *distribution function* $F(x)$ defined by (3.18). A relation exists which expresses $\phi(\omega)$ in terms of sampled values of $F(x)$,

$$\phi(\omega) = j\pi(\omega/\omega_0) \sum_{n=-\infty}^{\infty} F(n\pi/\omega_0) e^{-in\pi\omega/\omega_0}. \tag{3.58}$$

$$|\omega| \leq \omega_0$$

This sampling theorem was invented by *Tatian* [3.9] in order to compute the *optical transfer function* in terms of sampled values of the *edge response*.

Equation (3.58) is useful if the distribution function $F(x)$ is the basic data at hand, rather than the usual $p(x)$. With $F(x)$ known, $p(x)$ can only be found by numerically differentiating $F(x)$, which is a rather noise-sensitive operation. It often does not pay to use a sampling theorem that uses such error-prone $p(x)$

values as inputs. Under the circumstances of given $F(x)$ data, (3.58) is a much more accurate sampling theorem to use, since it is based upon the *direct* data.

Tatian also showed that if $p(x)$ is band limited, as is assumed here, so is $F(x)$. Therefore, $F(x)$ obeys its own sampling theorem

$$F(x) = \sum_{n=-\infty}^{\infty} F(n\pi/\omega_0)\,\text{sinc}(\omega_0 x - n\pi) \qquad (3.59)$$

for all x.

This would permit the distribution function to be constructed at any continuous x value from a set of discrete samples of itself. The more accuracy that is demanded in the construction, the higher the number of discrete samples that would be required.

3.2.4 Discrete Fourier Transforms and Fast Fourier Transforms

The discrete Fourier transform (DFT) of a sequence of one-dimensional numbers $\{f_n\}$ is defined as

$$F_m \equiv N^{-1} \sum_{n=0}^{N-1} f_n e^{-2\pi i m n/N} \qquad (3.60)$$

for $m = 0, 1, \ldots, K-1$.

The form of this expression resembles (3.56), which suggests that something like a FT of a function $f(x)$ is being attempted, based on sampled values $\{f_n\}$ of the function. That this is the case is shown next.

Correspondence Between DFT and FT, Derivation. A sampling theorem holds, we have found, when a function $f(x)$ is bandlimited, i.e., when its spectrum $F(\omega) = 0$ for all $|\omega| > \omega_0$, ω_0 finite. From the form of (3.56) our sampling theorem is

$$F(\omega) = \sum_{n=-\infty}^{\infty} f(n\pi/\omega_0)e^{-i n\pi\omega/\omega_0}, \qquad (3.61)$$

for $|\omega| \le \omega_0$,

where an irrelevant constant multiplier has been ignored. We want to show that the DFT (3.60) is equivalent to a sampling theorem (ST), (3.61), where $\{F_m\}$ represents sampled values $F(\omega_m)$ at discrete frequencies.

To do this, suppose function $f(x)$ is negligible outside a certain interval. As shown in Fig. 3.5a, let this function be sampled at points spaced a distance π/ω_0 apart. Denote the number of samples as N. Denote as region (1) samples at

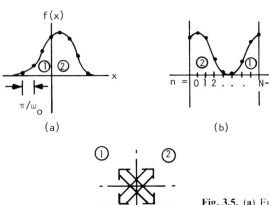

Fig. 3.5. (a) Function $f(x)$ to be Fourier transformed; dots denote sampled inputs $f(x_n)$. **(b)** As input into DFT. **(c)** Interchange of quadrants required for two-dimensional FT evaluation by the DFT

$x < 0$, and as region (2) samples at $x \geq 0$. Now, take region (2) and interchange it with region (1), as shown in Fig. 3.5b. Input these sampled values $f(n\pi/\omega_0) \equiv f_n$ into the DFT formula (3.60). What do we get?

As it was input, region (2) gives rise to a sum

$$N^{-1} \sum_{n=0}^{N/2-1} f_n e^{-2\pi i m n/N}$$

while region (1) gives a sum

$$N^{-1} \sum_{n=-N/2}^{-1} f_n e^{-2\pi i m(n+N)/N}.$$

Note the indexing of this last sum, which correctly samples the negative region (1) of $f(x)$ while giving the correct exponent values as they continue from the first sum.

But identically

$$e^{-2\pi i m(n+N)/N} = e^{-2\pi i m n/N}.$$

Using this in the second sum, and adding the two sums to form the DFT, its output obeys

$$F_m = N^{-1} \sum_{n=-N/2}^{N/2-1} f_n e^{-2\pi i m n/N}, \tag{3.62}$$

$$m = 0, 1, ..., N-1.$$

Now define index m to obey $\omega_m = 2m\omega_0/N$, and index n to obey $x_n = n\pi/\omega_0$. Then the DFT output is equivalent to sampling a function $F(\omega_m) \equiv F_m$, which obeys

$$F(\omega_m) = N^{-1} \sum_{n=-N/2}^{N/2-1} f(n\pi/\omega_0) e^{-in\pi\omega_m/\omega_0}. \tag{3.63}$$

$$\omega_m = 0, 2\omega_0/N, \ldots, 2\omega_0(N-1)/N.$$

The sum is indeed of the form (3.61) for the sampling theorem. Hence, the DFT operation *on interchanged data* (as described) gives rise to evaluation of the Fourier transform by means of the sampling theorem.

A secondary problem arises, in that the ST (3.61) formally represents the spectrum only within a band *centered on the origin* $|\omega_m| \leq \omega_0$, whereas the DFT output (3.63) evaluates ω within a band of the correct width $2\omega_0$, but displaced from the ST band by an amount ω_0 to the right. Thus, the DFT *half-band* $0 \leq \omega_m \leq 2\omega_0(N/2-1)$ corresponds directly to ST frequencies in that band; but what does the DFT *second* half-band $\omega_0 \leq \omega_m \leq 2\omega_0(N-1)/N$ correspond to?

From the form of DFT output (3.63)

$$F(\omega_0 + \Delta\omega) = F(-\omega_0 + \Delta\omega), \qquad \Delta\omega \geq 0$$

since $\exp(in\pi) = \exp(-in\pi)$. This means that the DFT second half-band (of frequencies $\omega_0 + \Delta\omega$) replicates the negative half-band (of frequencies $-\omega_0 + \Delta\omega$). This is, in fact, the analogous construction to the interchanged *input* curve of Fig. 3.5b.

In summary, then, the Fourier transform of a band limited function $f(x)$ that has effectively limited extension may be computed by use of the DFT, provided that a) the function's negative and positive argument regions are interchanged prior to being input, and b) it is realized that the first $N/2-1$ numbers output make up the positive-frequency domain of the FT, and the second $N/2$ numbers make up the negative-frequency domain.

The situation for two-dimensional functions is analogous. As shown in Fig. 3.5c, the *quadrants* must here be interchanged through the origin. Hence, quadrants (1) and (3) are interchanged, along with quadrants (2) and (4).

Reversibility of DFT Operation, Derivation. Here we ask whether the $\{f_n\}$ can be retrieved from knowledge of the $\{F_m\}$. With this aim, multiply DFT (3.60) by $\exp(2\pi imn'/N)$ and sum over $m = 0, \ldots, N-1$. This gives

$$\sum_{m=0}^{N-1} F_m e^{2\pi imn'/N} = N^{-1} \sum_{n=0}^{N-1} f_n \sum_{m=0}^{N-1} e^{2\pi im(n'-n)/N}.$$

Now the inner sum on the right-hand side may be recognized as a geometric series, which may be analytically summed to yield

$$\sum_{m=0}^{N-1} e^{2\pi i m(n'-n)/N} = \begin{cases} 0 & \text{for} \quad n \neq n' \\ N & \text{for} \quad n = n' \end{cases}. \tag{3.64}$$

Only one term then contributes to the double sum, namely $N f_{n'}$, so that

$$f_n = \sum_{m=0}^{N-1} F_m e^{2\pi i m n/N}. \tag{3.65}$$

We renamed $n' = n$ again.

This is often called the "reverse" DFT, since it is of precisely the same form as the DFT operation (3.60) except for a plus sign in the exponent (and unit multiplier replacing N^{-1}). The reverse DFT is also evaluated at points $n = 0, 1, ..., N-1$.

Significance of the Reverse DFT. By similar steps to the derivation that the DFT (3.60) is equivalent to a ST (3.63) for the spectrum F in terms of sampled values of f, it can be shown that the reverse DFT (3.65) is equivalent to a ST for f in terms of sampled values of spectrum F. We call this the reverse ST. In fact, the two results, ST, reverse ST, are perfectly symmetric in interchange of x for ω, etc., since the spacing $\Delta\omega$ of F values is $2\omega_0/N$ by (3.63), where N relates to the assumed limited extension $2x_0$ of $f(x)$ through

$$N\Delta x = N(\pi/\omega_0) = 2x_0.$$

This defines N. Hence, the frequency spacing is actually

$$\Delta\omega = 2\omega_0/[2x_0/(\pi/\omega_0)] = \pi/x_0, \tag{3.66}$$

exactly symmetric with spacing $\Delta x = \pi/\omega_0$.

The reverse ST, for f in terms of sampled values of F, can only be regarded as approximate, however, since by the assumption of $f(x)$ being band limited it cannot also be space limited as well. That is, if ω_0 is finite, x_0 cannot also be finite in (3.66).

On the other hand, for the most part this is not a real limitation on the accuracy of the reverse ST. In order for the primary ST of $\{F_m\}$ in terms of the $\{f_n\}$ to itself be true, function $f(x)$ must be limited in extension to the N numbers $\{f_n\}$. This was a vital assumption in the correspondence proof earlier in this section; see particularly step (3.63) where the finiteness of N is explicitly used. The upshot is that if the primary ST is to be true, so must be the reverse ST.

Sources of Error in Use of the DFT. The most common error made by a novice is to not interchange regions (1) and (2) before inputting $f(x)$ [or $F(\omega)$] into the DFT algorithm. What particularly "encourages" this mistake is the reversibility

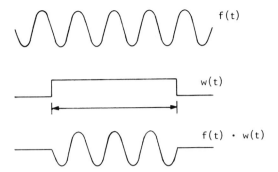

Fig. 3.6. The rectangular data window implied when a finite record of data is analyzed [3.10]

of the forward and reverse DFTs. A novice often assumes that if he starts with a sequence of numbers $\{f_n\}$, inputs these into the forward DFT, then performs the reverse operation and ends up with the same $\{f_n\}$, that this provides a check on his use of the algorithm! Obviously, it checks the correct performance of the two steps together, but it does not check either step *separately*! The output of the forward DFT step will not be the desired FT of $f(x)$ unless it is region reversed, as described. Similarly for the inverse DFT step.

A second important restriction is that the input to the DFT be wholly contained within its N values. As seen at derivation step (3.63), unless $f(x)$ falls to zero at its end points a *finite* Fourier transform will be output. This is called the "leakage" problem by *Bergland* [3.10], in a user-oriented paper on the FFT. This is equivalent to multiplication of the desired input by a rectangle function, or *to convolution by a* sinc(ω) *function* in the output (see Fig. 3.6). Consequently, *the output has superficial ripples.*

A way around this problem is to simply multiply the input numbers by a "window function" which is not as abrupt as a rectangle, therefore causing smaller false ripples in the output. Examples cited have been a) Tukey's "interim" data window, consisting of a raised cosine wave applied to the first and last 10% of the data, with unit weighting in between; b) a triangle window, $1 - |x|$; and others cited by *Bergland*. Another interesting possibility is to *post-process* the outputs of the DFT to reduce ripples, such as by convolution with the Hanning weights 1/4, 1/2, 1/4. This is equivalent to *preprocessing* with a raised cosine window function.

A word of caution: merely bracketing $f(x)$ with a few zeros will not work, because if $f(x)$ is abrupt before this operation it will be abrupt after it. It will still be multiplied by a rectangle function.

The third important restriction is that the number N of samples be high enough to properly sample the *highest* frequency component ω_0 present in the data. Otherwise, the problem called "aliasing" arises. This is the well-known "impersonation" effect whereby a high-frequency component appears to be of lower frequency (see Fig. 3.7). Quantitatively, a frequency component *higher* than the Nyquist frequency ω_N (the latter defined by the sampling rate N) by an

Fig. 3.7. An example of a high frequency "impersonating" a low frequency [3.10]

amount Δf *will appear to be lower* than ω_N by the same amount Δf. The amplitude of this superficial frequency will be one of the DFT outputs, which may be considerable.

The cure for this problem is to simply sample the curve $f(x)$ at the *correct* rate, namely at spacing $\Delta x = \pi/\omega_0 = 1/(2R)$ *or finer*, where $\omega_0 = 2\pi R$ and R cycles/length is the highest component frequency present in $f(x)$.

The Fast Fourier Transform (FFT). The FFT is simply a fast algorithm for computing the DFT in any number of dimensions. An example of the steps in the algorithm for the case $N = 8$ is given in [3.10].

The FFT algorithm has reduced DFT computer times from several minutes to less than a second. It has thereby opened to digital filtering a wide scope of application, ranging from acoustics to statistical simulation to image restoration. Also, the need for *analog methods* of performing the FT operation has been greatly reduced by the existence of the FFT. One commonly hears the expression "all-digital" systems nowadays.

Whereas conventional computation of the one-dimensional DFT requires nearly N^2 operations, use of the FFT reduces this figure to $(N/2) \log_2 N$ (each) complex multiplications, additions, and subtractions. For $N = 1024$, this represents a reduction in computation operations by more than a factor of $200:1$.

Earlier versions of the algorithm required N for each dimension to be a power of two. Later versions allow any integer for N, with the recommendation that N be close to a power of two for purposes of speed. Versions such as by *Singleton* [3.11] allow, in principle, *any size* for the Ns, by judicious use of disc storage in place of central memory.

Augmented Accuracy in FFT Use. If there is no leakage problem (see earlier discussion) then in practice the FFT will approximate the FT with vanishing error, provided that N is high enough to prevent "aliasing", as discussed. Whether N is sufficiently high can easily be ascertained by simply repeating the calculation for a value $2N$ and comparing outputs; insignificant change implies high accuracy.

However, tests such as these sometimes disclose that too high an N will be needed, from the standpoints of computer storage, time, and cost. In this event, accuracy can be improved by augmenting the input $\{f_n\}$ with an appropriate set of weights $\{w_n\}$ (see Sect. 2.4). The inputs are then $\{w_n f_n\}$, and the FFT calculates, in effect,

$$F(\omega_m) \equiv \Delta x \sum_{n=-\infty}^{\infty} w_n f(n\Delta x) e^{-i\omega_m n\Delta x}.$$

Table 3.1. Two-dimensional Simpson's rule weights. These should all be reduced by a factor 1/9

1	4	2	4	2	4	2	4	.	.	.	4	1
4	16	8	16	8	.	.	.	.	.	.	16	4
2	8	4	8	4	.	.	.	.	.	.	8	2
4	16	8	16	8	.	.	.	.	.	.	16	4
2	8	4	8	4	.	.	.	.	.	.	8	2
4	16	8	16	8	.	.	.	.	.	.	16	4
2	8	4	8	4	.	.	.	.	.	.	8	2
4	16	8	16	8	.	.	.	.	.	.	16	4
.	.	.	.	.	.	.	.	.	.	.	.	.
.	.	.	.	.	.	.	.	.	.	.	.	.
.	.	.	.	.	.	.	.	.	.	.	.	.
4	16	8	16	8	.	.	.	.	.	.	16	4
1	4	2	4	2	.	.	.	.	.	.	4	1

This may be recognized as a quadrature formula for F based on equispaced points at spacing Δx.

The purpose of weights $\{w_n\}$ is to effectively fit a series of smooth curves to successive points $f(n\Delta x)$ prior to integration. The hope is that the smooth curves will well approximate $f(x)$ *between* points $f(n\Delta x)$. As examples, unit weights fit the points with a sequence of steps, weights $(1/2, 1, 1, 1, ..., 1, 1/2)$ fit every two points with a connecting straight line (trapezoidal rule), and weights $(1/3, 4/3, 2/3, 4/3, ..., 4/3, 1/3)$ connect every three points with a parabola (Simpson's rule), etc., for higher order fits.

Such weights may also be found for two-dimensional evaluations. If $\{w_n\}$ is a good set of one-dimensional weights, two-dimensional weights

$$w_{mn} \equiv w_m w_n$$

may be employed. For example, see Table 3.1 for a two-dimensional set of Simpson's rule weights. *Abramowitz* and *Stegun* [3.12] give some *intrinsically* two-dimensional weights, i.e., not of the simple product form.

3.2.5 Central Limit Theorem

In Sect. 3.2.2, we found how to form the probability density $p_X(x)$ due to the sum of n independent r.v.'s $\{y_m\}$. The answer (3.48) was that the characteristic function $\phi_X(\omega)$ is the product

$$\phi_X(\omega) = \phi_{Y_1}(\omega)...\phi_{Y_n}(\omega) \tag{3.67}$$

of the individual characteristic functions.

Thus it must be that the functional form of the answer $\phi_X(\omega)$ will depend upon the form of the individual $\phi_{Y_m}(\omega)$, $m = 1, 2, ..., n$. In fact, this is true only to a very limited extent. Practically *regardless* of the form of the $\phi_{Y_m}(\omega)$, once a value $n \geq 4$ is used, $\phi_X(\omega)$ greatly resembles one, fixed distribution; namely, the normal curve! This is shown next.

Derivation. As will be seen, the basis for this derivation lies in the fact that a function convolved with itself many times over approaches a Gaussian curve shape.

Suppose a r.v. x is formed as the sum of n independent r.v.'s $\{y_m\}$

$$x = y_1 + y_2 + \ldots + y_n.$$

Suppose the $\{y_n\}$ to also have zero mean (this simplifies the proof) and to be identically distributed by any one density function $p_Y(y)$ and one characteristic function $\phi_Y(\omega)$. Then by the result (3.67) the characteristic function for x obeys

$$\phi_X(\omega) = [\phi_Y(\omega)]^n. \tag{3.68}$$

We next seek the limiting form for this $\phi_X(\omega)$ as n becomes large. Accordingly, expand $\phi_Y(\omega)$ by Taylor series. Then

$$\phi_X(\omega) = [\phi_Y(0) + \omega\phi_Y'(0) + 2^{-1}\omega^2\phi_Y''(0) + \mu\omega^3]^n.$$

But by (3.37), $\phi_Y(0) = 1$, $\phi_Y'(0) = i\langle y \rangle = 0$ since the $\{y_m\}$ are zero mean, and $\phi_Y''(0) = -\sigma_Y^2$; μ is some constant that need not be determined. Hence

$$\phi_X(\omega) = (1 - \sigma_Y^2\omega^2/2 + \mu\omega^3)^n.$$

Let us now define a new r.v.

$$s = x/\sqrt{n}$$

which is the required sum of r.v.'s $\{y_m\}$, divided by $\sqrt{n}$. Whereas with $n \to \infty$ the variance in x will increase unlimitedly [see result (3.50a)] as the sum of n variances, the new r.v. s has a *finite* variance. This is a desirable property, and we therefore seek the probability for s instead.

By the shift theorem (3.38a) $\phi_s(\omega) = \phi_X(\omega/\sqrt{n})$, so that

$$\phi_s(\omega) = [1 - \sigma_Y^2\omega^2/2n + \mu\omega^3/n^{3/2}]^n.$$

It is convenient now to take logarithms of both sides,

$$\ln\phi_s(\omega) = n\ln[1 - \sigma_Y^2\omega^2/2n + \mu\omega^3/n^{3/2}].$$

But as n is to be regarded as large, the [ ] term is very close to 1. Hence we may use the Taylor expansion

$$\ln(1 + b) = b + \eta b^2,$$

η constant. Then

$$\lim_{n \to \infty} \ln \phi_S(\omega) = n[-\sigma_Y^2 \omega^2 / 2n + \mu \omega^3 / n^{3/2} + \eta(-\sigma_Y^2 \omega^2 / 2n + \mu \omega^3 / n^{3/2})^2].$$

Now evaluating the right-hand side in the limit $n \to \infty$, *we see that only the first term in the [ ] remains.* Thus

$$\lim_{n \to \infty} \ln \phi_S(\omega) = -\sigma_Y^2 \omega^2 / 2,$$

or

$$\phi_S(\omega) = e^{-\sigma_Y^2 \omega^2 / 2} \tag{3.69}$$

for n large. As ϕ_S is Gaussian, by identity (3.41) so is r.v. s, and so

$$s = N(0, \sigma_Y^2), \tag{3.70}$$

which we set out to prove. The fact that $p_S(x)$ has this fixed *limiting* form is the "central limit" theorem.

The derivation also holds when r.v.'s $\{y_m\}$ have a finite mean, as the reader can easily verify. Furthermore, the central limit theorem holds under even more general conditions than assumed above. The $\{y_m\}$ do not have to all obey the same probability law, and they do not all have to be independent (see [Ref. 3.1, p. 267]). Finally, r.v.'s $\{y_m\}$ do not have to be continuous, as here assumed. The above derivation would hold for *discrete* r.v.'s as well. This fact by itself vastly broadens the scope of application of the central limit theorem.

How Large does n have to be? As a case in point, consider the $n = 3$ situation where y_1, y_2, and y_3 are identically distributed via $p_Y(y) = \text{Rect}(y)$,

$$\text{Rect}(y) \equiv \begin{cases} 1 & \text{for} \quad |y| \leq 0.5 \\ 0 & \text{for} \quad |y| > 0.5. \end{cases} \tag{3.71}$$

The Gaussian approximation and the exact answer (3.49) $p_X(x) = \text{Rect}(x) \otimes \text{Rect}(x) \otimes \text{Rect}(x)$ are shown in Fig. 3.8. The curve $p_X(x)$ is here three connected *parabolic* arcs, but their closeness to the normal curve (shown dashed) defined by (3.70) is remarkable.

Since a Rect function is about as far from resembling a Gaussian curve as any continuous $p(x)$ function, we may conclude from this exercise that when the $\{y_m\}$ are each characterized by a continuous density function *it will not take more than $n = 4$ of them to make their sum appear normal to a good approximation.* The central limit theorem is a strong statement.

For discrete r.v.'s $p_X(x)$ tends toward a sequence of equispaced impulses whose amplitude envelope is a normal curve. When the spacing between impulses is much less than the variance of the normal curve, for all practical purposes $p_X(x)$ acts like a normal curve.

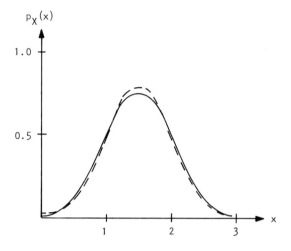

Fig. 3.8. Threefold convolution of a rectangle (———), compared with the closest Gaussian curve (- - -)

3.2.6 Some Applications to Optics

The central limit theorem applies fairly widely in optics, and also has some interesting digital consequences. These applications are not all statistical in nature. Some arise as purely a multiple-convolution phenomenon.

Cascaded Optical Systems. For example, linear optical systems are sometimes operated in "cascade", where the output image of one system is the input to the next. In this case, the net optical transfer function $\tau_{net}(\omega)$ is known to be a product over those of the individual systems, $\tau_m(\omega)$, $m = 1, 2, ..., n$,

$$\tau_{net}(\omega) = \tau_1(\omega)\tau_2(\omega)...\tau_n(\omega). \tag{3.72}$$

If n is the order of three or more, and the individual $\tau_m(\omega)$ are somewhat similar functions, then by the central limit theorem $\tau_{net}(\omega)$ should well approximate a Gaussian transfer function. The point spread function, which is the Fourier transform of $\tau(\omega)$, should then also be Gaussian.

Laser Resonator. In the laser resonator, optical waves are propagated back and forth between the resonator's end mirrors. Let these be rectangular, with separation b and width a. If $v(x_2)$ denotes the amplitude at coordinate x_2 on mirror 2 due to corresponding amplitude $v(x_1)$ on mirror 1, then by the Fresnel diffraction formula

$$v(x_2) = \gamma \int_{-a}^{a} dx_1 v(x_1) K(x_2 - x_1), \tag{3.73a}$$

where imaging kernel

$$K(x) = (\lambda b)^{-1/2} \exp(-i\pi x^2/\lambda b). \tag{3.73b}$$

In these equations, γ is a pure number, and λ is the light wavelength (see [3.13]).

Equation (3.73a) shows that the amplitude on mirror 2 is the amplitude on mirror 1 truncated for $|x_1| > a$, and then convolved with kernel $K(x)$. This process is repeated from mirror to mirror, so that the output wave after n propagations (3.73a) is the result of n successive pairs of operations (truncation, convolution).

If it were not for the truncation at each step we would have purely n successive convolutions, and again the central limit theorem would hold. The truncations alter the result, however, because they cut off the tails of each convolution output. This excites extra oscillations in each successive convolution, so we do not end up with the smooth Gaussian that the central limit theory gives. Such oscillatory functions, of course, ultimately find their way into the mode shapes for the laser.

However, if radio a/b is large enough *the effect of truncation will be small* in (3.73a), since $v(x_1)$ will effectively fall to zero before the rim values $x_1 = \pm a$ are attained. Now the resonator output after n reflections is purely due to n convolutions with kernel (3.73b), and hence should follow a Gaussian law. *Fox* and *Li* carried out these operations on a digital computer with the results shown in Fig. 1.1. Cases $n = 1$ and $n = 300$ of such "digital" propagation are shown. The $n = 300$ result is indeed close to a Gaussian shape.

Atmospheric Turbulence. The other type of application of the central limit theorem is purely statistical in nature. It arises from the addition of n random numbers. This is called a "random walk" phenomenon (see below).

For example, by one model of atmospheric turbulence, the turbulent atmosphere between light source and detector is imagined to consist of thin planes of spatially constant but timewise random optical phase (see [3.14]). These planes are oriented with their normals parallel to the line of sight connecting source and detector. Then the net instantaneous optical phase Φ_{net} at the detector is a sum

$$\Phi_{\text{net}} = \Phi_1 + \Phi_2 + \ldots + \Phi_n \tag{3.74}$$

over the individual phases Φ_m due to the thin planes. Here $\Phi_m = n_m \Delta t_m$, where n_m is the random index of refraction of the mth plane and Δt_n is its random thickness. As the turbulence ought to act *independently* from one plane to the next (or at least from one group of planes to the next), and as the phase fluctuations within each plane should follow about the same physical law, Φ_{net} satisfies the central limit theorem and hence should be normally distributed. This is, in fact, the usual presumption regarding $p(\Phi_{\text{net}})$ at a single point. More generally, for the joint $p(\Phi_{\text{net}}, \Phi_{\text{net}}')$ at two points, a Gaussian bivariate assumption is made.

The effect (3.74) is called a one-dimensional random walk phenomenon. Since each Φ_m can randomly be of any length or *sign*, a one-dimensional plot of the sum of the first m, with successively $m = 1, 2, \ldots, n$, will show that the sum randomly "walks" back and forth along the line.

3.2.7 Digital Consequences

A Gaussian function has some properties which strongly recommend it for computer use. Important gains in processing time or memory requirement result from these.

Also, the central limit theorem per se allows us to computer-generate normally random numbers from given uniformly random numbers. These points are discussed next.

Separability, and Reduction of Problem Dimensionality. A Gaussian function of radius

$$g(r) \equiv (2\pi)^{-1} \sigma^2 \exp(-r^2/2\sigma^2),$$
$$r^2 = x^2 + y^2 \tag{3.75}$$

is separable, i.e., may be expressed in the form

$$g(r) = g_1(x)g_2(y). \tag{3.76}$$

In fact, the Gaussian $g(r)$ is *the only* function having azimuthal symmetry which is also separable. This has some benefits for the image restoration problem.

In its discrete form, as processed by computer, the restoration problem is solution of the equations

$$i_{mn} = \sum_{j=1}^{N} \sum_{k=1}^{N} \hat{o}_{jk} s(m, j; n, k) + \text{noise}_{mn} \tag{3.77}$$

$$m = 1, \ldots, N, n = 1, \ldots, N$$

for an object estimate $\{\hat{o}_{jk}\}$, given image data $\{i_{mn}\}$, an estimated point spread function s, and unknown noise$_{mn}$. With s a *general* function of its coordinate indices, (3.77) must be solved for $\{\hat{o}_{jk}\}$ in a fully two-dimensional approach. Here s is a tensor of rank 4, and this gives rise to storage overflow problems in many cases.

Suppose, on the other hand, that s is separable,

$$s(m, j; n, k) = s_1(m, j)s_2(n, k) \tag{3.78}$$

since s is Gaussian. Because of the widespread applicability of the central limit theorem this is quite often a very good approximation. For example, in photographic imagery or for imagery through turbulence the Gaussian assumption is quite frequently made.

Then the overall two-dimensional problem (3.77) reads, after rearrangement,

$$i_{mn} = \sum_{j=1}^{N} s_1(m, j) \sum_{k=1}^{N} \hat{o}_{jk} s_2(n, k) + \text{noise}_{mn}. \tag{3.79}$$

We show next that in this situation the single two-dimensional restoring problem may be replaced by $2N$ *one-dimensional* restoring problems. We might note that this is not an intuitive effect. Intuition ordinarily leads one to believe that the object $\hat{o}_{jk}$ itself must be separable for this to be true.

Let the inner sum in (3.79) define an intermediate quantity $\hat{o}_{jn}^{(1)}$,

$$\sum_{k=1}^{N} \hat{o}_{jk} s_2(n, k) \equiv \hat{o}_{jn}^{(1)} . \tag{3.80a}$$

Then the problem (3.79) is equivalent to the problem

$$i_{mn} = \sum_{j=1}^{N} \hat{o}_{jn}^{(1)} s_1(m, j) + \text{noise}_{mn} , \tag{3.80b}$$

where $\hat{o}_{jn}^{(1)}$ is an intermediate "object" to be restored. This may be recognized to be a one-dimensional problem, for any fixed value of n (column number). Suppose a restoring scheme is to be chosen, as for example from *Frieden* [3.15]. Then it is first used in (3.80b) for value $n=1$ (first column); this comprises a restoring problem for object $\hat{o}_{j1}^{(1)}$, given image data i_{m1}, $m=1, \ldots, N$. In this way, the first column of the image is being deblurred in the vertical direction (along the column). The process is repeated for $n=2$ to produce the estimate $\hat{o}_{j2}^{(1)}$ of the deblurred second column; etc., over all n (columns). There are N such one-dimensional restoring problems in all, resulting in N restored columns $\hat{o}_{jn}^{(1)}$, $n=1, \ldots, N$.

With the N column objects $\hat{o}_{jn}^{(1)}$ so built up, these values are substituted *row-wise* into restoring problem (3.80a), where they act as intermediate image data, to enable the final *output* restoration $\hat{o}_{jk}$ to be formed. First, the known row object $\hat{o}_{1n}^{(1)}$ is used as data in (3.80a) to solve for output $\hat{o}_{1k}$; this is a one-dimensional restoring problem with deblurring now along k, i.e., in the horizontal direction. Next the known second row of data $\hat{o}_{2n}^{(1)}$ is used in (3.80a) to restore for output $\hat{o}_{2k}$; etc., for $j=3, \ldots, N$. There are N one-dimensional restoring problems required here.

In this manner the entire output $\{\hat{o}_{jk}\}$ is restored as a sequence of $2N$ one-dimensional restoring problems, i.e., N for the columns and then N for the rows. The main benefit of this piecemeal approach is often a vast reduction in central memory requirement. For the direct two-dimensional approach defined by (3.77) there are N^2 image values to be satisfied by N^2 unknown object values via a spread function tensor of rank 4. By contrast, any of the $2N$ one-dimensional problems involve only N image values and a two-dimensional spread function matrix. If the spread function obeys isoplanatism and a filtering approach is taken, then no benefit accrues from this approach. However, for certain nonlinear restoring methods, such as maximum entropy (see [3.15]), it is absolutely essential to reduce the dimensionality of the problem from two to one. Separability then saves the day.

Propagation of Matrix Coefficients; a Computational Advantage. In image processing work the user sometimes is confronted with generating a matrix of numbers c_{mn} defined by an integral of the form

$$c_{mn} = \int_a^b dx o(x) s(x_m - x) s(x_n - x),$$

$$m = 1, ..., N$$

$$n = 1, ..., N \tag{3.81}$$

$$x_n = n\Delta x.$$

The form of this integral might be called a "double convolution". For a general kernel function s this problem would ordinarily require $N^2/2$ numerical evaluations of the given integral. We shall show next that if s is Gaussian, instead only $2N$ numerical evaluations need be made. The rest of the coefficients c_{mn} are found very simply in terms of these $2N$ numbers by a technique of "numerical propagation" [3.16].

If s is Gaussian, then

$$c_{mn} = K \int_a^b dx o(x) \exp[-(x_m - x)^2/2\sigma^2 - (x_n - x)^2/2\sigma^2].$$

Then

$$c_{m+1,n-1} = K \int_a^b dx o(x) \exp[-(x_m + \Delta x - x)^2/2\sigma^2 - (x_n - \Delta x - x)^2/2\sigma^2]$$

$$= K \int_a^b dx o(x) \exp[-(x_m - x)^2/2\sigma^2 - (x_n - x)^2/2\sigma^2$$

$$- \Delta x^2/\sigma^2 - \Delta x(x_m - x)/\sigma^2 + \Delta x(x_n - x)/\sigma^2].$$

Consequently, due to some cancellation of terms

$$c_{m+1,n-1} = \exp\left[-\frac{\Delta x}{\sigma^2}(\Delta x + x_m - x_n)\right] c_{mn}. \tag{3.82}$$

This shows that knowledge of any element c_{mn} implies knowledge of its nearest-neighbor element diagonally downward to the left. Hence direct evaluation of the integral (3.81) need only be made along the top row and down the far-right column. All other elements may be generated from these by the propagation scheme (3.82). The arrows in Fig. 3.9 show the flow of element propagation. In this way an apparent requirement of $N^2/2$ quadrature evaluations is replaced with $2N$ such evaluations.

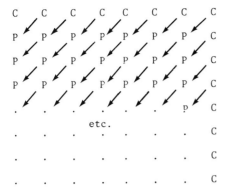

etc.

Fig. 3.9. Flow of numbers generated in turn by propagation rule, (3.82). Numbers marked C are calculated by direct evaluation of the integral, (3.81). All others, marked P, are propagated

Generating Normally Distributed Numbers from Uniformly Random Numbers.

In numerical simulation of noisy data, and in other types of Monte Carlo calculations, it is often necessary to generate independent, *normally random* numbers. For example, image noise is commonly modeled as being Gaussian random (normal, with zero mean), and uncorrelated from point to point.

However, the only random number generator that is ordinarily built into a computer library instead generates *uniformly* random numbers, in the interval $(0, 1)$. An example is the function $\text{RANF}(\cdot)$ of the CDC Scope library. Now these numbers have the desirable property of being uncorrelated, a property which takes some care in satisfying, and which is one-half of the requirements of our noise-generation problem. The question arises, then, as to whether it is possible to use these output numbers from RANF and somehow *transform them* into normally distributed numbers (with a required mean and required variance). In fact, there are a few different approaches to this problem, and to the more general one of transformation from one probability distribution to *any* other (see Sect. 3.4). Here we content ourselves with the simplest such approach, a mere addition of a few RANF outputs. This has the advantage of being a very fast operation, but has the disadvantage of *approximating* the normal case (as will be seen).

Suppose we add together every three successive outputs y_1, y_2, and y_3 from RANF $(\cdot)$ to form a new r.v.

$$x = y_1 + y_2 + y_3. \tag{3.83}$$

This is recognized as simply the case $n = 3$ of the derivation in Sect. 3.2.5. In particular, each of the $\{y_m\}$ here follows the *uniform* probability law. Then Fig. 3.8 gives the ensuing probability law for x, a sequence of three parabolic arcs which approximate a normal distribution. Hence, the new r.v. x will be approximately normal, as was required.

However, merely taking the sum as in (3.83) will not yield a prescribed mean m and variance σ^2 for r.v. x. For example, by taking the mean of both sides of (3.83) we see that $\langle x \rangle = \langle y_1 \rangle + \langle y_2 \rangle + \langle y_3 \rangle = 3\langle y \rangle = 3/2$.

This leads us to replace (3.83) by a slightly more general form

$$x = a(y_1 + y_2 + y_3) + b, \tag{3.84}$$

with constants a, b to be found such that x has the required two moments. The rest is algebra. Taking the mean of both sides and using $\langle y \rangle = 1/2$, requires

$$m = 3a/2 + b. \tag{3.85a}$$

Squaring both sides of (3.84) and taking the mean produces requirement

$$\langle x^2 \rangle \equiv \sigma^2 + m^2 = a^2(3\langle y^2 \rangle + 6\langle y \rangle \langle y \rangle) + b^2 + 6ab\langle y \rangle$$

by identity (3.16c), or

$$\sigma^2 + m^2 = 5a^2/2 + b^2 + 3ab \tag{3.85b}$$

since $\langle y^2 \rangle = 1/3$.

Equations (3.85a, b) may be solved for unknowns a, b. The solution is $a = 2\sigma$, $b = m - 3\sigma$. Hence, the required transformation is

$$x = 2\sigma(y_1 + y_2 + y_3) + m - 3\sigma. \tag{3.86}$$

A random variable x formed in this way from every three successive outputs of RANF($\cdot$) will be very close to a normal r.v., and will (exactly) have mean m and variances σ^2.

A measure of the degree to which x approximates a normal r.v. is the range of values that x defined by (3.86) can take on. A true normal r.v. can, of course, vary from $-\infty$ to $+\infty$. Using the extreme values for y of 0 and 1, (3.86) shows that x is confined to an interval

$$m - 3\sigma \leq x \leq m + 3\sigma.$$

In most simulation use this artificial constraint should not be serious, since the normal curve itself has 99.8 % of its events x confined to this interval.

If the degree of approximation is nevertheless unacceptable, the above procedure may be carried through for four successive outputs of RANF($\cdot$) instead; or indeed, for any number n required. The higher n is made, by the central limit, the closer density $p(x)$ will approximate the normal case.

3.3 Functions of Random Variables

The preceding Fourier theory involving characteristic functions, transfer theorems, sampling theorems, etc., is a stepping stone to what is sometimes called the "calculus of probability". This calculus has as its aim the solution to all statistical problems dealing with a set of random inputs into a system,

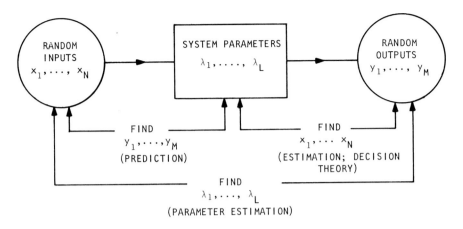

Fig. 3.10. Input-output view of statistical problems. Arrows point to given data, parentheses define the type of problem

which functionally forms random outputs. The inputs might be real or simulated, and the system into which these are input may be real or a mathematical model (see Fig. 3.10). The aim may be to establish the statistics of the outputs, given the inputs (the direct, or "prediction" problem); or the inputs, given the outputs and inputs (the problem of "parameter estimation"). Sometimes the statistical aim is to find particular numbers and, if so, with some measure of their reliability as measured by expected error or level of significance. When a discrete set of possible numbers is the unknown, the problem is simplified somewhat: to choosing the correct one. This is the discipline called "decision theory". Other times the aim is more modest: to establish the joint probability density for the unknown.

In preceding sections, we have developed the mathematical tools needed for solving these problems, except for one. The remaining tool of the calculus of probability comes into play when attacking a prediction problem. If a system with known parameters *functionally acts upon* some random inputs, what is the character of the outputs? In particular, we want to know what the joint probability density is for the outputs, given the probability law for the inputs and a known system function. The latter is assumed arbitrary, and is generally nonlinear.

3.3.1 Case of a Single Random Variable

The problem we consider here is to find the probability density $p_Y(x)$ for a r.v. y defined in terms of a r.v. x by a *functional relation*

$$y = f(x), \tag{3.87a}$$

when $p_X(x)$ is known. f might be considered a "system function" as described previously, with r.v. x the input to the system and r.v. y the output.

Let the inverse relation to (3.87a) be

$$x = f^{-1}(y). \tag{3.87b}$$

Now, for a given y there might be a unique root x, or a multiplicity of roots $x_1, ..., x_r$. This depends upon the form of function f. For example, if f is the squaring operation, then $y = x^2$ and $x = \pm \sqrt{y}$ for two roots. It is simplest to first consider the unique-root case.

Unique Root. The situation is most easily analyzed graphically, as in Fig. 3.11a. The vertical y axis consists of all permissible disjoint events

$$A_Y = (y \leq Y \leq y + dy), \ -\infty \leq y \leq \infty .$$

Consider one such event A_Y. Because to each y there is a unique x given by (3.87b), the same event A_Y may alternatively be described as event

$$A_X = (x \leq X \leq x + dx),$$

with x determined by (3.87b).

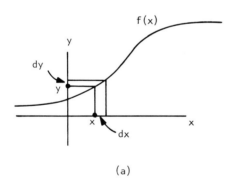

(a)

Fig. 3.11. (a) Unique-root case. For given y, there is one root x. (b) Multiple root case. For given y, there are two or more roots $x_1, x_2, ..., x_r$

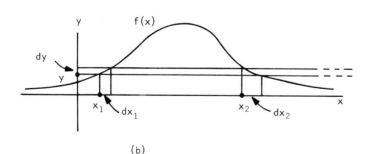

(b)

Therefore, the probability $P(A_Y)$ may be described alternatively as

$$P(A_Y) = P(y \le Y \le y + dy) = P(x \le X \le x + dx). \tag{3.88a}$$

Intuitively, what this means is that since an event in y has a unique correspondence to one in x, the relative number of times a value y will occur equals the relative number of times the corresponding value of x [via (3.87b)] will occur.

Then by definition (3.13) of probability density, (3.88a) becomes

$$p_Y(y)\,dy = p_X(x)\,dx. \tag{3.88b}$$

Hence by (3.87b),

$$p_Y(y) = p_X[f^{-1}(y)]/|y'| \tag{3.89}$$

is the required probability. y' is the derivative dy/dx. The absolute value is taken because dy and dx are both always positive, by definition. Note that since $p_Y(y)$ must be expressed purely in terms of y, y' must be expressed in terms of y as well.

Example from Geometrical Optics. As an example, consider the geometrical optics relation

$$1/y + 1/x = 1/F, \tag{3.90a}$$

with F a lens focal length and x, y conjugate distances from the lens. If $p_X(x)$ is known for the object conjugate distance, what is $p_Y(y)$ for the image conjugate distance? According to (3.89) we need to know $f^{-1}(y)$ and $y'(y)$. In our case

$$f^{-1}(y) \equiv x = \frac{Fy}{y - f},$$

and

$$y' = -\frac{(y - F)^2}{F^2}.$$

Then by (3.89),

$$p_Y(y) = \frac{F^2}{(y - F)^2}\, p_X\left(\frac{Fy}{y - F}\right), \tag{3.90b}$$

which is the general answer, for arbitrary $p_X(x)$.

To get the flavor of the distortion of object space manifest in (3.90b), consider the particular case of near equal conjugates, where all x values

$2F - F/2 \leq x \leq 2F + F/2$ are equally likely. This may be described by a probability

$$p_X(x) = \begin{cases} F^{-1} & \text{for} \quad 2F - F/2 \leq x \leq 2F + F/2 \\ 0 & \text{for all other } x. \end{cases} \qquad (3.90c)$$

Using this in (3.90b) yields

$$p_Y(y) = \begin{cases} \dfrac{F}{(y - F)^2} & \text{for} \quad \tfrac{5}{3} F \leq y \leq 3F \\ 0 & \text{elsewhere}. \end{cases} \qquad (3.90d)$$

This curve shows a much higher concentration of image events near $y = 5F/3$ than near $3F$.

Thus if a uniformly glowing light rod were placed on the x interval (3.90c) in object space, image intensity *along y* would follow the law (3.90d). In particular, the point $y = 5F/3$ would be nine times as bright as the point $3F$. This situation is illustrated in Fig. 3.12.

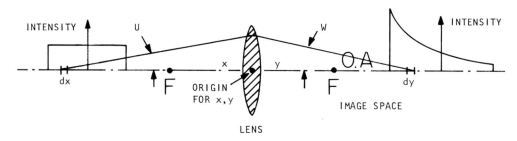

Fig. 3.12. Intensity distribution in image space due to uniform line object source. Both intensity curves describe light along the optical axis OA

Multiple Roots. Suppose the inverse relation (3.87b) to have many roots $x_1, \ldots, x_r$, for a given y. For example, this is the case if $y = x^2$, so that $x = \pm \sqrt{y}$ with $r = 2$. The situation is illustrated in Fig. 3.11b.

As in the one-root case, we consider an event y to occur. According to Fig. 3.11b this may be alternatively viewed as occurrence of the event x_1 or the event x_2 or ... or x_r. Now these r events are disjoint, by hypothesis (see paragraph following (3.14e)). Hence by the additivity property (3.2)

$$P(y \leq Y \leq y + dy) = P(x_1 \leq X \leq x_1 + dx_1) + \ldots + P(x_r \leq X \leq x_r + dx_r).$$

Note the need for subscripting the dx's, since as shown in Fig. 3.11b, *they are in general of different length depending upon the local slope value y'.*

Then by definition (3.13) of probability density,

$$p_Y(y)dy = p_X(x_1)dx_1 + \ldots + p_X(x_r)dx_r.$$ (3.91)

Finally, recalling that all $dy, dx_1, \ldots, dx_r$ are positive by hypothesis,

$$p_Y(y) = p_X(x_1)/|y'(x_1)| + \ldots + p_X(x_r)/|y'(x_r)|.$$ (3.92)

This is the r-root generalization we sought.

Illustrative Example. As an example, we return to the case of $y = x^2$, $x_1 = -\sqrt{y}$, $x_2 = \sqrt{y}$. Here $y' = 2x$, $y'(x_1) = -2\sqrt{y}$, $y'(x_2) = 2\sqrt{y}$, so that by (3.92)

$$p_Y(y) = [p_X(-\sqrt{y}) + p_X(+\sqrt{y})]/2\sqrt{y}.$$ (3.93)

If, furthermore, $x = N(0, \sigma^2)$, (3.93) immediately yields

$$p_Y(y) = \begin{cases} \dfrac{1}{2\sqrt{y}} \dfrac{1}{\sqrt{2\pi}\,\sigma} 2\exp(-y/2\sigma^2) & \text{for} \quad y \geq 0 \\ 0 & \text{for} \quad y < 0. \end{cases}$$ (3.94)

The zero region for y originates of course in the fact that if $y = x^2$ with x real, y can never be negative.

3.3.2 Case of n Random Variables, r Roots

Here we consider the most general situation, of a vector x of n r.v.'s transformed to a new vector of n r.v.'s y through a functional relation

$$y = f(x).$$ (3.95)

If density $p_X(x)$ is known, what is the new $p_Y(y)$?

An example might be the transformation from polar to rectangular variables, where $y_1 = x_1 \sin x_2$, $y_2 = x_1 \cos x_2$. The problem here is to find the joint probability density $p_{Y_1 Y_2}(y_1, y_2)$, if $p_{X_1 X_2}(x_1, x_2)$ is known. To be most general, we shall assume that the inverse relation

$$x = f^{-1}(y)$$ (3.96)

has r roots $x_{m1}, \ldots, x_{mr}$, r general, for each r.v. x_m, $m = 1, \ldots, n$.

In order to avoid cumbersome notation we first consider the particular case of $n = 2$ r.v.'s $\{y_1, y_2\}$, with $r = 2$ roots $\{x_{11}, x_{12}\}$ for y_1, and $\{x_{21}, x_{22}\}$ for y_2, in (3.96). The equivalence of events in x or y space implies

$$p_Y(y_1, y_2)dy_1 dy_2 = p_X(x_{11}, x_{21})dx_{11}dx_{21} + p_X(x_{11}, x_{22})dx_{11}dx_{22}$$
$$+ p_X(x_{12}, x_{21})dx_{12}dx_{21} + p_X(x_{12}, x_{22})dx_{12}dx_{22}.$$ (3.97)

In other words, the sum is now over all permutations of the r roots, four terms here or r^n in general.

Since also $dx_1 dx_2 = J(x_1, x_2/y_1, y_2) dy_1 dy_2$, where

$$J(x_1, x_2/y_1, y_2) = \det \begin{bmatrix} \partial x_1/\partial y_1 & \partial x_1/\partial y_2 \\ \partial x_2/\partial y_1 & \partial x_2/\partial y_2 \end{bmatrix}, \tag{3.98}$$

from (3.97) the answer is

$$p_Y(y_1, y_2) = p_X(x_{11}, x_{21}) |J(x_{11}, x_{21}/y_1, y_2)| + p_X(x_{11}, x_{22})$$
$$\cdot |J(x_{11}, x_{22}/y_1, y_2)| + p_X(x_{12}, x_{21}) |J(x_{12}, x_{21}/y_1, y_2)|$$
$$+ p_X(x_{12}, x_{22}) |J(x_{12}, x_{22}/y_1, y_2)|. \tag{3.99}$$

The notation

$$J(x_{11}, x_{21}/y_1, y_2) \equiv J(x_1, x_2/y_1, y_2) \Big|$$
$$x_1 = x_{11}$$
$$x_2 = x_{21}$$

is used, etc., for the other three terms.

The reader can easily generalize the result (3.99) to any n and r, although the *calculation* of r^n such terms may be tedious to say the least.

3.3.3 Calculation of Spot Intensity Profiles from Probability Curves

We showed in Sect. 3.3.1 and in Fig. 3.12 an example of how to calculate a geometrical intensity curve using basic principles of probability. As that particular problem has very limited practical use, we now want to broaden the view as much as possible.

Consider Fig. 3.13, where object and image planes are in fixed positions, and the spot intensity profile in the image due to a single object point Q is required. The lens system in between is a general one. Let any ray emanating from Q be specified by its *polar and azimuthal angles* x_1 and x_2, respectively. Imagine the ray to strike the image plane at *rectangular coordinates* y_1 and y_2. The density of such ray strikes as a function of (y_1, y_2) is called the "geometrical spot intensity" profile $p_{y_1 y_2}(y_1, y_2)$. It is a common figure of merit for lens system performance.

Now *the density of the ray strikes is*, by the law of large numbers (3.6), *precisely the probability density for these events*. Furthermore, suppose that the coordinates (y_1, y_2) relate to the angles (x_1, x_2) by a *known (ray-trace) relation*

$$(y_1, y_2) = f(x_1, x_2), \tag{3.100}$$

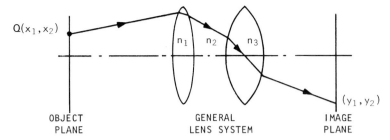

Fig. 3.13. The spot intensity problem. A ray emerges from fixed source point Q at coordinate *angles* x_1 (polar) and x_2 (azimuthal). It strikes the image plane at rectangular *space* coordinates y_1, y_2. If a fan of such rays leaves Q, what is the resulting intensity (density) of rays in the image plane?

and also that the probability density $p_{x_1 x_2}(x_1, x_2)$ for angles (x_1, x_2) is known. (For example, a uniform fan of rays is equivalent to a Rect function on x_1 and on x_2.) Then our problem of estimating the spot profile $p_{Y_1 Y_2}(y_1, y_2)$ function *is fully equivalent to establishing the probability density function $p_{Y_1 Y_2}(y_1, y_2)$ due to a transformation* (3.100) *of r.v.'s.* Aside from the beauty of the correspondence, this is a problem whose answer is already known.

According to the recipe (3.99), we simply have to know the Jacobian of the transformation at each of the roots (x_{1r}, x_{2r}) corresponding to output coordinates (y_1, y_2). In the vast majority of cases there will be only one such root[3]. The answer then is

$$p_{Y_1 Y_2}(y_1, y_2) = \begin{cases} \text{Abs det} \begin{bmatrix} \partial x_1/\partial y_1 & \partial x_1/\partial y_2 \\ \partial x_2/\partial y_1 & \partial x_2/\partial y_2 \end{bmatrix} & \text{for} \quad \begin{array}{l} a_1 \leqq y_1 \leqq b_1 \\ a_2 \leqq y_2 \leqq b_2 \end{array} \qquad (3.101) \\ 0 & \text{for } y_1, y_2 \text{ outside above intervals} \end{cases}$$

i.e., the Jacobian alone, since a uniform or Rect function ray fan was supposed for $p_{X_1 X_2}(x_1, x_2)$. Limiting coordinate values (a_1, b_1), (a_2, b_2) for (y_1, y_2) are determined by (3.100) when x_1, x_2 take on their extreme values defined by the pupil size.

Hence, the solution centers on knowing the partial derivatives in (3.101). These could be found, and exactly so, if the *functional form* for f in the ray-trace relation (3.100) were analytically known. However, this kind of knowledge is virtually never given: the tracing of rays through a complicated lens system does not lend itself to analytic expression.

Implementation by Ray Trace. There is an alternative, however, This is to *numerically* trace through the lens system each ray (x_1, x_2) and its differential counterpart $(x_1 + dx_1, x_2 + dx_2)$; these give rise to ray strikes (y_1, y_2) and

---

3 Multiple roots occur when the caustic bundle of intersecting rays also intersects the image plane. This does not ordinarily occur, but if it does, it is only at isolated points (y_1, y_2) of the plane.

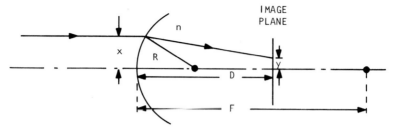

Fig. 3.14. Spot formation by a cylindrical surface

$(y_1 + dy_1, y_2 + dy_2)$. All these quantities are now known as *numbers*. Therefore, ratios $\partial x_1 / \partial y_2$, etc., may be formed as required in (3.101).

In practice, the calculation would start by assuming a uniform subdivision of input angles and their differentials. Given these, a ray trace (3.100) would be *directly* used to define the corresponding (y_1, y_2) in image space. [Note that in this way we avoid the difficult problem of *inverting* ray-trace relation (3.100) for unknown (x_1, x_2) in terms of known (y_1, y_2).] The price we pay for this unorthodox approach is determination of the required curve $p_{Y_1 Y_2}(y_1, y_2)$ at an *uneven spacing* of points (y_1, y_2), the latter due to the nonlinear nature of ray-trace relation (3.100).

However, this uneven spacing is not a severe price. It may be overcome by suitably interpolating between the points, or simply by using more rays.

The novel feature of the approach is that *each pair* (ray, differential ray) *of traced rays establishes with arbitrary precision a point on the spot intensity curve.* This is to be compared with the conventional approach of building up the spot curve as a histogram of ray strikes within narrow zones of the image plane. The latter is intrinsically an approximation because of the finite size of the zones, and also requires hundreds of rays to be traced to each zone in order to achieve acceptable error in the *single* estimated spot value.

This approach may also be derived from a deterministic point of view, using conservation of energy along each ray (see [3.17]).

Illustrative Example. To illustrate use of the approach (3.101), consider the one-dimensional system shown in Fig. 3.14. The lens system is a single cylindrical surface of radius R, index n, and paraxial focal length F. The image plane is located at distance D from the surface. The object point is at infinity. We want to find the spot intensity profile $p_Y(y)$ due to a uniform fan of rays $p_X(x) = \text{Rect}(x/3)$ (ignoring an irrelevant multiplicative constant). The reason we have chosen this problem is that *the functional relation (3.100) is known analytically here*,

$$y = x(1 - D/F) + x^3/2F^2(n/n - 1)[1 - (n/n - 1)D/F] \qquad (3.102)$$

to third order in x. Thus, the single derivative dx/dy here defining the Jacobian is known analytically, and also no ray-trace subroutines are needed.

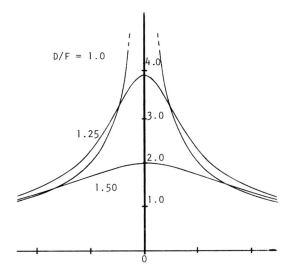

Fig. 3.15. Spot profiles at three different image plane positions D. Each curve is identified by its value D/F

The procedure is to define a uniform subdivision in y, invert the cubic polynomial (3.102) for the corresponding x values, evaluate dx/dy at these x, and then use (3.101) to compute $p_Y(y)$, which is here simply $|dx/dy|$. Resulting spot profiles are shown in Fig. 3.15, for three relative positions D/F of the image plane. Note that the closer the image plane comes to the focal point the more concentrated is the spot, right to the limit where the central maximum becomes infinite when the image plane is located at the paraxial focus. (This infinite value is, of course, an approximation of the geometrical ray approach taken here, and would not occur in a diffraction analysis.)

3.3.4 Calculation of the Geometrical MTF

The geometrical MTF is defined as the FT of the spot profile $p_{Y_1Y_2}(y_1, y_2)$. Of course, by definition (3.35) the *characteristic function* $\phi_{Y_1Y_2}(\omega_1, \omega_2)$ is also the FT of $p_{Y_1Y_2}(y_1, y_2)$. Hence the characteristic function here has an interesting physical significance.

An aid in the calculation of the MTF is that, by (3.101), $p_{Y_1Y_2}(y_1, y_2)$ has limited support (range of argument), so that sampling theorems hold for MTF and p in terms of sampled values of MTF (see derivation, Sect. 3.2.3). For simplicity, we show these in one dimension,

$$\text{MTF}(\omega) = \sum_{n=-\infty}^{\infty} \text{MTF}(n\pi/y_0)\,\text{sinc}(\omega y_0 - n\pi) \tag{3.103a}$$

and

$$p_Y(y) = \begin{cases} \pi/y_0 \displaystyle\sum_{n=-\infty}^{\infty} \text{MTF}(n\pi/y_0)e^{in\pi y/y_0} & \text{for } |y| \leq y_0 \\ 0 & \text{for } |y| > y_0. \end{cases} \tag{3.103b}$$

It is interesting that in the geometrical limit the spot profile p cuts off, i.e., has limited support, while in the diffraction limit the complementary quantity MTF cuts off instead.

These equations need sampled values $\text{MTF}(n\pi/y_0)$ as inputs. The latter may be conveniently computed via FFT operation upon the known $p_Y(y)$ at discrete y values $y_n \equiv ny_0/N$, $n = -(N-1), \ldots, N$ (see Sect. 3.2.4). Alternatively, some of the quadrature formulas of Barakat in Chap. 2 may be used.

3.4 Producing Random Numbers that Obey a Prescribed Probability Density

In the computer simulation of statistical phenomena, the user is often faced with the problem of generating random numbers that follow a required probability law. These numbers might, for example, be simulated Gaussian random data to test out an estimation procedure, or, they might be the random sample from a known probability law that is required at each step of a Monte Carlo calculation (see Sects. 1.6 and 3.4.3).

On the other hand, most computer libraries generate random numbers of only one variety – the uniformly random variable over the interval $(0, 1)$. For example, each call to the CDC *library function* RANF$(\cdot)$ generates a new number chosen *independently and uniformly* over the interval $(0, 1)$.

The question naturally arises, then, as to whether such uniformly random numbers may somehow be transformed by computer operation into numbers characterized by some other probability law, say the normal. In fact, we showed in Sect. 3.2.5 that the sum of three outputs from RANF is approximately normally distributed. Here we want to know if a procedure may be found for transforming to *any* prescribed probability law, call it $p_X(x)$.

Such a procedure may be found, as follows. Suppose a uniformly r.v. y is defined by successive outputs of RANF. Then y ranges over $(0, 1)$. We seek a functional relation $y = f(x)$ that will transform each number y_i to a new one x_i which is characterized by a prescribed density $p_X(x)$. Now by the transformation law (3.88b)

$$p_Y(y)dy = p_X(x)dx$$

or simply

$$dy = p_X(x)dx, \quad 0 \leqq y \leqq 1 \tag{3.104a}$$

for our uniform case. But (3.104a) may be regarded as a differential equation. Its solution is simply

$$y = \int_{-\infty}^{x} dx' p_X(x') \equiv F_X(x), \tag{3.104b}$$

the cumulative probability function for r.v. x.

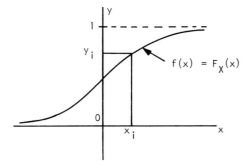

Fig. 3.16. Scheme for obtaining random numbers following a required density function $p_X(x)$. Curve $f(x)$ is the cumulative probability $F_X(x)$. A number y_i is chosen by the uniform random number generator RANF. The corresponding x_i from the curve follows the required law $p_X(x)$

This then is the required function $f(x)$ we sought for effecting the transformation. The situation is illustrated in Fig. 3.16.

The virtues of this approach are that a) it is exact, i.e., prescribed law $p_X(x)$ is exactly followed by number outputs $\{x_i\}$ (compare with the approximate approach in Sect. 3.2.7); b) it is easily programmed on the computer, either by direct use of the analytic function $F_X(x)$, if $p_X(x)$ is integrable, or, if not, by *numerically summing* $p_X(x_i)$ over x_i to form a sequence of $F_X(x_i)$ numbers, which are stored in memory and interpolated as needed.

The main drawback is that the function $F_X(x)$ must somehow be inverted for its root x_i at each input y_i value, and this is not usually possible analytically (although see illustrative case below). A numerical procedure must then be found for solving

$$F_X(x_i) - y_i = 0 \tag{3.105}$$

for the root x_i. The well-known Newton relaxation method is good for this purpose, because of its fast convergence property.

3.4.1 Illustrative Case

Since the trigonometric functions are easy to integrate and to invert analytically, let us suppose the required probability law to be

$$p_X(x) = \begin{cases} (a/2)\cos ax, & |x| \leq \pi/2a \\ 0, & |x| > \pi/2a. \end{cases} \tag{3.106}$$

This is a bell-shaped curve. By direct integration, it has a cumulative probability

$$F_X(x) = (1/2)(1 + \sin ax).$$

According to the recipe (3.104b) this expression is set equal to y, and then solved for $x(y)$ to define outputs x that follow the prescribed law. Doing so, we find that

$$x = a^{-1} \sin^{-1}(2y - 1), \qquad y \equiv \text{RANF}(\cdot). \tag{3.107}$$

Here, then, we have an *analytic answer* to the problem.

3.4.2 Normal Case

The normal law $p_X(x)$ would not be as easily accomplished as was the preceding. Its cumulative probability function is an error function, which cannot be analytically inverted for output x. Although the numerical approach suggested previously may be taken, or the approximate approach (3.86), an easier method exists. It is both analytic and exact.

Instead of seeking a transformation of a *single* r.v. y to do the job, as at the beginning of Sect. 3.4, why not seek a function of *two* r.v.'s y_1, y_2, each of which is uniformly random over $(0, 1)$? This, in fact, has an analytic answer.

Consider the transformation from (y_1, y_2) to outputs (x_1, x_2)

$$x_1 = m + \sigma(-2 \ln y_1)^{1/2} \cos 2\pi y_2, \tag{3.108a}$$

$$x_2 = m + \sigma(-2 \ln y_1)^{1/2} \sin 2\pi y_2. \tag{3.108b}$$

Use of transformation equations (3.99), with $r = 1$ root, shows that $p(x_1, x_2)$ is a product of normal laws, each with mean m and standard deviation σ. Then the marginal $p(x_1)$, or $p(x_2)$, is also a normal law with mean m and standard deviation σ, so that either of (3.108a, b) may be used to generate the required normal r.v.

3.4.3 The Monte Carlo Calculation

A research technique that makes much use of the methods described previously in this section is the Monte Carlo calculation. This technique attempts to simulate a given random process *event by event* by constructing random outputs in accordance with a known probability law. If $p(x)$ is the known probability law for the occurrence of experimental outcomes x_i, "typical" outcomes may be simulated by *selecting* or generating a sequence of events x_i which are typical of the known law $p(x)$. Methods of the preceding parts of Sect. 3.4 may be used, for example, to generate such numbers.

In practice most physical processes consist of random sampling, as just described, from *many laws* $p(x)$ *in sequence*. For example, consider the experiment where photons pass through a photographic emulsion, which is later developed to form an image. Any photon meets with many probability laws $p(x)$ *en route :* it can be absorbed or scattered by the emulsion surface, then by grains of the emulsion, etc., and each such phenomenon obeys a known probability law.

The Monte Carlo procedure is to trace each photon through the experiment, and to construct a random *intermediary output,* in turn, at each physical encounter, this output being the input to the next such encounter, etc., until it reaches the *final output* state (in this case, absorption somewhere, or scattering out of the emulsion). Each intermediary output state of the photon, as sampled from some one probability law, is made the intermediary *input* to the next (see, e.g. [3.18a]). It is instructive to describe the approach to this problem taken by *Depalma* and *Gasper* [3.18b].

Application to the Photographic Emulsion. The optical properties of photographic emulsions are very difficult to predict by analytic methods because of the large number of physical phenomena that characterize latent image formation. These properties, however, were accounted for by *DePalma* and *Gasper* [3.18b] on the basis of a classic Monte Carlo calculation. They tested a simple model by which incoming photons are either absorbed or scattered as they interact with particles within the emulsion. They modeled the optical properties of a photographic emulsion as resulting from absorption and scattering of incoming photons by the surface overcoat, by the silver halide grains within the emulsion, and by the undercoat base. The philosophy of the whole approach is that use of the *correct* probability laws governing absorption and scattering will cause the Monte Carlo calculation to predict the physically *observable* point spread function and modulation transfer function (MTF) of the emulsion.

Such agreement between Monte Carlo output and experimental observation would mean that the overall interactive model for the emulsion was probably correct. This is the empirical method of experimentation in action, with now *the computer replacing the laboratory.*

In order to carry through the calculation, all possible fates for a photon, as it passes through an emulsion, must be enumerated. Furthermore, a probability law has to be assigned to each fate. Figure 3.17 enumerates these possibilities. The presumed probability laws are given in [3.18b].

A uniformly random number generated by the computer allows a fate to be defined, in turn, by each probability law. The method of Fig. 3.16 is used to transform each uniformly random number into one characterized by the known probability law. A given photon is followed through the emulsion in this manner until it is either absorbed somewhere, is scattered out, or (arbitrarily) exceeds 250 events.

The point spread function is computed simply as the number of photon collisions within the volume dV of the emulsion lying beneath a differential surface area dA, i.e., $dV = t \cdot dA$, with t the emulsion thickness. Each collision is assumed to result in a developed grain. The MTF is computed as the modulus of the Fourier transform of the point spread function. As with all Monte Carlo

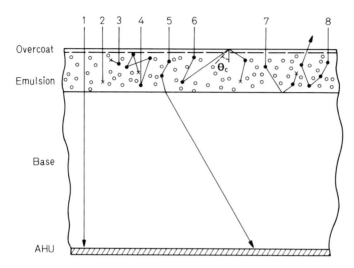

Fig. 3.17. Possible fates of a photon; ○=silver halide grain; ●= scattering event; ×=absorption event, θ_c= critical angle [3.18b]

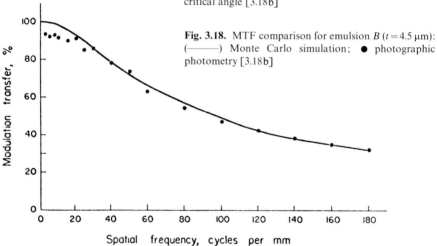

Fig. 3.18. MTF comparison for emulsion B (t=4.5 μm): (———) Monte Carlo simulation; ● photographic photometry [3.18b]

simulations, the accuracy in these outputs improves with the number of photons traced through. Specifically, the standard deviation in the output goes inversely with square root of the photon number (see Sect. 3.9.2). Acceptable accuracy in these quantities was accomplished by following the fates of a few thousand photons.

A typical MTF curve established in this way is shown by the solid curve in Fig. 3.18. The dotted curve is the *experimentally measured* MTF for the same emulsion. Agreement is seen to be quite good, implying that the interactive model was correct.

Application to Remote Sensing. Monte Carlo simulation has also been extensively used to predict radiative transfer through the ocean and clouds to a remote sensor above the atmosphere (see, for example, [3.19]). The problem was to construct the curve of *upward directed radiance*, in this problem defined as number of photons/area-steradian, versus *angle of observation* (the "nadir" angle from horizontal). Physical conditions are as follows. The sun is presumed to have a fixed zenith angle θ_0, the sky is cloudless but contains "typical" water droplets, a constant wind speed fans the ocean, the ocean water follows an idealized "clear ocean model", and the ocean bottom is totally absorbing. Because of the sheer number of differing physical phenomena involved here, there is no hope for an analytic solution; we have a tailor-made situation for a Monte Carlo approach.

Here the calculation consists in following the fate of a photon as it passes down through the atmosphere, interacts with the ocean surface, interacts with the ocean water, interacts with the ocean bottom, and then comes back up, going through the same interactions in reverse order. Each interaction is with a particle of the medium and is described by a known probability law governing absorption or scattering.

A radiance curve that was generated in this way followed the fate of about 1.5×10^6 interactions of photons with scattering and absorbing particles of the media involved. The result was curves of radiance versus nadir angle for a variety of solar zenith angles θ_0 and wind speeds. A typical plot is shown in Fig. 3.19. (Note: In these plots, angle ϕ denotes horizontal azimuthal angle from the sun's incident direction.)

A unique benefit of Monte Carlo methods pays off here. Because the user knows the fate of every photon everywhere in the atmosphere and ocean, he can likewise count photons crossing a small area *located anywhere*. Therefore, he can compute the radiance at the top of the atmosphere (as shown in Fig. 3.19), or within the atmosphere, just above or just below the ocean surface, etc. This property was exploited by *Plass* et al. to produce radiance curves for a variety of positions within the atmosphere and ocean.

3.4.4 Monte Carlo Formation of Optical Images

An optical image is, in reality, a random superposition of a finite number of photons, *whose placement in the picture is in accordance with a probability law on position.* This probability law is, in fact, the ideal image $i(x)$, i.e., the image which would be formed as the realization of an *infinity* of photon arrivals. Hence $i(x)$ represents both an intensity or density of events at position x, and simultaneously, the probability of a photon arrival at x, i.e., the "probability of x". This is a direct expression of the law of large numbers (3.6).

This correspondence between ideal image and probability density arises *physically* out of the quantum nature of light. For example, the diffraction pattern due to a point object (in particular) is well known to also represent the probability density for placement of photons.

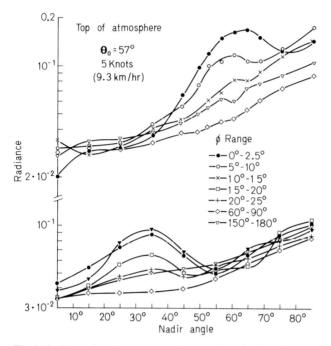

Fig. 3.19. Upward radiance at top of atmosphere for $\theta=32°$ (lower curves) and 57° and a wind speed of 5 knots (9.3 km/h) [3.19]

Since we have been dealing with the event-by-event simulation of probability laws, it might therefore seem possible to simulate the formation of an optical image by random photon arrivals. We consider this next.

The probability density $i(x)$ for the image relates to the object $o(x)$ and point spread function $s(x)$ by the convolution relation

$$i(x) = o(x) \otimes s(x).$$

(3.109)

Now for the particular case of $o(x) = \delta(x)$, this equation states that $i(x) = s(x)$. Hence, $s(x)$ represents, by the reasoning above, the *probability density* for position in the image due to a point source.

Furthermore, by similar reasoning $o(x)$ represents the *probability* in x for radiating photons.

Hence, the image-formation equation (3.109) alternatively represents the convolution of two probability densities to form a third. But by (3.44, 46), it then describes the probability for occurrence of a position value x_i in the image obeying

$$x_i \equiv x_o + x_s,$$

(3.110)

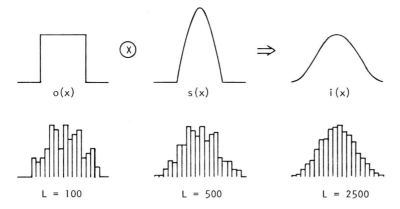

Fig. 3.20. Monte Carlo simulation of the random image due to L (finite) photon arrivals. Examples are given along the bottom row, for the indicated values L. These are constructed, event by event, using probability laws $o(x)$ and $s(x)$ given along the top row. The top right image $i(x)$ is the limit $L \to \infty$ for the random images

where x_o is a random position in the object and x_s is independently a random position in the spread function.

The latter relation tells us, then, how to simulate random formation of the image due to known object and spread functions (probability laws). *First generate a random sample x_o from probability law $o(x)$, then a sample x_s from law $s(x)$, and add the two samples.* The result is a position coordinate x_i whose frequency of occurrence, and hence whose image, follows the physical process (3.109) which we wanted to simulate.

The final problem is how to generate the two random samples x_o and x_s. If, as is usual, only the *uniform* random number generator is present, the approach taken in Fig. 3.16 may be used. For example, the cumulative probability law

$$F_x(x) = \int\limits_{-\infty}^{x} dx\, o(x) \tag{3.111}$$

would be used to generate values x_o. Note the further result that to generate values x_s, a cumulative law

$$F_x(x) = \int\limits_{-\infty}^{x} dx\, s(x) \tag{3.112}$$

would be used; this is precisely the *edge response function*. This correspondence is rather interesting, and by now expectable.

An Example. Suppose we want to Monte Carlo-simulate the photon image due to an object which is a rectangle function, and a spread function which is the cosine bell in (3.106). These are shown along the top of Fig. 3.20. By directly convolving them, the exact or signal image is obtained. This is the raised cosine shown at the right.

The random photon image is now formed, using the recipe of the preceding section: take a random sample x_0 from probability law $o(x)$, independently take a random sample x_s from probability law $s(x)$, add the two to form x_i; and repeat the procedure L times to form the histogram of events x_i. *This histogram is the required photon image due to L photon arrivals.*

If the object length is D, and a is the free parameter in $s(x)$, values x_0 and x_s may be formed from outputs of the *uniformly* random number generator RANF as

$$x_0 = D \ \text{RANF}(\cdot)$$

$$x_s = a^{-1} \sin^{-1}[2\,\text{RANF}(\cdot) - 1].$$

The latter was derived at (3.107); the former is a simple application of the approach (3.104) using the cumulative probability law (3.111) for $o(x)$.

Results of this simulation are shown along the bottom of Fig. 3.20 for three different values of L. These noisy images are to be compared with the signal image $i(x)$ in the figure. We see that for L as small as 100 the random image fluctuates wildly about $i(x)$, while for L of size 2500 or more the fluctuations start becoming insignificant.

We note in passing that this simulation method, when taken with L sufficiently large, asymptotically approaches the convolution (3.109). Hence the approach can also be thought of as *a method of forming an image from a known object $o(x)$ and spread function $s(x)$ without having to explicitly perform the convolution $o \otimes s$.* Oddly enough, random numbers form the image instead (just as in nature).

3.5 Application to Atmospheric Turbulence

Having constructed a calculus of probability, we now want to show how it has been applied to some of the important problems of optics. One of these is the study of weak atmospheric turbulence and its effect on image quality, or "seeing". Physically, the effect is caused by random fluctuations in local refractive index. A plane light wave passing through such a fluctuating medium becomes randomly corrugated. If many such waves emanate from a single point source, there results a random scatter of Airy-like discs in the image plane. These are often called "speckles", and form the net spread function $s(r)$ at any time t. We are interested in the statistics over time of the point spread function, and of the modulation transfer function $T(\omega)$. In particular, the long-term average values $\langle s(r) \rangle$, $\langle T(\omega) \rangle$ will be sought. In practice, this amounts to time exposures of 0.01 s or more.

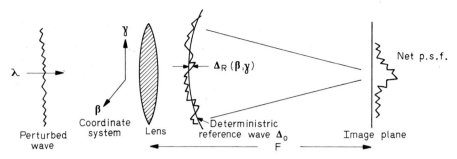

Fig. 3.21. Image formation in the presence of atmospheric turbulence. The source point is at infinity, to the left. Typical waves and the *psf* are shown "frozen" at any instant of time

Consider a lens system, as in Fig. 3.21, which is attempting to bring to a focus light from a distant point source. The light is quasi-monochromatic, of wavelength λ, and has been perturbed by atmospheric turbulence before entering the lens. At any instant of time, the net phase Δ at points (β, γ) across the pupil is composed of a deterministic contribution Δ_0 plus *a spatially random part* Δ_R (as sketched). Phase distribution $\Delta_0(\beta, \gamma)$ is the constant (in time) component due to system aberrations, while $\Delta_R(\beta, \gamma)$ is the random part due to the turbulence.

Coordinates (β, γ) are in the entrance pupil and are proportional to Cartesian distances (x, y), as

$$\beta = kx/F, \gamma = ky/F, k = 2\pi/\lambda. \tag{3.113}$$

The total wave front deformation at a pupil point (β, γ) obeys

$$\Delta(\beta, \gamma) = \Delta_0(\beta, \gamma) + \Delta_R(\beta, \gamma). \tag{3.114}$$

The modulation transfer in the image plane at distance F away is

$$T(\omega_1, \omega_2) = K \int\limits_{-\infty}^{\infty}\!\!\int d\beta d\gamma \, e^{ik[\Delta(\beta, \gamma) - \Delta(\beta - \omega_1, \gamma - \omega_2)]}, \tag{3.115}$$

the autocorrelation of the pupil function $\exp(ik\Delta)$. The integration limits will, from this equation onward, be infinite, and so we suppress them from the notation. The time average transfer function is then

$$\langle T(\omega_1, \omega_2)\rangle = K \int\!\!\int d\beta d\gamma \, e^{ik[\Delta_0(\beta, \gamma) - \Delta_0(\beta - \omega_1, \gamma - \omega_2)]}$$
$$\cdot \langle e^{ik[\Delta_R(\beta, \gamma) - \Delta_R(\beta - \omega_1, \gamma - \omega_2)]}\rangle \tag{3.116}$$

by (3.114). Note that the $\langle \ \rangle$ brackets have been brought *within* the integral to operate solely upon the randomly varying part. The expectation of a sum (or integral) is the sum of the expectations. To proceed further we have to define the statistics for Δ_R at any one point (β, γ).

3.5.1 Statistical Model for the Phase Fluctuations

As in all analyses of probabilistic effects, the key step is in selecting a *proper model* for the fluctuating quantities. Here, the ingenuity and imagination of the analyst come into full use. For, a good model is *both* a) descriptive of the phenomenon, and b) amenable to analysis. To permit b), often the *simplest* model that can satisfy a) with any degree of confidence is chosen. Hence, the choice is sometimes controversial, and only really verifiable when a proper laboratory experiment can demonstrate its correctness. The following model of atmospheric turbulence is commonly assumed. It is not controversial, at least for *weak* turbulence conditions.

● Assume that Δ_R obeys the central limit theorem, and is therefore normal at each point (β, γ). This can be justified on the grounds that Δ_R in the pupil is the sum total perturbation due to many *independent* perturbations on the way from source to pupil (see Sect. 3.2.6).

● Further, it is reasonable to suppose that Δ_R has zero mean, since phase fluctuations can be expected to go negative as often as positive. Then Δ_R is a Gaussian random variable.

● Let all statistical properties be invariant with positions (β, γ) in the pupil. We call this a property of "shift-invariant" statistics.

● Assume that each *pair of points* (β, γ), $(\beta - \omega_1, \gamma - \omega_2)$ has correlated Δ_R values, where such correlation is only a function of the *distance* $(\omega_1^2 + \omega_2^2)^{1/2} = \omega$ between them. This is a property of shift invariance for two points at a time, or a "second-order" shift invariance.

● A probability law that has the preceding properties is the Gaussian bivariate one [see (3.23)]. This law is also the "most likely" one, under the given circumstances (see Sect. 3.13.9). Hence, we shall assume that *the joint probability density for fluctuations Δ_R at the two pupil points (β, γ), $(\beta - \omega_1, \gamma - \omega_2)$ is Gaussian bivariate.* Furthermore, by shift invariance, it should have $\sigma_1 = \sigma_2$, and a correlation coefficient $\varrho = \varrho(\omega)$, i.e., only a function of the distance ω between the two points.

3.5.2 A Transfer Function for Turbulence

Consider the $\langle \ \rangle$ part of (3.116), where (β, γ) is fixed. Designate this as

$$\mathcal{T}_R(\beta, \gamma; \omega_1, \omega_2) \equiv \langle e^{ik[\Delta_R(\beta, \gamma) - \Delta_R(\beta - \omega_1, \gamma - \omega_2)]} \rangle . \tag{3.117}$$

Keeping in mind the fixed nature of β, γ, ω_1, and ω_2, let

$$\Delta_R(\beta, \gamma) \equiv \Delta_R ,$$
$$\Delta_R(\beta - \omega_1, \gamma - \omega_2) \equiv \Delta_R' . \tag{3.118}$$

Thus, Δ'_R describes a fluctuation at a fixed point *which is distance ω from the* point at which fluctuation Δ_R occurs. Equation (3.117) becomes

$$T_R(\beta,\gamma;\omega_1,\omega_2)=\langle e^{ik(\Delta_R-\Delta'_R)}\rangle. \tag{3.119}$$

Now the probability density

$$p_{GB}(\Delta_R,\Delta'_R) \tag{3.120}$$

describing the joint fluctuations Δ_R, Δ'_R was assumed to be Gaussian bivariate, and shift invariant, so that p_{GB} is *not a function of β, γ.* Thus by (3.119, 120),

$$T_R(\beta,\gamma;\omega_1,\omega_2)\equiv \iint d\Delta_R d\Delta'_R p_{GB}(\Delta_R,\Delta'_R)\, e^{ik(\Delta_R-\Delta'_R)}=T_R(\omega_1,\omega_2)\,\text{alone}. \tag{3.121}$$

Using this in (3.116), we see that T_R may be taken *outside* the $d\beta d\gamma$ integral. A cascading of transfer functions occurs,

$$\langle T(\omega_1,\omega_2)\rangle=T_0(\omega_1,\omega_2)\,T_R(\omega_1,\omega_2). \tag{3.122}$$

$T_0(\omega_1,\omega_2)$ is the *deterministic* transfer function

$$T_0(\omega_1,\omega_2)\equiv K\iint d\beta d\gamma\, e^{ik[\Delta_0(\beta,\gamma)-\Delta_0(\beta-\omega_1,\gamma-\omega_2)]}.$$

T_R evidently describes the image degradation due to random phase fluctuation *alone.* It may be regarded as a transfer function for turbulence *per se.*

3.5.3 Evaluation of $T_R(\omega_1,\omega_2)$

In order to evaluate the integral (3.121), let us use the definition (3.42) of characteristic function $\phi_{\Delta_R\Delta'_R}(\omega_1,\omega_2)$ for a general probability density $p(\Delta_R,\Delta'_R)$,

$$\phi_{\Delta_R\Delta'_R}(\omega_1,\omega_2)\equiv \iint d\Delta_R d\Delta'_R p(\Delta_R,\Delta'_R)\, e^{i(\omega_1\Delta_R+\omega_2\Delta'_R)}. \tag{3.123}$$

Compare with (3.121). It is precisely of the same form, with

$$T_R(\omega_1,\omega_2)=\phi_{\Delta_R\Delta'_R}(k,-k). \tag{3.124}$$

That is, T_R is a *given point $(k,-k)$ on the characteristic curve ϕ.* But the latter is known to be that due to a Gaussian bivariate case, with the specific form (3.43),

$$\phi_{\Delta_R\Delta'_R}(\omega_1,\omega_2)=e^{-1/2(\sigma_1^2\omega_1^2+\sigma_2^2\omega_2^2+2\varrho\sigma_1\sigma_2\omega_1\omega_2)}. \tag{3.125}$$

Therefore, by identity (3.124)

$$T_R(\omega_1,\omega_2)=e^{-1/2(\sigma_1^2 k^2+\sigma_2^2 k^2-2\varrho\sigma_1\sigma_2 k^2)}. \tag{3.126}$$

This can be reduced further.

By virtue of shift invariance, we had

$$\sigma_1 = \sigma_2$$

and

$$\varrho = \varrho(\omega).$$

Then (3.126) becomes

$$T_R(\omega_1, \omega_2) = e^{-k^2\sigma^2[1-\varrho(\omega)]} \equiv T_R(\omega). \tag{3.127}$$

Note that this could also have been arrived at by integration of (3.123), with a Gaussian bivariate form used for $p(\Delta_R, \Delta_R')$.

A final way of arriving at result (3.127) is worth mentioning because of its simplicity. Two-dimensional integrals are avoided. First, use the characteristic function (3.41) for a *single*, Gaussian r.v. x,

$$\langle e^{i\omega x} \rangle = e^{-\sigma_x^2\omega^2/2}. \tag{3.128}$$

Now compare this left-hand side with the right-hand side of (3.119). We see that by letting

$$\omega = k, \quad \text{and} \quad x = \Delta_R - \Delta_R' \tag{3.129}$$

(3.128) yields

$$T_R = e^{-\sigma_x^2 k^2/2}. \tag{3.130}$$

But by the second (3.129) and identity (3.16c),

$$\sigma_x^2 = \langle (\Delta_R - \Delta_R')^2 \rangle - \langle \Delta_R - \Delta_R' \rangle^2 = \langle (\Delta_R - \Delta_R')^2 \rangle$$

since Δ_R has zero mean,

$$= 2[\langle \Delta_R^2 \rangle - \langle \Delta_R \Delta_R' \rangle]$$
$$= 2[\sigma^2 - \sigma^2\varrho(\omega)]$$

by definition (3.26),

$$= 2\sigma^2[1 - \varrho(\omega)].$$

Substitution into (3.130) yields the desired result (3.127).

3.5.4 Discussion of Turbulence Transfer Function

The form $T_R(\omega)$ is seen by (3.127) to be uniquely fixed by the form for phase correlation function $\varrho(\omega)$. Note that by identities (3.113) *each pair of pupil points separated by length r translates into a spatial frequency* $\omega = kr/F$ *for* $T_R(\omega)$. Also, since the extreme values of $\varrho(\omega)$ are ± 1, we have from (3.127)

$$e^{-2k^2\sigma^2} \leqq T_R(\omega) \leqq 1 .$$

The upper bound acts as verification of the calculation. The lower bound expresses the fact that negative correlation $\varrho(\omega) = -1$ in phase (a cancellation effect) has the most adverse effect on contrast transfer, even worse than *zero* correlation.

Equation (3.127) shows that image quality varies directly with the degree to which there is correlation in phase in the pupil. For example, to see how bad an effect zero correlation has, suppose that $\sigma = \lambda/4$. This represents a modest fluctuation, by most standards. Then $k^2\sigma^2 = (2\pi/\lambda)^2 (\lambda/4)^2 = 2.5 \, \text{rad}$, and $T_R(\omega) = \exp(-2.5) = 0.08$ *at all frequencies*. This is severe loss of contrast. The effect for negative correlation is even worse, 0.0064 at all frequencies.

Conversely, result (3.127) shows that at any point separation r in the pupil for which there is perfect correlation $\varrho(r) = 1$, the corresponding spatial frequency $\omega = kr/F$ is passed with *no* loss of contrast. Hence we can have $T_R(\omega) = 1$ for nonzero ω, and even for high ω.

3.5.5 Evaluation of $T_R(\omega)$

To evaluate (3.127) *Hufnagel* and *Stanley* [3.20] used a specific functional form for $\varrho(\omega)$. This quantity is related to a more basic quantity used in turbulence theory, the "phase struction function",

$$D_\Delta(\omega) \equiv \langle |\Delta_R - \Delta_R'|^2 \rangle . \tag{3.131}$$

Squaring out (3.131) and taking expectations termwise,

$$D_\Delta(\omega) = \langle \Delta_R^2 \rangle + \langle \Delta_R'^2 \rangle - 2 \langle \Delta_R \Delta_R' \rangle$$
$$= 2\sigma^2 [1 - \varrho(\omega)] , \tag{3.132}$$

since $\langle \Delta_R^2 \rangle = \sigma^2$, and by definition (3.26). This is very nearly the exponent in result (3.127).

Experimentally, it is found that under conditions of weak turbulence, small-angle wave scattering, and single scattering

$$D_\Delta(\omega) = A\omega^{5/3} . \tag{3.133}$$

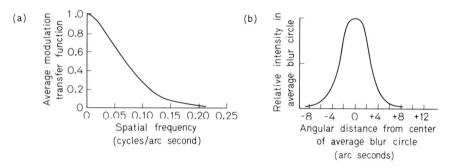

Fig. 3.22. Average transfer function (**a**) and average intensity distribution (**b**) for zenith viewing through whole earth's atmosphere [3.20]

Using this in (3.127),

$$T_R(\omega) = e^{-B\omega^{5/3}}, B \text{ a constant},\tag{3.134}$$

which is sometimes called the "five-thirds exponential power law".

This shows that the form of the MTF for long-term exposure imagery, $T_R(\omega)$, is something like a Gaussian. However, because $5/3 < 2$, high frequencies are not quite as strongly attenuated here. A typical form for $T_R(\omega)$ in daylight viewing is shown in Fig. 3.22a.

3.5.6 Resulting Point Spread Function (psf)

The long-term average point spread function (psf) $\langle s(x, y) \rangle$ is defined as

$$\langle s(x, y) \rangle = \langle \iint d\omega_1 d\omega_2 T(\omega_1, \omega_2) e^{i(\omega_1 x + \omega_2 y)} \rangle.$$

Taking the brackets within the integrals and using result (3.122), we get

$$\langle s(x, y) \rangle = \iint d\omega_1 d\omega_2 e^{i(\omega_1 x + \omega_2 y)} T_0(\omega_1, \omega_2) T_R(\omega).$$

Using the *convolution theorem*, we get

$$\langle s(x, y) \rangle = s_0(x, y) \otimes s_R(x, y)$$

where s_0 is the deterministic psf (the FT^{-1} of T_0), and

$$s_R(x, y) \equiv \iint d\omega_1 d\omega_2 e^{i(\omega_1 x + \omega_2 y)} T_R(\omega)$$

$$= 2\pi \int d\omega \omega J_0(\omega r) T_R(\omega) = s_R(r).$$

by rotational symmetry for T_R. Hence

$$s_R(r) = 2\pi \int d\omega \, \omega J_0(\omega r) e^{-B\omega^{5/3}} \qquad (3.135)$$

by (3.134).

This integral was evaluated numerically by *Hufnagel* and *Stanley*. For daytime viewing at zenith (straight up), they established the result shown in Fig. 3.22b. Thus, turbulence causes an average blur of about 6 arc s under these daytime conditions.

3.5.7 Higher Order Statistics

The mean value is of course the lowest order statistic one may take. Suppose the next higher order statistic, the second moment,

$$R_T(\omega_1, \omega_2; \omega_1', \omega_2') \equiv \langle T(\omega_1, \omega_2) \, T(\omega_1', \omega_2') \rangle$$

is required. This represents the joint behavior of the transfer function at *two* differing spatial frequencies. *Barakat* [3.21] solved this problem, and in fact solved the most general problem of establishing the *nth-order* moment of *T*. The approach is similar to that used in the derivation of (3.127), now using the characteristic function for n jointly normal r.v.'s. As an example, for the case $n = 2$ he found

$$R_T(\omega_1, \omega_2; \omega_1', \omega_2') = \exp(-2k^2\sigma^2) \iiint d\beta \, d\gamma \, d\beta' \, d\gamma'$$

$$\cdot \exp[k^2\sigma^2(\varrho_{12} - \varrho_{13} + \varrho_{14} + \varrho_{23} - \varrho_{24} + \varrho_{34})], \quad (3.136)$$

where ϱ_{mn} is the correlation coefficient (3.26) for phase $\varDelta_R$ at the two corresponding pupil points (see Ref. [3.21], Eq. (A6) and preceding).

Unfortunately, many of these correlation coefficients are evaluated at points depending specifically upon integration variables β, γ, β', γ', so that the exponential in (3.136) cannot be pulled outside the integral, as we did when calculating the mean, $\langle T(\omega_1, \omega_2) \rangle$. Hence, we do not get a nice separation into deterministic and random factors, as in (3.122). The integral (3.136) must be evaluated numerically.

3.6 Application to Laser Speckle

Anyone who has seen a laser beam in reflection off a wall, or in transmission, has seen laser speckle. It has a granular appearance, whereby the laser light appears to be broken up into a random pattern of grains (see Fig. 3.23). The effect is particularly bothersome because a) the frequency of occurrence of

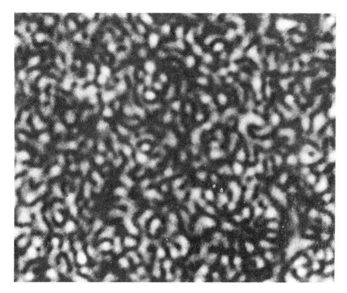

Fig. 3.23. Speckle pattern produced by laser illumination [3.22]

random speckle intensity falls off rather slowly (single exponential) with intensity, so that large intensity excursions are common; b) the standard deviation of these fluctuations *increases linearly* with mean intensity level in the light beam, so that increasing the signal level does not buy a loss in speckle effect; and c) all phase values from 0 to 2π in the beam are *equally* likely, which is about as random as phase can be.

It is an interesting exercise in probability to derive these properties a) to c). This analysis follows the general approach taken by *Dainty* [3.23].

3.6.1 Physical Layout

As illustrated in Fig. 3.24, suppose a uniformly bright, collimated light beam of wavelength λ to be incident upon a diffuser. Let the light be linearly polarized, for simplicity. Then *a speckle pattern will be formed in all planes beyond the diffuser*. In particular, we shall examine the statistics of the pattern in the plane *B* located distance *R* from the diffuser. This speckle pattern could be observed by simply imaging plane *B* onto a screen, by use of any convenient lens.

3.6.2 Game Plan for the Analysis

As discussed above, we want to establish the probability laws $p_I(x)$ and $p_\phi(x)$ for intensity and phase of the speckles in the plane *B*. To accomplish this, we

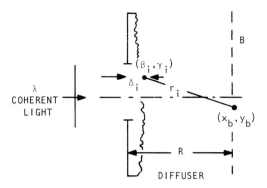

Fig. 3.24. Physical setup for producing a speckle pattern

shall make use of the transformation relations

$$I = U_{re}^2 + U_{im}^2$$
$$\phi = \tan^{-1}(U_{im}/U_{re}),$$

(3.137)

where U_{re}, U_{im}, respectively, are the real and imaginary parts of the complex light amplitude U at a point (x_b, y_b) in plane B. If joint probability $p_{U_{re}U]m}(x, y)$ can be established first, the law $p_{I\phi}(v, w)$ follows by a transformation (3.99) of random variables. With $p_{I\phi}$ known, the required laws p_I, p_ϕ are found by marginal integration (3.14e) of $p_{I\phi}$. Hence, we first set out to find $p_{U_{re}U_{im}}(x, y)$.

3.6.3 Statistical Model for Laser Speckle

We shall show here that by a reasonable and yet simple *statistical model* (see comments in first paragraph, Sect. 3.5.1), U_{re} and U_{im} each obey the central limit theorem. Hence they are normally distributed. The assumptions of the model are denoted by ● in the following. A last assumption is given later in Sect. 3.6.5.

  ● If R is not too small, the light amplitude U at any point (x_b, y_b) in plane B relates to the amplitude in the diffuser by the well-known Fraunhofer integral formula.

  ● To keep the analysis simple, assume that the diffuser consists of $N \gg 1$ uncorrelated, contiguous areas called "scattering spots". Within each scattering spot the amplitude is perfectly correlated. This is a statistical model which has been used with success in other problems as well. For example, in Sect. 3.7 or in *Korff* [3.24].

  ● Let r_i (see Fig. 3.24) connect the image point (x_b, y_b) with the center of the ith spot. Then if the spot area Δa is sufficiently small, the Fraunhofer integral formula becomes well approximated by a discrete sum

$$U(x_b, y_b) \equiv U = \Delta a \sum_{i=1}^{N} e^{ikr_i}/\lambda r_i.$$

(3.138)

● Now r_i will differ from R by a small amount. Therefore, we make the usual approximation of $r_i \simeq R$ in the denominator of (3.138),

$$U = (\Delta a / \lambda R) \sum_{i=1}^{N} e^{i k r_i} . \tag{3.139}$$

3.6.4 Marginal Probabilities for Light Amplitudes U_{re}, U_{im}

We next want to show that U obeys the central limit theorem (see Sect. 3.2.5), in each of its real and imaginary parts.

From the geometry of Fig. 3.24,

$$r_i = [(R - \Delta_i)^2 + (\beta_i - x_b)^2 + (\gamma_i - y_b)^2]^{1/2} , \tag{3.140}$$

where Δ_i is the diffuser thickness at point (β_i, γ_i). Of course, $\Delta_i \ll R$. Then (3.140) is well approximated by

$$r_i = (R - \Delta_i) + (2R)^{-1} [(\beta_i - x_b)^2 + (\gamma_i - y_b)^2] \tag{3.141}$$

or simply

$$r_i = A_i - \Delta_i , \tag{3.142}$$

where A_i is all the deterministic terms in (3.141).

Substitution of (3.142) into (3.139) gives

$$U = c \sum_{i=1}^{N} e^{i k (A_i - \Delta_i)} , \quad c = \Delta a / \lambda R . \tag{3.143}$$

Does U obey the central limit theorem?

By hypothesis, each scattering spot i has an independent phase Δ_i. Therefore, each term of the sum (3.143) is an independent r.v. Let us assume further that the statistics in Δ across the diffuser are invariant with position i. Then, except for the deterministic factor $\exp(i k A_i)$, each term of the sum (3.143) is identically distributed as well as independent. Of course, N is very large. These are the ground rules described in Sect. 3.2.5 for satisfying the central limit theorem. Hence, each of U_{re} and U_{im} are normal r.v.'s.

Having established that the marginal probabilities $p_{U_{re}}$ and $p_{U_{im}}$ are each normal, we now ask what the *joint* probability $p_{U_{re}U_{im}}$ is. (This quantity is not, of course, uniquely fixed by the marginal laws.) For example, if U_{re} and U_{im} are *correlated*, the joint probability in question might be the normal bivariate one. If they are not correlated, we must assume the joint law to be a simple product of the two marginal laws. Therefore, we have to determine the state of correlation.

3.6.5 Correlation Between U_{re} and U_{im}

Directly from (3.143), the correlation in question obeys

$$\langle U_{re} U_{im} \rangle = c^2 \sum_{m,n} \langle \cos k(A_m - \Delta_m) \sin k(A_n - \Delta_n) \rangle$$

$$= c^2 \sum_{m \neq n} \langle \cos k(A_m - \Delta_m) \rangle \langle \sin k(A_n - \Delta_n) \rangle$$

$$+ c^2 \sum_n \langle \cos k(A_n - \Delta_n) \sin k(A_n - \Delta_n) \rangle \tag{3.144}$$

according to whether $m = n$ or not. The sum $m \neq n$ separates into the given product of expectations because Δ_m and Δ_n are independent, by the statistical model. The second sum was for $m = n$.

● In order to evaluate the averages in (3.144), we have to fix the statistics of Δ. It is reasonable to assume that a physical diffuser has *uniform randomness* for its total phase $k\Delta$. All this presumes is that $p(\Delta)$ has a $\sigma \gg \lambda$, since then $\langle (k\Delta)^2 \rangle = (2\pi)^2 \langle \Delta^2 \rangle / \lambda^2 \gg (2\pi)^2$, so that many cycles of phase are a common occurrence. In summary, the final assumption of our statistical model is that

$$p_{k\Delta}(\theta) = (2\pi)^{-1} \operatorname{Rect}(\theta/\pi). \tag{3.145}$$

Then

$$\langle \cos k(A - \Delta) \rangle = (2\pi)^{-1} \int_{-\pi}^{\pi} d\theta \cos(kA - \theta) = 0,$$

$$\langle \sin k(A - \Delta) \rangle = 0$$

and

$$\langle \cos(kA - \theta) \sin(kA - \theta) \rangle = 0.$$

Therefore, U_{re} and U_{im} do not correlate.
These results also imply that

$$\langle U_{re} \rangle \equiv c \sum_{n=1}^{N} \langle \cos k(A_n - \Delta_n) \rangle = 0$$

and

$$\langle U_{im} \rangle = 0.$$

Therefore, each of U_{re} and U_{im} is a *Gaussian* r.v., in particular.

3.6.6 Joint Probability Law for U_{re}, U_{im}

We have thereby established that the joint law is a simple product of Gaussian marginal laws

$$p_{U_{re}U_{im}}(x, y) = (\pi\sigma^2)^{-1} \exp[-(x^2 + y^2)/\sigma^2]. \tag{3.146}$$

Here

$$\sigma^2 \equiv \langle |U|^2 \rangle = \langle U_{re}^2 + U_{im}^2 \rangle = \langle U_{re}^2 \rangle + \langle U_{im}^2 \rangle$$

$$= c^2 \sum_{n=1}^{N} \langle \cos^2 k(A_n - \Delta_n) \rangle + c^2 \sum_{n=1}^{N} \langle \sin^2 k(A_n - \Delta_n) \rangle$$

as at (3.144), or since each $\langle \rangle = 1/2$,

$$\sigma^2 = Nc^2 = N(\Delta a/\lambda R)^2 \tag{3.147}$$

by identity (3.143).

3.6.7 Probability Laws for Intensity and Phase

Continuing the game plan of Sect. 3.6.2, we want to find the joint law $p_{I\phi}(v, w)$ through the transformation (3.137) of old r.v.'s U_{re} and U_{im} to new variables I and ϕ. This is a unique ($r=1$ root) transformation. By using the general approach (3.99) with $r=1$,

$$p_{I\phi}(v, w) = p_{U_{re}U_{im}}(x, y) \left| J\left(\frac{x, y}{v, w}\right) \right|. \tag{3.148}$$

Now

$$J\left(\frac{x, y}{v, w}\right) \equiv det \begin{bmatrix} \partial x/\partial v & \partial x/\partial w \\ \partial y/\partial v & \partial y/\partial w \end{bmatrix},$$

where by the transformation (3.137)

$$U_{re} = I^{1/2} \cos\phi \quad \text{or} \quad x = v^{1/2} \cos w$$

and

$$U_{im} = I^{1/2} \sin\phi \quad \text{or} \quad y = v^{1/2} \sin w.$$

Thus

$$J\left(\frac{x, y}{v, w}\right) = det \begin{bmatrix} 2^{-1}v^{-1/2}\cos w & -v^{1/2}\sin w \\ 2^{-1}v^{-1/2}\sin w & -v^{1/2}\cos w \end{bmatrix}$$

$$= 2^{-1}\cos^2 w + 2^{-1}\sin^2 w = 1/2.$$

Using this result in (3.148),

$$p_{I\phi}(v, w) = 2^{-1}p_{U_{re}U_{im}}(v^{1/2}\cos w, y^{1/2}\sin w). \tag{3.149}$$

This would be true for *any* joint law $p_{U_{re}U_{im}}$. In the particular case (3.146), (3.149) becomes

$$p_{I\phi}(v, w) = \frac{1}{2\pi\sigma^2} e^{-v/\sigma^2} \text{Rect}(w/\pi), \tag{3.150}$$

where $v \geq 0$.

3.6.8 Marginal Law for Intensity, for Phase

Following the prescription (3.14e), (3.150) integrates dw over interval $(-\pi, \pi)$ to give

$$p_I(v) = \sigma^{-2} \exp(-v/\sigma^2), \tag{3.151a}$$

or it integrates dv over interval $(0, \infty)$ to give

$$p_\phi(w) = (2\pi)^{-1} \text{Rect}(w/\pi). \tag{3.151b}$$

These are what we set out to find.

In summary, under the assumptions of the given statistical model, *speckle intensity follows a negative exponential law* (3.151a), *and speckle phase follows a uniform law* (3.151b).

The fact that (3.151a) falls off so slowly with intensity v accounts for the very random and grainy appearance in a speckle pattern. Quantitatively, this slow fall off makes the speckle fluctuations comparable with the mean intensity level in the pattern, as shown next.

3.6.9 Signal-to-Noise (S/N) Ratio in the Speckle Image

The signal-to-noise ratio, denoted as S/N, describes the extent to which an image is corrupted by noise. It is defined as the mean intensity value $\langle I \rangle$ over the standard deviation for intensity σ_I. These quantities may easily be found from the known law (3.151a) for $p_I(v)$. Directly,

$$\langle I\rangle=\sigma^{-2}\int_0^\infty dv\,v\exp(-v/\sigma^2)=\sigma^2, \tag{3.152}$$

after an integration by parts. Further,

$$\langle I^2\rangle=\sigma^{-2}\int_0^\infty dv\,v^2\exp(-v/\sigma^2)=2\sigma^4 \tag{3.153}$$

again integrating by parts. Then by identity (3.16c)

$$\sigma_I^2\equiv\langle I^2\rangle-\langle I\rangle^2=\sigma^4. \tag{3.154}$$

Using (3.152, 154)

$$S/N\equiv\langle I\rangle/\sigma_I=\sigma^2/\sigma^2=1. \tag{3.155}$$

This result shows specifically how noisy a process speckle is. *On the average, its fluctuations equal the mean signal level!* This accounts for the extremely grainy appearance in a speckle image.

It is possible to reduce the noise level by averaging adjacent image points. Many such "speckle reduction" schemes have been proposed (see, e.g., the survey *Dainty* [3.25]). One of the simplest of these approaches is to scan the speckle image with a finite aperture. The output of such a scan is the convolution of the noisy speckle image with a "pillbox" spread function, which performs a running average or smoothing effect upon the image. It is a useful exercise in probability to analyze this technique, and this is done in Sect. 3.7.

3.6.10 Monte Carlo Simulation of Speckle Patterns

Suppose it is desired to construct a "typical" speckle intensity pattern upon the computer. How may this be done? As usual, suppose we have access to the uniformly random numbers between 0 and 1 generated by the library function RANF($\cdot$). Let the latter be denoted by values y.

Since we know the probability law (3.151a) obeyed by intensity, we may use the approach of Fig. 3.16 to generate typical values of intensity from given numbers y. The cumulative probability law must be formed. It is

$$F_I(x)=\sigma^{-2}\int_0^x dv\exp(-v/\sigma^2)=1-\exp(-x/\sigma^2).$$

Therefore we set

$$1-\exp(-x/\sigma^2)=y,$$

which has the analytic solution

$$x = -\sigma^2 \ln(1-y).$$ (3.156)

x is the simulated intensity value in question.

In order to obtain a spatial intensity pattern, it is necessary to place the generated intensities x at positions in the image plane. How should this be done? According to a model of *Goodman* [3.26], a speckle image consists of uncorrelated speckles of a characteristic size a. Hence, the simulated intensity values x (which are indeed uncorrelated) should simply be placed, in turn, at positions $(x_m, y_n) = (ma, na)$, m, $n = 1, \cdots, N$ across the image plane. An $N \times N$ point simulation will result.

Computer simulation of speckle patterns has been carried through by *Fujii* et al. [3.27]. They questioned the model of *independent* scattering spots in the diffuser, based on the reasoning that a smooth diffuser, as encountered in high-quality optical systems, ought to have significant correlation across its face. Accordingly, they simulated formation of the speckle image as if the diffuser were Gaussian random at each point but correlated from point to point. The authors note that their resulting speckle images are more in compliance with experimental observation than when independent Gaussian randomness is assumed in the simulation.

3.7 Speckle Reduction by Scanning Aperture; the χ-Square Distribution

The chi-square, or gamma, distribution is a widely occurring probability law. The main purpose of this section will be to show the kind of statistical model that gives rise to the law. We shall follow the development of *Goodman* [3.26].

One direct way of reducing speckle is by picking up the speckled image with a scanning aperture of finite area A. The aperture automatically averages the speckles falling within it at each aperture position. Of course, resolution is lost in this manner but it is often a worthwhile tradeoff with speckle reduction.

Such use of a scanning aperture is, of course, equivalent to defocussing the speckle image, or to moving the image back and forth during a finite exposure time. Hence the analysis that follows applies to these physical operations as well.

The ultimate aim of the calculation is to predict the resulting increase in S/N ratio due to aperture averaging. As in Sect. 3.6, this will be found by determining the probability density for total intensity within the aperture, at any position in the image. This will introduce us to the chi-square distribution, a very important law because of its widespread physical applicability.

As usual, a statistical model must be devised, and this is denoted by dots.

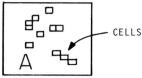

SCANNING APERTURE

Fig. 3.25. Geometry of scanning aperture. It encloses a fixed number M of statistically independent amplitude "cells"

● Assume the speckle image to consist of *uncorrelated speckles*, or cells, of a characteristic size. This model coincides with the "scatter spot" model of Sect. 3.6.3 for the diffuser. Let aperture A contain M of these cells, as illustrated in Fig. 3.25.

● The total amplitude U (complex) inside the aperture then obeys

$$U = \sum_{m=1}^{M} U_m, \tag{3.157}$$

where U_n represents the complex amplitude from the mth cell. As the U_m are by hypothesis independent, U is the output of a random walk process (see Sect. 3.2.6).

By (3.157), the total intensity v, and net phase w, obey

$$v = \sum_{m=1}^{M} (x_m^2 + y_m^2), \qquad w = \tan^{-1}\left(\sum_m y_m \Big/ \sum_m x_m\right), \tag{3.158}$$

where x_m, y_m are U_{re}, U_{im} for cell m. We are particularly interested in establishing $p_I(v)$, the density for output intensity from the aperture.

3.7.1 Probability Density for Output Intensity $p_I(v)$

The first of Eqs. (3.158) may be rewritten as

$$v = \sum_{m=1}^{M} x_m^2 + \sum_{m=1}^{M} y_m^2. \tag{3.159}$$

Now, by (3.146), the marginal probabilities are known as

$$p_{X_m}(x) = p_{Y_m}(x) = (\pi\sigma^2)^{-1/2} \exp(-x^2/\sigma^2), \tag{3.160}$$

where σ is independent of m, by (3.147).

In view of the quadratic dependencies in (3.159), we then note that the *square* of X_m (or Y_m) is distributed as

$$p_{X_m^2}(x) = \pi^{-1/2}\sigma^{-1}x^{-1/2}\exp(-x/\sigma^2), \qquad x \geq 0, \tag{3.161}$$

by transformation law (3.92). Intensity v is then the sum of $2M$ of such r.v.'s, and these are independent by the model. Since they are identically distributed we may drop subscript m.

It is convenient now to use characteristic functions. By (3.161)

$$\Phi_{X^2}(\omega) = \pi^{-1/2}\sigma^{-1} \int_0^\infty dx\, x^{-1/2} \exp(i\omega x - x/\sigma^2). \tag{3.162}$$

This is a special case of the more general integral

$$I(v) \equiv \int_0^\infty dx\, x^{v-1} \exp(i\omega x - x/\sigma^2). \tag{3.163}$$

In fact,

$$\Phi_{X^2}(\omega) = \pi^{-1/2}\sigma^{-1} I(1/2). \tag{3.164}$$

To evaluate (3.163), use the change of variable

$$t = -(i\omega x - x/\sigma^2).$$

Then

$$I(v) = (1/\sigma^2 - i\omega)^{-v} \int_0^\infty dt\, t^{v-1} \exp(-t)$$
$$= \sigma^{2v}(1 - i\omega\sigma^2)^{-v} \Gamma(v). \tag{3.165}$$

The integral defined $\Gamma(v)$, the gamma function. Using $\Gamma(1/2) = \pi^{1/2}$, and (3.164),

$$\Phi_{X^2}(\omega) = (1 - i\omega\sigma^2)^{-1/2}. \tag{3.166}$$

This is the characteristic function for U_{re}^2 or U_{im}^2 at one of the M independent speckles.

By (3.159) and the independence of random variables x_m and y_m, the net characteristic function obeys

$$\Phi_I(\omega) = \prod_{m=1}^{2M} \Phi_{X^2}(\omega) = [\Phi_{X^2}(\omega)]^{2M} \tag{3.167}$$

since all $2M$ are identically distributed.

Hence by (3.166)

$$\Phi_I(\omega) = (1 - i\omega\sigma^2)^{-M}. \tag{3.168}$$

The probability density having this characteristic function is the sought-after result.

By (3.163), $I(M)$ defines the characteristic function for a probability $x^{M-1} \exp(-x/\sigma^2)$. By result (3.165), this characteristic function is

$$\sigma^{2M} \Gamma(M)(1 - i\omega\sigma^2)^{-M}. \tag{3.169}$$

Compare this with (3.168). This is precisely $\sigma^{2M} \Gamma(M) \cdot \Phi_I(\omega)$. Hence a probability density of

$$p_I(x) = \sigma^{-2M} [\Gamma(M)]^{-1} x^{M-1} \exp(-x/\sigma^2) \tag{3.170}$$

would have precisely (3.168) as its characteristic function. This is our required probability for total intensity.

This probability density is called the "chi-square" distribution. As a check on the result, for $M=1$ it goes over into the result (3.151a) for *single point* observation of the speckle image.

For further remarks on the degree of accuracy in the result (3.170), and a more exact approach to the subject, see the chapter by *Goodman* in [3.25].

The chi-square distribution has an entirely different use as a specifier of "significance" in experimental results (see Sect. 3.17).

3.7.2 Moments and S/N Ratio

The moments of (3.170) are best obtained by successive differentiation of its characteristic function (3.168). To directly use (3.170) instead in moment integrals would be very cumbersome.

From (3.168)

$$\Phi_I'(\omega) = iM\sigma^2(1 - i\omega\sigma^2)^{-M-1}$$

and

$$\Phi_I''(\omega) = i^2 M(M+1)\sigma^4(1 - i\omega\sigma^2)^{-M-2}.$$

Then

$$\langle I \rangle = M\sigma^2 \quad \text{and} \quad \langle I^2 \rangle = M(M+1)\sigma^4. \tag{3.171}$$

Using

$$\sigma_I^2 \equiv \langle I^2 \rangle - \langle I \rangle^2$$

we have

$$\sigma_I^2 = M\sigma^4. \tag{3.172}$$

As might be expected, σ_I^2 for the aperture varies directly with aperture size. However, so does the mean signal level $\langle I \rangle$, by (3.171). Again defining a S/N ratio by

$$S/N \equiv \langle I \rangle / \sigma_I ,$$

from (3.171, 172)

$$S/N = M^{1/2} . \tag{3.173}$$

This shows the advantage of aperture averaging. The S/N in the speckle image directly increases as the square root of the aperture area.

Of course aperture averaging is not entirely beneficial, since it is equivalent to convolution of the image with a square window function, and this must result in a *loss of spatial resolution*. Work on speckle reduction is still going on.

3.8 Statistical Methods

To this point we have been dealing with problems of *predicting* statistical properties of data (e.g., S/N ratio) from known or inferred probability laws. These are problems of the discipline called "probability theory".

On the other hand, there is a wide class of problems that is complementary and reverse to these. This is where a particular set of data is *given*, and we want to somehow estimate from these the probablity law, or some property of this such as the mean, that formed the data. This type of problem falls within the domain of "statistics".

One of the basic goals of statistics is to arrive at an answer, *based solely upon data at hand*. Whatever operations we subject the data to, these should be as free as possible of assumptions as to the underlying probability laws that caused the data. Ideally, the analysis should be "distribution free". For this reason, the goals of statistical theory are often modest. Rather than seek a definite number as the answer, sometimes the aim is simply to know that the number arrived at is "probably" correct within certain error bounds; or, that the sample of film at hand is "probably" of a different type than another; or that the data at hand are "significant"; or that enough tests have been made upon a manufactured item to be "confident" that its failure rate may be bracketed.

Subsequent sections of this chapter deal with statistical problems of this type, as they arise in optics. For the sake of brevity, we shall, however, not cover in any depth such well-worked subjects as estimation theory and pattern recognition. These cover a prohibitively broad scope of material, and besides this, have already received a great deal of exposure in the optical community.

Conventional statistical methods, however, have not been used extensively in optical research. We hope by this exposition to show how naturally and freely many optical problems may be so treated.

3.9 Estimating a Mean from a Finite Sample

Consider this most basic problem of statistics. The speed of light c is known to be approximately 3.0×10^8 m/s, from the result of one experiment. The standard deviation in c due to this experiment is judged to be

$$\sigma_c = 0.1 \times 10^8 \text{ m/s}.$$

In an attempt to obtain a more accurate value for c, someone suggests repeating the same experiment a number N of times, and estimating the true c by taking an arithmetic average

$$\bar{c} \equiv N^{-1} \sum_{n=1}^{N} c_n \tag{3.174}$$

of the results $\{c_n\}$. The arithmetic average (3.174) when taken over experimental data (as here) is often called the "sample mean".

Is this a sound approach? Does the sample mean improve indefinitely with the number N of samples? If so, how large must N be for the expected error in $\bar{c}$ to be less than 1%? By comparison, the error of $\pm 0.1 \times 10^8$ amounts to a 3% relative error for any *one* experiment.

3.9.1 Statistical Model

It is reasonable to suppose that each experiment is performed by the identical procedure, so that 1) each output c_n is in reality a sample from *the same* probability law.

Next, we shall suppose that the experimental procedure is deterministically (in the absence of errors) sound, so that 2) the mean of the probability law is exactly the true value, c. Then for any n,

$$\langle c_n \rangle = c. \tag{3.175}$$

[Note: This is not an ensemble average as in (3.174). It is the ideal mean of the one probability law describing all the outputs.] What (3.175) states is that there is no *systematic error* present in the experiments that would lead to an average *bias away* from the true value c. This is a strong assumption to make, as most experimental procedures do suffer at least some systematic error or bias.

Finally, let us ideally assume 3) the experiments to be truly *independent*, or, there is zero correlation between any two outputs c_m and c_n, $m \neq n$,

$$\langle (c_m - c)(c_n - c) \rangle = \delta_{mn} \sigma_c^2 \tag{3.176}$$

by definition (3.26). δ_{mn} is the Kronecker delta.

3.9.2 Analysis

We want to know what error to expect by use of the sample mean formula (3.174). A good measure of error is the standard deviation $\sigma_{\bar{c}}$ of the sample mean $\bar{c}$ from the true value c. This is easily computed on the basis of the statistical model above.

By definition

$$\sigma_{\bar{c}}^2 \equiv \langle (c - \bar{c})^2 \rangle$$

$$= N^{-2} \left\langle \sum_n \left[(c - c_n) \right]^2 \right\rangle$$

by (3.174),

$$\sigma_{\bar{c}}^2 = N^{-2} \sum_n \sum_m \langle (c - c_m)(c - c_n) \rangle$$

after squaring out,

$$\sigma_{\bar{c}}^2 = N^{-2} \sum_{n=1}^{N} \sigma_c^2$$

by lack of correlation (3.176), so that

$$\sigma_{\bar{c}} = \sigma_c / \sqrt{N} . \tag{3.177}$$

This famous result states that, yes, the error in the estimate $\bar{c}$ does indeed *decrease indefinitely* with number of experiments N. However, the effect is a rather slow one, because of the square-root dependence on N.

Equation (3.177) may be recast as a requirement on N, given a required relative error $e \equiv \sigma_{\bar{c}}/c$ in the sample mean. By (3.177),

$$N = (\sigma_c / ec)^2 . \tag{3.178}$$

This relation may be used to solve the problem posed at the outset, of how large N must be for accomplishing error $e = 1\%$,

$$N = (0.1 \times 10^8 / 0.01 \times 3.0 \times 10^8)^2$$

$$= 11 \text{ experiments.}$$

3.9.3 Discussion

This result can of course be generalized to the case where N independent and unbiased determinations of *any experimental quantity c* are known, and from these N numbers a better estimate of c is sought. Also, note that the derivation assumed nothing about the *form* of the probability law obeyed by outputs c: whether normal, inverse exponential, or whatever. Hence, the result (3.177). is *distribution free*, and has widespread applicability.

A further generalization is noted. Although we assumed that each experiment was operationally identical, leading to model assumption 1), this assumption is not really necessary for 1) to be true. Hence, each output c_n from a *different* operational experiment might still be a sample from the same probability law, or nearly so. Much use is made of this generalization. The universal constants (such as c) given in physical tables are usually sample means (3.174) over many different types of experiments.

In this author's opinion, the weakest assumption made in the derivation is number 2), that the theoretical mean of the experiment is *exactly* the true value c. In reality, all experimental procedures suffer *some* systematic bias away from the true value. The existence of such bias will cause result (3.177) to break down at sufficiently high N. That is, even with very high N the error $\sigma_{\bar{c}}$ will remain finite.

3.9.4 Error in a Discrete, Linear Processor

Rather than perform a simple average (3.174), in image processing it is common to form an output $\bar{c}$ from N *finite image values* $\{c_n\}$ *as the weighted superposition*

$$\bar{c} \equiv \sum_{n=1}^{N} w_n c_n \bigg/ \sum_{n=1}^{N} w_n. \tag{3.179}$$

This is often termed a "linear processor", of the image data $\{c_n\}$ lying within the finite "window" $\{w_n\}$. This window is placed upon image values $(c_1, \cdots, c_N)$, then upon $(c_2, \cdots, c_{N+1})$, etc., the operation (3.179) performed at each placement, to form respective outputs $\bar{c}_1, \bar{c}_2$, etc.

The weights $\{w_n\}$ are numbers selected so as either to smooth the data $\{c_n\}$, in which case they are all positive, or to enhance the resolution in $\{c_n\}$, in which case some are negative. The form (3.179) includes division by $\{w_n\}$ so as to force conservation of energy in the sum $\sum \bar{c}_m$ over all outputs $\bar{c}_m$ (we have suppressed subscript m) with that of the data sum $\sum c_n$.

Note that the form (3.179) includes the particular case (3.174) of pure data averaging, in the case where all $w_n = 1$. This permits a simple check on the results below.

We are interested in the situation where data values $\{c_n\}$ consist of true or signal values $\{C_n\}$ plus independent noise value $\{e_n\}$.

$$c_n = C_n + e_n. \tag{3.180}$$

Noise is supposed to be zero mean and independent,

$$\langle e_n \rangle = 0, \qquad \langle e_m e_n \rangle = \sigma_c^2 \delta_{mn}, \tag{3.181}$$

as in (3.175, 176).

We further suppose that the weights $\{w_n\}$ have been chosen so that when they operate upon noiseless data the result is the ideal value c (which might represent a restored ideal object value, e.g., or a smoothed image signal value). That is,

$$\sum_{n=1}^{N} w_n C_n \bigg/ \sum_{n=1}^{N} w_n = c. \tag{3.182}$$

This being the ideal output, the mean-square error is

$$\sigma_{\bar{c}}^2 \equiv \langle (c - \bar{c})^2 \rangle$$

as in the preceding Sect. 3.9.3. This error is then

$$\sigma_{\bar{c}}^2 = \langle [c - \sum w_n (C_n + e_n) / \sum w_n]^2 \rangle$$

by (3.179, 180), or

$$\sigma_{\bar{c}}^2 = \langle (\sum w_n e_n)^2 \rangle / (\sum w_n)^2$$

by (3.182). Then squaring out the numerator and using independence (3.181) yields

$$\sigma_{\bar{c}}^2 = \sigma_c^2 \frac{\displaystyle\sum_{n=1}^{N} w_n^2}{\left(\displaystyle\sum_{n=1}^{N} w_n\right)^2}. \tag{3.183}$$

This symmetric expression depends only upon the data error σ_c and the weights. As a check, for the case of unit weights $w_n = 1$ we once again get expression (3.177) corresponding to the simple arithmetic average.

To see the effect of the weights on the output error $\sigma_{\bar{c}}^2$, consider first the case of *data smoothing*, where all $w_n \geq 0$. This corresponds to pure apodization in the case of image processing. If the ratio of weights factor in (3.183) is denoted as r, identically

$$r = \frac{(\sum w_n)^2 - \displaystyle\sum_{m \neq n} w_m w_n}{(\sum w_n)^2}.$$

Since all $w_n \geq 0$ here, we see that

$$r < 1. \tag{3.184}$$

Hence, by (3.183) the *output error is less than the data error,*

$$\sigma_{\bar{c}}^2 < \sigma_c^2. \tag{3.185}$$

This is a good state of affairs, but does not imply getting something for nothing, since relation (3.182) is still presumed to hold, i.e., that the weights correctly process the signal. However, the set of weights satisfying (3.182) will not always turn out to be positive, as assumed here. For example, consider the following case.

If the image $\{c_n\}$ is a *blurred version* of the object (of ideal value c at the one output point considered), some of the weights now have to be *negative* in order to enforce (3.182) (see, e.g., [3.28]). In this case, r will usually exceed 1, and if any significant increase in resolution (such as a factor of 2 or more) is demanded, will *greatly exceed* 1. Then the result (3.183) predicts a *noise-boost* phenomenon. In this case, *the weights $\{w_n\}$ are primarily intended to boost resolution, via* (3.182), *rather than to decrease noise via* (3.183). Evidently, this tradeoff will be acceptable only if σ_c in (3.183) is small enough. Linear methods of restoring images always suffer such a tradeoff, directly because of (3.183).

3.10 The Binomial Distribution

Basic to an understanding of statistics is the notion of a binary experiment. An example is the experiment consisting of the flip of a coin. The output must either be "head" or "tail", and is therefore binary. Many real situations may be modeled in this way (see Sect. 3.11, for example).

Suppose a coin is flipped N times. *We want to know the probability $P_N(m)$ of acquiring m heads* (and by implication $N - m$ tails). The coin may not be "fair", i.e., have equal probability of head and tail. An abbreviated derivation of the law obeyed by $P_N(m)$ is given next; *Parzen* [3.29] has the more complete proof.

3.10.1 Derivation

The statistical model for this experiment is the following:
- Each experiment is independent of the others.
- Each experimental output is a sample from the same binary probability law, with probability p of a "head", and $q = 1 - p$ of a "tail".

By these assumptions, the probability of obtaining m heads on m *particular* trials (say, flip numbers 2, 5, 7, and 10) is simply p^m. This is irrespective of the outcomes for the remaining $N - m$ trials. These could be heads or tails in any order.

If in addition we demand *all tails* in the remaining $N - m$ trials we have a net probability of

$$p^m q^{N-m}. \tag{3.186}$$

This is what we have stipulated, in fact.

Now the *total* probability of getting m heads and $N - m$ tails takes into account *all possible* sequences of heads and tails having m heads total. By the model above, each such sequence has the same elemental probability (3.186). Therefore the desired probability is

$$P_N(m) = W_N(m) p^m q^{N-m}, \tag{3.187}$$

where $W_N(m)$ is the total number of sequences of flips which give rise to m heads.

$W_N(m)$ may also be thought of as the number of sets of m indistinguishable elements that may be formed out of a total of N elements. This is known to describe the binomial coefficient (see [3.29])

$$W_N(m) = \frac{N!}{m!(N-m)!} \equiv \binom{N}{m}. \tag{3.188}$$

Hence, the answer is

$$P_N(m) = \binom{N}{m} p^m q^{N-m}. \tag{3.189}$$

3.10.2 Characteristic Function, Moments, S/N

The characteristic function is, by definition (3.39),

$$\phi_N(\omega) = \sum_{m=0}^{N} e^{i\omega m} \binom{N}{m} p^m q^{N-m}.$$

To evaluate this sum we write it as

$$\phi_N(\omega) = \sum_{m=0}^{N} \binom{N}{m} (p e^{i\omega})^m q^{N-m}$$

and compare it with a mathematical identity called the binomial theorem,

$$(a+b)^N \equiv \sum_{m=0}^{N} \binom{N}{m} a^m b^{N-m}.$$

Directly the answer is

$$\phi_N(\omega) = (pe^{i\omega} + q)^N .$$ (3.190)

The moments may be found as usual by successively differentiating (3.190). In this manner we easily obtain the mean and variance

$$\langle m \rangle = Np$$ (3.191)

and

$$\sigma_m^2 = Np(1 - p).$$ (3.192)

Finally, from these last two, the S/N ratio for a binomial experiment is

$$S/N \equiv \langle m \rangle / \sigma_m = [Np/(1 - p)]^{1/2} ,$$ (3.193)

showing an increase with $N^{1/2}$ and a maximum with p for $p = 1$ (only "heads", therefore no randomness).

3.11 Estimating a Probability

With this groundwork laid, we may attack a very basic problem of statistics. This is how to compute a probability on the basis of a set of data, and more importantly how much error to expect in the computed value.

The most direct and common method of estimating a probability is to use the law of large numbers (3.6) in a finite form

$$\hat{p} = m/N, \quad N \text{ finite}.$$ (3.194)

Here $\hat{p}$ is the estimate of p, the probability of the event in question, and m is the number of times the event occurs in N trials. This estimate will be in error because N is finite. We want to know how serious the error is.

In order to estimate the error, we have to model the statistics of the physical situation. This consists of N independent repetitions of an experiment whose outcomes are either the event or the non event. But this is precisely the model we assumed in Sect. 3.10.1 for the *binomial process*. Hence, we may use in particular the moment results (3.191, 192) for the occurrence of m.

3.11.1 Error Analysis

The expected error in the estimate $\hat{p}$ can be defined by the variance of error

$$e^2 \equiv \langle (p - \hat{p})^2 \rangle ,$$ (3.195)

where brackets denote an average over a great many determinations (3.194) with fixed N. Combining (3.194) and (3.195),

$$e^2 = N^{-2}\langle(Np-m)^2\rangle$$

$$= N^{-2}\sigma_m^2$$

by moment (3.191),

$$= N^{-2}Np(1-p)$$

by moment (3.192), or

$$e^2 = N^{-1}p(1-p). \tag{3.196}$$

This shows that the error becomes arbitrarily small as $N\to\infty$, which is not startling and, in fact, proves the law of large numbers (3.6).

It is more useful to define a relative error $\varepsilon \equiv e/p$ and recast (3.196) as

$$N = \frac{1-p}{p\varepsilon^2}. \tag{3.197}$$

This may be used for calculating the sample size N required of a *prescribed* accuracy.

Result (3.197) shows that if the event in question is rare, i.e., p is very small, then N must be very large to meet a prescribed ε. The rare event requires much observation for its probability to be estimated with any accuracy.

Also, noting that $\varepsilon < 1$, since N varies inversely as the *second* power of ε then N must be very large if ε is to be modestly small. An example points this up.

3.11.2 Illustrative Example

Computers contain a large number of binary components, which are either in an "on" or an "off" state. A *properly functioning component* is as apt to be on as off in the long run. It is desired to test one of these elements for "fairness", i.e., whether it has a bias toward being on more than being off in the long run. A "fair" component would have a probability p of being on of exactly $1/2$. An "unfair" component should be replaced.

A proposed method for measuring p is to simply count up the number m of times the component is on during N observations, and form ratio m/N. How large must N be to estimate fairness with 1% accuracy?

Using (3.197) with $\varepsilon = 0.01$ and $p = 1/2$ (the component is probably close to being fair), we obtain $N = 10{,}000$ observations required.

3.12 The Multinomial Distribution

A binary experiment, described in Sect. 3.10, has but two possible outcomes. The statistics of a binary experiment were established in Sect. 3.10. Knowing these statistics, we were able in Sect. 3.11 to analyze a method for estimating the probability of an event.

Suppose *we now want to find a method for estimating the joint probability of occurrence of M distinct events.* It turns out that we then have to know the statistics of an *M'ary* experiment. This is an experiment with M possible outcomes. An example is the tossing of a die, which has $M=6$ possible outcomes.

3.12.1 Derivation

Regarding the die experiment, let this be repeated N times. Let m_1 describe the number of times die value 1 appears, etc., for $m_2, \cdots, m_M$, with $M=6$ here. We want to know the joint probability $P_N(m_1, \cdots, m_M)$.

The analysis is completely analogous to the binary case of Sect. 3.10, so that we can be brief here. We follow the same steps as in the binary derivation.

Any one sequence of trials giving rise to the required m_1 events 1, m_2 events 2, $\cdots$, m_M events M *will have the same* probability of occurrence

$$p_1^{m_1} p_2^{m_2} \cdots p_M^{m_M}. \tag{3.198}$$

The product form is the result of independence from trial to trial, and independence among the outcomes.

Therefore, we have only to enumerate the *number of ways* $W(m_1, \cdots, m_M)$ the events in question can occur and multiply this by (3.198) to form the answer.

$W(m_1, \cdots, m_M)$ may be thought of as the number of sets of m_1 indistinguishable elements of type 1, and m_2 indistinguishable elements of type 2, etc., that may be formed out of a total of N elements. This is known to describe the multinomial coefficient (see [3.29])

$$W_N(m_1, \cdots, m_M) \equiv \frac{N!}{m_1! \cdots m_M!}. \tag{3.199}$$

Combining (3.198, 199), we therefore have

$$P_N(m_1, \cdots, m_M) = \frac{N!}{m_1! \cdots m_M!} p_1^{m_1} \cdots p_M^{m_M} \tag{3.200}$$

where $N = m_1 + \cdots + m_M$.

3.12.2 Illustrative Example

At a party for 27 people, prizes of the following kind were to be distributed one to a person: 4 noisemakers, 10 paper hats, 8 balloons, and 5 water pistols. All the noisemakers are identical, etc., for the other prizes. In how many ways can the prizes be distributed among the party goers?

This is the number of ways of forming $M=4$ sets consisting of $m_1=4$ (indistinguishable elements, $m_2=8$ elements, $m_3=10$ elements, and $m_4=5$ elements, respectively. The answer is then the multinomial coefficient

$$\frac{(4+8+10+5)!}{4!\,8!\,10!\,5!}$$

or about 8 quadrillion.

3.13 Estimating an Unknown Probability Distribution

Determining an unknown probability distribution from given data is a central problem of statistics. We touched on this problem in Sects. 3.1.12 (end) and 3.11. The chief problem usually lies in the sparsity of the data. For example, suppose only a few moments of the random variable are known. This situation cannot, of course, *uniquely* define an unknown probability law. Here we show that with insufficient data to uniquely determine a probability law, the law which has *maximum entropy* is the best estimate in a certain sense. This method was first proposed by *Jaynes* [3.30] in 1968.

3.13.1 Approach

Suppose an experiment (say, rolling a die having *unknown fairness*) is repeated N times. Each repetition has possible outcomes $i=1, 2, 3, \cdots, M$, and m_i represents the number of times outcome i occurs over the N experiments. With $\{p_i\}$ the *unknown probabilities*, of course

$$\sum_{i=1}^{M} p_i = 1. \tag{3.201}$$

Assume that N is so large that the m_i satisfy the law of large numbers (3.6) with arbitrary precision, so that

$$m_i = N p_i. \tag{3.202}$$

The $\{p_i\}$ are to be regarded as unknowns. Let us further assume that the $\{m_i\}$ are not direct observables. [If they were, we could simply use (3.202) to directly solve for the $\{p_i\}$. End of problem.]

Instead, suppose the observable data to consist of quantities $\{F_k\}$, where

$$\sum_{i=1}^{M} f_k(i) p_i = F_k, \qquad k = 1, 2, \ldots, K, \tag{3.203}$$

with

$$K < M - 1. \tag{3.204}$$

Thus, the $\{F_k\}$ are expected values of some function of the outcomes i. For example, with $f_k(i) = i^k$, the $\{F_k\}$ are the kth moment m_k of $\{p_i\}$. Data $\{F_k\}$ may arise either out of observing their *approximate values* from the N experiments, or simply as "prior knowledge" independent of the N experiments.

Note that, if $K = M - 1$, the $K + 1$ linear equations (3.201, 203) would be sufficient for uniquely solving for the unknown $\{p_i\}$. However, it is more usual to have insufficient data, i.e., a situation where there are more unknowns $\{p_i\}$ than equations. In this case, we have an underconstrained problem at hand. This means *that there is an infinity of sets* $\{p_i\}$ that could give rise to the observed $\{F_k\}$.

Here we ask, which of these sets is the "most likely" to have given rise to the $\{F_k\}$? An answer is provided by the result (3.199). This states that each set $\{m_i\}$ [or $\{p_i\}$, via (3.202)] has a known and generally *different* degeneracy W. *Knowing nothing else about the* $\{m_i\}$, *it is logical to choose it as the set that has maximum degeneracy* $W(m_1, \cdots, m_M)$.

Hence our solution is $\hat{p}_i = m_i/N$, with $\{m_i\}$ chosen to satisfy

$$\frac{N!}{m_1! m_2! \cdots m_M} = \text{maximum}, \tag{3.205}$$

as a supplement to the data equations (3.203). This was Jaynes' solution to the problem of insufficient data.

3.13.2 A Criterion Based on Entropy

It turns out to be more convenient to maximize the ln of (3.205) which by Stirling's approximation

$$\ln(u!) \simeq u \ln u$$

becomes

$$- \sum_{i=1}^{N} m_i \ln m_i = \text{maximum}. \tag{3.206}$$

[The term $N \ln N$ is an additive constant that does not affect the solution $\{m_i\}$, and so is absorbed into the right-hand side of (3.206)].

Using (3.202), we see that

$$-\sum m_i \ln m_i = -\sum N p_i \ln N p_i = -N \sum p_i \ln p_i - N \ln N \sum p_i$$

$$= -N \sum p_i \ln p_i - N \ln N.$$

Hence the principle (3.206) becomes

$$-\sum_{i=1}^{M} p_i \ln p_i = \text{maximum}, \tag{3.207}$$

where again a multiplicative constant and an additive constant have been absorbed into the right-hand side.

The left-hand quantity is called the "entropy" of the distribution $\{p_i\}$, and is denoted by H. Hence, we have established the important principle that, *given insufficient data for estimating a probability distribution, the probability distribution which has a maximum entropy and satisfies the data is the most likely*. It is most likely in the sense that it is defined by outcome occurrences $m_1, \cdots, m_M$, which can be realized in the maximum number of ways.

3.13.3 Explicit Solution

But the $\{p_i\}$ obeying (3.207) must also obey the constraint equations (3.201, 203) due to *the data*. Standard use of Lagrange multipliers μ, $\{\lambda_i\}$ tacked onto the basic requirement (3.207), as in

$$-\sum_i p_i \ln p_i + \mu \left(\sum_i p_i - 1 \right) + \sum_{k=1}^{K} \lambda_k \left[\sum_i f_k(i) p_i - F_k \right]$$

$$= \text{maximum}, \tag{3.208}$$

allows for the constraints.

We may now find the set $\{\hat{p}_i\}$ that accomplishes the maximum. By setting $\partial/\partial p_i$ of (3.208) equal to zero, in turn for $i = 1, 2, \cdots, M$, we get

$$-1 - \ln \hat{p}_i + \mu + \sum_{k=1}^{K} \lambda_k f_k(i) = 0,$$

with solution

$$\hat{p}_i = \exp \left[-1 + \mu + \sum_{k=1}^{K} \lambda_k f_k(i) \right]. \tag{3.209}$$

Thus, the required probability distribution is always an exponential function. The precise answer depends upon the Lagrange multiplier values μ, $\{\lambda_k\}$ used in (3.209). These are solved for by substituting the form (3.209) for $\hat{p}_i$ into the constraint equations

$$\sum_i \hat{p}_i = 1$$

$$\sum_i f_k(i)\hat{p}_i = F_k, \quad k = 1, 2, ..., K . \qquad (3.210)$$

These comprise $K + 1$ equations in the $K + 1$ unknowns μ, $\{\lambda_k\}$, so that a *unique solution* now results.

In summary, the extremum requirement (3.205) on maximum degeneracy has changed a situation where there is an infinity of solutions to one where there is a unique solution, *the maximum likely.*

3.13.4 Example

The first two moments of a random variable i are known. Find $\{p_i\}$, $i = 1, 2, \cdots, N \gg 2$. Here the constraint equations (3.210) are

$$\sum_i \hat{p}_i = 1$$

and

$$\sum_i i^k \hat{p}_i = m_k, \quad k = 1, 2 .$$

Thus $f_k(i) = i^k$, $F_k = m_k$, and the estimate of $\{\hat{p}_i\}$ is from (3.209)

$$\hat{p}_i = \exp[-1 + \mu + \lambda_1 i + \lambda_2 i^2] .$$

Thus, $\hat{p}_i$ is a quadratic exponential.

Rather than go the final step and solve for the parameters μ, λ_1, and λ_2 that satisfy the three constraints, we proceed to the simpler problem where the random variable i is replaced by a continuous random variable x.

3.13.5 Transition to a Continuous Random Variable x

The entire derivation carries through if each p_i is represented as an integrated segment of a continuous $p(x)$ curve,

$$p_i \equiv \int_{x_i}^{x_i + \Delta x} p(x) dx .$$

We choose Δx small enough that the approximation

$$p_i = p(x_i)\Delta x$$

is good to whatever degree of accuracy we want. Substituting this into principle (3.208), we get

$$-\sum_i \Delta x\, p(x_i)\ln p(x_i) - \sum_i \Delta x\, p(x_i)\ln \Delta x$$

$$+\mu\left[\sum_i p(x_i)\Delta x - 1\right] + \sum_{k=1}^{K} \lambda_k\left[\sum_i f_k(x_i)p(x_i)\Delta x - F_k\right]$$

$$= \text{maximum}.$$

This is to be evaluated in the limit $\Delta x \to 0$.

The second sum here may be evaluated as the additive constant (albeit large)

$$-\ln \Delta x$$

which does not affect the maximization. Hence it may be ignored. [Note that the left-hand side of (3.208) can be added to by any constant, without affecting the maximization. Choose the constant $+\ln \Delta x$. Then it is exactly cancelled here, *before* taking the $\lim \Delta x \to 0$.]

The remaining sums converge toward corresponding integrals, and we get

$$-\int dx\, p(x)\ln p(x) + \mu[\int dx\, p(x) - 1]$$

$$+ \sum_{k=1}^{K} \lambda_k[\int dx\, f_k(x)p(x) - F_k] = \text{maximum}. \qquad (3.211)$$

The integration limits go over all x.

This is the estimation principle for a *continuous* random variable x. It is basically a principle of maximum entropy

$$H \equiv -\int dx\, p(x)\ln p(x) = \text{maximum} \qquad (3.212)$$

for the *continuous* probability density $p(x)$ to be estimated.

3.13.6 The Smoothness Property; Least Biased Aspect

This result has an interesting *numerical* property. If a function $p_1(x)$ has an entropy H_1, and a new function $p_2(x)$ is formed from $p_1(x)$ by perturbing $p_1(x)$ toward a smoother curve, then *the new entropy H_2 must exceed H_1* (see Fig. 3.26). Hence, by maximum entropy we really mean *maximally smooth*.

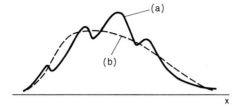

Fig. 3.26. Curves (a) and (b) are two probability curves obeying a constraint F_k on area. The smoother curve (b) has the higher entropy H

In probabilistic terms this means least biased toward any particular value of x. That is, $p(x)$ satisfying maximum entropy has a minimum of spikes about particular events x. This is a correct tendency, since with insufficient data $\{F_k\}$ to uniquely determine $p(x)$, we would want an estimate of $p(x)$ to be as equanimous or impartial in x as the data would allow.

3.13.7 Solution

Problem (3.211) is very easy to solve. The Lagrangian (or integrand) L for dx is

$$L[x, p(x)] = -p(x)\ln p(x) + \mu p(x) + \sum_k \lambda_k f_k(x) p(x).$$

Hence L does not have terms $dp(x)/dx$, and the well-known solution is the Euler-Lagrange equation

$$\partial L/\partial p(x) = 0. \tag{3.213}$$

Taking this derivative,

$$-1 - \ln\hat{p}(x) + \mu + \sum_k \lambda_k f_k(x) = 0,$$

or

$$\hat{p}(x) = \exp\left[-1 + \mu + \sum_k \lambda_k f_k(x)\right]. \tag{3.214}$$

The coefficients μ, λ_k are found by substituting form (3.214) into the $K+1$ constraint conditions in (3.211).

3.13.8 Maximized H

The maximum in H attained by the solution (3.214) is

$$H_{\max} \equiv -\int dx\, \hat{p}(x)\ln\hat{p}(x),$$

which by substitution of (3.214) becomes simply

$$H_{\max} = -1 + \mu + \sum_k \lambda_k F_k. \tag{3.215}$$

3.13.9 Illustrative Example

This is analogous to the previous, discrete example. Suppose that nothing is known about a random variable x except its mean $\bar{x}$ and variance σ_x^2. What is the most likely $p(x)$ to have these two moments?

Here

$$f_1(x) = x, \qquad f_2(x) = (x - \bar{x})^2,$$
$$F_1 = \bar{x} \quad \text{and} \quad F_2 = \sigma_x^2.$$

Then by (3.214)

$$\hat{p}(x) = \exp[-1 + \mu + \lambda_1 x + \lambda_2 (x - \bar{x})^2]. \tag{3.216}$$

Parameters λ_1, λ_2, μ are found by substitution of (3.216) into the constraint equations

$$\int dx\, \hat{p}(x) = 1$$

$$\int dx\, f_k(x)\hat{p}(x) = F_k, \qquad k = 1, 2. \tag{3.217}$$

It is not hard to show that μ, λ_1, and λ_2 satisfying these constraints yield

$$\hat{p}(x) = (2\pi)^{-1/2}\sigma_x^{-1} \exp[-(x - \bar{x})^2/2\sigma_x^2]. \tag{3.218}$$

That is, x is a *normal* random variable. *The normal curve is then the smoothest and most equiprobable law (by Sect. 3.13.6) consistent with knowledge of the first two moments.* Notice in fact that it shows bias toward only one value, the mean. There is only one maximum to the curve, at the mean value, and the curve tapers off about the maximum in an optimally smooth way.

Other applications of the overall approach have been made by *Wragg* and *Dowson* [3.31]. These authors have computer-programmed the algorithm, and applied it to realistic data consisting of $k > 2$ moments.

We note in passing that the Gram-Charlier estimate (3.30) of a probability law cannot coincide with a maximum likely solution (3.214), except in the particular case (3.218). The maximum likely estimate must always be a pure exponential (3.214), whereas the Gram-Charlier is a Gaussian *times a polynomial.*

3.14 A Well-Known Distribution Derived

We shall show next that the estimation procedure makes sense on physical grounds.

Suppose N particles with average energy $\langle E \rangle = kT$ are enjoying Brownian motion. What is the most likely probability law $p(E)$ for describing the energy E of a particle?

The data we have at hand about the random variable E are evidently the first moment

$$\int_0^\infty dE\, E\hat{p}(E) = kT, \tag{3.219}$$

and the ever-present normalization

$$\int_0^\infty dE\, \hat{p}(E) = 1. \tag{3.220}$$

According to (3.214), the solution for $\hat{p}(E)$ is

$$\hat{p}(E) = \exp(1 + \mu + \lambda_1 E). \tag{3.221}$$

Parameters μ and λ_1 are found by making the solution (3.221) satisfy the two constraint equations (3.219, 220). The result is

$$\mu = 1 - \ln(kT), \quad \lambda_1 = -(kT)^{-1},$$

so that by (3.221)

$$\hat{p}(E) = (kT)^{-1} e^{-E/kT}. \tag{3.222}$$

This is the Boltzmann distribution!

In fact, the Boltzmann distribution *is known to be the true* probability law for the given physical situation. This lends credence to the estimation procedure we have used.

It also shows that the Boltzmann distribution has the special properties we derived for a solution (3.214). That is, it is the single *most probable* law, also the smoothest, most equiprobable and consequently most random, law consistent with a single average energy constraint on the particles.

As a corollary, if Nature required some additional constraint on the particles, such as a maximum permissible E or a second moment for E, a *different* probability law $p(E)$ would result by use of solution (3.214). So, since the Boltzmann law is observed to be true, *there must be only the one constraint* $\langle E \rangle$ on the particles.

Finally, all this ties in with the second law of thermodynamics, according to which the entropy of the universe must always be increasing. Since the estimate (3.222) *already has maximum entropy*, via property (3.212), it shows that *a general estimate* (3.214) *has a built-in bias toward satisfying the second law*. This is a healthy tendency for a general estimation procedure to have, and makes the whole approach believable.

3.15 Optical Applications

The principle (3.207) of maximum entropy may be applied to photons as well. We give two examples below.

3.15.1 Estimation of an Object Scene Using Maximum Entropy

An optical object is a two-dimensional array of radiating photons. For purposes of estimating it, subdivide the object into finite cells of spatial extent Δx. Let object cell (x_i, y_j) have m_{ij} photons that will radiate to the observer over the time T of observation (exposure) (see Fig. 3.27). We want to estimate these as $\hat{m}_{ij}$. We follow the approach of *Frieden* [3.32]. This is an approximation to the quantum optical calculation of *Kikuchi* and *Soffer* [3.33].

Suppose that the photons radiate independently, and that they number N in all, i.e.,

$$\sum_{i,j=1}^{M} \hat{m}_{ij} = N .\tag{3.223}$$

N takes on the role of total light flux from the object. Assume this to be known.

Let nothing be known about the distribution $\{m_{ij}\}$, except for its *conjugate image* i_{mn},

$$i_{mn} = \sum_{i,j=1}^{M} \hat{m}_{ij} s(m-i, n-j), \quad m=1, 2, \cdots, K, \quad n=1, 2, \cdots, K \tag{3.224}$$

observed as data. s is the point spread function. What is the maximum likely set $\{m_{ij}\}$ consistent with the data (3.223, 224)? This problem is highly suggestive of the derivation (3.201–210), and we proceed accordingly.

The number of ways W of attaining a set $(m_{11}, m_{12}, \cdots, m_{MM})$ is the multinomial coefficient

$$W = \frac{N!}{m_{11}! m_{12}! \cdots m_{MM}!} .$$

We seek the set $\{m_{ij}\}$ that attains the maximum in W. This is the most degenerate object, or the one which could have occurred in the maximum number of ways. In this sense, it is the most likely object as well.

PHOTONS

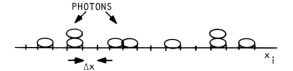

x_i

Δx

Fig. 3.27. A model distribution of photons across a line of the object. These photons will later be detected in the image plane

Taking the ln, and attaching on the constraints (3.223, 224) as before, we have an estimation principle

$$-\sum_{i,j} \hat{m}_{ij} \ln \hat{m}_{ij} + \mu(\sum \hat{m}_{ij} - N)$$

$$+ \sum_{m,n} \lambda_{mn} \left[\sum_{i,j} \hat{m}_{ij} s(m-i, n-j) - i_{mn}\right] = \text{maximum}.$$

The first term on the left is the *spatial entropy* across the object, and we see that it wants to be maximized, subject to the indicated Lagrange constraints.

The preceding may be solved by setting $\partial/\partial \hat{m}_{ij} = 0$, yielding

$$\hat{m}_{ij} = \exp\left[-1 + \mu + \sum_{m,n} \lambda_{mn} s(m-i, n-j)\right]. \tag{3.225}$$

This is the maximum likely and maximum entropy object. We may use it as an estimate of the true object that satisfies constraints (data) (3.223) and (3.224).

Note that this object representation is explicitly positive. It also *exceeds the optical bandwidth* 2Ω for s if the $\{\lambda_{mn}\}$ are finite. For, by (3.225)

$$\hat{m}_{ij} = A\{1 + \sum \lambda_{mn} s(m-i, n-j) + [\sum \lambda_{mn} s(m-i, n-j)]^2/2! + \cdots\}$$

in a Taylor expansion. But the first sum is band limited to $(-\Omega, \Omega)$, the second to $(-2\Omega, 2\Omega)$, etc. Hence, with the $\{\lambda_{mn}\}$ large enough that the nth Taylor sum is significant, m_{ij} is band limited to interval $(-n\Omega, +n\Omega)$. In practice, n is commonly of size 3–5, allowing an extrapolation by these multiples.

Examples of maximum entropy estimates (3.225) are given in Figs. 1.14b and 1.15b.

3.15.2 A Return to the Speckle Phenomenon

The formation of statistical speckle images was discussed in Sect. 3.6, with the result (3.151a) for the probability $p_I(x)$ of intensity value I. When combined with identity (3.152), this becomes

$$p_I(x) = \langle x \rangle^{-1} \exp(-x/\langle x \rangle). \tag{3.226}$$

This was derived on the basis of the *detailed statistical model* of Sect. 3.6.3 for phase fluctuations across the diffuser.

We note that (3.226) is usable only if the average value $\langle x \rangle$ of intensity is known. Indeed, this is the only parameter assumed known in (3.226). Suppose, in fact, that *nothing was known about the formation of speckle, except this piece of datum*. That is, we did not choose to model the diffuser's phase distribution, either through ignorance or choice. What would the maximum entropy approach of *Jaynes* give us as an estimate $\hat{p}_I(x)$?

In fact, we went through precisely this analysis in Sect. 3.14, in deriving the Boltzmann law (3.222). There, as well as here, the only data constraint on the maximum entropy solution was the mean value of x (there energy). The resulting solution was (3.222), and this is precisely of our derived form (3.226) for speckle!

Hence, for the case of speckle imagery,

$$\hat{p}_I(x) = p_I(x). \tag{3.227}$$

The maximum-entropy estimate equals the true law.

What can be made of this correspondence? It appears that the statistical model of Sects. 3.6.3 and 3.6.5 chosen for formation of speckle coincides with *actual* (not just estimated) formation of the image according to maximum entropy. What this means is that the details of the model allowed for *maximum randomness* in intensity I. In fact, examination of the details of the model – *uniformly* random phase over $(0, 2\pi)$, statistical *independence* from one scatter spot to the next – bears this out.

Furthermore, we can generalize this result. What if the diffuser model *had not* been maximally random? Suppose, for example, there was instead a degree of correlation between different scatter spots? We would not expect the simple law (3.226) to follow now. However, neither would the maximum entropy result follow this law. The existence of a known correlation dependence between scatter points would in turn *reflect itself in a new constraint upon the intensity I,* which means new data. Hence, the maximum entropy estimate would now have *two constraints* – the old one on mean intensity and this new one – to obey. Accordingly, a new maximum entropy estimate would result, and it seems reasonable to expect that this one would *remain equal* to the newly derived speckle distribution $p_I(x)$ as well.

In other words, a maximum entropy estimate $p(x)$ *is as true* as are the details of the constraints $\{F_k\}$ imposed upon it. If *all* the physical constraints $\{F_k\}$ are accounted for, and the input data are 100 % accurate, then we can expect the estimate $\hat{p}(x)$ *to equal* the true law $p(x)$.

Conversely, *incomplete* knowledge of the constraints leads to an estimate $\hat{p}(x)$ which is only an approximation to the true $p(x)$, but however a "smoothest" or least-biased approximation, as discussed in Sect. 3.13.6.

Moreover, as was exemplified with the Boltzmann law derivation (3.222), no matter what degree of completeness characterizes the "inputs" $\{K_k\}$, the estimate $\hat{p}(x)$ *is always in compliance* with the second law of thermodynamics.

For these reaons, we believe the maximum entropy method of *probability estimation* to be the best one available. As for *general estimation problems* in optics, whenever the unknowns can be physically modeled as a probability distribution (as in Sect. 3.15.1) the approach is applicable.

3.16 Linear Regression

In previous sections we have *assumed* certain statistical models to fit given physical phenomena, such as laser speckle. Here we take up the complementary problem of establishing or *estimating* the particular model that fits new and unknown phenomena.

Suppose a new type of film is discovered. It has *unknown development characteristics*, so an experiment is conducted to find these. Specifically, the effects of exposure time t, light level E, and developer temperature T upon film density D are sought. By testing five different samples of the film, the data in Table 3.2 are obtained. *Can a functional relation $D(t, E, T)$ be estimated from these data?*

This problem is frequently encountered in statistics. In general, a parameter y depends on M other variables $x_1, \cdots, x_M$ in an unknown way. We want to establish the dependence $y(x_1, \cdots, x_M)$ by observing N data "points" $(y, x_1, \cdots, x_M)$ as seen in Table 3.3. Each row of data corresponds to a different experiment. Each column of data represents the numerical values taken by that variable over the experiments.

In the "unknown film" case a form for the dependence $D(t)$ alone is suggested by plotting the dependence $D(t)$ indicated in Table 3.2. This is shown by the dots in Fig. 3.28. The dependence seems erratically linear, i.e., perhaps linear plus a random variable. The dashed line, for example, could be viewed as a fit to the data. This kind of quasi-linear behavior is observable in diverse

Table 3.2. Data for the unknown film

D	t [min]	E [m Cd s]	T [°C]
2.6	18.0	1.0	20.0
2.0	12.0	1.0	21.1
1.6	10.0	0.8	18.8
0.7	8.0	0.1	19.6
0.2	3.0	0.07	20.8

Table 3.3. Data in the general case

y	x_1	x_2		x_M
y_1	x_{11}	x_{21}	$\cdots$	x_{M1}
y_2	x_{12}	x_{22}	$\cdots$	x_{M2}
.	.	.	$\cdots$	.
.	.	...	$\cdots$	.
.	.	.	$\cdots$	.
y_N	x_{1N}	x_{2N}	$\cdots$	x_{MN}

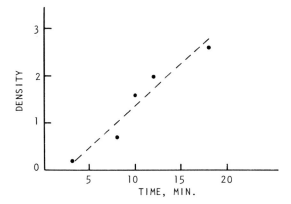

Fig. 3.28. Density versus exposure time alone

phenomena, for a limited range of experimental variation. Also, since it is the *simplest* type of dependence (and the smoothest) it is often *assumed* as a model form, and is called a "linear model". A good introductory reference to this subject is *Smillie* [3.34].

We should note that instead of linearity in a variable, x_n, the observer might know or suspect that the relation $y(x)$ is linear in, say, $\log x_n$. Must the linear model in all the $(x_1, \cdots, x_M)$ be abandoned because of this one nonlinearity in an x variable? No, for by simply renaming $t_n = \log x_n$, a linear theory holds for y in terms of the new variable and all the remaining $\{x_n\}$. This renaming procedure can be extended to two or more such nonlinear variables, as well.

3.16.1 The Linear Model

By the linear model it is in general assumed that the dependence $y(x_1, \cdots, x_M)$ is of the form

$$y = \alpha_0 + \alpha_1 x_1 + a_2 x_n + \cdots + \alpha_M x_M + u \tag{3.228}$$

with u a random variable that perturbs the data away from an ideal linear dependence. Parameter u is intended to represent all *unknown* effects that can possibly influence y.

The coefficients $\{\alpha_m\}$ fix the answer to the particular physical problem. Note that the relative sizes of the $\{\alpha_m\}$ adjust to the different units taken for the different physical quantities $\{x_m\}$.

Assumption of the linear form (3.228) really derives from a state of complete ignorance about the physical phenomena involved. This has its parallel with the estimation principle (3.212) for an unknown probability law $p(x)$. By (3.212) the unknown $p(x)$ is *also maximally smooth*, in a certain sense. The unifying principle is perhaps that the greater the state of ignorance we are in about a particular physical process, the smoother we ought to assume it to be. To assume unwarranted oscillations is to imply knowledge that simply does not exist.

By the same token, the linear model can be wrong enough to be misleading in its predictions about the phenomenon. This must be kept in mind. Remember that the Earth used to be modeled linearly, its shape presumed *flat*,[4] prior to Columbus. One of the predictions of this model was of course that Columbus would sail off its edge. *Caveat emptor!*

3.16.2 Criterion for Solution

Ultimately, we can solve for the unknown $\{\alpha_m\}$ by substituting the data from Table 3.3 into (3.228). A system of linear equations in unknowns $\{\alpha_m\}$ results. However, usually there are many more data than there are unknowns $\{\alpha_m\}$. This results from the human propensity for producing more data rather than thinking up new potential physical causes $\{x_m\}$. For example, see Table 3.2 where $N=5$ whereas $M=3$. We could easily double N by further repetition of the experiment.

Hence if we substitute the data values from Table 3.3 into the linear model (3.228) we end up with a "tall" system of N linear equations in $M+1$ unknowns $\{\alpha_m\}$, $N>M+1$. This is an over constrained situation which does not have an exact solution $\{\alpha_m\}$.

We therefore seek the best *inexact* solution, using the criterion of minimum squared error to define "best". That is, we want the set of $\{\hat{\alpha}_m\}$ which satisfies

$$\sum_{n=1}^{N} \left(y_n - \hat{\alpha}_0 - \sum_{m=1}^{M} \hat{\alpha}_m x_{mn} \right)^2 = \text{minimum}. \tag{3.229}$$

Notice that if the linear model (3.228) *really is* correct, in fact the minimum achieved is precisely

$$\sum_{n=1}^{N} u_n^2,$$

the cumulative error due to all unknown effects. By seeking the minimum in (3.229) we are tacitly assuming that the unknown effects tend to be small and to randomly "balance out" over many experiments.

---

4 It seems to be a human quirk to readily accept a linear or "flat" theory and to initially reject nonlinear theories as "controversial". Of course the ancient Greeks already knew the Earth was round, even having computed its radius with astonishing accuracy. However, this "theory" was chosen to be ignored by their successors. This has parallels today. Nonlinear image restoring methods are still mistrusted and shunned, except when a truly difficult restoring problem exists. Some people have remarked that they feel uneasy if they *don't* see Gibbsian artifact oscillations in the output!

3.16.3 Solution

This is obtained in the usual way, by setting $\partial/\partial \hat{\alpha}_m$ of (3.229) equal to zero for each of $m = 0, 1, \cdots, M$. The mth equation so obtained is

$$\sum_{n=1}^{N} x_{mn}\left(y_n - \hat{\alpha}_0 - \sum_{k=1}^{M} \hat{\alpha}_k x_{kn}\right) = 0.$$

This is linear in unknowns $\{\hat{\alpha}_k\}$. Moreover, the system of equations is square, so there is now a *unique solution*

$$\hat{\boldsymbol{\alpha}} = ([X^T][X])^{-1}[X]^T \boldsymbol{y}. \tag{3.230}$$

Matrix $[X]$ is formed from the data as

$$[X] \equiv \begin{pmatrix} 1 & x_{11} & x_{21} & \cdots & x_{M1} \\ 1 & x_{12} & x_{22} & \cdots & x_{M2} \\ \vdots & \vdots & \vdots & & \vdots \\ 1 & x_{1N} & x_{2N} & \cdots & x_{MN} \end{pmatrix}$$

and $\boldsymbol{y}$, $\hat{\boldsymbol{\alpha}}$ are vectors

$$\boldsymbol{y} \equiv (y_1 \, y_2 \cdots y_N)^T$$
$$\hat{\boldsymbol{\alpha}} \equiv (\alpha_0 \, \alpha_1 \cdots \alpha_M)^T.$$

Computer implementation of the solution (3.230) is quite easily carried out, since many standard algorithms exist for taking the required inverse and transpose operations.

3.16.4 Return to Film Problem

The data in Table 3.2 were input into solution (3.230). The resulting $\{\alpha_m\}$ when substituted into linear model (3.228) predicts the dependence

$$\hat{D} = -0.285 + 0.099t + 0.996E + 0.005T \tag{3.231}$$

for the estimated film density $\hat{D}$. The relation is reasonable regarding the plus signs for the coefficients, since this correctly implies that D increases with t, E, and T.

3.16.5 "Significant" Parameters

From the very small size for the coefficient of T, it appears that D may not depend very strongly on T, at least over the range of T tested out. To check this hypothesis, we need a measure of the contribution of T to the variability of $\hat{D}$ in (3.231). That is, *if the variation of the $\{T_n\}$ data values causes $\hat{D}$ to fluctuate strongly, then T is a strong or significant contributor to $\hat{D}$,* and conversely.

A measure of variability is of course the variance. Hence, we propose to first compute the variance σ_D^2 in $\hat{D}$ over the ensemble of data. This indicates how strongly all the variables t, E, T as a whole contribute to D. Next, we carry through the same calculation, now ignoring the contribution of T in (3.231). Call the result $\sigma_D'^2$. This tells us how strongly variables t and E *alone* contribute to D. Therefore the difference in the two variances σ_D^2, $\sigma_D'^2$ indicates how strongly T *by itself* contributes to D. A small difference points up a weak dependence on T, and conversely. If weak, T is called *insignificant.*

It is customary to compute the variance from the *mean data* value

$$\bar{y} \equiv N^{-1} \sum_{n=1}^{N} y_n \tag{3.232}$$

rather than from the mean *linear model* value $N^{-1}\sum \hat{y}_n$. In practice the two means do not differ that much usually. The variance is then called the *sample variance*, and obeys

$$\sigma_y^2 \equiv N^{-1} \sum_{n=1}^{N} (y_n - \bar{y})^2. \tag{3.233}$$

The two sample variances in question turn out to be

$$\sigma_D^2 = 0.754 \quad \text{and} \quad \sigma_D'^2 = 0.766.$$

The difference in these is 0.012, numerically small, but is it small enough to consider T insignificant? We have to apply some probability theory to the problem.

Now parameters $\{x_m\}$ are statistically independent contributors to y (for example, t certainly does not influence E). Then by linear form (3.228) the variance in y should be a weighted sum of variances in the $\{x_m\}$.

$$\sigma_y^2 = \sum_{m=1}^{M} \alpha_m^2 \sigma_m^2 \equiv \sum_{m=1}^{M} \mu_m^2. \tag{3.234}$$

The variances here are assumed representable by *ensemble* variances over the N data. If all terms μ_m^2 were equal this would mean equal "strength" for all the parameters $\{x_m\}$. In this case each μ_m^2 would have the size

$$\mu_m^2 = M^{-1}\sigma_y^2.$$

Hence *the strength of a parameter $\{x_m\}$ can be judged by its variability μ_m^2 relative to value $M^{-1}\sigma_y^2$.*

For example, in the film problem the value 0.012 actually represents μ_T^2 since by independence $\sigma_D^2 = \mu_t^2 + \mu_E^2 + \mu_T^2$ and we formed $\sigma_D^2 - (\mu_t^2 + \mu_E^2)$ to yield 0.012. Also, here $M^{-1}\sigma_y^2$ is $3^{-1} \times 0.754$ or value 0.251. Since $0.012 \ll 0.251$ we conclude that T is indeed a weak contributor to film density D. T is an insignificant factor.

One of the principal aims of *regression analysis* is to find which of the M proposed contributors $\{x_m\}$ to data y are the most significant, and which may be neglected. Obviously the approach used above may be applied one by one to all of the $\{x_m\}$ and a ranking made from the largest to smallest contributions μ_m^2. In this manner the unknown phenomenon y becomes better understood insofar as its real causes.

3.16.6 Actual Regression Work on Basic H&D (Hurter and Driffield) Curve Shape

One of the most elegant pieces of statistical research in optics was performed by *Simonds* [3.35], using regression analysis.

Photographic density D is related to log exposure E in the typical manner shown in Fig. 3.29. However, the precise shape of the curve will depend upon many conditions: film type, development effects such as concentration and temperature of developer, time duration in developer, etc.

Simonds suspected that, when developed under identical conditions, *a wide variety of films would have similar* H&D (Hurter and Driffield) *curves*. This suggests that any film in the test set could be represented as a superposition

$$D(x_i) = \bar{D}(x_i) + \alpha_1 D_1(x_i) + \alpha_2 D_2(x_i) + \cdots + \alpha_M D_M(x_i)$$
$$i = 1, 2, \cdots, 10 \tag{3.235}$$

of some *small subset* of curves $\{D_m(x)\}$ selected from the test set. Here

$$\bar{D}(x_i) \equiv M^{-1} \sum_{m=1}^{M} D_m(x_i)$$

and M is small. In (3.235), $\{x_i\} \equiv \{\log E_i\}$ represents a fixed subdivion of log exposure values at which all H&D curves were observed. There were 10 of these

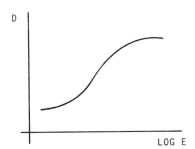

D

LOG E

Fig. 3.29. A typical H &D sensitometric curve

on the 101 curves of the test set. In the context of Tables 3.2 or 3.3, each value x_i designates a new "experiment".

This is evidently a problem in finding significant "parameters", where by parameter here we mean an entire curve $D_m(x_i)$. The problem is to find the subset of such curves which, when used as $D_m(x_i)$ on the right side in (3.235) best *represents* the entire set of 101. [Of course each of the 101 would require a *different* set of coefficients $\{\alpha_m\}$ in (3.235).] Insignificant curves $D_m(x_i)$ would be dropped.

Hence, the optimum set $\{\hat{D}_m(x)\}$ is sought as the solution to a *double* minimization procedure. First, choose a trial set $\{D_m(x)\}$. This may contain considerably fewer than 101 curves, since not all are *significant* (see Sect. 3.16.5). See how well these can be made to fit the kth experimental curve $D_k(x)$ of the set through choice of weights $\{\alpha_m\}$, by solving

$$\sum_{i=1}^{10}\left[D_k(x_i)-\bar{D}(x_i)-\sum_{m=1}^{M}\alpha_m D_m(x_i)\right]^2 \equiv \sigma_k^2 \equiv \text{minimum} \tag{3.236}$$

for the $\{\alpha_m\}$. This has the solution (3.230).

This is done for each value of $k=1, 2, \cdots, 101$. The total mean square error of fit to the 101 is then

$$\sigma^2 \equiv \sum_{k=1}^{101} \sigma_k^2.$$

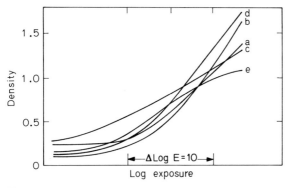

Fig. 3.30. Five H &D curves generated by adding the characteristic vectors of density variability to the mean curve in various amounts, as listed below [3.35]

Curve	α_1	α_2	α_3	α_4
a	0	0	0	0
b	0	-2	-2	0
c	2	2	-2	2
d	0	-2	2	-2
e	0	2	2	0

The process is repeated for another choice of $\{D_m(x)\}$, resulting in another value for σ^2. That set $\{D_m(x)\}$ which causes a *minimum* σ^2 is an intermediate solution. Finally, those curves of this set which do not significantly affect the variability σ_D of the density data are dropped from the set (see Sect. 3.16.5).

It was found in this way that a value $M = 4$ sufficied to accurately represent the class of 101 curves! Hence H&D variability is restricted enough to be fit by four basis curves. Or, *any* H&D *curve may be described by four numbers*.

To illustrate the variability attainable by the four basis curves, Fig. 3.30 shows a range of H&D curves which are generated by the use of coefficients $\{\alpha_m\}$ listed in the table beneath it.

3.17 The Chi-Square Test of Significance

We have already encountered the word "significance" in Sect. 3.16.5. There it was defined to mean strength of contribution to an observed effect. A significant parameter of an experiment would strongly affect the output of the experiment.

Here we ask if the *outputs themselves* are significant. By significant, we now mean strongly different from pure chance outputs. An example makes this clear. Suppose a coin is flipped 5000 times and heads appear 2512 times. If the coin were "fair", heads would appear very close to 2500 times. The question to ask about the experimental output 2512 is, does it *significantly differ* from the pure chance figure 2500? If it does, this is called a significant result, on the grounds that it implies something unusual about the physical makeup of the coin. It implies that there is a physical phenomenon at work which bears looking into.

In general, significance tests are performed upon experimental data to judge whether the experiment really implies that a new or hypothesized physical effect is probably present. *A physical effect really means a systematic bias away from a state of randomness.* Hence a test to measure the extent to which data are random also measures the extent to which they are significant. The more random are the data, the less significant they are.

In order to devise a test of randomness, or significance, of data we have to return to the chi-square distribution derived in Sect. 3.7. We have to see when it arises *in general*, and cast it in a standard form for later use.

3.17.1 Standard Form for the Chi-Square Distribution

The chi-square distribution (3.170) was found to arise out of a particular physical effect, speckle averaging. From the derivation, a chi-square distribution in a random variable z can be seen to hold whenever

$$z = \sum_{n=1}^{N} x_n^2, \quad x_n = N(0, \sigma^2), \tag{3.237}$$

N finite, where the x_n are independently chosen from the same, Gaussian, probability law.

This *standard form* of the problem corresponds to the speckle problem we considered if one makes replacements $2M \to N$, $\sigma^2 \to 2\sigma^2$ in (3.168, 170). The results are

$$p_Z(z) = (\sqrt{2}\sigma)^{-N}[\Gamma(N/2)]^{-1} z^{N/2-1} \exp(-z/2\sigma^2) \tag{3.238}$$

and

$$\Phi_Z(\omega) = (1 - 2i\omega\sigma^2)^{-N/2}. \tag{3.239}$$

The standard problem (3.237) arises in many physical problems. It also may be *contrived*, to be used as a test of significance on certain data. The latter is shown next.

3.17.2 Devising a Test for Significance (A useful reference for this section is *Brandt* [3.36])

This use of the chi-square distribution is much more prevalent than physical uses. In fact, it can be applied to nearly any set of experimental data!

Let there be N possible outcomes for an event (say, $N = 6$ for a roll of a die), and let the events be independent. Suppose the discrete probabilities P_i, $i = 1$, $2, \cdots, N$ for outcomes of the event are assumed as known. Let a large number L of events be observed, with r_i the observed number of outcomes i, for $i = 1, 2, \cdots, N$. This constitutes one experiment.

With $\{P_i\}$ *fixed*, and the experiment repeated, a new set of $\{r_i\}$ will be obtained. These will in general differ from those of the first experiment. Hence, the $\{r_i\}$ are actually random variables. We regard one such set of data $\{r_i\}$.

We want to know whether the observed $\{r_i\}$ are consistent with the presumed $\{P_i\}$. If they are *not*, we call the experiment "interesting", or in fact "significant". By this we mean that the observed $\{r_i\}$ could not have occurred merely as a random outcome of the $\{P_i\}$. Hence, the data are governed by an effect other than mere chance. They are "significant".

And so, we want to devise a test of the $\{r_i\}$ data which will meausre their departure from what one would expect as consistent with the $\{P_i\}$. In fact, consistent data would obey $r_i \simeq LP_i$ for L observed outcomes, L large. This is based on the law of large numbers (3.86).

One obvious measure of this type is a merit function or *statistical measure*

$$\chi \equiv \sum_{i=1}^{N} (r_i - LP_i)^2. \tag{3.240}$$

Thus if χ is large the data are significant.

It turns out that a better statistical measure of significance is

$$\chi^2 \equiv \sum_{i=1}^{N} \frac{(r_i - LP_i)^2}{LP_i},$$ (3.241)

called a "chi-square test" of the data $\{r_i\}$. Recalling that the $\{P_i\}$ are merely constants, this is closely related to form (3.240).

If χ^2 is large, we want to state that the data are significant. But *how large is large?* Suppose we observe a value χ_0^2 and know that the probability

$$P(\chi^2 \geq \chi_0^2) = 0.05.$$ (3.242)

We may then conclude that value χ_0^2 is so large as to be highly unlikely to be consistent with the $\{P_i\}$. We then say that the *data are significant at the 5% level.*

We therefore have to know the probability density for χ^2. This is shown to be chi-square next.

3.17.3 Probability Law for χ^2-Statistic

Consider a single random variable r_i defined in the previous paragraph. What are its statistics? Note first that $P(r_i) \neq P_i$. That is, for a die value, i, $P_i = 1/6$ whereas $P(r_i)$ represents the probability of "spread" in occurrence of values r_i when the experiment consisting of L die rolls *is repeated over and over.*

To get a handle on r_i, we can represent it as a sum

$$r_i = \sum_{l=1}^{L} n_{li}, \quad L \text{ large}$$ (3.243)

formed over outcomes $l = 1, 2, \cdots, L$ of a single experiment. Quantity n_{li} is a "counter", i.e.,

$$n_{li} \equiv \begin{cases} +1 \text{ if outcome } l \text{ has the outcome } i \\ 0 \text{ if outcome } l \text{ does not have outcome } i. \end{cases}$$

Now the n_{li} are independent over l, since the events (say, rolling of a die) are independent. Also, each n_{li} is governed by the *same* binary probability law

$$P(n_{li} = 1) = P_i$$

$$P(n_{li} = 0) = 1 - P_i$$ (3.244)

independent of l. For example, $P_i = 1/6$ for any one die value i, and this is true at all trials l.

Therefore, r_i obeys the central limit theorem, and is normal (see Sect. 3.2.5).

Also, from (3.243)

$$\langle r_i \rangle = L \langle n_i \rangle = L[1 \cdot P_i + 0 \cdot (1 - P_i)]$$
$$= LP_i.$$

Therefore, a new random variable

$$x_i' \equiv r_i - LP_i$$

would be Gaussian, as would another choice

$$x_i \equiv \frac{r_i - LP_i}{(LP_i)^{1/2}}. \tag{3.245}$$

Hence the data test form (3.241) is actually

$$\chi^2 = \sum_{i=1}^{N} x_i^2 \tag{3.246}$$

with each of the x_i Gaussian. However, this is not in the standard form (3.237) because a) the variances $\sigma_{x_i}^2 = 1 - P_i$ and hence are not equal, and b) the $\{x_i\}$ are not all independent. The former may be shown from properties (3.243–245). The latter follows from the fact that

$$\sum_{i=1}^{N} r_i = L.$$

Combining this with (3.245) leads to the remarkable result

$$\sum_{i=1}^{N} x_i P_i^{1/2} = 0. \tag{3.247}$$

This shows that, instead, $N-1$ of the $\{x_i\}$ are independent.

If (3.247) is solved for x_N, and this is substituted into (3.246), there results an expression for χ^2 which is quadratic, with cross terms $x_i x_j$. By a process of completing the square, it is then possible to define a new set of $N-1$ independent random variables y_i which are linear combinations of the x_i, and which have the required constant variance. In fact, $\sigma_y^2 = 1$. *Papoulis* [Ref. 3.1, p. 252] shows this procedure for specific cases $N = 2$ and 3.

Thus

$$\chi^2 = \sum_{i=1}^{N-1} y_i^2, \quad y_i = N(0, 1)$$

which each y_i independent. Comparison with the form (3.237) shows that χ^2 is a chi-square random variable, so that

$$P_{\chi^2}(z) = 2^{-(N-1)/2}\{\Gamma[(N-1)/2]\}^{-1}z^{(N-3)/2}\exp(-z/2). \tag{3.248}$$

Then we may evaluate our criterion for significance

$$P(\chi^2 \geq \chi_0^2) = \int_{\chi_0^2}^{\infty} dz\, p_{\chi^2}(z). \tag{3.249}$$

This gives a numerical value to the probability that an experimental value χ_0^2 for χ^2 will be exceeded. If this P is small, *then the data were significant*. Tables exist for evaluating the integral (3.249). Note that it is only a function of χ_0^2 and N (see, for example, [Ref. 3.12, pp, 978–983]). Alternatively, (3.249) may be evaluated on the computer, using any convenient numerical integration scheme (see Chap. 2 for details).

3.17.4 When Is a Coin Fixed?

We return to the coin problem mentioned at the outset. A coin was flipped 5000 times and heads appeared 2512 times. Is this datum significant, i.e., is it a large departure from the statistics $P_{\text{head}} = P_{\text{tails}} = 1/2$? Notice that here "significance" means biased away from "fairness". We want to know if the coin was "fixed". We have $L = 5000$, $N = 2$, $P_1 = P_2 = 1/2$, $r_1 = 2512$ and $r_2 = 2488$. Then $LP_1 = LP_2 = 2500$, and by (3.241)

$$\chi_0^2 = \frac{(2512-2500)^2}{2500} + \frac{(2488-2500)^2}{2500} = 0.115. \tag{3.250}$$

A table of χ^2, for value $\chi_0^2 = 0.115$ and $N = 2$, discloses $P(\chi^2 > 0.115) = 0.73$. This is not very small. Hence value 0.115 is consistent with chance $(P_1 = P_2 = 1/2)$ as defined. The datum is *not* significant; the coin is probably fair.

The same table shows a required $\chi_0^2 = 3.84$ to get $P(\chi^2 > \chi_0^2) = 0.05$. This would be *significant*. Data that would cause this large a χ_0^2 are $r_1 = 2570$ and $r_2 = 2430$ for the coin-flipping problem.

3.17.5 When Is a Vote Decisive?

This may be considered a controversial use of the chi-square test.

The faculty of a certain graduate department met to vote on whether to continue the foreign language requirement. The vote was *19 to 15* against continuing the requirement. The presider at the meeting declared that this was a "decisive" vote, but one professor disagreed, noting that if but three voters had changed their minds, the decision would have been turned around. Who was right?

Let us analyze the situation from the standpoint of an interested observer, who is not a voter, and who wishes to judge the "mood" (yes or no) of the faculty. To him, each vote decision (yes or no) is not predictable before the vote is made. Each vote decision is then a random variable with two possible outcomes. The outcomes are the data that will help him to decide on the true mood and on its decisiveness.

Suppose the observer had wanted to judge the "bias" of an unknown coin, instead of the "mood" of the faculty. That is, he wanted to know the actual probability p of a head. He has the following evidence for making the judgment on bias: A group of L people flip, in turn, the same coin once each. From the L outcomes as data he can test for significant departure from a "fair" coin $P = \frac{1}{2}$, for example. The χ^2-test may be used for this purpose, as we did previously.

Now he returns to the "mood" determination. The observer's evidence, or data, here are the L independent votes made. These data correspond to the L independent coin flips made above. The coin flips were samples from the one probability law governing the coin's bias. Likewise, here, *the L votes may be regarded as samples from the one probability law governing the faculty's mood overall*. On this basis, he may use the χ^2-test to judge the mood or bias from a $P = \frac{1}{2}$ state.

To test for mood, then, we want to test the data (vote tally) for significant departure from a $P_1 = P_2 = \frac{1}{2}$ statistic. Here $L = 19 + 15 = 34$, $N = 2$, $P_1 = P_2 = \frac{1}{2}$, $r_1 = 19$, and $r_2 = 15$. Then $LP_1 = LP_2 = 17$, and

$$\chi_0^2 = \frac{(19-17)^2}{17} + \frac{(15-17)^2}{17} = 0.47 . \tag{3.251}$$

A table of χ^2 shows $P(\chi^2 > 0.47) = 0.48$. Hence value 0.47 is not overly large, and is consistent with equanimity ($P_1 = P_2 = \frac{1}{2}$). Working backward, to yield a $P(\chi^2 > \chi_0^2) = 0.05$ would have required a $\chi_0^2 \approx 4.0$, or a vote of *23 to 11* on the issue. Hence a 2:1 majority would have been needed to characterize the vote as decisive!

3.17.6 Generalization to L Voters

It is interesting to generalize the last calculation. Suppose L people vote, with two alternatives possible. What margin of vote beyond $L/2$ is needed to define a decisive vote? Since $N = 2$, this still requires a $\chi_0^2 = 4.0$ for confidence at the 0.05 level. Let v = necessary vote for one alternative. Then by (3.241) we have to solve

$$\frac{2(v - L/2)^2}{L/2} = 4.0$$

for v. The solution is simply

$$v = L/2 + \sqrt{L} \, .$$

Hence, *the votes must be at least as extreme as* $L/2 \pm \sqrt{L}$. Examples follow.

If $L = 100$ (number of U.S. Senators), this requires a $60:40$ vote. A two-thirds majority *is, in fact, required* in the Senate. (Could the founding fathers have known some statistics?)

If instead $L = 10^8$ (voters in U.S. presidential election), a margin of 10,000 votes ensures a decisive vote! This is somewhat surprising, as it means that *all* U.S. presidential elections have been decisive! Also, perhaps this result justifies the simple majority rule that (notwithstanding electoral college complications) applies for U.S. presidential elections.

3.17.7 Use as an Image Detector

We found in Sect. 3.4.4 how to create a photon statistical image on the computer (see Fig. 3.20). These images were used in the following study.

Suppose an observer is told that a noisy image he has received is either random noise (as defined below) or is a statistical image of *any object*. The observer has difficulty in making the judgment because there are a limited number of photons in the picture, and this causes the image of a real object to visually resemble pure noise. *Is there a way for him to make an educated guess as to which of the two alternatives is true?*

The chi-square test provides a way. Suppose, as in Fig. 3.20, the data consist of $N = 20$ photon number counts (r_i, $i = 1, \ldots, 20$) across the image. These are given to be formed independently, by the placement of L photons in all. The hypothesis we want to test is that these $\{r_i\}$ are consistent with pure noise, the latter specified as *uniformly random* probabilities $P_i = 1/20$, $i = 1, \ldots, 20$ for photon position across the image. Since all the $\{P_i\}$ are equal, the noise image would tend to be flat, or gray in appearance.

Accordingly we form a χ^2 statistic (3.241)

$$\chi_0^2 \equiv \sum_{i=1}^{20} (r_i - L/20)^2 / (L/20) \tag{3.252}$$

for data departure from an ideal gray state $\{L/20\}$. If χ_0^2 is *sufficiently large*, we surmise that the data are *significantly far* from the gray state to indicate that *noise is not present: a real object is, instead.*

We Monte Carlo-simulated noisy images of the rectangle shown in Fig. 3.20. *Thus, in these tests a real object was always present.* Since we know "ground truth", we can judge the effectiveness of the proposed method.

From the noisy images previously generated in Fig. 3.20, the higher the photon count L is, the less the image resembles random noise. This would make the proposed test (3.252) more apt to be correct for L large. We therefore want to see *how small* L can be to still allow the test to reach the correct conclusion.

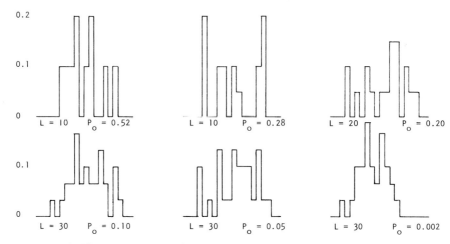

Fig. 3.31. Significance tests on six noisy images

We arbitrarily decide to adopt a 5% confidence level of acceptance. This means that we agree to accept the hypothesis of a real object, if the χ_0^2 value obtained is so large that $P(\chi^2 \geq \chi_0^2) = 0.05$ or less. Here we use the χ^2 test with $N - 1 = 19$ "degrees of freedom".

Figure 3.31 shows some typical results of the experiments. Each plot is of a Monte Carlo-created image of the rectangle due to the number L of photons indicated beneath it. Also indicated there is the value of $P(\chi^2 > \chi_0^2) \equiv P_0$ corresponding to the χ_0^2 (not shown) for that image. Remember that the value $P_0 = 0.05$ is critical.

The images are shown in order of decreasing P_0 from left to right, and downward. The top-left image is so noisy that 52% of the time random noise would give rise to it or something more random. It is not significant. The bottom right image shows a strong enough resemblance to the rectangle image of Fig. 3.20 that its probability of occurrence consistent with pure noise is nearly infinitesimal, $P_0 = 0.002$. It is very significant. The in between curves are at intermediate stages of development away from randomness and toward the rectangle image. Note that the bottom middle curve is the first to be significant on the 5% level.

Regarding total photon number L required for accurate discrimination, we found that for $L = 10$ a significance level $P_0 = 0.05$ was seldom attained, whereas for $L = 30$ it nearly always was attained. This is the kind of tendency we expected, since for a great number of photons the image is so regular that there is no problem of distinguishing it from random noise.

This was, of course, merely one example of use of the χ^2-test upon image data. More generally, the test may be used as a vehicle for deciding upon the presence of any *hypothetical signal* $\{P_i\}$ within a given noisy image. Such signal hypotheses as weak stars, tumors, submarine wakes, and diseased crops are potential candidates for the test. Moreover, the confidence level in use actually represents the probability that a decision, to accept the test image hypothesis, *is wrong*. This is a very important thing to know, and is a real attribute of the test. The test should prove particularly useful in medical diagnostic imagery and in aerial surveillance, where decisions on "significant" departure from standard images are, again, crucial.

3.18 The Probable Error in a Sample Mean: Student's *t*-Distribution

This is a famous example of how statistical methods can be contrived to overcome a problem of inadequate (in fact, missing) information.

Suppose, as in Sect. 3.9, N values of the speed of light c are determined by N independent experiments, and the *sample mean*

$$\bar{c} \equiv N^{-1} \sum_{n=1}^{N} c_n \tag{3.253}$$

is taken. The $\{c_n\}$ are the experimental values of c. The purpose of taking the sample mean is to obtain an improved estimate of c, the true value of the speed of light. The latter is also presumed to be the *theoretical mean* of the probability law whose outputs are the $\{c_n\}$. Thus, we assume

$$c_n = c + e_n, \tag{3.254}$$

where

$$\langle c_n \rangle = c \tag{3.255}$$

and consequently the average error

$$\langle e_n \rangle = 0. \tag{3.256}$$

Since the experiments are independent, we also assume the $\{e_n\}$ to be independent. *We want to know how accurate the sample mean* (3.253) *is.*

This type of problem is widely encountered. For example, a noisy image is scanned with a *finite aperture* in order to beat down speckle (see Sect. 3.7). How accurate a version of the signal image is this scanned image? We shall continue to use the particular notation $\{c_n\}$, while simultaneously addressing the more general problem.

This problem is of course directly answerable if the variance σ_c^2 in the $\{c_n\}$ outputs is known. By the result (3.177), the mean-square error $\sigma_{\bar{c}}^2$ in the sample mean (3.253) obeys simply

$$\sigma_{\bar{c}}^2 = \sigma_c^2 / N. \tag{3.257}$$

Again, this requires σ_c^2 to be known, if a *numerical* value is to be obtained for $\sigma_{\bar{c}}^2$.

Suppose, on the other hand, that σ_c^2 is not known. This is a situation of ignorance regarding the accuracy in the experimental data. When does such a situation arise?

3.18.1 Cases Where Data Accuracy Is Unknown

If an experiment is of the "quick-and-dirty" variety, where large errors are expected, the user can pretty well estimate the expected error σ_c^2 in the data. However, in the opposite case *where a highly refined experiment is performed*, the errors are liable to be so small as to be difficult to estimate with any degree of assurance. For example they may easily be off by a factor of 2 or more. With this amount of uncertainty, it might be inadvisable to use the estimate of the error in any quantitative way, such as in (3.257).

In another situation, widely encountered, one experimenter reads the published work of another. Not having himself performed the experiment, he would rather avoid using the claims on accuracy of the published values. These might be overly optimistic, he believes. In this case, he would like to estimate the error $\sigma_{\bar{c}}^2$ *independent* of the published value of σ_c^2. That is, he *purposely puts himself* in a state of ignorance regarding σ_c^2. Can $\sigma_{\bar{c}}^2$ still be estimated?

Broadening the former a little, we can see that this problem would arise whenever experimental results $\{c_n\}$ are published, but where the reader has limited access to knowledge of the accuracy of the data, either because a) these were simply not published, or because b) the reader suspects that some sources of error may have been overlooked by the experimenter.

Then there are some data which *by their nature* preclude knowledge of their accuracy. The phenomenon giving rise to the data is so poorly understood, or so rare, as to preclude a reliable figure for σ_c. An example of the former is the rate of incidence c_n of UFO reports, from year to year $n = 1, 2, \ldots$. The latter is exemplified by the yearly discovery rate of new fundamental particles.

Finally, there are physical problems where *the unknown quantity per se defines an unknown σ_c.* For example, consider the problem where the underlying signal c represents an *unknown density* level on a grainy (noisy) photographic emulsion. The noise is *density dependent*, so that σ_c is again unknown. If a finite aperture scans the emulsion, each output of the aperture is a sample mean. The problem of estimating the error $\sigma_{\bar{c}}$ in this sample mean is then precisely our problem once again.

3.18.2 Philosophy of the Approach; Statistical Inference

This is a good example of a problem in statistics. Basically, all the experimenter has at his disposal is the data $\{c_n\}$. From these, he wants to form a measure of the error σ_c^2 in the sample mean over the data, which must be independent of the unknown factor σ_c^2 describing its intrinsic accuracy. How could this possible be done?

Could a replacement for knowledge of the theoretical variance be observation of the *sample* variance in the data? Let us define this as a quantity S^2, where

$$S^2 \equiv N^{-1} \sum_{n=1}^{N} (c_n - \bar{c})^2, \tag{3.258}$$

$\bar{c}$ formed at (3.253). Indeed, since the experiments are independent, as $N \to \infty$ it should asymptotically be true that $S^2 \to \sigma_c^2$. Due to the law of large numbers (3.6) a theoretical probability law and all its averages are asymptotically approached by the histogram of the data. Or simply, theoretical averages approach ensemble averages.

One way to use S is to attempt to replace the exact (3.257) by

$$\sigma_{\bar{c}}^2 = \lim_{N \to \infty} S^2/N. \tag{3.259}$$

But, this formula is not very useful, since by hypothesis we want to know $\sigma_{\bar{c}}^2$ for *finite N*. A new tactic must be sought.

Let us try now the basic method of statistics called *statistical inference*. This somewhat resembles the "indirect proof" of mathematics, where a test hypothesis is made and then is shown to be inconsistent with other theorems. Hence the hypothesis is rejected.

In the method of statistical inference, a hypothesis is made about the observable, here sample mean $\bar{c}$. The hypothesis is that it has resulted from the presence of the particular value $\hat{c}$ of c. Thus $\hat{c}$ is a test or a trial value for the unknown c. Now if $\hat{c}$ is correct, the *test statistic* $(\bar{c} - \hat{c})$ ought to be "small". The sample mean tends to equal the true value.

Conversely, too large a departure in $\bar{c}$ from $\hat{c}$ implies that the test hypothesis $\hat{c} = c$ *is wrong*. Hence, if quantity $(\bar{c} - \hat{c})$ is observed to be overly large, the hypothesis $\hat{c}$ is rejected. The grounds for this rejection are that the sample mean $\bar{c}$ contradicts the assumption that $\hat{c} = c$. Now, what do we mean by "overly large"?

There is, in fact, a certain, small probability that the observed *large* number $(\bar{c} - \hat{c})$ could have occurred *as a purely random fluctuation* from the *correct* $\hat{c} = c$. In fact, even larger fluctuations could have occurred, again purely as a random fluctuation from $\hat{c} = c$. If such fluctuation occurred, we would be wrong to reject the hypothesis that $\hat{c} = c$. How are we to know, then, when to reject the hypothesis?

If the probability of the large value $(\bar{c} - \hat{c})$ being exceeded is very small, say 0.05 or less, and we know this numerical probability, then we know when to reject the hypothesis c. The grounds are that the observed sample mean $\bar{c}$ is *improbably far* away numerically from the hypothetical mean $\hat{c}$. We say, then, that we reject the hypothesis with 0.05 (5%) confidence. Often, the 1% confidence level is used instead.

What hypothesis values $\hat{c}$ *will be accepted*, instead? The particular number $\hat{c} \equiv \bar{c}$ can never be rejected, since then $(\bar{c} - \hat{c}) = 0$ identically, and the probability of a fluctuation occurring that is greater than or equal to 0 is exactly 50% (see below). Of course 50% is not a reasonable confidence level for rejection. In a similar way, values of $\hat{c}$ *near to* $\bar{c}$ will be accepted. Finally, when either value

$$\hat{c} = \bar{c} \pm \Delta c \tag{3.260}$$

is tested, it will define just a large enough fluctuation $(\bar{c} - \hat{c}) = \pm \Delta c$ to be rejected.

The answer to the error estimation problem is then the following. Sample mean $\bar{c}$ is correct to $\pm \Delta c$ with confidence 5% (or whatever).

3.18.3 Forming the Statistic

The statistic we proposed to use for testing the hypothesis $\hat{c}$ was $(\bar{c} - \hat{c})$. *Any quantity proportional to this statistic* would also suffice, by the same reasoning. We use this fact below to form a statistic proportional to $(\bar{c} - \hat{c})$ *which does not require knowledge of the unknown* σ_c.

The procedure outlined above requires knowing the probability that a value $(\bar{c} - \hat{c})$ is exceeded. This requires knowledge, in turn, of the probability density for $(\bar{c} - \hat{c})$. We try to find this next.

By (3.253–256)

$$\bar{c} - \hat{c} = N^{-1} \sum_{n=1}^{N} c_n - \hat{c}$$

$$= c - \hat{c} + N^{-1} \sum_{n=1}^{N} e_n$$

$$= N^{-1} \sum_{n=1}^{N} e_n \tag{3.261}$$

since the statistic is tested under the assumption that the test hypothesis $\hat{c}$ *is correct* (the "indirect proof" spoken of previously).

Let us assume next that the errors $\{e_n\}$ are Gaussian random variables, in addition to the previous assumptions of zero mean and independence. By the central limit theorem of Sect. 3.2.5 this is very often the case.

Then from (3.261) the statistic $(\bar{c} - \hat{c})$ is a Gaussian random variable whose variance is $N^{-2}(N\sigma_c^2)$ or $N^{-1}\sigma_c^2$. Also, the related statistic

$$x \equiv (\sqrt{N}/\sigma_c)(\bar{c} - \hat{c}) \tag{3.262}$$

must be a Gaussian random variable with *unit variance* (independent of σ_c). The trouble with this statistic is that to form it requires knowledge of the quantity σ_c^2 *which we have been assuming to be unknown* (see Sect. 3.18.1).

How about, then, replacing division by σ_c in (3.262) with division by quantity S defined in (3.258)? As discussed below that equation, S is after all a reasonable approximation to σ_c. Hence, we form a new statistic

$$y \equiv (\bar{c} - \hat{c})/S. \tag{3.263}$$

This quantity is formed independent of an assumption of knowing σ_c. But is the probability density for y also independent of σ_c? This is shown next to be the case, basically because both numerator and denominator of (3.263) are proportional to σ_c, which cancels.

From the form of defining relation (3.258) the random variable S^2 is proportional to a sum of squares of N random variables $(c_n - \bar{c})$. By (3.253, 254), these random variables are not all independent. However, *von Mises* [3.37] shows that $(N-1)$ are. Hence, S^2 is proportional to a chi-square random variable of $N-1$ degrees of freedom. In fact,

$$S^2 = (\sigma_c^2/N)z, \tag{3.264}$$

where z is chi-square with $N-1$ degrees of freedom. We can now combine results.

Consider the new statistic very closely related to y,

$$t \equiv \sqrt{N-1}\,(\bar{c} - \hat{c})/S. \tag{3.265}$$

By (3.262, 264)

$$t = \sqrt{N-1}\,x/\sqrt{z}. \tag{3.266}$$

We found before that x is Gaussian with unit variance, and z is chi-square with $N-1$ degrees of freedom. Then, *neither the formation (3.265) of the t-statistic, nor the random variable t defined in (3.266) depends in any way upon the unknown quantity* σ_c. This solves the problem. We have found a statistic that permits a decision to be made about the likelihood of a test hypothesis $\hat{c}$, without requiring knowledge of the data accuracy σ_c!

The size of a number t, and more precisely, its probability of being that large or larger, now determines our decision on the acceptability of an hypothesis $\hat{c}$. Accordingly, we must establish the probability density for t.

3.18.4 Student's *t*-Distribution; Derivation

The derivation of probability law $p_T(t)$ is actually quite easy, not even encountering any difficult integrations. The plan is to first form the joint probability density $p_{XZ}(x, z)$, then from this to establish $p_{TZ}(t, z)$ via the random variable transformation (3.266), and finally to integrate out over z to establish the marginal $p_T(t)$. We carry through these operations next.

Because x and z are independent, by identity (3.8)

$$p_{XZ}(x, z) = p_X(x) p_Z(z).$$

With the known forms for $p_X(x)$ and $p_Z(z)$,

$$p_{XZ}(x, z) = (2\pi)^{-1/2} \exp(-x^2/2)$$
$$\cdot 2^{-(N-1)/2} [\Gamma(N-1)/2]^{-1} z^{(N-3)/2} \exp(-z/2). \tag{3.267}$$

We can transform this to the corresponding law $p_{TZ}(t, z)$ by regarding (3.266) as a transformation of random variables from the old x to the new t. There is a single root x for each t, so that by identity (3.88b)

$$p_{TZ}(t, z)dt = p_{XZ}(x, z)dx$$
$$= p_{XZ}[z^{1/2}(N-1)^{-1/2}t, z] z^{1/2}(N-1)^{-1/2}dt.$$

Cancelling the dt factors on both sides, and substituting in the form (3.267) for p_{XZ},

$$p_{TZ}(t, z) = (2\pi)^{-1/2}(N-1)^{-1/2}2^{-(N-1)/2}[\Gamma(N-1)/2]^{-1}$$
$$\cdot e^{-(z/2)[1+t^2(N-1)^{-1}]} z^{(N-3)/2}.$$

Finally, integrating out over z we obtain the marginal

$$p_T(t) = \frac{\Gamma(N/2)}{\Gamma(N-1)/2} [(N-1)\pi]^{-1/2} \left(1 + \frac{t^2}{N-1}\right)^{-N/2}, \tag{3.268}$$

which is what we set out to find.

This is known as "Student's distribution", after the mathematician Student (pseudonym of W. S. Gosett), who contrived it in 1908 to solve the general problem of this section [3.38].

3.18.5 Some Properties of Student's t-Distribution

This distribution depends upon t only through t^2. Hence, $p_T(t)$ is even in t and

$$\langle t \rangle = 0. \tag{3.269}$$

The variance may be found by directly integrating out $t^2 \cdot p_T(t)$. The result is

$$\sigma_T^2 = \frac{N-1}{N-3}, \tag{3.270}$$

or unit variance for N moderately large.

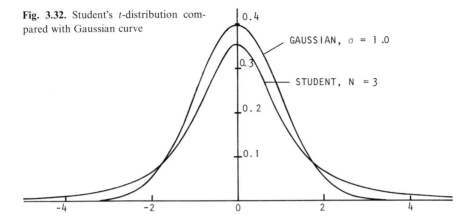

Fig. 3.32. Student's t-distribution compared with Gaussian curve

Unless N is very small (4 or less), $p_T(t)$ is very close to a *Gaussian curve* with unit variance. To show this, from (3.268) the t-dependence is

$$\left(1+\frac{t^2}{N-1}\right)^{-N/2}.$$

Calling this y,

$$\lim_{N\to\infty}\ln y=\lim_{N\to\infty}-\frac{N}{2}\ln\left(1+\frac{t^2}{N-1}\right)$$

$$=-\frac{t^2}{2}\lim_{N\to\infty}\frac{N}{N-1}$$

$$=-t^2/2.$$

Consequently,

$$\lim_{N\to\infty}p_T(t)\propto e^{-t^2/2},\qquad\qquad(3.271)$$

a Gaussian with unit variance.

To show how close Student's distribution is to a Gaussian, it is plotted in Fig. 3.32 for the case $N=3$, along with the unit variance Gaussian.

Tables of the integral

$$P(|t|\leq t_0)\equiv 2\int_0^{t_0}dt p_T(t)\qquad\qquad(3.272)$$

exist, as functions of t_0 and N (the only free parameters) for example, see [Ref. 3.12, p. 990]). Or, the integral (3.272) may be evaluated numerically, by means of Gauss quadrature or some other approach (see Chap. 2 for details).

3.18.6 Application to the Problem; Student's *t*-Test

The procedure we have derived, in summary, is to form a value of $t = t_0$ from the N data $\{c_n\}$ and the test hypothesis c via

$$t_0 = (N-1)^{1/2}(\bar{c} - \hat{c})/S, \tag{3.273}$$

where $\bar{c}$ is the sample mean (3.253) and S^2 is the sample variance (3.258). Next, look up the corresponding value of $P(|t| \le t_0)$ in tables of the Student distribution. Then $1 - P(|t| \le t_0)$ is the probability that the value t_0 will be exceeded, even though (by assumption) $\hat{c}$ is correct. If this probability is *less than* a prescribed *confidence level*, say 0.05, then the value $\hat{c}$ is rejected as a possible value of c. In words, the normalized average fluctuation (3.273) in the $\{c_n\}$ away from the test $\hat{c}$ is too large to be reasonably expected. Conversely, if $1 - P$ exceeds the confidence level, then the test $\hat{c}$ is accepted as a possible value of c. *In this manner, a range* $\pm \Delta c$ *of acceptable* $\hat{c}$ *is constructed, and* $\pm \Delta c$ *is the* estimated uncertainty in the sample mean $\bar{c}$.

3.18.7 Illustrative Example

In an attempt to reduce image noise, a slowly varying image is scanned with a small aperture. The output of the aperture at each of its positions is the sample mean over the data within it. (This problem is statistically equivalent to the speed of light determination problem discussed previously.)

At each position in the image, the aperture contains four image points, e.g., the data in Table 3.4. The output image value is the mean; there $\bar{i} = 2.0$. By how much is this liable to be in error from the signal value within the aperture? That is, if the true $i = 2.0 \pm \Delta i$, what is Δi? (See last paragraphs of Sect. 3.18.2.)

If we assume that each

$$i_n = i + e_n, \tag{3.274}$$

where i is the unknown signal value and the $\{e_n\}$ are independent and Gaussian, then we may use Student's *t*-test to decide on any hypothesis $\hat{i}$ for i. [See the paragraph prior to (3.262).]

Table 3.4. Image values within aperture at one scan position

n	i_n
1	2.0
2	3.0
3	1.0
4	2.0

Let us adopt a 5% confidence level. For the case $N=4$ at hand, tables of Student's distribution show that a value $t_0=3.182$ just barely flunks the t-test, i.e., its probability of being exceeded is *less than* 0.05. To see what test hypotheses $\hat{i}$ this corresponds to, from Table 3.4, $S^2=0.5$. Hence, by (3.273), for any test $\hat{i}$

$$t_0=\sqrt{3}(2.0-\hat{i})/\sqrt{0.5}.$$

Setting this equal to 3.182, we find this to result from a just rejected hypothesis

$$\hat{i}_{rej}=2.0-1.3.$$

Since $p_T(t)$ is even in t, the same t_0 would result from an $\hat{i}$ on the other side of the mean, or

$$\hat{i}_{rej}=2.0+1.3.$$

We conclude that the data at hand imply no tighter estimate of the signal value i than

$$i=2.0\pm1.3, \tag{3.275}$$

for a confidence level 5%. A lower confidence level would permit even wider latitude in acceptable $\hat{i}$ values, i.e., more uncertainty than ±1.3.

We emphasize once again that this calculation has been made *without having to know* the accuracy σ_i in each data value i_n. Herein lies the power of the approach.

Finally, it is highly instructive to observe the effect of data fluctuation upon our estimate of the spread $\pm\Delta i$ in possible i values. Suppose, for example, that the data were now a little "tighter" around the mean of 2.0 than in the preceding table, as in Table 3.5. Here S^2 is smaller, at value 0.125. Now we have

$$t_0=\sqrt{3}(2.0-\hat{i})/\sqrt{0.125}.$$

Once again equating this to 3.182 (since $N=4$ still),

$$\hat{i}_{rej}=2.0+0.6.$$

Table 3.5. As in Table 3.4, but now less fluctuation

n	i_n
1	2.0
2	2.5
3	1.5
4	2.0

Therefore, the data now imply an accuracy of

$$i = 2.0 \pm 0.6 \qquad (3.276)$$

in the sample mean, with confidence level of 5% (as before).

This is tighter, by a factor of 2, than the preceding result (3.275). This shows that the variance *in the data* plays the same role in defining probable error as does the *theoretical standard deviation* σ_i for each datum [see (3.257)]. Hence, when the latter is not known (as presumed here), *empirical observation* of the data variation takes its place entirely. This is a very important result, with ramifications on estimation methods which are today, 70 years after Gossett, still being felt (see, e.g., [3.39]).

3.18.8 Other Applications

The *t*-test has other uses as well. For example, it may be used to decide whether two specimens of data probably (at some level of confidence) have the same mean (see [3.36]). This allows a decision to be made on whether the two specimens arose from identical physical processes. For example, two samples of uniformly exposed film are given, and we want to test whether they are probably pieces of the same film.

Or, the failure rates over the years are given for brand X and brand Y, and from these we wish to determine whether brand Y is an improvement over brand X.

Or, two weak stars are observed to have nearly equal brightnesses. How long a time exposure is needed to have confidence at 5% that they are not equal? There are potentially many uses of the *t*-test in optical research.

3.19 The *F*-Test on Variance

If the *t*-test may be used to test the hypothesis that two sets of data have the same mean, the *F*-test does likewise for their variances. With N given data $\{c_n\}$, define the sample variance s^2 by

$$s^2 \equiv (N-1)^{-1} \sum_{n=1}^{N} (c_n - \bar{c})^2 . \qquad (3.277)$$

[Notice the similarity to S^2 of (3.258).] If two sets of data $\{c_n\}$ and $\{c'_n\}$ consisting, respectively, of N and N' numbers have identical variances then *the ratio of their sample variances*

$$s^2/s'^2 \equiv f_0 \qquad (3.278)$$

should be close to 1. f_0 is called the "f-ratio" statistic. The "F-test" consists in deciding from the size of f_0 whether to accept the hypothesis that the two variances are indeed equal.

If as before all data are normally distributed, then if the variances are equal (the test hypothesis), the probability density for f may be found. In complete analogy to the derivation of $p_T(t)$ in Sect. 3.18, we find

$$p_F(f) = Kf^{1/2(N-1)-1}(1+rf)^{-1/2(N+N')+1},$$

where

$$K = \frac{\Gamma[1/2(N+N')-1]}{\Gamma[1/2(N-1)]\,\Gamma[1/2(N'-1)]}\, r^{1/2(N-1)} \tag{3.279}$$

and

$$r = \frac{N-1}{N'-1}.$$

This is sometimes called "Snedecor's F-distribution", after Snedecor [3.40].

Now if the two data sets have the same variance, ratio f_0 can either exceed 1 or be less than 1. Consider the former case $f_0 > 1$ first. The probability $P(f > f_0)$ is easily computed from the known density (3.279), by numerical quadrature, and is tabulated widely (see, e.g., [Ref. 3.12, pp. 986–989]).

Since the values of $P(f > f_0)$ are computed on the basis of equal variances for the two data sets, if the observed statistic $f_0 > 1$ of (3.278) is so large that $P(f > f_0)$ is very small, then as usual we choose to reject the hypothesis of equality. Again, a value $P(f > f_0) = 0.05$, or a "5 % confidence level", is often used as the decisive value.

If, on the other hand, $f_0 < 1$, then by merely interchanging the names of the two sets so that the larger of S^2 and S'^2 is in the numerator of (3.278), we once more obtain a case $f_0 > 1$, and may treat it as before.

3.19.1 Application to Image Detection

In photographic imagery, the variance of noise increases with signal density level. Suppose an image scene is either empty, consisting only of photographic noise caused by a background signal level, or has somewhere superimposed upon the background a feature of interest. The feature, if it is present, is uniform with an unknown signal level of its own. Can the scene be tested for the hypothesis that the feature is present? This problem is for example encountered in medical diagnostic imagery, where tumors are to be detected.

Imagine the image to be subdivied into subareas, each containing a finite number of data values. We can test each subarea for the presence of the feature

Fig. 3.33. Three demonstrations of F-test feature extraction. In each row, the feature on the right was extracted from the image in the middle! The true feature is shown on the far left. S/N is unity in all three cases (Illustration courtesy of Professor Peter Bartels, University of Arizona)

based on the fact that where the feature is present, its signal adds to that of the background, *increasing the local variance of noise*. This, in turn, increases the *total* variance of intensity. Hence, the pertinent statistic is the ratio of the sample variance (3.277) over the subarea to the variance over an image subarea where the feature is *known not to be* present. If this value f_0 is near 1, we reject the hypothesis that the foreground feature exists there. This test is performed in sequence over the subareas, each subarea defining a single pixel in the output picture.

Bartels and *Subach* [3.41] have carried through this test by computer simulation. In order to create gray-tone pictures, they generate a local gray value *linear with the local value of* $P(f > f_0)$. This gray-scale coding is given the name "significance probability mapping". Their test feature was a white object (see Fig. 3.33), so that a high $P(f > f_0)$ signifies a high probability of local blackness, which is in compliance with their gray-scale mapping.

Each of the three rows of photos in Fig. 3.33 contains three images. On the left is the test feature, to be superimposed somewhere within the square background field shown in the middle. Both the feature and the background were generated with signal level equal to standard deviation. Hence, the signal-to-noise ratio S/N in the simulated data is *unity*.

A subarea size of $N = N' = 200$ data points was chosen. This defines the pixel size in the right-hand images. The F-test was performed in each subarea, as described previously. The right-hand images are the outputs of the test. These indicate a very good job of feature extraction, considering what the unaided eye can discern in the middle images. Note that the finite subarea size defines the blur spot size in the outputs. The result is a tradeoff between sensitivity of detection and spatial resolution, since the F-test is more discriminating as N and N' increase. Nevertheless, that the method even works with a *signal-to-noise ratio of unity* is quite remarkable and holds promise for future applications.

References

3.1   A. Papoulis: *Probability Random Variables and Stochastic Processes* (McGraw-Hill, New York 1965)
3.2   A. de Moivre: *The Doctrine of Chances*, 3rd ed., 1756 (photographically reprinted by Chelsea Publ., New York 1967)
3.3   A. Kolmogoroff: *Foundations of the Theory of Probability* (English transl.) (Chelsea, New York 1933)
3.4   G. N. Plass, G. W. Kattawar, J. A. Guinn: Appl. Opt. **16**, 643 (1977)
3.5   C. Cox, W. Monk: J. Opt. Soc. Am. **44**, 838 (1954)
3.6   R. M. Bracewell: *The Fourier Transform and Its Application* (McGraw-Hill, New York 1965)
3.7   R. Barakat: Opt. Acta **21**, 903 (1974)
3.8   E. L. O'Neil: *Introduction to Statistical Optics* (Addison-Wesley, Reading, Mass. 1963)
3.9   B. Tatian: J. Opt. Soc. Am. **55**, 1014 (1965)
3.10 G. D. Bergland: IEEE Spectrum **6**, 44 (1969)
3.11 R. C. Singleton: IEEE Trans. AU-**15**, 91 (1967)
3.12 M. Abramowitz, I. A. Stegun (eds.): *Handbook of Mathematical Functions* (National Bureau of Standards, Washington, D. C. 1964) pp. 892, 893
3.13 A. G. Fox, T. Li: Bell Sys. Tech. J. **40**, 453 (1961)
3.14 R. W. Lee, J. C. Harp: Proc. IEEE **57**, 375 (1969)
3.15 B. R. Frieden: "Image enhancement and restoration", in *Picture Processing and Digital Filtering*, 2nd ed., ed. by T. S. Huang, Topics in Applied Physics, Vol. 6 (Springer, Berlin, Heidelberg, New York 1979)
3.16 R. S. Hershel: Optical Sciences Center, University of Arizona, private communication (1978)
3.17 K. Miyamoto: "Wave optics and geometrical optics in optical design", in *Progress in Optics*, Vol. 1, ed. by E. Wolf (North Holland, New York 1961)
3.18a G. I. Marchuk, G. A. Mikhailov, M. A. Nazaraliev, R. A. Darbinjan, B. A. Kargin, B. S. Elepov: *The Monte Carlo Methods in Atmospheric Optics*, Springer Series in Optical Sciences, Vol. 12 (Springer, Berlin, Heidelberg, New York 1980)
      b J. J. DePalma, J. Gasper: Phot. Sci. Eng. **16**, 181 (1972)
3.19 G. N. Plass, G. W. Kattawar, J. A. Guinn: Appl. Opt. **14**, 1924 (1975)
3.20 R. E. Hufnagel, N. R. Stanley: J. Opt. Soc. Am. **54**, 52 (1964)
3.21 R. Barakat: Opt. Acta **18**, 683 (1971)
3.22 L. I. Goldfischer: J. Opt. Soc. Am. **55**, 247–253 (1965)
3.23 J. C. Dainty: Opt. Acta **17**, 761 (1970)
3.24 D. Korff: Opt. Commun. **5**, 188 (1972)
3.25 J. C. Dainty (ed.): *Laser Speckle and Related Phenomena*, Topics in Applied Physics, Vol. 9 (Springer, Berlin, Heidelberg, New York 1975)
3.26 J. W. Goodman: Proc. IEEE **53**, 1688 (1965)
3.27 H. Fujii, J. Vozomi, T. Askura: J. Opt. Soc. Am. **66**, 1222 (1976)
3.28 B. R. Frieden: J. Opt. Soc. Am. **64**, 682 (1974)
3.29 E. Parzen: *Modern Probability Theory and its Applications* (Wiley, New York 1960)
3.30 E. T. Jaynes: IEEE Trans. SSC-**4**, 227 (1968)
3.31 A. Wragg, D. C. Dowson: IEEE Trans. IT-**16**, 226 (1970)
3.32 B. R. Frieden: J. Opt. Soc. Am. **62**, 511 (1972)

3.33 R.Kikuchi, B.H.Soffer: J. Opt. Soc. Am. **67**, 1656 (1977)
3.34 K.W.Smillie: *An Introduction to Regression and Correlation* (Academic Press, New York 1966)
3.35 J.L.Simonds: J. Phot. Sci. Eng. **2**, 205 (1958)
3.36 S.Brandt: *Statistical and Computational Methods in Data Analysis* (North Holland, Amsterdam 1970)
3.37 **R**.von Mises: *Mathematical Theory of Probability and Statistics* (Academic Press, New York 1964) p. 407
3.38 Student: Biomctrika **6**, 1 (1908)
3.39 C.Stein: *Proceedings Third Berkeley Symposium on Mathematics, Statistics, and Probability* **1** (University of California Press, Berkeley 1955) p. 197
3.40 F.Snedecor: *Statistical Methods*, 5th ed. (Iowa State Univ. Press, Ames 1962)
3.41 P.H.Bartels, J.A.Subach: "Significance probability mapping, and automated interpretation of complex pictorial scenes", in *Digital Processing of Biomedical Images*, ed. by K.Preston, M.Onoe (Plenum Press, New York 1976) pp. 101–114

4. Optimization Methods in Optics

A. K. Rigler and R. J. Pegis

With 16 Figures

Optimization, in general, makes a system or process perform as well as possible with respect to a given set of criteria, without violating an associated set of constraints. This is an extremely general concept in everyday life, with countless applications both optical and nonoptical, technical and nontechnical in nature. A simple optical example would be the tuning of a television set until the picture conforms to a subjective visual "best" criterion. On the nonoptical side, a comparable example would be the planning of a vacation trip to visit six cities, while spending the least amount of driving time between cities. These two examples can illustrate the importance of careful modeling and prior agreement among all parties, concerning the criterion of merit and the constraining side conditions.

When an optimization problem, be it technical or otherwise, is approached by more than one person, it is, in the interests of credibility, desirable that their respective solutions be the same. Even with precise mathematical formulation, this agreement cannot always be guaranteed; when subjectivity and hidden differences in criteria are involved, it is most unlikely to be achieved. In our television example, any family member with normal vision can probably tune the TV set to please the rest of the family; a color-blind person may be able to satisfy no one but himself. In the technical areas as well, one must never overlook the influence of subjectivity and unintentionally disguised differences in criteria, for even with the most carefully posed mathematical models, different computer programs in the hands of different users may produce considerable variation in designs that can be explained by these factors. The correctness of the computer code and the applicability of the mathematics may always be questioned and tested, but the individuality and artistry of the designer, based on preferences and prejudices derived from his experience, will always be present and will have a bearing on the final results. This subjectivity is not necessarily undesirable; only when its presence is forgotten or ignored will it lead to trouble.

The influence of constraints is no less important than the performance criterion in the solution of an optimization problem. An illustration can be seen in the vacation trip plans mentioned above. The speed limit is an obvious constraint that affects driving time. Other factors which could act as constraints might evolve from the mother's interest in the overnight accommodations along the route, or perhaps from the children's desire for a side trip to an amusement park. Such constraints will clearly modify the route that would be selected when time is the only consideration, and may narrow the range of alternatives to only a few routes.

These two trivial examples suggest that a criterion of merit must be agreed upon and specified in advance, and that constraints may often be the controlling factors in the process of finding an optimal solution to any problem. Success in large-scale technical optimization depends in great measure on attention to the same considerations.

After such a problem has been formulated as a mathematical model, then a procedure to obtain the solution must be selected from a very large collection of mathematical and computational tools. Many of these tools are general purpose in nature and can be expected to succeed for a wide range of problems. On the other hand, certain disciplines present characteristics in their problems that can be exploited by special-purpose procedures. The education of a designer is incomplete without some exposure to the mathematical methods available, their strengths and weaknesses, and their range of applicability.

Optical design has traditionally given rise to numerous and difficult optimization problems, and at the same time, has motivated significant research towards their solution. As long as methods of evaluation have been available, it has been possible for designers to work towards optimal designs by the construction of change tables, interpolation, and trial and error. Mechanical calculators and early computers helped this process enormously.

When the truly large-scale digital computers arrived in the 1960s, it became possible to automate not only the evaluation of optical systems, but the decision-making algorithms for improving these solutions as well. It was at this point that the optics industry seriously turned to the problem of formalizing and quantifying the previously loose and subjective process by which designers worked towards optimizing prototypes. From that time on, much has been written about machine-oriented design methods, of which only a small sample can be included here.

The intersection of the fields of optics and optimization is much too large to be covered in detail by a survey paper. We shall comment upon several aspects of each discipline in the hope that the mathematically inclined reader will find in optics a source of practical, interesting, and difficult problems to solve, while the optics-oriented person may be motivated to a deeper study of the mathematical tools available. Among our references, a few have extensive bibliographies. In particular, the texts by *Himmelblau* [4.1], *Lawson* and *Hanson* [4.2], and *Ortega* and *Rheinboldt* [4.3] and a recent Russian survey paper by *Polyak* [4.4] cover the mathematical aspects rather well. In optics, *Jamieson*'s [4.5] reference list includes many of the important sources on optimization in lens design.

Section 4.1 of this chapter presents four diversified sources of optimization problems in optics. In the second, Sect. 4.2, we review the parallel development of optimization techniques by optical designers and by mathematicians, establish the notation to be used, and discuss the mathematical background of optimization. Section 4.3 presents a number of actual optimization algorithms which the designer has available, and finally Sect. 4.4 displays and discusses examples of solutions to some of the typical design problems.

4.1 Origins of Optimization Problems in Optics

Optimization problems that have their origin in an optical context range in complexity from simple curve fitting as practised by a numerical analyst following the guidance of *Isaacson* and *Keller* [4.6] to the myriad details of an automobile headlamp as described by *Donohue* and *Joseph* [4.7]. In this section, we shall describe the formulation of optimization problems from curve fitting, thin film filter design, the design of imaging optics, and illumination systems. The reader will recognize other examples from his own experience.

4.1.1 Curve Fitting

When using empirical data in computation, it is often desirable to replace tabular data by an explicit formula that contains equivalent information, perhaps with random measurement errors suppressed. The set of coordinate pairs (t_i, y_i), $i=1, 2, ..., n$ is to be represented by a mathematical model,

$$y=f(x;t), \tag{4.1}$$

where x is a vector of m parameters to be determined. The evaluation of the model gives a set of n equations,

$$y_i=f(x;t_i)+\varepsilon_i, \quad i=1, 2, ..., n, \tag{4.2}$$

where ε is a vector of discrepancies. The selection of parameters x when $n\geq m$ to

$$\underset{x}{\text{Minimize}} \sum_i \varepsilon_i^2 \tag{4.3}$$

is an optimization problem known as *least squares* or *regression*. When the model $f(x;t)$ is linear in x, we have the classic linear least-squares problem that forms the basis for several of the algorithms to be discussed later in this chapter. The linear problem can be solved with special attention to statistics as in the text by *Draper* and *Smith* [4.8] or with emphasis on the numerical difficulties as in the book by *Lawson* and *Hanson* [4.2].

When $f(x;t)$ is nonlinear in x, the minimization problem is said to be nonlinear. A simple nonlinear example from curve fitting is a rational function. While a polynomial in t is linear in its coefficients, a quotient of polynomials is not.

At times, the minimization of the sum of squared error is unsuitable and a different criterion must be chosen. The Chebyshev criterion is

$$\underset{x}{\text{Minimize}} \ \underset{i}{\text{Maximum}} \ |\varepsilon_i| \ . \tag{4.4}$$

Several algorithms have been proposed to solve this case. *Stiefel's* [4.9] exchange, *Osborne* and *Watson* [4.10], or *McBride* and *Rigler* [4.11] attack it directly, using linear programming as a tool; in the conventional least-squares routine, the ε_i are raised to a large integer power before squaring to approximate the infinity norm, while *Lawson* [4.12] replaces (4.4) by

$$\underset{x}{\text{Minimize}} \sum_i \omega_i \varepsilon_i^2 \tag{4.5}$$

with an algorithm prescribed to choose the weights ω_i. Lawson's algorithm is inefficient for calculation but provides important assurance that weights used in this manner do have mathematical justification. It suggests also that personal judgment in choosing the ω_i for other purposes has a possibility of rigorous mathematical support.

Besides the curve fitting to merely generate a recipe for calculation, it is often necessary to infer something about the underlying structure of the data. Spectroscopic data resemble a mountain range of peaks and valleys with physical considerations dictating the form of $f(x; t)$; the peaks are often described by Lorentz functions or by Gaussian distributions. The point of the optimization is to identify the location and shape parameters of the actual physical problem. This is a much harder problem than simply fitting a curve, since a good fit may occur with very little information content in the parameters. This lack of information in a good fit is mentioned in [4.13]; another good example of this annoying phenomenon occurs when a linear combination of decaying exponential functions is fitted to an empirical curve, as in [4.14]. Discussion of the spectroscopic data fitting problem has appeared in a number of papers, for example [4.15–17].

4.1.2 Thin Film Filter Design

While curve fitting is an analytic process, many of the techniques may be turned to the more difficult problem of synthesis. An application occurs in the optimal design of thin film interference filters.

Multilayer thin film filters reflect, absorb, and transmit light in a complicated way, depending on both the construction parameters and the mode of use. The variables in the mode of use are the wavelength, angle of incidence, and polarization.

While dielectric multilayers with equal optical thickness in all layers can be designed in closed form by algebraic means, see [4.18], optimum performance over a given wavelength range is usually achieved by varying thickness.

Especially where absorption bands are involved, the designer has to perform the final optimization of the filter with given tables of indices of refraction, and with only thickness variables to adjust.

A simple but illustrative multilayer filter optimization problem is the design of an antireflection coating for a given range of angles of incidence. Classical solutions can be computed at any one incidence angle and polarization, but they deteriorate as the incidence angle and polarization are changed. The incidence angle and wavelength ranges are sampled discretely to give a collection of individual "targets" for the optimization. The details of this example are discussed in Sect. 4.4.2.

4.1.3 Lens Design

The most widely known problem of design in optics is that of imaging devices. It has been an art as well as an engineering science and has been influenced by the digital computer more than any of the other aspects of optical optimization discussed here. The problem changes with the requirements so that one set of specifications cannot begin to illustrate all of the variations. Among the realistic published problems that might be studied is the "symposium lens", described by *Feder* [4.19].

The disadvantage of such "standard" problems is that it is frequently difficult to decide which of two lens designs is "best". This points up a very basic difficulty in the optimization of lenses: while it is obvious that certain rays must pass the lens in certain prescribed ways, it is not at all obvious which rays should be weighted and in what manner, nor what complex functions of ray data should have their target values designated. These decisions will come out of the designer's experience and are examples of the subjectivity mentioned earlier.

In a typical lens optimization problem, the designer will know the desired focal length and magnification, the spatial constraints, and the desired quality. A large body of existing art usually will indicate the approximate complexity and form of the elements. In the actual optimization, the parameter list will include curvatures and thicknesses, and sometimes aspheric coefficients of the surfaces. The targets will include first-order properties, ray results, functions of ray data, and frequently aberration coefficients computed from series expansions of an aberration model. Constraints will appear in the form of geometrical restrictions on the size and shape of the lens or its elements.

The design of lenses for image formation also can occasion simpler but less publicized optimization problems. First-order layouts can be difficult to establish when a design has geometrical constraints. This is especially true in the case of zoom lenses, where multiple positions are sought for the lenses to accomplish magnification changes. Geometric models have been used to aid in the first-order design problem, [4.20, 21], but they become unwieldy when the number of variables and constraints is large.

The algebraic formulation of constrained optimization problems for fixed-focus and zoom systems and the subsequent solution of these problems by nonlinear optimization algorithms is a somewhat uncultivated optical field.

4.1.4 Illumination Design

As difficult as the lens design problem may be, the illumination problem can be worse, especially in its variety. A familiar example is an overhead fixture whose reflecting and refracting surfaces are so shaped that a given source will produce a required intensity distribution on a work plane while suppressing glare and other annoying characteristics. More stringent directional requirements can be found in the specification of an automobile headlamp [4.7], a color television lighthouse [4.22], or an airport runway light [4.23]. The latter device is interesting in that it is intended to be looked at, rather than to be the means by which a nonluminous object becomes visible. The specifications establish a distribution of intensity in a rectangle positioned in the air above a marker beyond the end of the runway. As an airplane approaches to land under either instrument or visual rules, it will pass through the rectangle if the airplane is properly positioned in space. The runway lights will be clearly visible to the pilot, weather conditions permitting. The specifications include a complementary distribution of intensity outside of the rectangle. The sharp cutoff at the boundary of the "window" from high intensity inside to relatively low intensity outside gives the pilot an easy visual check on his position. When the plane is misaligned with the runway, the lights will appear to be correspondingly dim. Figure 4.1 is a sketch indicating the general aspects of this problem.

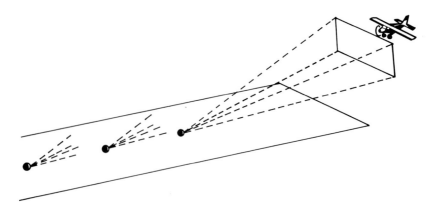

Fig. 4.1. Airport runway lights, an illustration of an illumination design problem. Fixtures imbedded in the runway are designed to produce a prescribed intensity distribution in the "window" through which the airplane approaches the runway

4.2 Mathematical Background of Optimization

Before the advent of the high-speed digital computer, the optimization of a process or device was a goal to which designers aspired, but except in rare instances, no practical methods were available to attain that goal. Fortunately, computer designs are not always necessary to the success of an enterprise; businesses have been profitable, battles have been won, and planets have been discovered without the benefit of electronic computers. The definition of optimum can be set forth clearly in mathematical form, yet its practical attainment may be impossible and success in design is often measured in terms of progress made up to the time that the search is abandoned. In his introduction to a conference on optimization, *Hyde* [4.24] suggests that many a solution is declared to be optimal to coincide with the exhaustion of the budget allocated for optimization. This section reviews the development of the mathematics involved in obtaining and verifying a solution, and avoids the political and economic aspects of paying for it.

4.2.1 Remarks on the Historical Development

Mathematicians have often considered the problem of finding extreme points of a function, and the names of early contributors such as Newton, Cauchy, Gauss, and Lagrange are common-place in today's literature. Unfortunately, the amount of computation required to study their suggestions was so extensive that significant testing was impossible until the middle of the twentieth century. In the early 1950s, the prospects of automating tedious computation led designers to pursue the goal of optimal solutions, following the recommendations of the old masters. Very soon it became apparent that more mathematical development was needed in order to produce a satisfactory algorithm. Although the burden of evaluating mathematical models was eased by the new computing power, the naive search procedures fell short of the engineers' hopes.

   During the 1950s, progress by lens designers and progress by the mathematical community developed almost independently. Lens designers reviewed the old literature for search algorithms and invented their own variations and improvements. Two papers by mathematicians were influential, [4.25, 26], but for the most part, the opticians and mathematicians worked independently and have had relatively little exchange of ideas to the present time.

   The 1960s offered an impressive increase in the size and speed of digital computers to the effect that both optical designers and mathematicians were encouraged to invent and test new algorithms to take advantage of their new and faster computers. In particular, papers by *Davidon* [4.27] and *Fletcher* and *Powell* [4.28] on the variable metric method and by *Grey* [4.29] on the *QR* decomposition were clearly new and exciting. Confidence of the researchers was reflected in their titles, "Automatic Design...". As realism prevailed, "Semi-Automatic..." became the preferred descriptor.

By the end of the decade, the optics community had settled upon search procedures based either on the *Levenberg* [4.25] or the *Grey* [4.29] idea. The major lens design codes that are available commercially today use one or both of these methods. Since both work well and the evaluation portion for optical design is relatively expensive, the attention of researchers was diverted to solving other classes of problems rather than continuing with inventing and testing new algorithms.

The 1960s saw a proliferation of algorithms from mathematics and some considerable effort was made to test subroutines and modularize them for general purpose use. The search for a "best" algorithm turned out to be a failure on the grounds that the definition of best varies from one situation to another. Nevertheless, general conclusions were to the effect that the methods originating from *Levenberg's* [4.25] and *Davidon's* [4.27] papers were reliable and that special characteristics such as a least-squares objective should be considered in the selection of an algorithm. During this time, new journals appeared that encouraged publication of work in these areas: Applied Optics, Mathematical Programming, and the Journal of Optimization Theory and Applications. Of course, the older outlets in operations research, mathematics, and optics continued to welcome contributions. A complete bibliography alone could fill this volume.

During the past few years, the success of the large lens design codes has changed the emphasis from search methodology to redefining aspects of the objective functions, t the matching of problem to algorithm, to the use of time sharing and other new services of commercial computer centers, and to the attack on other large-scale applications. The mathematical activity has shifted also from the emphasis on new methods to a study of the ones we have. New definitions and theory on convergence and convergence rates and the attempts to take advantage of special properties of the problem have become more persistent themes in publication.

The independent development of our subject by mathematicians and opticians has led to notation and jargon difficulties that further obstruct communication. As we proceed with a more detailed description of the subject of mathematical programming, we shall attempt to point out the variations in usage.

4.2.2 Nonlinear Programming

The problem that has been called *mathematical programming* is the following:

$$\text{Minimize} \quad f(x), x = (x_1, x_2, ..., x_m)^t, \qquad (4.6)$$

$$\text{Subject to} \quad g_k(x) \geq 0, \ xk = 1, 2, ..., n, \qquad (4.7)$$

$$h_k(x) = 0, \ xk = n+1, ..., K. \qquad (4.8)$$

This problem arises in many areas of applied science and is also interesting to mathematicians and worthy of study for its own sake. Because of the broad range of sources, the descriptive language is not consistent from one area to the next and the unifying influence of the mathematician is too recent to have reached all contributors. We shall attempt to use the language most common to mathematics and shall point out some of the variations in usage that have developed among the optical designers.

The function $f(x)$ will be called the *objective function*. Our formulation is such that $f(x)$ is to be minimized so that a natural description is "cost function". It might represent actual cost in money, weight, time, distance, or it may be made up of a combination of several elements. To the lens designer, it may represent the aberrations that degrade an image. On the other hand, maximization of a function may be more natural: profit, return on investment, energy transfer, or any measure of a desirable attribute. We can include this maximization option in our formulation (4.6–8) by considering $-f(x)$.

The functions $g_k(x) \geqq 0$ and $h_k(x) = 0$ are called *constraints*. The equality constraints (4.8) reduce the dimension of the problem either implicitly or by explicit solution and substitution. The inequalities (4.7) reduce the set of eligible points to a subset of E^m. This set is known as the *feasible region* or *feasible set*. On the other hand, the constraint functions (4.7, 8) may be absent or so generous that they might as well be missing, in which case we speak of an *unconstrained minimization* problem.

Lens designers have tended to use "merit function" or "performance index" and "boundary conditions" to describe (4.6, 7), respectively, see [4.30], and "defect" has been associated with ε in (4.2). "Construction parameters" refer to those independent variables associated with physical quantities and "target values" are the intended values of terms in the objective, i.e., the y_i in (4.2).

The mathematical programming problem (4.6–8) is stated in very general terms and to consider every aspect would lead us away from the theme of this volume. Three special types should be mentioned, however, in spite of their absence in detail. The first is *linear programming* in which the objective function and all of the constraints in (4.6–8) are linear functions. This problem is of great importance, a mathematical and computational theory is well established, and every computer center has a reliable subroutine for obtaining the solution. Its appearance in optics is rare and at that, it is usually in the context of a subproblem in a more general setting. The interested reader is referred to any standard book on the subject, such as the text by *Hadley* [4.31]. The second special category is *integer programming*, where one or more of the independent variables are further restricted to take on only integral values. The automation of these solutions is considerably more difficult and because the designer in optics prefers to reserve to himself the judgment on inserting and deleting elements, we again refer the interested reader to a textbook, for example [4.32, 33]. Finally, *optimal control*, requiring time-dependent dynamic solutions, has an extensive literature of its own of which an accessible example will appear in every technical library. A suitable reference is the book by *Tabak* and *Kuo* [4.34]. It should be mentioned further that our problems are deterministic; *stochastic programming* is excluded from our discussion.

The vector $x^* = (x_1^*, x_2^*, ..., x_m^*)^t$ which satisfies (4.6–8) is called the *optimal point* and the value of the objective function at that point $f(x^*)$, is called its *optimal value*. Taken together, $[x^*, f(x^*)]$ is the *optimal solution*. We distinguish between the cases for which (4.6) holds for all feasible x and those for which $f(x^*) \leq f(x^*)$ only for a small neighborhood of x^*. The latter points are called *local optima*, while the former is called the *global optimum*.

Many practical situations yield only a global solution which can be guaranteed beforehand. In other instances, lens design included, local solutions are possible. Most of the algorithms that have been developed to solve (4.6–8) converge to a local solution. In many instances there is little reason to choose between two local solutions so that the lack of a global guarantee may not be a serious defect. On the other hand, the designer's dissatisfaction may be the only influence to motivate a continued search; personal expertise is still a most important factor in the success of an optimization project.

A property useful to ensure that a solution will be global is convexity. This is a subject with a wealth of literature, both theoretical and practical in nature, so that reference can be made to standard works such as *Rockafellar* [4.35]. In order to show the consequences for nonlinear programming, however, the definitions and a few remarks about them may be appropriate here.

A domain D of E^m is said to be *convex* if for any two points, x_1 and $x_2 \in D$ and any scalar $\lambda \in [0, 1]$, $x = \lambda x_1 + (1 - \lambda)x_2$ is also a member of D. A function $f(x)$ is said to be *convex* over a convex domain if for any two points, x_1 and $x_2 \in D$, and any scalar $\lambda \in [0, 1]$,

$$f[\lambda x_1 + (1 - \lambda)x_2] \leq \lambda f(x_1) + (1 - \lambda) f(x_2). \tag{4.9}$$

That is, the function is never greater along a line joining two points than their linear interpolation. If strict inequality holds, $f(x)$ is said to be *strictly convex*. When the reverse inequalities hold, $f(x)$ is said to be *concave*.

If the convex function $f(x)$ is differentiable, it lies entirely to one side of its tangent plane at any point in D. Furthermore, if the second partial derivatives exist, the *Hessian* matrix (the matrix whose elements are $\partial^2 f / \partial x_i \partial x_j$) will be positive definite. Finally, over D, the $f(x)$ has only one minimum and if it occurs in the interior of D, it can be found where the gradient vector $\nabla f = (\partial f / \partial x_1, \partial f / \partial x_2, ..., \partial f / \partial x_m)^t = 0$. A problem of the form (4.6–8) specialized so the $f(x)$ is convex, the $g_k(x)$ define a convex feasible region, the $h_k(x)$ are absent, and all $x_j \geq 0, j = 1, 2, ..., m$ is called a *convex programming* problem; its optimum is guaranteed to be global. Several special situations are illustrated in Figs. 4.2, 3.

A minimum of (4.6) may occur at an interior point of the set defined by (4.7) or it may occur on the boundary. At a boundary point, one or more of the inequality constraints (4.7) will become strict equalities, in which case they are said to be *active constraints*. Conditions that may be used to verify an alleged solution must take into account the objective function and the constraints,

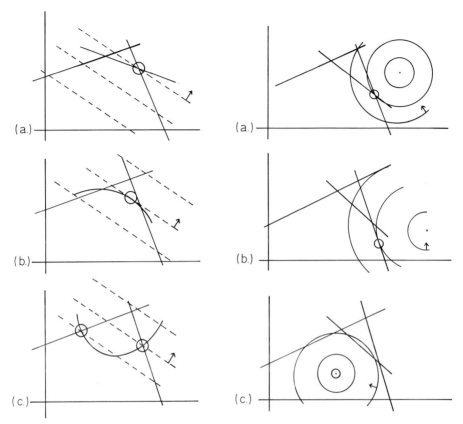

Fig. 4.2a–c. Three classes of mathematical programs. In increasing order of difficulty, (a) a linear program, (b) a linear objective with nonlinear constraints forming a convex feasible region, and (c) a nonconvex region with local solutions

Fig. 4.3a–c. Quadratic programs illustrating three types of solution points. (a) Solution at a corner of the feasible region, (b) solution on an edge, and (c) solution in the interior

whether they be active or inactive. If the problem is unconstrained and $f(x)$ is differentiable at x^*, then a necessary condition for x^* to be a local minimum is that

$$\nabla f(x^*) = 0, \tag{4.10}$$

that is, x^* is a *stationary point* of $f(x)$. If we add to this the requirement that the Hessian matrix at x^* be positive definite, then we have both necessary and sufficient conditions that x^* be a local minimum of $f(x)$. Note that $f(x)$ may have a minimum without these conditions, $f(x) = |x|$ being an example where $f(x)$ is not differentiable at the solution $x^* = 0$.

When both equality and inequality constraints are present, the conditions are more complicated (see [4.1]). Suppose that x^* is a local minimum; then $f(x)$ cannot decrease along any smooth curve from x^* into the feasible region. Let v be the tangent vector to such an arc at x^* and let the inner product of two vectors be denoted by $\langle \cdot, \cdot \rangle$. Then the nonzero vectors v can be separated into three classes, having the properties

	Inequality constraints	Equality constraints	Objective
V_1	$\left\{ \begin{array}{l} \langle v, \nabla g_j(x^*)\rangle \geq 0 \\ \text{for active constraints} \end{array} \right\} \cap \left\{ \begin{array}{l} \langle v, \nabla h_j(x^*)\rangle = 0 \\ \text{for } j=n+1, ..., K \end{array} \right\} \cap \left\{ \begin{array}{l} \langle v, \nabla f(x^*)\rangle \geq 0 \\ \end{array} \right\}$		
V_2	$\left\{ \begin{array}{l} \langle v, \nabla g_j(x^*)\rangle \geq 0 \\ \text{for active constraints} \end{array} \right\} \cap \left\{ \begin{array}{l} \langle v, \nabla h_i(x^*)\rangle = 0 \\ \text{for } j=n+1, ..., K \end{array} \right\} \cap \left\{ \begin{array}{l} \langle v, \nabla f(x^*)\rangle < 0 \\ \end{array} \right\}$		
V_3	$\left\{ \begin{array}{l} \langle v, \nabla g_j(x^*)\rangle < 0 \\ \text{for at least one} \\ \text{active constraint} \end{array} \right\} \cup \left\{ \begin{array}{l} \langle v, \nabla h_j(x^*)\rangle \neq 0 \\ \text{for at least one} \\ \text{constraint} \end{array} \right\}$		

If V_2 is empty, the existence of Lagrange multipliers can be proved. A Lagrange function is constructed from (4.6–8),

$$L(x, \lambda, \mu) = f(x) - \langle \lambda, g(x)\rangle + \langle \mu, h(x)\rangle, \tag{4.11}$$

where λ and μ are vectors of Lagrange multipliers, dimensioned n and $K-n$, respectively. If x^* is a local solution of (4.6–8), $f(x)$, $g_j(x)$, $h_j(x)$ are differentiable, V_2 is empty, then λ^* and μ^* exist such that

$$h_j(x^*) = 0, \qquad j = 1, 2, ..., n, \tag{4.12}$$

$$g_j(x^*) \geq 0, \qquad j = n+1, ..., K, \tag{4.13}$$

$$\lambda_j^* g_j(x^*) = 0 \qquad j = n+1, ..., K, \tag{4.14}$$

$$\mu_j^* \geq 0 \qquad j = n+1, ..., K, \tag{4.15}$$

$$\nabla L(x^*, \lambda^*, \mu^*) = 0. \tag{4.16}$$

These conditions are the *Kuhn-Tucker* necessary conditions [4.36]. The usefulness of these conditions depends upon the ability to verify that V_2 is indeed empty. One such condition is the first-order *constraint qualification*. Let $\bar{x}$ be a feasible point of (4.6–8) and suppose that $g(x)$ are differentiable and for active $g(x)$ there is a smooth curve terminating at $\bar{x}^*$ and consisting entirely of feasible points for which the $g(x)$ are not active. A feasible point can be said to be *consistent* with the constraints, and if points exist for which $g(x) > 0$ for all constraints, then such a point is *superconsistent* [4.37].

When the constraint qualification is imposed as a hypothesis, then the Kuhn-Tucker conditions (4.12–16) hold. The emptiness of V_2 can be assured by the constraint qualification, which in turn can be established by the linear independence of the gradients of the $h(x)$ and the active components of $g(x)$ at x^*. Proofs of these statements depend upon Farkas' lemma on linear inequalities; *Fiacco* and *McCormick* [4.38] provide the proofs, extended theory, and a number of examples to illustrate the applicability or failure of (4.12–16). It must be kept in mind that the Kuhn-Tucker theory applies to local minima and any information about the global solution must be obtained from stronger hypotheses, such as convexity.

Too often in practice, it is difficult to verify that the convergence conditions hold. The designer must exercise his judgment without support from theory. This is recognized in several papers on optical design by the emphasis on the semi-automatic nature of the process.

4.2.3 Search Algorithms

Nonlinear problems rarely can be solved explicitly. An initial guess followed by a systematic strategy for improvement is the usual way that a problem is attacked. We shall mention three broad categories of methods here, with details given in Sect. 4.3.

Unconstrained Objectives

First, let us reconsider the remarks on the minimum of an unconstrained convex function. In the neighborhood of its solution, with suitable differentiability assumptions, it can be represented by a positive definite quadratic form using Taylor's theorem. Looking at the problem in reverse, we are led to a rather general approach to formulating search algorithms. At an estimate of a minimum, either local or global, we express the objective function in terms of its Taylor's series, truncated after the quadratic term. The stationary point where $\nabla f = 0$ can be found by solving a set of simultaneous linear equations, whose coefficient matrix is the Hessian, known to be positive definite when the estimate is "close" to the solution. The solution of the linear equations may be carried out by elimination in one total step or in m single steps suitably chosen. When $f(x)$ is not purely quadratic, this process gives a new estimate of the solution, not necessarily a better one. Any algorithm for minimizing a general function that minimizes a positive definite quadratic form in m or fewer steps is said to possess *property Q*. Several of the methods in popular use do have property Q^1.

---

1 Sometimes called quadratic convergence. We prefer to reserve this descriptor for rates of convergence.

The search algorithms for locating a minimum of an unconstrained function take the form

Step 0.   Guess $x^{(0)}$ (4.17)

Step i. $x^{(i+1)} = x^{(i)} + \Delta x^{(i)}$ $i = 1, 2, ..., m$

              $\Delta x^{(i)} = \omega^{(i)} \alpha^{(i)} s^{(i)}$

              $s^{(i)}$ is a search direction, $\alpha^{(i)}$ is calculated step length, and $\omega^{(i)}$ is a predetermined relaxation parameter. $\omega^{(i)}$ is often chosen to be 1.0 but there may be advantages in using other values.

Step $m+1$.   Spacer step. This step may be exactly the same as the previous m steps, it may be quite different with its purpose being acceleration or enforcement of descent, or it may be missing entirely. Convergence criteria are checked here and the sequence terminated or restarted with the current solution serving as $x^{(0)}$.

Features that distinguish the several different methods for minimizing a function include the calculation of the search directions $s^{(i)}$, the step length calculations $\alpha^{(i)}$, the relaxation parameters $\omega^{(i)}$, the initial guess $x^{(0)}$, and the details of the spacer step.

Property Q is not necessary for a search algorithm to be successful, although the feature is surely desirable. Its presence will depend upon the details in the calculation of the steps $\Delta x^{(i)}$. Other characteristics of search algorithms that are of interest include their capability of following narrow curved valleys far removed from a minimum and the rates of convergence in a neighborhood of a minimum. The valley-following trait is often derived by a heuristic argument, while convergence rates are given by precise mathematical definitions. *Ortega* and *Rheinboldt* [4.3] define asymptotic convergence rates in analogy with the Cauchy ratio and the d'Alembert root test for convergence of series. In particular, *superlinear* and *quadratic* convergence rates are associated with several of the search algorithms in common use. This rate amounts to the exponent of the error norm in the comparison of successive iterates. Familiar cases of superlinear and quadratic rates of convergence for functions of one variable are explained in detail by *Isaacson* and *Keller* [4.6] in their discussion of false position and Newton's method. These convergence rates are characteristic of method and solution taken together. For example, Newton's method to find the zeros of $f(x) = x^2(1-x)$ has asymptotic convergence rates of 1 and 2 associated with solutions 0.0 and 1.0, respectively.

In the past few years, these convergence rates of iterative processes have received considerable theoretical attention. They are derived under the assumptions that a solution x^* exists and the guess $x^{(0)}$ is sufficiently close to x^*, and that a large number of steps in the process have already been taken. *Ortega* and *Rheinboldt* [4.3], for example, are careful to point out these assumptions; other authors may not be so explicit. These asymptotic properties are interesting and at times useful, but they tell us little about the early stages of the optimization where the estimates $x^{(i)}$ are far from x^*, nor do they provide much information about the prospects of arriving at a global or a local solution with a reasonable amount of calculation.

Attention to Constraints

A second category of methods attempts to solve the constrained optimization problem with explicit use of the constraints in determining the search directions and step lengths. We can classify these further into special case algorithms, gradient projection methods, and cutting plane methods. The first of these is likely to be of value to the experienced professional user having many cases with the same characteristics to be exploited. Included in this class will be *quadratic programming* algorithms specially designed for the case where (4.6) is a quadratic form and (4.7, 8) are linear. $x \geq 0$ is also included among the constraints. *Wolfe* [4.39] derived an algorithm making use of the Kuhn-Tucker conditions and a modification of the simplex method from linear programming. Several other authors have discussed this problem, most of them treating it as an extension of linear programming. A second special case worth mentioning here is *geometric programming*. This is a transformation technique devised by *Zener* [4.40], whereby problems of a special form are replaced by simpler problems having only linear constraints. Geometric programming has been discredited by some practitioners as being too specialized for their realistic problems. On the contrary, we believe it to be more useful than is generally supposed and since it has a specific optics application, a more detailed commentary is given in Sect. 4.3.

Gradient projection methods tend to follow the scheme (4.17) with restrictions placed upon the directions of search $s^{(i)}$ and the step lengths $\alpha^{(i)}$. The basic step requirement is to produce a decrease in the objective function. If the estimate $x^{(i)}$ is strictly inside of the feasible region, the step may be taken to the minimum in that direction or to a constraint, whichever is closer. If one or more of the constraints are active, a projection on them provides a suitable descent direction. If the active constraints are linear, the process just described is executed; otherwise, the projection may be feasible only in a small neighborhood of $x^{(i)}$.

The third category uses cutting planes described by *Kelley* [4.41] and is important to us in that the method is well suited to an implementation of geometric programming. This class of algorithms approximates the constraints and the objective by linear functions, thus producing a linear program to be solved. The solution is tested for the nonlinear problem and if infeasible, a linear constraint is inserted into the constraint set, separating the current estimate from the feasible set. Feasibility in the linear program is then restored by a single step of the dual simplex method from linear programming. Figure 4.4 indicates several LP approximations where the feasible region is convex and the objective function is linear.

When the original constraints are linear, as in the transformed geometric program, only the objective function needs to be approximated. The process is

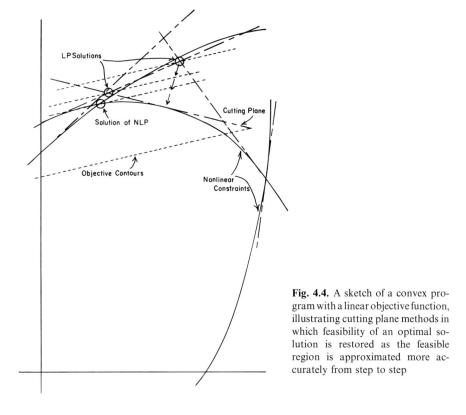

Fig. 4.4. A sketch of a convex program with a linear objective function, illustrating cutting plane methods in which feasibility of an optimal solution is restored as the feasible region is approximated more accurately from step to step

repeated until convergence is achieved. Because of the simplicity of the dual simplex steps, this method can be quite efficient when it is applicable.

Penalty and Barrier Methods

An intermediate approach to the constrained problem is to convert to a sequence of approximating unconstrained problems. This has been suggested many times; one of the earlier papers was by *Courant* [4.42]. Optical designers have made use of penalties, sometimes with little success. *Feder* [4.43] specifically advised against their use. Presumably, he reconsidered in a later paper [4.30] where he refers to *Grey's* [4.44] paper which completed the cycle by referencing [4.42]. In the 1960s, the process was formally studied in a mathematical structure and called SUMT: *sequential unconstrained minimization technique* by *Fiacco* and *McCormick* [4.38]. The method consists of forming a new objective function by augmenting (4.6) with a penalty when the constraint is violated. The more severe the penalty, the better approximation its minimum makes to the true solution. These methods have had considerable theoretical study and some of the difficulties that may have motivated Feder's negative comments are explained by *Murray* [4.45, 46]. The SUMT methods in a number of variations control feasibility in several of the large-scale optical design programs available today.

Convergence from a Poor First Guess

A consideration yet to be mentioned is the capability of the algorithms to improve a crude guess. Both theory and success in practice are rather haphazard at this point. Other than existence theory of general iterative processes, the derivations and explanations of suitable methods are based on intuition. An ability to align search directions with the valley being followed is most important to the designer. The methods to achieve this alignment will be mentioned in the discussion of each search algorithm in Sect. 4.3.

4.3 Algorithms for Nonlinear Optimization

The nonlinear programming problem has been attacked by designers from several engineering and scientific disciplines as well as by applied mathematicians. Consequently, a large number of algorithms is available from which to choose. The effectiveness of any particular procedure depends partly upon its own characteristics and partly upon the problem to which it is applied. We present the details of only a few of these many algorithms; our selection has been based upon a mathematical classification of methods and upon the types of problems from optics to which they appear to be well suited. Any such selection is open to criticism; indeed, it is possible to compare several computer programs with each other using several standard test problems and have each method rank "best" for one of the problems [4.47].

Optimization problems occur naturally in one of two broad categories, unconstrained and constrained objectives. As we mentioned earlier, these are not entirely distinct since one method of treating constraints amounts to augmenting the unconstrained objective function with penalties.

4.3.1 Unconstrained Objectives

Among the various ways that algorithms might be classified, the order of derivatives required is a commonly used basis for organization. As one might expect, the additional information about the problem carried in the derivatives leads to a solution in fewer steps. On the other hand, differentiation may introduce cumbersome arithmetic processes and cost more in the long run than a less sophisticated algorithm.

Second Derivative Methods

The objective function (4.6) to be minimized is $f(x)$, $x=(x_1, x_2, ..., x_m)^t$. Given a starting point x^0, $f(x)$ may be represented by a Taylor's series about x^*, and the solution truncated after the second-order terms

$$f(x^*) = f(x^0) + \langle (x^* - x^0), \nabla f_0(x^0) \rangle + 1/2 \langle (x^* - x^0), H_0(x^* - x^0) \rangle,$$

where $H_0 = [\partial^2 f(x^0)/\partial x_i \partial x_j]$ is the Hessian matrix at x^0 and $\langle \cdot, \cdot \rangle$ denotes the inner product of two vectors. A necessary condition for a stationary point at x^* is $\nabla f(x^*) = 0$

$$\nabla f(x^*) = \nabla f(x^0) + H_0(x^* - x^0) = 0. \tag{4.18}$$

Then a step that goes from x^0 to x^* is

$$\Delta x = x^* - x_0 = -H_0^{-1}(\nabla f_0), \tag{4.19}$$

under the condition that the Hessian matrix H_0 is nonsingular.

If $f(x)$ were truly a quadratic form, then this single step, involving the correction of all m variables, produces the correct answer. That is, the calculation possesses "property Q". If derivatives of higher order cannot be neglected in the Taylor's series, then the single step, $x^* = x^0 + \Delta x$ does not produce the solution, only a new guess. Repeating this cycle gives us Newton's algorithm.

Nothing was included in the description above to assure convergence to the stationary point or to guarantee a minimum instead of a maximum or saddle point. The existence of a minimum follows from the further assumption that $F(x)$ is convex, that is, H is positive definite. If $F(x)$ is convex, then a comparison of $F(x^*)$ with $F(x^0)$ informs us of an overshot and possible divergence. A step length parameter α allows us to solve a minimization problem in one dimension,

$$\operatorname*{Min}_{\alpha} F(x^0 + \alpha s),$$

where $s = -H_0^{-1}(\nabla F_0)$. The result is the modified Newton's method.

There have been numerous other variations published concerning Newton's method. They have been directed generally toward improving performance of algorithms intended to minimize a sum of squares.

When Newton's method is attempted with a singular or nearly singular Hessian matrix, the calculation may fail entirely or, perhaps even worse, the steps will be erratic and vacillatory, perhaps even diverging unless descent is enforced. The nonlinear least-squares problem is often confronted with extreme ill conditioning, especially if the normal equations formulation is used. The normal equation matrix is not the Hessian matrix unless the problem is truly quadratic but both are troubled by near singularity and they are amenable to the same repair. The ill condition is manifest geometrically by level contours of the objective function forming very narrow and closed curves. Even linear least squares are inclined to this difficulty which tends to introduce and magnify roundoff and other errors. Reference [4.2] is devoted to the numerical aspects of linear least-squares problems.

The unfortunate effects of the ill condition have motivated several efforts to correct the difficulty. One of these, by *Greenstadt* [4.48], decomposes the Hessian matrix into its eigenvector representation

$$H = \sum_i^m \lambda_i \mathbf{v}_i \rangle \langle \mathbf{v}_i \,. \qquad (4.20)$$

The notation $\cdot \rangle \langle \cdot$ indicates the outer product or matrix product of two vectors. The zero and negative eigenvalues are now replaced with suitably chosen positive values; the new matrix is now positive definite and the calculation is stabilized.

A different approach to damping was introduced by *Levenberg* [4.25] and in the following years the method has been reinvented, renovated, and modified by several authors, including *Marquardt* [4.49, 50] and *Morrison* [4.51]. *Levenberg's* paper on nonlinear least squares was taken up by optical designers who used the term "damped least squares", descriptive of the stabilizing action. Early contributions in the optics literature on damping came from *Wynne* [4.52] and *Meiron* [4.53].

Marquardt designed his algorithm as a compromise between the Newton step which causes the oscillation and the guaranteed but slow descent of the gradient method. In terms of the original idea of simply augmenting the diagonal of the normal equation coefficients, this seems like an entirely different algorithm. Several different arguments for the optimal selection of the damping coefficient have been published, for example [4.54, 55]. *Jones* [4.56] proposes a search along a curve to obtain the best combination of the two directions. This has merit when the number of total steps is important but suffers when evaluation of the objective function is very expensive.

The "compromise" argument can be derived from a sketch, i.e., Fig. 4.5. A method based upon a quadratic approximation will take a step to the center of the elliptical contour. A pure gradient step is orthogonal to the tangent to the contour and when the problem is ill conditioned, the two directions are nearly orthogonal. Since both steps are derived on the basis of reasonable assumptions, a compromise is suggested in the form of a linear combination. The two steps are

$$\Delta x_a = H^{-1} \mathbf{V} f$$

and

$$\Delta x_b = \mathbf{V} f \,.$$

Then

$$\Delta x = \Delta x_a + \mu \Delta x_b$$

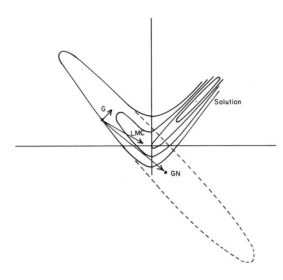

Fig. 4.5. Contours of a nonlinear objective function and illustration of the gradient (G), the Gauss-Newton (GN), and the Levenberg-Marquardt compromise (LMC) directions

or

$$(H + \mu I)\Delta x = -\nabla f \tag{4.21}$$

can be solved directly. This final form suggests the term "damping factor" to describe μ.

The numerical effect is, to increase the diagonal elements of the coefficient matrix, making it more positive definite. It has been noted that the scalar matrix μI can be replaced by a diagonal matrix with positive entries, thus attending to the variables individually. Another variation is multiplicative damping where the diagonal elements of H are multiplied by positive damping factors, greater than unity. The sketch indicates how the compromise enhances the valley following capabilities of either algorithm.

First Derivative Methods

One of the first search methods to come to mind is "steepest descent", originally proposed by Cauchy. Although the algorithm is practically useless in its purpose of solving problems, a review of its reasons for failure may be instructive. The steps are simple and easy to program and the justification for them seems to be quite reasonable; unfortunately, Cauchy's method, based on the best tactics, also leads to poor overall strategy.

The function $f(x)$ evaluated at a particular point x^0 has a numerical value, $f(x^0) = b$. Those other points of the domain at which $f(x) = b$ define a contour or surface. Since our desire is to change $f(x)$, we move from this surface in the direction of greatest change, that is, we use the direction of the negative gradient or direction of steepest descent as the search direction. Specifically, the iteration is given by the equations

$$x^0 \quad \text{initial guess}$$
$$\Delta x^i = -\alpha_i \nabla f(x^i). \tag{4.22}$$

α_i is the scalar that minimizes $f[x^i - \alpha_i \nabla f(x^i)]$ as a function of α.

$$x^{i+1} = x^i + \Delta x^i.$$

The method was not properly tested until the early days of automatic high-speed digital computation. Early lens design programs attempted to optimize by this method but after a period of frustation the method was abandoned. *Feder* recounts some of these projects in his papers [4.30, 43] as does *Stavroudis* [4.57] in a 1964 survey for a computer-oriented audience. At the same time Cauchy's method was being tried and discarded by optical designers, the problem was studied by mathematicians including *Forsythe* [4.58] and *Akaike* [4.59] who eventually gave precise mathematical reasons for the failure.

One reason with intuitive appeal that is often cited is the dependence of the gradient upon the scaling of the independent variables. If all level contours were circles, the gradient method would converge in one step. The rescaling of the independent variables to round out the contours will improve the performance of any algorithm and is generally recommended as a part of the pre-computation analysis of a problem. When the contours are flattened and the guess is unfortunate, the gradient zigzags across the valley. A few steps of the gradient method applied to minimize

$$f(x_1, x_2) = 0.2575 x_1^2 - 0.8574 x_1 x_2 + 0.7525 x_2^2 - 0.1726 x_1 + 0.2097 x_2 - 0.9322 \tag{4.23}$$

are listed in Table 4.1 and illustrated in Figs. 4.6, 7.

Table 4.1. Gradient steps and conjugate direction steps in the minimization of the function depicted in Fig. 4.6. Successive approximations to the Hessian's inverse are included. The conjugate gradient and the Davidon-Fletcher-Powell methods take identical steps for this problem

	x_0	s_0	x_1	s_1	x_2	s_2	x^3
Gradient method	10.0000	0.1695	10.0915	−0.1880	8.9665	0.1476	...
	6.0031	−0.6708	5.6411	−0.0475	5.3568	−0.5842	...
Conjugate gradient method	10.0000	0.1695	10.0915	−0.1747	1.9994	0.0000	
	6.0031	−0.6708	5.6411	−0.1002	0.9997	0.0000	

Davidon-Fletcher-Powell	Steps as in conjugate gradient

$$H_0 = \begin{bmatrix} 1.0 & 0.0 \\ 0.0 & 1.0 \end{bmatrix} \quad H_1 = \begin{bmatrix} 0.7848 & 0.3034 \\ 0.3034 & 0.7548 \end{bmatrix} \quad H_2 = H^{-1} = \begin{bmatrix} 37.6193 & 21.4303 \\ 21.4303 & 12.8736 \end{bmatrix}$$

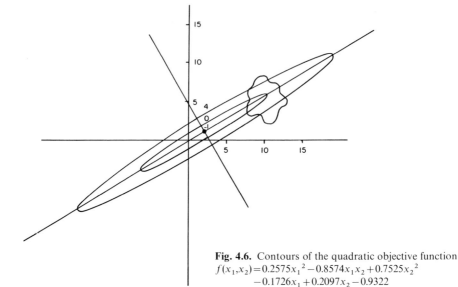

Fig. 4.6. Contours of the quadratic objective function
$f(x_1,x_2)=0.2575x_1{}^2-0.8574x_1x_2+0.7525x_2{}^2$
$-0.1726x_1+0.2097x_2-0.9322$

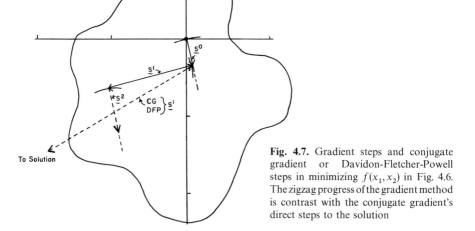

Fig. 4.7. Gradient steps and conjugate gradient or Davidon-Fletcher-Powell steps in minimizing $f(x_1,x_2)$ in Fig. 4.6. The zigzag progress of the gradient method is contrast with the conjugate gradient's direct steps to the solution

At about the same time, a new algorithm by *Hestenes* and *Stiefel* [4.26] using descent methods was being developed to solve symmetric linear equations by minimizing the associated quadratic form. The new routine conducted a search in a direction suggested by the local gradient but altered in such a manner that after *n* steps, a linearly independent set of directions has been explored. This does minimize the quadratic form and solves the linear equations, but today the routine is seldom used for that purpose. At the time of its inception, computer memory was scarce or practically nonexistent. The problems of solving elliptic partial differential equations led to large sparse symmetric matrices for which one of this new class of algorithms maintained sparseness throughout the calculations. Although the memory problem was solved by advances in hardware technology, the algorithms remain as the foundation of a class of effective optimization methods for nonlinear problems.

The idea of conjugate directions follows from the attempt to search through a set of directions that form a basis for the vector space of m dimensions. The independence alone does not produce property Q as can be seen by considering the coordinate direction vectors. Given the symmetric and positive definite matrix A, we attempt to minimize

$$f(x) = c + \langle b, x \rangle + 1/2 \langle x, Ax \rangle . \tag{4.24}$$

Suppose that we have a set of m vectors $\{p^i\}$, $i = 1, 2, \ldots, m$ available that has the property of A conjugacy or A orthogonality,

$$\langle p^i, Ap^j \rangle = 0, \quad i \neq j$$

$$\langle p^i, Ap^i \rangle = 1 .$$

For the moment, we avoid the question of how we obtain $\{p^i\}$; at least one such set exists, the eigenvectors. Then, commencing at a guess x_0, the values of x are improved by searching in the direction $p^1, p^2, \ldots, p^m$ sequentially. At the ith step,

$$x^{i+1} = x^i + \lambda_i p^i ,$$

where λ_i minimizes the one-dimensional problem

$$\min f(x^i + \lambda p^i) = \min [c + \langle b, x^i + \lambda p^i \rangle + 1/2 \langle x^i + \lambda p^i, A(x^i + \lambda p^i) \rangle]$$

$$df/d\lambda = \langle p^i, b + Ax^i \rangle + \lambda = 0 .$$

Thus, the step length $\lambda_i = \langle -p^i, \nabla f_i \rangle$. It is easy to show that a true quadratic is minimized in m steps or fewer so that any conjugate direction algorithm has property Q.

Nothing we have done so far suggests a method for obtaining $\{p^i\}$ except the eigenvector calculation, a formidable problem in its own right. The several conjugate direction algorithms are distinguished first by their method of obtaining $\{p^i\}$. Two of this class have been used in optical design codes while a third has been used with real success in curve fitting and design in other fields. The first was the conjugate gradient method. *Feder* [4.43] apparently was the first to use this method for optical design and may have been the first to apply the method to any nonlinear problem. The paper by *Fletcher* and *Reeves* [4.60] in 1964 certainly increased the awareness of the algorithm. The details are as follows:

$$g^{(0)} = \nabla f(x^{(0)}), \quad p^{(0)} = -g^{(0)}.$$

For $i = 1, 2, ..., m$

$$x^{i+1} = x^i + \lambda_i p^i$$

$$\lambda_i \text{ minimizes } f(x^i + \lambda p^i)$$

$$g^i = \nabla f(x^i)$$

$$p^{i+1} = -g^{i+1} + (\langle g^{i+1}, g^{i+1} \rangle / \langle g^i, g^i \rangle) p^i.$$

The process may continue, be reset to the beginning, or a spacer step may be taken.

We shall carry through the steps required to minimize the quadratic form (4.23). The results are tabulated in Table 4.1, and are sketched in Figs. 4.6, 7.

Experimental evidence from all sources known to us indicates that this routine may require more steps than its competitors, but the minimal storage requirements and moderate amount of calculation suggest that it always be considered when choosing an algorithm.

A more powerful procedure of a similar nature was suggested by *Davidon* [4.27] and expanded upon by *Fletcher* and *Powell* [4.28]. The use of the DFP algorithm in major optical design programs seems to be limited to experiments by *Feder* [4.43] and by *Jamieson* [4.5] who tentatively rejected it. Nevertheless, the method is popular in many fields including data fitting so that some discussion here is in order.

We have already seen that conjugate direction methods will solve a symmetric and positive definite set of linear equations (4.18) in m steps. Furthermore if the set $\{p^i\}$, $i = 1, 2, ..., m$ were eigenvectors, both A and A^{-1} can be represented as a sum of outer products, that is, if $Ap^i = \lambda_i p^i$, $i = 1, 2, ..., m$, then

$$A = \sum \lambda_i p^i \rangle \langle p^i / \langle p^i, p^i \rangle$$

and

$$A^{-1} = \sum 1/\lambda_i p^i \rangle \langle p^i / \langle p^i, p^i \rangle.$$

This will also be true for other sets of conjugate directions. Let $\{p^i\}$ be conjugate with respect to A. Then

$$A^{-1} = \sum p^i \rangle \langle p^i / \langle p^i, Ap^i \rangle.$$

If the sum is incomplete, that is, less than m terms appear, it can act as an approximate inverse. When A^{-1} is known, a quadratic form is minimized in one step. Otherwise, if H_i is the ith approximation to the inverse obtained at the ith step, the direction of search for the next step is

$$p^{i+1} = -H_i \nabla f(x^{i+1}).$$

The results of the search will minimize $f(x)$ in the p^{i+1} direction and are used to define the next appropriate inverse H_{i+1}

$$H_{i+1} = H_i + p^i\rangle\langle p^i/\langle p_i, A p_i\rangle + B_i,$$

where B_i is a further correction term to be determined. At the ith step, we require p^i to be conjugate with respect to A to the previous steps $p^1, p^2, \ldots, p^{i-1}$. Furthermore, H_i is to behave as A^{-1} in the subspace spanned by $p^1, p^2, \ldots, p^i$. That is, $H_{i-1} A p^k = p^k$, $k = 1, 2, \ldots, i-1$, and as a result

$$-\langle p^k, A p^i\rangle = \langle p^k, A H_{i-1} g^i\rangle = \langle p^k, g^i\rangle = 0 \tag{4.25}$$

because the gradient is orthogonal to all previous search directions. B_i is constructed so that

$$H_i A p^k = p^k$$
$$[H_{i-1} + (p^i\rangle\langle p^i)/\langle p^i, A p^i\rangle + B] A p^i = p^i \tag{4.26}$$

or

$$(H_{i-1} + B_i) A p^i = 0.$$

Since $f = A + \langle b, x\rangle + 1/2\langle x, Ax\rangle$ and $\nabla f = g + Ax$, we have

$$g^{i+1} - g^i = A(x^{i+1} - x^i) = x_i A p^i$$

and (4.26) is written as

$$(H_{i-1} + B_i)(g^{i+1} - g^i) = 0.$$

Let $y^i = g^{i+1} - g^i$. Then

$$(H_{i-1} + B_i) y^i = 0$$

and an easy solution of these equations is obtained from

$$H_{i-1} y^i = -B_i y^i$$

by multiplication by $H_{i-1}y^i$.

$$H_{i-1}y^i\rangle\langle H_{i-1}y^i = -\langle y^i, H_{i-1}y^i\rangle B_i,$$

or $B_i = -H_{i-1}y_i\rangle\langle H_{i-1}y_i/\langle y_i, H_{i-1}y_i\rangle$.
Furthermore, since $\langle p^k, g^{i+1}\rangle = 0$,

$$B_i A p^k = 0, \quad k = 1, 2, ..., i-1.\tag{4.27}$$

Finally, the Davidon-Fletcher-Powell algorithm can be summarized for the *i*th stage.
1) $d^i = -H_{i-1}g^i$.
2) Find λ_i to minimize $q_i(\lambda) = F(x^i + \lambda d^i)$.
3) $x^{i+1} = x^i + \lambda_i d^i, \ y^i = g^{i+1} - g^i$.
4) $H_i = H_{i-1} + \lambda_i d^i\rangle\langle d^i/\langle g_i, H_{i-1}g_i\rangle - H_{i-1}y^i\rangle\langle H_{i-1}y^i/\langle y_i, H_{i-1}y_i\rangle$
where $(H_0 = I)$.

This algorithm has been generally accepted as an excellent method for unconstrained minimization problems. It is not the best for all cases [4.47] but seems to be quite reliable.

The Davidon-Fletcher-Powell and the conjugate gradient methods have been shown to take identical steps when the function to be minimized is indeed a quadratic and they start at the same point, but the DFP appears to locate the minimum at less expense for more general functions. Although the CG algorithm takes less computer memory and both have similar asymptotic behavior near the solution, the DFP apparently has a more favorable ability to follow a narrow curved valley to the neighborhood of the solution.

Another algorithm in the conjugate direction class was developed by *Grey* [4.29] to minimize an objective function consisting of a sum of squares. His motivation was the optical design problem, and the algorithm has been developed since to be competitive with other popular gradient algorithms.

The algorithm attempts to minimize the sum of squares of nonlinear functions

$$J = 1/2 \sum_{i=1}^{N} f_i^2(x), \quad x = (x_1, x_2, ..., x_m).$$

Linearization of the equations

$$f_i(x) = 0, \quad i = 1, 2, ... N$$

about point x_0 gives

$$f_i(x^0) + \sum_j (\partial f_i/\partial x_j)\Delta x^j, \quad i = 1, 2, ... N.$$

If this set of linear equations $A\Delta x = b$ is solved for Δx and a new estimate $x^1 = x^0 + \Delta x^0$ used to repeat the process, we have an implementation of the

Gauss-Newton method. *Hartley* [4.61] improved the performance by enforcing descent with a search in one dimension

$$\underset{\lambda}{\text{Min}} \, J[x^{(i)} + \lambda \Delta x^{(i)}] \, .$$

The linear least-squares problem to be solved at each step can be treated by the normal equation approach or by a direct attack on the rectangular coefficient matrix, the QR transformation. Orthogonalization by the Gram-Schmidt process or by Householder transformations has become popular in recent years. *Grey* anticipated this in his algorithm for the nonlinear problem

$$A\Delta x = b$$

$$\Phi S \Delta x = b$$

$$\Phi^t \Phi = I$$

$$S \Delta x = \Phi^t b$$

$$\Delta x = S^{-1} \Phi^t b \, .$$

The Gram-Schmidt or the Householder process generates a matrix Φ with mutually orthogonal columns and an upper triangular transformation. The solution Δx is obtained by a simple back substitution.

   Grey observed that the orthogonalization proceeds one column at a time and that by defining a new coordinate system u in which

$$\Delta u = S \Delta x \, ,$$

a relaxation of each coordinate in turn can be carried out with updating and reevaluation of the f_i's.

   The updating after the Δu_i relaxation leads to a demonstration of conjugate directions, [4.62],

$$S \Delta x_i = \Delta u_i \, ,$$

where $\Delta u_i = (0, 0, ..., \Delta u_i, 0, ... 0)^t$. Then $\langle \Phi u^i, \Phi u^j \rangle = 0$, $i \neq j$, and

$$\langle S \Delta x^i, S \Delta x^j \rangle = \langle \Delta x^i, S^t S \Delta x^i = 0 \rangle$$

or the Δx^i are conjugate with respect to $S^t S$ and thus the method has property Q. Finally, after m steps are taken in the nonlinear case, it is prudent for both theoretical and practical reasons to insert a spacer step [4.63].

   A more traditional method is the Hartley variation of the Gauss-Newton algorithm. This routine linearizes each term and solves the linear least-squares problem for a step direction, then conducts a one-dimensional search for a minimum. The linear problem is often solved by a direct attack on the rectangular matrix equation. The QR transformation is one of the most stable and effective numerically for solving the linear problem.

A recent variation on this theme has been developed by *St. Clair* and *Rigler* [4.17] for the problem of curve fitting to spectroscopic data. The Grey orthogonalization is applied in blocks, identified with the natural groupings of the variables in the model, such as the individual line shapes. Block size of one yields Grey's original routine while block size of m gives an implementation of the Gauss-Newton-Hartley method.

Descent Methods Without the Use of Derivatives

Of course, the derivatives that were the basis of the previous section can be estimated by finite differences. The Davidon-Fletcher-Powell routine was studied by *Stewart* [4.64] using difference methods instead of derivatives. Grey's method also may be programmed using finite difference. For the problems where the evaluation of derivatives is extremely complicated and tedious, this approach is generally used.

Although the desirable properties of the methods using first derivatives are preserved by difference methods, it is not necessary. *Powell* [4.65] has shown that a conjugate direction method can be constructed by purely algebraic and geometric arguments. The paper by *Shah* et al. [4.66] follows similar reasoning.

Suppose that two different starting points x^1 and x^2 are chosen and a search for a minimum in the direction p is conducted from each. If the function to be minimized is a positive definite quadratic form, then $x^2 - x^1$ is conjugate to p. Let $f(x) = c + \langle b, x \rangle + 1/2 \langle x, Ax \rangle$

$$\nabla f_1 = Ax^1 + b$$
$$\nabla f_2 = Ax^2 + b$$
$$\langle p, Ax^1 + b \rangle = 0$$
$$\langle p, Ax^2 + b \rangle = 0$$
$$\langle p, A(x^2 - x^1) \rangle = 0 .$$

More generally, if the search for each minimum is made along k conjugate directions, then the vector joining the first and last of these points is conjugate to all of these directions. Powell's algorithm requires m independent directions to start, $p^1, p^2, ..., p^m$.

Then,
1) λ^0 minimizes $f(x^0 + \lambda p^0)$
   $x^1 = x^0 + \lambda^0 p^0$.
2) x_i minimizes $f(x^i + \lambda p^i)$, $i = 1, 2, ..., m$
   $x^{i+1} = x^i + \lambda_i p^i$.
3) $p^i = p^{i+1}$, $i = 1, 2, ..., m-1$.
4) $p^m = x^{m+1} - x^1$, $x^0 = x^{m+1}$.
5) Return to 1 unless convergence is confirmed.

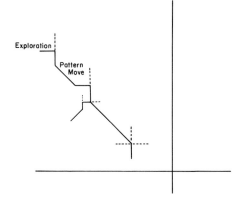

Fig. 4.8. Direct search steps, distinguishing the exploration phase and the pattern move phase

This algorithm has been quite effective in practice although we know of no instance where it has been used in optics.

A very crude search procedure with an entirely unsatisfactory asymptotic rate of convergence nevertheless has been remarkably effective in following valleys to the neighborhood of the solution. The location of the neighborhood may be sufficient for the purpose at hand, or a more sophisticated algorithm may take over at this stage. *Hooke* and *Jeeves* [4.67] called their method "direct search" and *Weisman* et al. [4.68] published an implementation of it suitable for constrained problems as well.

The method consists of a set of "exploratory" steps in the coordinate directions followed by a "pattern" move. This cycle is repeated until convergence is reached. The steps are as follows:

Exploration phase: Assume a value of Δx_i, $i = 1, 2, ..., m$, and begin at a "base point", x^B.

1) $i = 1$, $F = f(x^B)$, $x^B = (x^1, x^2, ..., x^m)$.
2) Trial point $x = (x^1, x^2, ..., x^{i-1}, x^i + \Delta x^i, x^{i+1}, ..., x^m)$.
3) If $f(x) < F$, $F = f(x)$, $i = i + 1$, go to 2.
4) If $f(x) \geq F$, $x = x - (0, ..., 0, 2\Delta x_i, 0, ..., 0)$.
5) If $f(x) < F$, $F = f(x)$, $i = i + 1$, go to 2.
6) Otherwise reset x, $i = i + 1$, go to 2.
7) After m variables have been explored, we have arrived at point $x^{\bar{B}}$, a new base point.

Pattern move: Extrapolate from two successive base points.

$$x = x^B + (x^B - x^{\bar{B}}).$$

Restart the exploration at x or x^B depending upon which gives the better value of $f(x)$, unless convergence has been achieved. A decision on expanding or contracting Δx_i will be made at this stage, before the restart. Figure 4.8 illustrates the nature of the exploration and pattern moves.

A somewhat different direct search method was suggested by *Rosenbrock* [4.69]. These direct methods may be painfully slow near the final optimized solution but are reputed to be quite competitive in the early stages of an optimizing sequence. The Hooke and Jeeves method has been used for optical calculations, in the context of illumination [4.92].

Search in One Dimension

Almost all of the algorithms for minimizing a function of several variables have a need to locate the minimum of a function of one variable. In this section, we shall discuss two different approaches to this problem. One first assumption is made about the function.

Definition: The function is said to be *unimodal* in $[a, b]$ if the slope changes sign no more than once in $[a, b]$.

A precise statement of the consequence of unimodality is the following lemma: Let $f(x)$ be unimodal in $\lfloor a, b \rfloor$. Then it is necessary to evaluate two and no more than two distinct interior points before the minimum can be located in a proper sub interval of $[a, b]$. Let $a < x_1 < x_2 < b$. If $f(x_1) > f(x_2)$, the minimal lies in $[x_1, b]$; otherwise it lies in $[a, x_2]$. In Fig. 4.9, the interval $[a, x_1]$ is discarded.

Two general classes of algorithms are employed to locate the minimum. One of these plans a systematic strategy for placing the experiments in an optimum fashion, with no regard for the behavior of the function itself. Bisection, golden section, and Fibonacci searches are examples of this class. On the other hand, the information about the function values may be used to estimate the minimum and thus suggest a suitable location for the next guess. Interpolation formulas are used to approximate the function and are differentiated and solved for their minimum. With three points, a quadratic interpolation locates the fourth experiment. If directional derivatives are available, two points determine a cubic. Generally, the lowest order curve is best to avoid

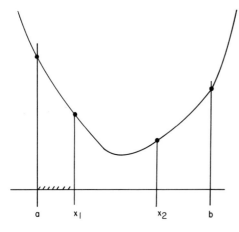

Fig. 4.9. A unimodal function on $[a, b]$. The interval is reduced to $[x_1, b]$ by two experiments at x_1 and x_2

the artifacts possibly introduced by the interpolation. The details of two of these are given as illustrations.

The Fibonacci search [4.74] is based upon the sequence of numbers $Z_0 = 1$, $Z_1 = 1$, $Z_n = Z_{n-1} + Z_{n-2}$. Given a priori tolerance decisions, the number of searches and the strategy for placement are predetermined. A simple example illustrates the method. Given the interval $[0, 4]$ and a tolerance of 0.2, place the experiments to guarantee this final interval using a minimum number of evaluations. First, the Fibonacci sequence

n	0	1	2	3	4	5	6	7	9	10	...
Z_n	1	1	2	3	5	8	13	21	34	55	...

suggests that the total interval be divided into 21 subintervals of equal size $h = 4/21 < 0.2$.

The first two experiments are placed at $8h$ and $13h$, a symmetric distance from either end. It does not matter which end of the interval is discarded since one of the two new experiments at distance $5h$ from one end has already been done. Thus we place the next experiment symmetrically in the reduced interval.

The function $f(x)$ is evaluated by a subroutine; here

$$f(x) = x^2 - 3.2x + 8 .$$

Step 1. $f(a)\quad = 8.0$
$f(8h)\ = 5.445805$
$f(13h) = 6.207710$
$f(4)\quad = 11.2,\ h = 4/21 = 0.190476.$

The assumption of unimodality allows us to discard $(13h, 4.0)$; a new experiment is placed at $5h$.

Step 2. $f(0)\quad = 8.0$
$f(5h)\ = 5.859410$
$f(8h)\ = 5.445805$
$f(13h) = -6.207710.$

This time we discard $[0, 5h]$. The process is continued with the symmetric placement of successive experiments, in each case $Z_j h$ from the outer end of the larger subinterval. The index j is systematically reduced to zero to locate the minimum at $8h \pm h$.

$\quad\quad 7h = 1.333333,\quad f(7h) = 5.511111$
$\quad\quad 8h = 1.523810,\quad f(8h) = 5.445805$
$\quad\quad 9h = 1.714286,\quad f(9h) = 5.453061.$

The reputation of the Fibonacci search as being most efficient may be misleading without an additional word of explanation. This sequence guarantees a preassigned tolerance in a minimum number of steps; the objection to be raised is the fact that all of these steps must be taken.

An interpolation polynomial may be constructed and differentiated to locate the minimum of the approximate function. This idea has been developed into very effective algorithms for minimizing functions of one variable. One of these, attributed to Davies, Swann, and Campey (DSC) by *Box* et al. [4.70] acts in two phases. The first stage is a crude search to bracket the minimum within an interval. The second stage constructs an interpolating quadratic whose minimum is used to approximate the minimum of the original function.

Step 1. Given $x_0, f(x_0)$
          Evaluate $f(x_0+h)$
                    $f(x_0+2h)$.

If these three points do not bracket the minimum, then additional experiments are placed at x_0+4h, x_0+8h, ..., until the bracket is attained. Then one additional experiment is placed to halve the last interval. Then the appropriate three of the four equidistant points are selected for entry into step 2. If the process is not successful, it will be repeated in the opposite direction.

Step 2. Given three points $x_0<x_1<x_2$ that bracket the minimum, we construct a quadratic interpolating polynomial, $f(x)=a+bx+cx^2$.

$$\begin{bmatrix} 1 & x_0 & x_0^2 \\ 1 & x_1 & x_1^2 \\ 1 & x_2 & x_2^2 \end{bmatrix} \begin{bmatrix} a \\ b \\ c \end{bmatrix} = \begin{bmatrix} f_0 \\ f_1 \\ f_2 \end{bmatrix}.$$

Since the minimum of the parabola occurs at

$$\bar{x} = -b/2c,$$

it is unnecessary to find a in order to estimate the minimizing point. In assessing the validity of the estimate, a is needed to compare $f(\bar{x})$ with $a+b\bar{x}+c\bar{x}^2$.

$$c=f_0/(x_1-x_0)(x_2-x_0)-f_1/(x_1-x_0)(x_2-x_1)$$
$$+f_2/(x_2-x_1)(x_2-x_0)$$
$$b=f_0(x_1+x_2)/(x_1-x_0)(x_2-x_0)+f_1(x_0+x_2)/(x_1-x_0)(x_2-x_1)$$
$$-f_2(x_0+x_1)/(x_2-x_1)(x_2-x_0)$$
$$a=f_0-bx_0-cx_0^2. \tag{4.29}$$

This interpolation scheme can be checked using the last three entries from the previous calculation.

$$x_0=1.333333 \quad f_0=5.511111$$
$$x_1=1.523810 \quad f_1=5.445805$$
$$x_2=1.714286 \quad f_2=5.453061.$$

Equations (4.29) produce

$$a = 8.000094$$
$$b = -3.2000067$$
$$c = 0.999997$$
$$\bar{x} = 1.600038$$
$$f(\bar{x}) = 5.439979 .$$

Thus to the accuracy allowed by round-off error in these expressions, we have produced the correct location of the minimum of the quadratic interpolation polynomial and, of course, the minimum of the function itself in this particular example.

The DSC search stops at this point. Of course it is possible to reinitiate the process from step 1. *Himmelblau* [4.1] suggests that the DSC search followed by iteration of the quadratic is better than either alone. He also claims that in the context of minimizing in many variables, the interpolation method is better than Fibonacci when the function evaluation is at all complicated and time consuming.

The reasoning behind the use of the one-dimensional search is that many of the conjugate direction properties hold rigorously only when the minimum is found in each step direction. In fact, far away from x^*, the validity is lost because of the nonlinearity. Thus, a crude search or even a step required only to be in descent may serve nearly as well. If the function were truly quadratic or nearly so as in the neighborhood of x^*, the size linear prediction steps is sufficient to find the minimum. The implementation of Grey's method in the optical design context usually omits the linear search while in the curve fitting application it is included. The subject of linear search is still a subject for research [4.71].

4.3.2 Techniques for Constrained Problems

The presence of constraints complicates the majority of practical problems. Quite often the constraints are placed individually upon the variables, and the reasoning that motivates the constraints may be obvious. For example, variables that denote a physical quantity are often constrained to take on only nonnegative values. Amounts of ingredients in a mixture, physical distance between points, and time increments will all be nonnegative. These quantities may truly be independent variables and appear explicitly in the formulation of an objective function or they may be expressed as functions of the independent variables.

Constraints may be placed on variables to guard against a perfectly reasonable mathematical solution but one which is unacceptable in practice. For example, going out of business will reduce costs and may possibly even maximize profit. Yet the problem might be incompletely specified. If profit is constrained to exceed a minimum amount, we might be able to arrive at an operational solution.

Constraints on Terms of the Objective Functions

At times a constraint may be needed to place an upper limit to a term in an objective function that is intended to be minimized. This may occur as a way to suppress a Gibbs' phenomenon in the least-squares fitting of trigonometric series. An engineering illustration occurs in the design of a thin film filter where such an effect might indicate the presence of an active element that is impossible to achieve. Besides constraining the individual terms of the objective function, a Chebyshev approximation, directly or by weighted least squares using Lawson's program, can be used to suppress unwanted variations in the objective. In our example in Sect. 4.4, we use the $2p$ norm as an approximation to the infinity norm.

Lagrange Functions

Constraints expressed as functions of the independent variables may appear in the form of equalities or inequalities. The former may allow us to solve explicitly for one independent variable and by substitution, reduce the dimension of the space. The implicit function theory of calculus regarding this point may encourage or perhaps deny the possibility of substitution but provides little help in the actual work. The classic Lagrange multiplier theory can be applied when explicit substitution is difficult or impossible. Although this approach is theoretically satisfactory, in practice it too may be unusable. The Kuhn-Tucker theory discussed in Sect. 4.2 can be used to inform us of the nature of an alleged solution; only in favorable special cases do we derive a constructive approach to a solution starting with the Kuhn-Tucker conditions.

Penalty and Barrier Methods

Although the various theories based on the Lagrange function

$$L(x, \lambda, \mu) = f(x) + \langle \lambda, g \rangle + \langle \mu, h \rangle$$

are not used often, the form of $f(x, \lambda, \mu)$ suggests a variation that is often successful. The expression for $f(x, \lambda, \mu)$ amounts to altering the objective, maximizing with respect to the λ and μ variables while simultaneously minimizing with respect to x's. If the added function is chosen to penalize the objective when the approximate solution is infeasible, or perhaps when the constraint is nearly active but feasible, then an algorithm can act upon the augmented objective function as being unconstrained. This technique was formally proposed by *Carroll* [4.72] as a *created response surface*, and later,

Fiacco and *McCormick* [4.38] developed a theory and computer program SUMT: *sequential unconstrained minimization technique.*

We shall attempt to illustrate SUMT with a simple numerical example before discussing its difficulties. Suppose we are to solve the constrained optimization problem

Minimize $4 - x^2$,

Subject to $x \geq 0$,

$x \leq 1$.

The solution: $x = 1$, $f(1) = 3$.

Since we know the solution to this example, let us use it to illustrate the Kuhn-Tucker necessary conditions.

$$L(x, \lambda) = 4 - x^2 - \lambda(1 - x) + \lambda_2 x,$$

$$\partial L / \partial x = -2x + \lambda_1 + \lambda_2 = 0, \tag{4.30}$$

$$\partial L / \partial \lambda_1 = -1 + x = 0, \tag{4.31}$$

$$\partial L / \partial \lambda_2 = x = 0. \tag{4.32}$$

To be a stationary point, the contradictory equations (4.31, 32) must be resolved. The solution $x = 1$ requires that $\lambda_2 = 0$ by (4.14); then $\lambda_1 = 2$. Thus all (4.12–16) hold. A maximum can be verified to lie at $x = 0$ by similar analysis. The saddle point nature of the Kuhn-Tucker point can be verified by perturbation of the numerical values.

An unconstrained minimization of $F(x, r)$ or $f(x)$ under the penalties $p_i(x)$ is formulated to have continuous derivatives, to leave interior minima undisturbed, and to penalize the objective severely at infeasible points.

$$p = \begin{cases} x^2, & x < 0 \\ 0, & 0 \leq x \leq 1 \\ (x - 1)^2 & x > 1. \end{cases}$$

The augmented objective function is now

$$F(x; r) = 4 - x^2 + rP(x)$$

$$= 4 - x^2 + r \begin{cases} x^2 & x < 0 \\ 0 & 0 \leq x \leq 1 \\ (x - 1)^2 & 1 < x. \end{cases}$$

The critical points are found where $dF/dx = 0$.

$$F'(x;r) = -2x + r \begin{cases} 2x & x < 0 \\ 0 & 0 \leq x \leq 1 \\ 2(x-1) & 1 < x \end{cases}$$

$$= \begin{cases} 2x(-1+r) \\ -2x = 0 \\ 2(-x+rx-r). \end{cases}$$

One of these indicates a maximum or saddle point at $x=0$. The other

$$x(r-1) - r = 0$$

or

$$x^* = r/(r-1) = 1/(1-1/r)$$

lies outside of the feasible region but as the penalty is made more severe, $r \to \infty$, the solution approaches the correct value $x=1$

$$\begin{aligned} F(x^*;r) &= 4 - [r/(r-1)]^2 + r[r/(r-1)-1]^2 \\ &= 4 - [r/(r-1)]^2 + r[1/(r-1)]^2 \\ &= 4 - (1-1/r)r^2/(r-1)^2. \end{aligned}$$

This value approaches the correct minimum of 3 from below as might be expected.

   In engineering design, the data are often so crude to begin with that a slight violation of a constraint is unimportant. Furthermore, the constraint may have been placed arbitrarily in the first place. On the other hand, at times feasibility may be much more important than optimality. In such cases, a somewhat different style of SUMT may be used that prevents a constraint from becoming active. Barrier methods augment the objective function with functions that become infinite on the boundary

$$F(x;r) = f(x) + rB(x),$$

where

$$B(x) = \ln[b - g(x)]$$

or

$$B(x) = [b - g(x)]^{-1}.$$

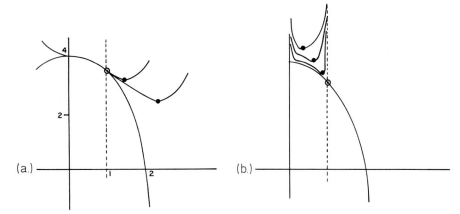

Fig. 4.10a, b. SUMT solutions to minimize $4-x^2$ on $[0,1]$. **(a)** Penalty, **(b)** barrier. The sequences of the approximate unconstrained solutions (solid dots) approach the constrained solutions (open dots)

The previous example leads to a barrier function such as

$$B(x)=1/x+1/(1-x)$$

and the augmented objective is

$$f(x,r)=4-x^2+r(1/x+1/1-x)$$
$$dF/dx=2x+r[-1/x^2+1/(1-x)^2]=0$$
$$-2x^3(1-x)^2+r[x^2-(1-x)^2]=0.$$

This will be more difficult to solve, but the graph of $F(x;r)$ indicates how the solution behaves as a function of r. The critical point of $F(x;r)$ is feasible but not optimal. Nevertheless, as $r\to0$, the critical point of F approaches the solution; see the illustrations in Fig. 4.10.

One drawback to the barrier method is that an infeasible point can never lead to a feasible solution.

The basic idea of SUMT is very attractive since we have rather good algorithms available to solve the unconstrained problem. Unfortunately, the objective function becomes so distorted by the penalties that it is unusually difficult to minimize. Even worse than distortion of contours and descent directions is the introduction of singularities of the Hessian matrix in the neighborhood of the constraint [4.45, 46].

This is illustrated by a classic test problem where an equality constraint is incorporated as a penalty [4.69]

Minimize $(1-x_1)^2$

Subject to $x_2=x_1^2$

becomes

$$f(x_1, x_2) = (1 - x_1)^2 + r(x_1^2 - x_2)^2 .$$

To be specific, $r = 100$ produces Rosenbrock's test function.

$$F = (1 - x_1)^2 + 100(x_1^2 - x_2)^2$$

$$\nabla F = \begin{bmatrix} -2(1 - x_1) + 400x_1(x_1^2 - x_2) \\ -200(x_1^2 - x_2) \end{bmatrix}$$

$$H = \begin{bmatrix} 2 - 400x_2 + 1200x_1^2 & -400x_1 \\ -400x_1 & 200 \end{bmatrix} .$$

A check for singularity tests the determinant of H for zero.

$$|H| = 400 - 80000x_2 + 240000x_1^2 - 160000x_1^2 = 0$$

$$80000x_1^2 + 400 = 80000x_2$$

or

$$x_2 = x_1^2 + 1/200 .$$

The constraint $x_2 = x_1^2$ has a curve within 0.005 units above it on which the augmented objective has a singular Hessian matrix.

Fiacco and McCormick solve a sequence of problems, systematically changing r to increase the emphasis on the constraint. They prove that the sequence of solutions converges to the desired constrained optimum. The solution from the most recent value of r acts as a first guess for the next. The advantages of a good first guess offset the problems of distortion and singularity to some extent. Furthermore, the methods of Levenberg [4.25] or Greenstadt [4.48] that force the Hessian matrix to be positive definite are directly applicable here.

Explicit Treatment of Constraints

One approach to the constrained problem is to linearize all constraints and objection function and solve the resulting linear program. The repetition of this process leads to the sequence of approximate solutions described by Griffith and Stewart [4.73]. This "method of approximate programming" is given in several textbooks [4.1, 74] and since it is not often used in the context of optics, we shall proceed to another algorithm.

Projection methods or feasible direction methods are used in the general area of nonlinear programming. The ideas are adapted for treatment of certain types of constraints and lead to a sort of hybrid algorithm for use in optical design. In this routine, the algorithm has the form

    I) Select a feasible point $x^{(k)}$.
    II) Feasible direction determined, $s^{(k)}$.
    III) λ_k is chosen to min $f[x(k) + \lambda s^{(k)}]$ but to ensure that $x^{k+1} = x^{(k)} + \lambda_k s^{(k)}$ is still feasible.

The various algorithms that have been proposed differ in the selection of $s^{(k)}$.

Gradient projection is a term that describes the local change of a function in a direction identified by the constraints. The method of *Rosen* [4.75, 76] is a descent method coupled with the orthogonal projection of the descent direction onto a linear manifold of linearized active constraints.

Let A be the gradient matrix of the active constraints.

$$A = \begin{bmatrix} \partial g_1/\partial x_1 \dots \partial g_1/\partial x_m \\ \cdot \; \cdot \; \cdot \; \cdot \; \cdot \; \cdot \; \cdot \; \cdot \\ \partial g_k/\partial x_1 \dots \partial g_k/\partial x_m \end{bmatrix},$$

$$p = I - A^t(AA^t)^{-1}A,$$

$$s^{(k+1)} = \nabla f(x^k) - A^t\{(AA^t)^{-1}A\nabla f\} = p\nabla f,$$

where the elements of $(AA^t)^{-1}A\nabla f$ indicate whether or not additional progress can be made. When an element is negative, the corresponding constraint can be removed from the constraint basis. The similarity to the simplex strategy for linear programming should be obvious. For linear constraints, the method takes large steps along the constraints.

Geometric Programming

An algorithm for minimizing nonlinear objectives subject to nonlinear constraints was proposed by *Zener* [4.40] and extended by many mathematicians. Although applications may appear from almost any source, the method apparently has received regular use only among chemical engineers. A thorough description of the original form appears in the book by *Duffin* et al. [4.37] and generalizations are discussed in more recent papers by *Blau* and *Wilde* [4.77], *Avriel* et al. [4.78], and others. We describe the method briefly here, then illustrate its use in Sect. 4.4 by solving a simple optical prototype design in *Delano's* [4.20] $y\bar{y}$ variables, using a computer program by *Dembo* [4.79].

Geometric programming is based upon the classic inequality between the arithmetic and geometric means. It is easy to convince oneself by performing the arithmetic, that $(x_1 + x_2)/2 \geq (x_1 x_2)^{1/2}$. More generally, it is true that

$$\delta_1 U_1 + \delta_2 U_2 + \dots + \delta_n U_n \geq U_1^{\delta_1} U_2^{\delta_2} \dots U_n^{\delta_n}, \tag{4.33}$$

where the U_i are nonnegative numbers, otherwise arbitrary, and the δ_i are positive weights that satisfy the condition $\sum_i \delta_i = 1$. Proofs of this geometric inequality abound in mathematical analysis literature; *Beckenbach* and *Bellman* [4.80] list several.

A change of variables $\mu_i = \delta_i U_i$ leads to a different form of the geometric inequality.

$$g_0 = \mu_1 + \mu_2 + \ldots + \mu_n \geq (\mu_1/\delta_1)^{\delta_1}(\mu_2/\delta_2)^{\delta_2}\ldots(\mu_n/\delta_n)^{\delta_n}. \tag{4.34}$$

Equality holds when $\mu_1 = \mu_2 = \ldots = \mu_n$.

We now concentrate on the right-hand side. Suppose that each μ_i has the special form

$$\mu_i = c_i t_1^{\alpha_{i1}} t_2^{\alpha_{i2}} \ldots t_m^{\alpha_{im}}, \tag{4.35}$$

where c_i is a positive constant, the t_j are positive variables, and the exponents α_{ij} are arbitrary real numbers. Such a function is called a posynomial and constitutes a basic element in the theory of geometric programming. Its importance is apparent when substituted into the right-hand side of (4.34).

The function

$$\begin{aligned} V(\boldsymbol{\delta}, \boldsymbol{t}) &= (\mu_1/\delta_1)^{\delta_1}(\mu_2/\delta_2)^{\delta_2}\ldots(\mu_n/\delta_n)^{\delta_n} \\ &= (c_1/\delta_1)^{\delta_1}(c_2/\delta_2)^{\delta_2}\ldots(c_n/\delta_n)^{\delta_n} \\ &\quad \times (t_1^{d_1} t_2^{d_2} \ldots t_m^{d_m}), \end{aligned} \tag{4.36}$$

where

$$d_j = \sum_i \delta_i \alpha_{ij}, \; j = 1, 2, \ldots, m,$$

is also a posynomial. Its constant

$$n(\boldsymbol{\delta}) = \prod_i (c_i/\delta_i)^{\delta_i} \tag{4.37}$$

is called the dual function. If we maximize $n(\boldsymbol{\delta})$ subject to the linear constraints

$$\sum_i \delta_i = 1, \tag{4.38}$$

and

$$d_j = 0, \; j = 1, 2, \ldots, m, \tag{4.39}$$

the parameters t_j do not enter into the calculation. Equations (4.38, 39) are called the normality and orthogonality conditions, respectively.

At the maximum, the solution in the δ_i variables gives the fraction of the total objective function that each μ_i contributes at the minimizing point.

The primal variables or construction parameters are still unknown but may be obtained from the dual solution by solving

$$\mu_i(t) = \delta_i V(\delta), \, i = 1, 2, ..., n. \qquad (4.40)$$

Constraints of the form

$$g_k(t) \leq 1, \, k = 1, 2, ..., p, \qquad (4.41)$$

where $g_k(t)$ are also posynomials are easy to incorporate into this framework. We need a form for the geometric inequality where the weights are not normalized.

Let $\Delta_i = \lambda \delta_i$, $i = 1, 2, ..., n$ be the unnormalized weights so that we can write

$$[g_0(t)]^{\lambda_0} \geq (\mu_1/\Delta_1)^{\Delta_1} (\mu_2/\Delta_2)^{\Delta_2} ...) \mu_n/\Delta_n)^{\Delta_n} \lambda^\lambda. \qquad (4.42)$$

The same substitution in each constraint leads to

$$1 \geq [g_k(t)]^{\lambda_k} \geq (\mu_{k_1}/\Delta_{k_1})^{\Delta_{k_1}} (\mu_{k_2}/\Delta_{k_2})^{\Delta_{k_2}} ...(\mu_{k_n}/\Delta_{k_n})^{\Delta_{k_n}} \lambda_k^{\lambda_k}. \qquad (4.43)$$

Multiplication gives

$$[g_0(t)]^{\lambda_0} \geq (\mu_1/\Delta_1)^{\Delta_1} ...(\mu_{k_n}/\Delta_{k_n})^{\Delta_{k_n}} \lambda_0^{\lambda_0} \lambda_1^{\lambda_1} ... \lambda_k^{\lambda_k}. \qquad (4.44)$$

A new normalization condition is $\lambda_0 = 1$ and the orthogonality conditions are imposed as before. At this stage of the derivation, we can rename the weights as δ_i.

The original form of this problem has since been generalized to include negative values of c_i (or subtraction of posynomials). The generalized geometric programming problem is posed as follows:

$$\text{Minimize} \quad p_0(t) - Q_0(t), \qquad (4.45)$$
$$_t$$

$$\text{Subject to} \quad p_k(t) - Q_k(t) \leq 1, \, k = 1, 2, ..., P, \qquad (4.46)$$

$$0 < t_j^{LB} \leq t_j \leq t_j^{UB}, j = 1, 2, ..., m, \qquad (4.47)$$

where $P_k(t)$ and $Q_k(t)$ are posynomials. The difference of two posynomials is called a signomial.

It is desirable that $Q_k(t)$ be absent on the grounds that a global solution will be found. The result obtained by solving the generalization may, however, be satisfactory and may well be global. When $Q_k(t)$ is present, we obtain a solution by constructing an approximating sequence of posynomial programs as follows.

The signomial constraints are rewritten as a quotient of posynomials, $P_k(t)/[1+Q_k(t)] \leq 1$. The fundamental inequality is applied to $1+Q_k(t)$, producing a smaller monomial term to be used in the denominator of the constraint. This process of using the inequality to replace a posynomial of several terms by a monomial has been called "condensation". The sequence of conventional geometric programs produced by condensation may be solved by any suitable method.

The process we call geometric programming is not necessarily to be considered as a solution algorithm; rather it is a process of formulating problems in a manner that is systematic and which may suggest especially efficient solution algorithms. In addition, the choice of solving either the primal or the dual may be made on the basis of ease of solution or of the information obtained.

A posynomial geometric program has the related dual maximization problem

Maximize $\underset{\delta}{n(\delta)}$

Subject to $\lambda_0 = 1$,
$$d_j = 0, j = 1, 2, ..., m, \tag{4.48}$$

where the constraints are all linear and $\log n(\delta)$ is concave. Thus, the dual offers several possibilities for the selection of efficient solution procedures. In particular, approximation by linear programming can be effective, as in Kelley's [4.41] cutting plane algorithm.

Linear programming is also applicable to the primal problem. If each posynomial of the primal is further reduced by condensation to a monomial term, then logarithmic transformation produces a linear program to be solved by a standard simplex or dual simplex algorithm. Dembo's [4.79] program GGP uses this technique; in our experience, it is the most efficient geometric programming code available.

A brief numerical example follows to help clarify the notation:

Minimize $\underset{t}{3/t_1 + 8t_1 t_2 + 5/t_2^2 + 8t_2}$ $\tag{4.49}$

is replaced by

Maximize $\underset{\delta}{(3/\delta_1)^{\delta_1} (8/\delta_2)^{\delta_2} (5/\delta_3)^{\delta_3} (8/\delta_4)^{\delta_4}}$, $\tag{4.50}$

Subject to $\delta_1 + \delta_2 + \delta_3 + \delta_4 = 1$
$-\delta_1 + \delta_2 \qquad = 0$
$\delta_2 - 2\delta_3 + \delta_4 \quad = 0.$ $\tag{4.51}$

The second problem is solved by a one-dimensional search on $\delta_3 \in [0, 1/3]$. A crude search gives $\delta = [0.208, 0.208, 0.264, 0.320]^t$ $v(\delta) = 22.6639$. The corresponding $t = [0.6364, 0.9066]$, $f(t) = 22.6657$. Thus the minimum value of the objective function is bracketed within an interval $(22.6639, 22.6657)$.

4.4 Examples and Computational Results

This section is intended to present some illustrative problems and solutions and to reference a sample of the commercially available optimization codes for optical problems. It should be pointed out in advance that large-scale optimization programs for any purpose are expensive to develop, so it is anticipated that the details of their inner workings are held proprietary by the developers. Nevertheless, it is possible to comment qualitatively about the approaches taken by the various commercial codes.

4.4.1 Curve Fitting with Chebyshev Objective

While least-squares curve fitting techniques are well known to workers in optics, their extension to objective functions other than sums of squares of errors is less well understood.

Consider the problem of fitting a Fourier cosine series to the following even function:

$$f(x) = 1, \qquad 0 < x < \pi/2$$
$$f(x) = 10, \qquad \pi/2 < x < \pi.$$

This square-wave function has a difficult corner at $x = \pi/2$, where the "Gibbs phenomenon" [4.81] causes the representation to overshoot by much more than the average error.

Classical Fourier series are already optimal in the least-squares sense, so there is nothing to be gained by further least-squares optimization. The Gibbs phenomenon is a necessary ingredient in the least-squares solution.

In many cases such problems have easily computed Chebyshev solutions [4.82]. More often they do not, and the incorporation of Chebyshev criteria into optimization algorithms is not trivial.

An alternative approach which captures most of the power of the Chebyshev norm is the minimization of the sum of the $2p$ powers of the errors in the representation, where p is a large positive integer. Thus the actual algorithm remains least squares, to be solved using orthogonalization methods or not, as the user prefers.

To carry this out within the framework of an existing optimization code we define new system discrepancies

$$\varepsilon_i' = (\varepsilon_i)^p = [y_i - f(x; t_i)]^p,$$

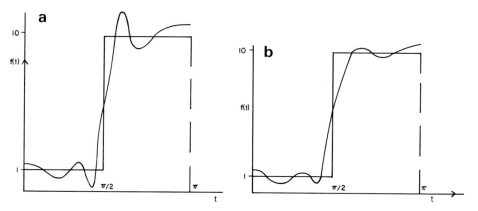

Fig. 4.11a, b. Suppression of Gibbs' phenomenon in fitting of a discontinuous function by trigonometric series. (**a**) Cosine series, least squares; (**b**) cosine series, Chebyshev

where p is an integer greater than one. We now consider the minimization of

$$\sum_i (\varepsilon_i')^2$$

as an independent optimization problem. In this way the Fourier series problem proposed and similar curve fitting problems may be solved within conventional optimization procedures but with a near-Chebyshev norm. The difference between the two solutions may be inferred from Fig. 4.11.

4.4.2 Thin Film Filter Design

While multilayer optical thin film filters frequently may be designed by closed-form methods, it is seldom possible to handle all possible constraints or to vary all possible parameters in a closed mathematical synthesis. For example, the method of *Delano* and *Pegis* [4.18] handles performance specifications at only a single constant incidence angle, and uses as variables only the layer refractive indices. Ideally, a multilayer filter design program should allow the user to specify reflection or transmission targets at a variety of incidence angles and wavelengths, and to accomplish the design goal, it should permit the variation of thickness as well as index variables.

A number of highly successful optimization programs are known to the authors. *Baumeister* [4.83] pioneered in the development of least-squares optimization codes for thin film filters. *Dobrowolski* [4.84] has developed multilayer optimization programs which add layers when needed and permit the "growing" of a complex filter from a simple starting design. *MacIntyre* [4.85] has created a damped least-squares thin film package available for use through CDC Cybernet, wherever that commercial service is available.

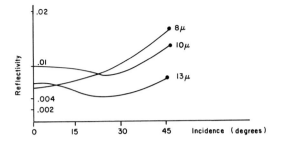

Fig. 4.12. Evaluation of reflectivity of a three-layer antireflection coating for germanium for three wave lengths and a range of incidence angles

Undoubtedly, other codes exist but they are most likely to be proprietary to companies in the multilayer film business.

In the following example, the authors demonstrate the use of Grey's orthonormal optimization procedure on a three-layer antireflection coating for germanium. The wavelength range is 8.0 to 13.0 μ while the incidence range is from normal to 45°.

As a prototype, the algebraic solution at normal incidence was computed using the closed-form method of *Delano* and *Pegis* [4.18]. This classical solution was excellent at normal incidence but deteriorated rapidly with increasing incidence angles, giving reflectivities in excess of 10% at 45°.

Five iterations of the orthonormal method led to the solution shown in Fig. 4.12. This three-layer design with individual layers of silicon, zinc sulfide, and barium flouride on a germanium substrate had a reflectivity below 1.8% over the entire range of wavelengths and incidence angles requested in the original specifications.

4.4.3 Spectroscopic Peak Resolution

The appearance of a curve may not suggest the proper model to use in order to obtain a "correct" fit. An artificial example constructed by *Ekenberg* [4.13] makes an interesting illustration and a difficult optimization problem. Our purpose here is to show how a standard algorithm can be modified to suit a special class of problems with considerable enhancement of its capability.

The problem was generated by evaluating the function

$$f(t) = \sum_{k=1}^{2} \alpha_k \exp[-c(\beta_k - t)^2/\gamma_k^2], \tag{4.52}$$

where

$$\begin{aligned}
c &= 4\ln(2) \\
\alpha_1 &= 89.13259 \quad \alpha_2 = 71.76958 \\
\beta_1 &= 3.41095 \quad \beta_2 = 2.82991 \\
\gamma_1 &= 1.66706 \quad \gamma_2 = 1.61194.
\end{aligned} \tag{4.53}$$

The values of t were 55 equally spaced points in [0.0, 5.4]. This superposition of two Gaussian curves has the appearance of one Gaussian and can be fit very well by a single peak. In practice, the noise in the data will overwhelm any discernable difference between a fit by one or by two Gaussians.

We assume that it is known at the outset that two Gaussians should be used, and with the starting values

$$\alpha_1 = 81.1020 \quad \alpha_2 = 67.5251$$
$$\beta_1 = 3.2111 \quad \beta_2 = 3.0817$$
$$\gamma_1 = 1.7813 \quad \gamma_2 = 1.7795.$$

Three versions of Grey's basic routine were applied. The first is Grey's original version updating one variable at a time, the second is a block orthogonalization where the partitions are identified with the individual Gaussians, and finally all variables are simultaneously updated. After the sequence has considered all variables, *Cornwell*'s [4.47] extrapolation step is taken. Although it is quite possible that another method or these more carefully programmed might perform better, one compares these in a more meaningful way by using the same program for all three. The distinction is made by providing the partitioning parameter as input.

After 400 steps through the six variables the routine was stopped, with Grey's method showing a square sum error of 0.11 while the Gauss-Newton-Hartley method had an error measure of 6.6. On the other hand, the partitioned version halted of its own accord after 99 steps with an objective function value of 0.00002 and a correct solution [values given in (4.53)]. This result emphasizes the need for preliminary analysis to assure a compatible matching of method to problem.

4.4.4 Optical Imaging System Design

Hyde's [4.24] remark that the "optimum solution" is the best one has achieved when the money runs out was made in the context of lens design. While the remark is valid for any expensive computer-aided design project, it is especially true in lens design. It is never clear how far a given lens can be improved, nor which of two optimized lenses is better. It would be easy to find two designs which would be ranked in one order by one performance index and in the reverse order by a different measure of quality. It is at this point where differences in purpose and experience of the designers enter and should be recognized. Many hours have been spent debating the merits of two optimization algorithms when the differences being discussed arose from the fact that two separate mathematical problems had been solved.

There are available today many computer programs for optical imaging system design. These tend to be very large and expensive programs with enormous development cost. They are seldom bought and sold, but more often are licensed or used on a royalty basis. Three such programs which are fairly readily available are ACCOS V, COOL, and ZOOM GENII.

ACCOS V is a proprietary product of Scientific Calculations, Inc. [4.86]. The time-sharing version of this system is available through National CSS, Inc. [4.87]. The optimization procedure is damped least squares, with penalty functions for treating the constraints.

COOL is a proprietary product of David Grey Associates [4.88]. The optimization procedure is the orthonormal nonlinear least-squares algorithm. Constraints are handled by penalty functions, with variations developed by *Grey* [4.44].

ZOOM GENII is a proprietary product of Genesee Computer Center, Inc. [4.89]. The optimization procedure used is the damped least-squares algorithm, with a number of heuristic additions to speed convergence.

Other proprietary programs exist as well as programs in governmental laboratories and a few in the public domain. The latter tend to be obsolete or skeletal in nature but could certainly function in the hands of an experienced designer. It is pointless to argue the relative merits of these lens optimization programs. Examples can be found to favor one technique or to frustrate another. These examples prove little about the overall capabilities of a design system, although they often give insight into the nature of the optimization algorithms.

A classic example of a design specification that favors one algorithm over another is the optimization of a long focal length triplet with excessive and undesirable chromatic aberration. When the curvatures are varied, they affect the first order and color severely. What the system needs, of course, is lens bending, but this is a simultaneous combination of parameter changes. In this example, the orthonormal method will find the lens bendings immediately, whereas any total step method such as damped least squares with no coordinate transformations may encounter prohibitive difficulties with derivatives.

The reader interested in the difficulties involved in comparing optimizations of the same lens under different programs should consult the study by *Hopkins* and *Unvala* [4.90].

Very little has been published about the use of optimization techniques in the early stages of a lens design or in the search for new prototypes. *Jamieson* [4.5] includes the text of a small optimization program in FORTRAN II in his book. He sets target values for the Seidel aberrations S_I, S_{II}, S_{III}, and S_V, and minimizes the errors in the least-squares sense using the damped least-squares algorithm. He says, "The main use of such a program is, for instance, to generate feasible starting systems for more detailed optimization, or the exploration of parameter space of specific types of optical systems." He also suggests that such a tool would be useful in the study of zoom systems.

Pegis et al. [4.91] have described a program which links orthonormal optimization with the $y\bar{y}$ diagram of *Delano* [4.20]. Most optimization techniques which can handle constraints work quite well in first-order optics, and for this reason, their relative neglect is surprising, especially for zoom systems where intuitive methods are difficult.

As a simple example of the use of optimization methods in first-order design, consider a triplet of thin lenses in air with zero sum of powers and a number of spatial constraints. This problem illustrates how one can handle one of the fundamental difficulties of first-order models: angle variables are good for powers but not separations, while height variables are good for separations but not powers. Our example is intended to demonstrate the use of the $y\bar{y}$ variables and the geometric programming optimization technique.

In the $y\bar{y}$ method of first-order design, the paths of the paraxial marginal and principal rays through the system are plotted together as a series of connected line segments on a graph of y against $\bar{y}$. The object and image points are on the $\bar{y}$ axis, the stop is on the y axis and many first-order optical properties find simple application in the diagram. In particular, separations between elements turn out as areas, while stop and conjugate shifts are represented by shearing the diagram. This is a very powerful technique originally intended as a visual aid for first-order design planning. In this instance, it is a visual aid for optimization problem formulation.

We choose the marginal and principal paraxial rays y and $\bar{y}$, as the natural variables of the system. The objective function is

$$J = \sum_{i=0}^{3} [(u_{i+1} - u_i)^2 + (\bar{u}_{i+1} - \bar{u}_i)^2] \tag{4.54}$$

to control the speeds of the elements [4.91]. The angle variables $u_i, \bar{u}_i$ are expressed in terms of the height variables $y_i, \bar{y}_i$ and the separations d_i. The natural constraints are those imposed on conjugate separation, clear apertures, lens length, and the sum of powers.

First, it is necessary to exhibit this as a geometric program. All variables are necessarily positive so that a translation is used to assure us that this requirement is satisfied,

$$\begin{aligned} y_i &= t_i - L \\ \bar{y}_i &= \bar{t}_i - L. \end{aligned} \tag{4.55}$$

Separations are redundant, given the ray heights and the Lagrange invariant Q; they are needed as explicit variables, however, in order to express the objective as a signomial.

$$\begin{aligned} d_i &= (y_i \bar{y}_{i+1} - \bar{y}_i y_{i+1})/Q \\ u_i &= (y_{i+1} - y_i)/d_i \\ \bar{u}_i &= (\bar{y}_{i+1} - \bar{y}_i)/d_i. \end{aligned} \tag{4.56}$$

Clearly (4.54) is a signomial (difference of two posynomials) in the variables t_i, $\bar{t}_i$, and d_i.

The mechanical constraints are also signomials in these variables. Clear aperture constraints are $|y_i| + |\bar{y}_i| \leq L/2$ where L is the diameter. This is equivalent to four signomial constraints for each element. The lens length and the conjugate separation constraints are directly expressed as posynomials in the separation d_i. It is easy to see that these constraints can all be formulated as $P(t, \bar{t}, d) - Q(t, \bar{t}, d) \leq 1$ as required by geometric programming theory.

Finally, we have several constraints of the equality type (4.8), explicitly disallowed in the formalism of geometric programming. *Blau* and *Wilde* [4.77] show that these constraints can be included if the designer has prior knowledge of their influence and can pose the constraint in such a manner that it will be active in the optimization. Power of an element is expressed as

$$(u_i \bar{u}_{i+1} - \bar{u}_i u_{i+1})/Q \tag{4.57}$$

which is a signomial in $t, \bar{t}, d$ variables, and thus the sum of the powers of the elements is suitable for a constraint. If we choose to hold this sum to a specific value (zero, in our example), we violate the requirement that constraints be inequalities. But, recognizing that the optimization process will act in opposition, we require that the sum of powers be nonpositive.

Equality constraints can always be replaced by two inequalities, $\geq$ and $\leq$. This is contrary to the intent in geometric programming, which is to allow a variable or a posynomial some freedom to change. The skill of the designer may aid as in the treatment of powers. Otherwise, trial and error or the development of a new type of insight may be necessary. A systematic trial process can use $\geq$ and $\leq$ pairs but with a narrow band of slack between the two corresponding limits. After one execution of the program, those active constraints can have the bound reset to the correct value and the corresponding reversed and inactive constraints are discarded. The redundant variables d_i and their connection with y_i, $\bar{y}_i$, and Q must be maintained in this manner.

We show a three-element lens of dimension 4×4 units, working $2:1$ at a distance of 31 units. With (4.54) as the objective and the sum of powers constrained to be zero, and with the appropriate mechanical constraints, we obtained the solution shown in Fig. 4.13 and Table 4.2 using *Dembo's* [4.79] generalized geometric programming code, written for general-purpose use. The entire calculation was completed in about 7 s on an IBM 370/168.

4.4.5 Illuminating Systems

Until very recently, illuminating systems have been optimized by trial and error, either on a computer or in a laboratory. The computational problems involved in just the evaluation of an illuminating system are considerable, since there is no a priori knowledge of the order in which a given ray will intersect

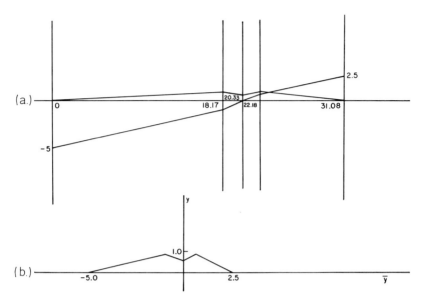

Fig. 4.13a, b. First-order optimized solution of a three-element 2:1 copy lens. (a) Ray trace, (b) y, $\bar{y}$ diagram

Table 4.2. Optimized data obtained by geometric programming for the $y, \bar{y}$ diagram of a three-element copy lens. Included are ray heights y_i and $\bar{y}_i$, separations d_i, ray angles u_i and $\bar{u}_i$, and powers K_i. The spaces are numbered according to the immediately preceding surface

Surface	y	$\bar{y}$	d	u	$\bar{u}$	K
0	0.0000	−5.0000				
			18.17	0.0500	0.2183	0.2111
1	0.9086	−1.0338				
			2.16	−0.1418	0.4365	−0.4967
2	0.6018	−0.0894				
			1.85	0.1571	0.3921	0.2880
3	0.8928	0.6370				
			8.92	−0.1000	0.2087	
4	0.0000	2.5000				

any or all of them. In addition, tilted and decentered surfaces, asymmetric surfaces, and segmented or faceted surfaces are common. The optimization is further complicated by the fact that a very small parameter change which makes one more ray get through the system acceptably should not make a large change in the objective function.

Vogl et al. [4.92] have described a design optimization scheme in use at the Westinghouse Research Laboratories. In this scheme, two models are possible, the "aperture flash mode" and the "field patch mode".

In aperture flash mode, a set of observation points is preselected in the target plane, and at each point the lit area of the system aperture is computed. This computation involves the tracing of a grid of rays and interpolation between rays for more detail. Since the source is modeled as being Lambertian, all of the flashed areas have equal brightness, independent of aspect angle. Thus the area of the flash is proportional to the energy landing at that point on the target surface, and the objective function is the weighted sum of squares of differences between actual and target values at these points. In this mode, the orthonormal least-squares method of optimization has been used successfully.

In the field patch mode, the aperture is divided into a grid of elemental segments, with a pinhole associated with each. Each segment may define a faceted surface, perhaps with power in the facet. The light distribution on the target plane due to the energy coming through a pinhole is evaluated; the power of the facet partially determines the shape of the illuminated patch while the tilt of the facet helps to determine its position.

The optimization process consists of moving the illuminated patches so that they overlap to produce the desired illumination distribution. The amount and direction of the displacement needed for each patch determines the tilt needed for each prismatic facet. *Vogl* et al. [4.92] called this process *shuffling* and applied a version of the *Hooke* and *Jeeves* [4.67] direct search optimization technique to carry it out.

Compared to the state of the art in computer-aided lens design, illumination programs are relatively crude and experimental in nature. Research on computer-aided methods continues, proceeding in several different directions.

In two recent papers, *Schruben* [4.93, 94] has posed an illumination design problem from a strictly mathematical point of view, leading to an elliptic type boundary value problem. The solution of this problem determines the shape of the reflector. At the present time, it is not clear that her formulation offers any computational advantages over the direct attack by a nonlinear optimization algorithm. However, the work is important because it does place the problem in a mathematical setting where the choice can be made between solving a differential equation or minimizing a functional. As a historical note, it is appropriate to mention that this choice between differential equation and variational principle that appears so often in mathematical physics and engineering was one of the motivations in the development of numerical methods in the 1950s, including the conjugate gradient algorithm [4.26].

Quite a different application of newly developed computer science capabilities is a study underway by *Hankins* [4.95] of a computer graphics approach to the field patch mode mentioned above. The equipment network consists of a minicomputer, a graphics tablet, and a graphics terminal consisting of a keyboard and cathode ray tube display, supervised by an IBM 360/50 which in turn is peripheral to a 370/168. Using pressure pen graphics input and cathode ray tube output, she sketches and displays a trial system. Rays are traced through pinholes in the aperture, and the illuminated patches on the target plane are displayed and their size, shape, and position assessed visually. Figure 4.14 indicates this manual variation on the figure from [4.92]. Many of the mathematical methods which are useful for graphics work may be found in the text by *Rogers* and *Adams* [4.96]. The freehand curves are represented within

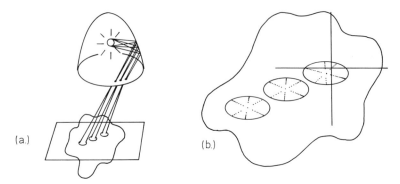

Fig. 4.14a, b. A sketch of an illuminator. (**a**) Source, reflector, and field patch mode of operation. The entire configuration is described to a computer by digitized pressure pen data. (**b**) Illuminated patches on a work plane

the minicomputer by splines fit to the pressure pen data by the least-squares methods of [4.2].

Changes in the system as well as the original specifications are input via the graphics facility and processed by a minicomputer. The quality of design will certainly depend upon many subjective factors and if the program were used alone, it would amount to an experimental tool, in effect, little different from traditional laboratory equipment. However, with the ease of data transfer from the minicomputer to its large-scale supervisor, this graphics technique is promising as a method of data input and preparation of a good first guess supplied to a major design code.

One of the features of lighting fixtures that aids immensely in achieving a successful design is the loose tolerances that may be allowed compared to the very stringent requirements that tend to be associated with the specifications of an imaging system. This is not always the case, however, and the color television lighthouse gives us an example where the requirements are very strict. This device illustrates the design of an analog computer. It is an essential part of the manufacturing process of color television picture tubes and is described in the patents by *Epstein* et al. [4.97]. The following description of the process is taken from one variety of tube that has been produced. A nontechnical article is available in [4.98].

On the faceplate of the picture tube, a matrix of three-color triads of phosphor dots is fixed by exposure to ultraviolet radiation. Each colored spot is to be illuminated in the tube when in operation, by an electron beam from one of a triad of electron guns located in the neck of the tube. Each gun carries the signal corresponding to one color and, to produce the visual effect, each must excite its own and only its own color of phosphor dots.

To avoid interference as the three electron beams scan the entire faceplate, a mask with one hole per color triad is placed between the phosphor and the electron guns. Each hole acts as a pinhole camera that places an electron image of the three guns onto the faceplate. For the tube to operate correctly, the

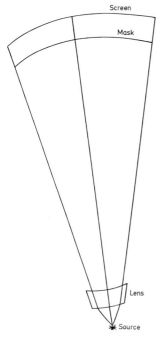

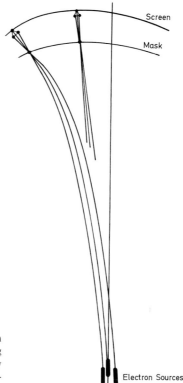

Fig. 4.15. A sketch of the TV lighthouse. The solution of the design problem is a prescription for the refracting surfaces. The light rays from the source are refracted by the lens so as to have a prescribed distribution of directions as they pass through the aperture mask to fix the colored phosphor dots on the screen

Fig. 4.16.

Fig. 4.16. A diagram of the picture tube for which the lighthouse is an analog computer. The electrons carrying the signal for one color pass through the aperture mask to illuminate the phosphor dots of the corresponding color

phosphor triad and the electron triad must coincide over the entire faceplate of the tube.

In the manufacturing process, the screen is coated with phosphor of one color, the aperture mask is set in place, and the phosphor dots are printed by exposure to ultraviolet light passing through the holes in the mask. The system is rotated through 120° and the process is repeated for each of the other colors.

The objective of the manufacturing process is to align the color dots behind the apertures so that the electron beams coincide exactly with their corresponding phosphors all over the tube face. That is, the direction cosines of the rays of ultraviolet fixing illumination as they pass through each aperture must coincide with the direction cosines of the corresponding electron trajectory at the aperture. Figures 4.15, 16 indicate geometric configurations.

The objective of the process is precisely the objective of the nonlinear optimization algorithm used to design the optical elements in the lighthouse.

Although the emphasis was on the description and calculation with optical surfaces of unusual character, the paper by *Vogl* et al. [4.22] presents a design of this analog by the orthonormal optimization process that minimized the sum of squares of the differences between the optical and the electron direction cosines. The "solution" is a prescription for the lens surface; a sketch showing a solution for one color is given in [4.22].

A final remark about this problem points out how such a problem could be attacked by a fully computational method or by a semiautomatic process. Since the boundary conditions that specify the electric and magnetic fields used to focus and deflect the three beams are known as well as the field equations and the equations of motion, it would be possible to calculate the electron trajectories beforehand, to provide the standard by which the objective function is formed. Indeed, this approach was taken by *Bloomburgh* et al. [4.99]. On the other hand, if a tube is operating, albeit less than satisfactory, an experimental determination of the electron trajectories is possible from observation of the face of the tube under operating conditions. If the location of the dot of phosphor is known from the characteristics of the optical elements that placed it there, then comparison through a microscope with the electron beam location gives the quantitative data to form the optimization objective function. Although the latter method of obtaining the data may be less satisfying to one mathematically inclined, it was effective and at much less cost, and provided the data for the objective function in [4.22].

4.5 Conclusion

It should be clear from the foregoing discussion and examples that optimization techniques can be applied to a wide range of problems in optics. What may not be quite so clear is the degree of problem analysis that is required before the application can be programmed. It is very necessary to understand all of the idiosyncrasies of an evaluation before letting it be driven by an optimization procedure. At the same time it is necessary to understand how a given optimization procedure handles system defects, constraint violations, and system blow-up before selecting that optimization procedure for linking with one's own problem.

By and large, all of the existing and tested optimization procedures will do reasonably well on a well-set problem. With the cost of computing decreasing every year, it is worth questioning what practical gain arises from changing procedures for a few percentage points in computing efficiency. What is much more significant in developing an optimization application is building a good performance index with the intended optimization procedure in mind. Some obvious questions which arise are

1) Is the model differentiable? Can repeated evaluations with slightly changed parameters yield accurate derivatives? How important are derivatives to the optimization method?

2) Does the model permit constraint violations to be monitored continuously?
3) What happens when a parameter change prevents evaluation (blow-up)?
4) Can weights be assigned to reflect the importance of the targets in a way that will be used by the optimization procedure in a numerically stable manner?

Attention to these questions in the early stages of planning any optimization application will make it possible to couple the evaluation and optimization procedures in a meaningful way.

4.6 Postscript

During the time between the completion of the above manuscript and its transformation into print, quite a large number of additional publications on the theory and practice of optimization have come to our attention. These might be divided, for the purposes of this paper, into three general classes: mathematical programming, optics, and general applications. A few remarks and representative items to augment our references are appropriate here.

Among the many recent contributions to the mathematical programming literature are papers on sensitivity analysis and tolerancing [4.100–104], a renewed interest in conjugate gradient algorithms [4.105–107], new studies of an approach to the solution of the unconstrained problem by way of an integration scheme [4.108, 109], a number of articles on generalized geometric programming, including two entire journal issues on the subject [4.110], and discussion of modularization of general purpose algorithms for varied usage [4.111]. We have used the routines described in [4.111] and found them to be quite satisfactory.

Thin film filter design, tolerance and sensitivity analysis in lens design, energy collection, objectives that include production and marketing considerations, illumination, and comparisons of specific computer programs for lens design have been discussed in the literature directed to the optics community [4.112–115].

Communication between the optics and the optimization researchers is still sketchy; however, two recent conference proceedings that are devoted primarily to mathematical or engineering considerations have included attempts to broaden the awareness among mathematical programmers of the optical origins of interesting problems [4.116, 117].

References

4.1   D.M.Himmelblau: *Applied Nonlinear Programming* (McGraw-Hill, New York 1972)

4.2   C.L.Lawson, R.J.Hanson: *Solving Least Squares Problems* (Prentice-Hall, Englewood Cliffs 1974)

4.3   J.M.Ortega, W.C.Rheinboldt: *Iterative Solution of Nonlinear Equations in Several Variables* (Academic Press, New York, London 1970)

4.4   B.T.Polyak: J. Sov. Math. **5**, 97 (1976)

4.5   T.H.Jamieson: *Optimization Techniques in Lens Design* American Elsevier, New York 1971)

4.6   E.Isaacson, H.B.Keller: *Analysis of Numerical Methods* (Wiley, New York, London, Sydney 1966)

4.7   R.J.Donohue, B.W.Joseph: Appl. Opt. **14**, 2384 (1975)

4.8   N.R.Draper, H.Smith: *Applied Regression Analysis* (Wiley, New York, London, Sydney 1966)

4.9   E.L.Stiefel: In *On Numerical Approximation*, ed. by R.E.Langer (University of Wisconsin Press, Madison 1959) p. 217

4.10   M.R.Osborne, G.A.Watson: Comput. J. **12**, 63 (1969)

4.11   W.E.McBride, A.K.Rigler: Comput. J. **19**, 79 (1976)

4.12   C.L.Lawson: "Contributions to the Theory of Linear Least Maximum Approximation", Ph. D. Dissertation, University of California, Los Angeles (1961)

4.13   B.Ekenberg: Behand. Inf. Tid. **15**, 385 (1975)

4.14   C.Lanczos: *Applied Analysis* (Prentice-Hall, Englewood Cliffs 1956)

4.15   R.Mireles: J. Opt. Soc. Am. **56**, 644 (1966)

4.16   C.M.Lederer: In *Radioactivity in Nuclear Spectroscopy*, ed. by J.H.Hamilton and M.C.Manthuruthil (Gordon and Breach, New York 1972) p. 73

4.17   D.C.St.Clair, A.K.Rigler: In *Computer Science and Statistics: Eighth Annual Symposium on the Interface*, ed. by J.W.Frane (Health Sciences Computing Facility, University of California, Los Angeles 1975)

4.18   E.Delano, R.J.Pegis: In *Progress in Optics VII*, ed. by E.Wolf (North-Holland, Amsterdam 1969) p. 69

4.19   D.P.Feder: Appl. Opt. **2**, 272 (1963)

4.20   E.Delano: Appl. Opt. **2**, 1251 (1963)

4.21   F.J.Lopez-Lopez: "The Application of the Delano $y\bar{y}$ Diagram to Optical Design"; Ph. D. Dissertation, University of Arizona, Tucson (1973)

4.22   T.P.Vogl, A.K.Rigler, B.R.Canty: Appl. Opt. **10**, 2513 (1971)

4.23   "Inset Light Fixtures for Airport Runways and Taxiways", Department of Transport, Canada, Spec. No. 1271 (1968)

4.24   W.L.Hyde: In *Recent Advances in Optimization Techniques*, ed. by A.Lavi and T.P.Vogl (Wiley, New York, London, Sydney 1966) p. 1

4.25   K.Levenberg: Q. Appl. Math. **2**, 164 (1944)

4.26   M.R.Hestenes, E.L.Stiefel: J. Res. Nat. Bur. Stds. **49**, 409 (1952)

4.27   W.Davidon: "Variable Metric Methods for Minimization", A.E.C. Res. and Dev. Rept. ANL-5990, Argonne Nat. Lab., Lemont, Ill. (1959)

4.28   R.Fletcher, M.J.D.Powell: Comput. J. **6**, 163 (1963)

4.29   D.S.Grey: J. Opt. Soc. Am. **53**, 672, 677 (1963)

4.30   D.P.Feder: In *Recent Advances in Optimization Techniques*, ed. by A.Lavi and T.P.Vogl (Wiley, New York, London, Sydney 1966) p. 5

4.31   G.Hadley: *Linear Programming* (Addison-Wesley, Reading, Mass., Palo Alto, London 1962)

4.32   R.S.Garfinkel, G.L.Nemhauser: *Integer Programming* (Wiley, New York, London, Sydney 1972)

4.33   H.M.Salkin: *Integer Programming* (Addison-Wesley, Reading, Mass., Palo Alto, London 1975)

4.34   D.Tabak, B.C.Kuo: *Optimal Control by Mathematical Programming* (Prentice-Hall, Englewood Cliffs 1971)

4.35   R.T.Rockafellar: *Convex Analysis* (Princeton University Press, Princeton 1969)

4.36   H.W.Kuhn, A.W.Tucker: In *Proc. 2nd Berkeley Symposium on Mathematical Statistics and Probability*, ed. by J.Neyman (University of California Press, Berkeley 1951) p. 481

4.37   R.J.Duffin, E.L.Peterson, C.Zener: *Geometric Programming – Theory and Application* (Wiley, New York, London, Sydney 1967)

4.38   A.V.Fiacco, G.P.McCormick: *Nonlinear Programming; Sequential Unconstrained Minimization Techniques* (Wiley, New York, London, Sydney 1968)

4.39   P. Wolfe: Econometrica **27**, 382 (1959)
4.40   C. Zener: Proc. Nat. Acad. Sci. **47**, 537 (1961)
4.41   J. E. Kelley: J. SIAM **8**, 703 (1960)
4.42   R. Courant: Bull. Am. Math. Soc. **49**, 1 (1943)
4.43   D. P. Feder: J. Opt. Soc. Am. **52**, 177 (1962)
4.44   D. S. Grey: In *Recent Advances in Optimization Techniques*, ed. by A. Lavi and T. P. Vogl (Wiley, New York, London, Sydney 1966) p. 69
4.45   W. Murray: In *Proc. 6th Internat. Symposium on Mathematical Programming* (Princeton University Press, Princeton 1967)
4.46   W. Murray: J. Opt. Th. Appl. **7**, 189 (1971)
4.47   L. W. Cornwell, A. K. Rigler: Appl. Opt. **11**, 1659 (1972)
4.48   J. L. Greenstadt: Math. Comput. **21**, 360 (1967)
4.49   D. W. Marquardt: J. SIAM **11**, 431 (1963)
4.50   D. W. Marquardt: Technometrics **12**, 591 (1970)
4.51   D. D. Morrison: SIAM J. Num. Anal. **5**, 83 (1968)
4.52   C. G. Wynne: Proc. Phys. Soc. London **73**, 777 (1959)
4.53   J. Meiron: J. Opt. Soc. Am. **55**, 1105 (1965)
4.54   D. R. Buchele: Appl. Opt. **7**, 2433 (1968)
4.55   D. F. Shanno: SIAM J. Num. Anal. **7**, 366 (1970)
4.56   A. Jones: Comput. J. **13**, 301 (1970)
4.57   O. N. Stavroudis: In *Advances in Computers V5*, ed. by F. L. Alt and M. Rubinoff (Academic Press, New York, London 1964)
4.58   G. E. Forsythe: Numer. Math. **11**, 57 (1968)
4.59   H. Akaike: Ann. Inst. Stat. Math. Tokyo **11**, 1 (1959)
4.60   R. Fletcher, C. M. Reeves: Comput. J. **7**, 149 (1964)
4.61   H. O. Hartley: Technometrics **3**, 269 (1961)
4.62   N. A. Broste: "An Orthonormal Optimization Technique: Theory, Implementation, and Application"; Ph. D. Dissertation, Carnegie-Mellon University, Pittsburgh (1968)
4.63   L. W. Cornwell, R. J. Pegis, A. K. Rigler, T. P. Vogl: J. Opt. Soc. Am. **63**, 576 (1973)
4.64   G. W. Stewart: J. Assoc. Comput. Mach. **14**, 72 (1967)
4.65   M. J. D. Powell: Comput. J. **7**, 303 (1964)
4.66   B. V. Shah, R. J. Buehler, O. Kempthorne: J. SIAM **12**, 74 (1964)
4.67   R. Hooke, T. A. Jeeves: J. Assoc. Comput. Mach. **8**, 212 (1961)
4.68   J. Weisman, C. F. Wood, L. Rivlen: In *Process Control and Applied Mathematics*, ed. by L. H. Krone (Am. Inst. Chem. Eng., New York 1965) p. 50
4.69   H. H. Rosenbrock: Comput. J. **3**, 175 (1970)
4.70   M. J. Box, D. Davies, W. H. Swann: *Nonlinear Optimization Techniques* (Oliver and Boyd, Edinburgh 1969)
4.71   L. C. W. Dixon: In *Numerical Methods for Nonlinear Optimization*, ed. by F. A. Lootsma (Academic Press, New York, London 1972) p. 149
4.72   C. W. Carroll: Oper. Res. **9**, 169 (1961)
4.73   R. E. Griffith, R. A. Stewart: Manage. Sci. **7**, 379 (1961)
4.74   L. Cooper, D. Steinberg: *Methods of Optimization* (W. B. Saunders, Philadelphia, London, Toronto 1970)
4.75   J. B. Rosen: J. SIAM **8**, 181 (1960)
4.76   J. B. Rosen: J. SIAM **9**, 514 (1961)
4.77   G. E. Blau, D. J. Wilde: Can. J. Chem. Eng. **47**, 317 (1969)
4.78   M. Avriel, R. Dembo, U. Passy: Int. J. Num. Meth. Eng. **9**, 149 (1975)
4.79   R. S. Dembo: *GGP: A Computer Program for the Solution of Generalized Geometric Programming Problems* (McMaster University, Hamilton, Ont. 1975)
4.80   E. F. Beckenbach, R. Bellman: *Inequalities*, Ergebnisse der Mathematik, Vol. 30 (Springer, Berlin, Heidelberg, New York 1965)
4.81   H. S. Carslaw: *Introduction to the Theory of Fourier's Series and Integrals*, 3rd ed. (Macmillan, London 1930)

4.82 S.Karlin, W.J.Studden: *Tchebycheff Systems with Applications in Analysis and Statistics* (Interscience, New York 1966)

4.83 P.W.Baumeister: J. Opt. Soc. Am. **52**, 1149 (1962)

4.84 J.A.Dobrowolski: Appl. Opt. **4**, 937 (1965)

4.85 R.T.MacIntyre: Genesee Computer Center, 20 University Avenue, Rochester, New York 14605

4.86 ACCOS V: Scientific Calculations, Inc. 110 Allen's Creek Road, Rochester, New York 14618

4.87 National CSS, Inc., 300 Westport Avenue, Norwalk, Conn. 06851

4.88 COOL: David Grey Associates, 60 Hickory Drive, Waltham, Mass. 02154

4.89 ZOOM GENII: Genesee Computer Center, Inc., 20 University Avenue, Rochester, New York 14605

4.90 R.E.Hopkins, H.A.Unvala: In *Lens Design with Large Computers, Proceedings of the Conference*, ed. by W.L.Hyde (Institute of Optics, Rochester 1967) p. 11-1

4.91 R.J.Pegis, T.P.Vogl, A.K.Rigler, R.Walters: Appl. Opt. **6**, 969 (1967)

4.92 T.P.Vogl, L.C.Lintner, R.J.Pegis, W.M.Waldbauer, H.A.Unvala: Appl. Opt. **11**, 1087 (1972)

4.93 J.S.Schruben: J. Opt. Soc. Am. **62**, 1498 (1972)

4.94 J.S.Schruben: J. Opt. Soc. Am. **64**, 55 (1974)

4.95 J.A.Hankins: Unpublished Report – Computer Science Department, University of Missouri – Rolla (1976)

4.96 D.F.Rogers, J.A.Adams: *Mathematical Elements for Computer Graphics* (McGraw-Hill, New York 1976)

4.97 D.W.Epstein, P.E.Kaus, D.D.Van Ormer: "Manufacture of Color – Kinescopes", U. S. Pat. 2,817,276, 24 Dec. 1957

4.98 "Color Television", in *McGraw-Hill Encyclopedia of Science and Technology V3* (McGraw-Hill, New York 1971) p. 316

4.99 R.Bloomburgh, R.Jones, J.King, J.Pietrolewicz: IEEE Trans. BTR-**11**, 50 (1965)

Bibliographic Supplement:

4.100 J.J.Dinkel, G.A.Kochenberger: Math. Prog. **15**, 261–267 (1978)

4.101 R.L.Armacost: "Sensitivity Analysis in Parametric Nonlinear Programming"; Ph.D. Dissertation, George Washington University (1976)

4.102 J.D.Buys, R.Gonin: Math. Prog. **12**, 281–284 (1977)

4.103 A.V.Fiacco: Math. Prog. **10**, 287–311 (1976)

4.104 J.J.Dinkel, G.A.Kochenberger, S.N.Wong: Trans. Math. Software **4**, 1–14 (1978)

4.105 A.Buckley: Math. Prog. **15**, 200–210 (1978)

4.106 A.Buckley: Math. Prog. **15**, 343–348 (1978)

4.107 D.P.O'Leary: "Hybrid Conjugate Gradient Algorithms"; Ph.D. Dissertation, Stanford University (1975)

4.108 P.T.Boggs: SIAM J. Num. Anal. **14**, 830–843 (1977)

4.109 C.A.Botsaris: J. Math. Anal. & Appl. **63**, 729–749 (1978)

4.110 J. Opt. Th. Appl. **26**, Nos. 1, 2 (1978)

4.111 K.Brown, M.Minkoff, K.Hillstrom, L.Nazareth, J.Pool, B.Smith: "Progress in the Development of a Modularized Package of Algorithms for Optimization Problems", in Ref. 4.116

4.112 D.C.Dilworte: Appl. Opt. **17**, 3372–3375 (1978)

4.113 J.Dobrowolski, D.Lowe: Appl. Opt. **17**, 3039–3050 (1978)

4.114 R.E.Fischer (ed.): *Computer-Aided Optical Design*, Proc. SPIE, Vol. 147, Bellingham, Wash. (1978)

4.115 I.Powell: Appl. Opt. **17**, 3361–3367 (1978)

4.116 L.C.W.Dixon (ed.): *Optimization in Action* (Academic Press, New York 1976)

4.117 L.C.Wellford (ed.): *Application of Computer Methods in Engineering* (University of Southern California, Los Angeles 1977)

5. Computers and Optical Astronomy

L. Mertz

With 3 Figures

Observational astronomy has always depended on digital expression and manipulation of observational data, just as with any experimental science. The automation of digital computers has not only facilitated the pursuit but has come to guide the course of contemporary astronomy. This chapter traces the history and influence of computers on a broad range of the many facets in observational optical astronomy.

5.1 Archeological Computers and Positional Astronomy

5.1.1 Stonehenge

The interrelation between computers and optical astronomy dates back thousands of years. The earliest extant astronomical computer known appears to be Stonehenge, and its purpose appears to have been the prediction of eclipses (see Fig. 5.1). The most notable feature of Stonehenge is not the impressive array of trilithons, but the ring of 56 chalk-filled Aubrey holes that are equispaced on a 90 m diameter circle surrounding the more recently constructed central trilithons. The number 56 has a threefold numerological significance in relation to eclipses.

The year of 365.25 days can be approximately counted as $56(13/2) = 364$ days. Likewise the lunar month is approximately 56/2 days. As seen from the earth the sun moves around the ecliptic once a year. In the course of each lunar month the moon moves around a great circle that is inclined to the ecliptic by $5°9'$. However that great circle of the moon's orbit precesses so that the intersections (nodes) with the ecliptic rotate around the ecliptic with an 18.61 year cycle. The necessary and sufficient condition for an eclipse is that the sun-earth-moon locations be colinear, and that happens when a new or a full moon occurs sufficiently near to a node. That circumstance provides the third numerologically significant relation whereby $56/3 = 18.67 \approx 18.61$ years.

The requisite counting, base 56, for eclipse prediction then follows the prescription of moving a sun location marker counterclockwise by two holes every thirteen days, moving a moon location marker counterclockwise by two holes each day, and by moving a node location marker clockwise by three holes each year. When the three markers are on the same hole or are distributed on two diametrically opposite holes an eclipse will occur. That is the nature of the computer.

Fig. 5.1. Aerial view of Stonehenge. The heelstone is at bottom center. Aubrey holes which have been uncovered are shown at middle left [Ref. 5.1, Fig. 2.2, p. 21]. (Photo courtesy of Controller of Her Britannic Majesty's Stationery Office. British Crown Copyright)

Of course it is necessary not only to initialize the marker locations, but to make occasional corrections because the numerology is not exact. It is the other elements of Stonehenge, such as the heelstone and certain reference stones, that are found to provide alignments permitting observational calibration of the initial sun, moon, and node marker locations and for occasionally correcting these locations.

5.1.2 The Renaissance and Introduction of Electromechanical Calculators

So much time has elapsed since the era of Stonehenge that actually we can only surmise its use from the remnants. The Renaissance brought a renewed interest and fascination in astronomy. The Copernican revolution and Kepler's laws of planetary motion represented enormous intellectual strides that permitted detailed long-term prediction of planetary positions. Then with the invention of the telescope ushering in the modern era of observational astronomy, there grew a need for ephemerides (a tabular statement) of the lunar and planetary positions. Although the necessary ephemerides were indeed produced for many years using manual computation, the work was extremely laborious.

Electromechanical calculators called Hollerith machines served as a prelude to modern electronic computers. In 1935, *Eckert* [5.2] published "The Computation of Special Perturbations by the Punched Card Method", which gave numerical and operational procedures for the actual use of the Hollerith machines for calculation of planetary motions.

Subsequently [5.3] around 1950 the heliocentric coordinates of Jupiter, Saturn, Uranus, Neptune, and Pluto were tabulated at forty day intervals from 1653 to 2060 by numerical integration using the IBM selective sequence electronic calculator. Over five million multiplications and divisions and seven million additions and subtractions of large numbers were performed by the machine, and the 300 page volume containing approximately one-and-one half million figures was published in 1951.

5.2 Telescope Automation

5.2.1 Rudimentary Aiming at Celestial Objects

Another impact of the advent of computers on observational astronomy is from their application as control elements for telescopes. Although most very small telescopes are pointed by looking and aiming just as with hand-held binoculars, that procedure is thoroughly impractical for large high-magnification telescopes. The traditional procedure for pointing the large telescopes had been to first make a small finder chart by copying the vicinity of the desired target from a star atlas. Each observer accumulates a collection of finder charts for those elected objects that he deems interesting. Finder charts for newly interesting objects are often published. Objects within the solar system move rapidly, however, so a fresh finder chart is needed for each occasion.

Having the finder chart, the next step had been to ascertain the sidereal time[1] of the commencement of the observation. For this purpose observatories maintained accurate sidereal clocks so that the time would be readily available at the last minute. Subtraction of the desired right ascension from that time, usually performed on scratch paper, gave the desired hour angle. The telescope was then slewed in declination and hour angle until two large scribed setting circles on the respective axes indicated those desired coordinates. With good fortune, the position would be close enough so that the observer could recognize the pattern of stars seen in a relatively low-power finder telescope and identify them according to the finder chart. Slow motion control of the telescope was finally used to zero in on the target.

---

1 Sidereal time is based on a sidereal day being the time for one earth rotation with respect to the stars. 366.2425 sidereal days equal 365.2425 mean solar days.

The first computational simplification of the task was the introduction of the driven polar setting circle so that the circle would directly read right ascension rather than hour angle. Telescopes having a driven circle must be initialized, usually at the start of each night.

New telescopes are most often equipped with angle encoders on their axes and stepper motors for position control. These features are readily interfaced to minicomputers to provide closed-loop control of both the positions and velocities for each axis. Electronic sidereal clocks, directly interfaced to the same minicomputer, have replaced the mechanical clocks so the observer may now remain oblivious to the intricacies of sidereal time. At the present stage of development the precision of the automated control system is typically about 1/4 min of arc, which is about an order of magnitude better than for previous generation telescopes. Although the 1/4 min precision is still insufficient to dispense with finder charts, it is sufficient to considerably speed up the recognition process.

5.2.2 More Sophisticated Pointing Corrections

Substantially more significant benefits of computer control for the telescopes are just beginning to come into practice. For example, with computers it is readily possible to account for deviation due to atmospheric refraction. The computation involves solving the zenith angle, correcting the zenith angle, and resolving the correction into equatorial coordinates for the telescope axes. An old often-used policy of a small deliberate misalignment of the polar axis accompanied with a small deliberate reduction of the drive rate gave only approximate compensation for the atmospheric refraction and applied only to the most commonly observed portions of the sky.

The telescope azimuth appears as part of the zenith angle calculation, and can be used to ensure that the dome remains aligned so as not to obstruct light from entering the telescope. That monitoring had usually been one function of the observer. An exception had been the 5-m (200-inch) Hale telescope, shown in Fig. 5.2, which for many years had an analog computer in the form of a small model "phantom" telescope with a rod along its optic axis that would physically steer an azimuth gimbal corresponding to the dome (see Fig. 5.3). Minicomputer control rendered the "phantom" telescope obsolete.

Another refinement, ignored in the absence of computers, is automatic updating of positions from the ephemeris epoch, usually 1950, to the present epoch. That task is readily accomplished under computer control.

High-resolution angle encoders in conjunction with the computers are making it very worthwhile to pursue this higher accuracy of telescope steering. The control system of the 3.9-m Anglo-Australian telescope (AAT) presents a very advanced example [5.5] of such an endeavor. The corrections that are incorporated, with the coefficients expressed in arcseconds, are attributed as follows:

elevation of the polar axis,

$$\Delta H = +79.4 \sin h \tan \delta$$
$$\Delta \delta = +79.4 \cos h,$$

azimuth of the polar axis,

$$\Delta h = -17.6 \cos h \tan \delta$$
$$\Delta \delta = +17.6 \sin h,$$

collimation error,

$$\Delta h = +10.0 \, s\delta,$$

nonperpendicularity of axes,

$$\Delta h = -1.6 \tan \delta,$$

tube flexure,

$$\Delta Z = +2.0 \sin Z,$$

horseshoe flexure,

$$\Delta h = -18.9 \sin h \, s\delta,$$

where h, δ, and Z are hour angle, declination, and zenith angle, respectively. For the last correction, the form as well as the coefficient are empirically determined. The results of these corrections have reduced the rms pointing errors from 55 to 2.5 arcsec. Finder charts are no longer necessary. Even more important, there is a significant reduction in the acquisition time wasted between observations, and coordinates for discovered objects are directly available. The tracking rates for the AAT are determined from the changing pointing corrections so that no cumulative errors develop. The difference between the telescope itself and its mathematical model is the only small error remaining.

5.2.3 Automation Philosophy

The character of the automation of large telescopes, of which the AAT is but one example, has benefited greatly from experience with radio telescopes. The automation of radio telescopes preceded that of optical telescopes, and with the automation radio telescope design quickly evolved from the clumsy equatorial arrangement to the mechanically more convenient alt-azimuth mounting.

Fig. 5.3. The 5-m Hale telescope still uses this "phantom" telescope to *1)* provide a horizon limit for automatic controls, *2)* keep the dome shutter aligned with the real telescope, *3)* indicate zenith angle, and *4)* keep the canvas wind screen aligned with the telescope. (Photo courtesy of Hale Observatories)

Fig. 5.2. The 200-inch Hale telescope and dome on Palomar Mountain, photographed by moonlight [5.4]. (Photo courtesy of the Hale Observatories; photograph copyright by the California Institute of Technology and Carnegie Institution of Washington)

Admittedly it was somewhat easier for radio telescopes since they did not need such high pointing precision. Furthermore optical astronomy has traditionally been a very conservative field and so far only a very few optical telescopes with alt-azimuth mountings have been undertaken; notably the Soviet 6-m telescope and the multiple mirror telescope at Mount Hopkins in Arizona. Their operation is completely contingent on the existence of computers to control the steering.

Along with the hardware developments of automation there have evolved schools of philosophy and software development pertaining to the automation. The conservative stance of optical astronomers created a philosophy that the automation be considered as a supplementary accessory attached to an otherwise fully traditional telescope. Computers were considered to be neither sufficiently reliable nor sufficiently versatile to depend upon and in any case astronomers were accustomed to having certain buttons to push as well as setting circles to read.

A counter philosophy [5.6] considers the computers, including software, to be more reliable than the mechanical drives of the telescopes. According to this philosophy it is preferable to simplify the mechanisms as much as possible, such as by not having separate drive motors for slew, set, and guide along with their mechanical differentials. Even the sidereal clock is eliminated by computing sidereal time from local time. It is in this way that maximum overall reliability and efficiency are obtained. Experience is tending to vindicate this computer-oriented philosophy. The most outspoken proponent of this philosophy, Moore, has furthermore developed the computer language FORTH that has become widely accepted in the astronomical community because of its simplicity, its convenience, and its suitability to the problems of astronomical equipment and observations.

5.2.4 Eyes for the Computer

The vast majority of astronomical observations have been recorded using photography since its introduction about a century ago. The combination of acceptable sensitivity and extraordinary recording capacity has maintained the photographic emulsion as the dominant information storage medium in astronomy. Scanning microdensitometers act as the eyes so that computers may see the information. Early scanning microdensitometers concentrated on photometric precision, scanned in a hardware established sequence, and punched the results on paper tape. The major refinements have been computer-controlled scanning and recording on magnetic tape.

The character of astronomical images containing sharp star images on an unexposed background sets them apart from ordinary pictures so that specialized techniques are desirable for the control of the scanning. The GALAXY machines and their successors the COSMOS machines [5.7] at Edinburgh have been developed specifically to accommodate the character of astronomical images, excluding useless information while retaining and recording the astronomically important information concerning positions and magnitudes of star images and identification of nebular images.

These kinds of machines form a vital link giving the computers access not only to currently obtained information but also to archival information. Microcomputers are now occasionally used as the controllers for these kinds of machines as well as for new optical instrumentation. Controversies of policy, as to whether to use central minicomputer control or special microcomputer control for the instrumentation are developing. These controversies are reminiscent of the controversies of a decade ago between large central computer facilities and small distributed facilities. The trend seems to be not only that the smaller dedicated microcomputers are becoming more versatile and more competitive but that the distinctions are eroding.

5.3 Photometric Data Processing

5.3.1 Linearity and Atmospheric Corrections

The most straightforward portions of our astronomical knowledge are based on the photometry of stars. Eyeball estimates of the relative brightness of stars formed the original basis for the logarithmic magnitude scale; five magnitudes corresponds to a factor of one hundred in brightness. Although the eye remains an important detector because of the ubiquity of visual observers, more objective magnitude estimates are now available using photographic or photoelectric photometry. The nonlinear response of the photographic emulsion requires careful calibration so as to minimize the span of the interpolated relative magnitude estimates. The core of the photographic star image is often saturated so that the image diameter serves as the photometric measure, and if care is exercised to avoid spurious influences the probable error may be as small as about ± 0.05 magnitude.

Precise absolute photometry requires photoelectric techniques. The photocells themselves have a quite linear response; uncertainties about the atmosphere introduce the major source of error. Careful work requires many measurements on a clear night, so as to estimate the atmospheric attenuation on the basis of its increase with zenith angle. There is a substantial amount of statistical fitting involved and the complexity is suited to present-day programmable pocket calculators. Larger scale electronic computers are nevertheless most often used since the pocket calculators have only recently become available.

5.3.2 Variable Stars

Variable stars have long shown as a flaw in the immutability of the starry sky. Mira, the first to be discovered, is conspicuously variable to the naked eye, displaying a more than thousandfold brightness variation with a fairly regular period of 330 days. Auspiciously the phenomenon of variability has proven to offer key and crucial information concerning the nature of the universe.

For many years variable stars were identified only when their brightness variation was conspicuous. Repeated observations could then be folded according to guessed periods, and once the period was known continued folding, modulo that period, would lead to a reproducible light curve. Under the circumstances that procedure worked remarkably satisfactorily. Large numbers of two important classes of variable stars were sorted out, eclipsing binaries and pulsating stars.

Eclipsing Binary Stars

Eclipsing binaries are important not only because their prevalence bears upon the origin of stars, but because they present rare opportunities to ascertain the masses, as well as certain other characteristics, of stars. The traditional approach [5.8] to the determination of orbits for eclipsing binaries has not been one of analysis, but rather one of constructing relatively idealized models and comparing the light curves the models would give with the actual observed light curves. One then judiciously adjusts the parameters of the model until the light curves are in reasonable agreement.

Certain of the integrals involved in ascertaining the light curves from a binary star model are particularly difficult to calculate and early work even resorted to constructing tangible models on polar coordinate paper, overlaying the two model "stars" and adding squares for integration. Since then voluminous tables have been compiled by Russell and Merrill for the computations involved in model development.

Frequency Analysis. The behavior of these variable stars is periodic and periodic functions are the grist of harmonic analysis. The aptness of the Fourier series (frequency domain as opposed to time domain) representation of the variability has been recognized by *Kopal* [5.9] and *Kitamura* [5.10], who find that it not only facilitates the determination of the orbital elements of eclipsing binaries, but that it is also less susceptible to the effects of small errors. The reason for the lower susceptibility is that Fourier analysis involves integration using the whole light curve, thereby legitimately smoothing the observations. Errors in the light curve tend to appear principally as very high harmonics that may be duly recognized and suppressed.

The Fast Fourier Transform. It is noteworthy that the thrust of their approach was developed prior to the advent of the fast Fourier transform (F.F.T) algorithm. The fast Fourier transform algorithm [5.11] has found ubiquitous applications and has profoundly influenced the technology and use of numerical computation. The algorithm is a factoring procedure that reduces the work of transforming a sequence of n samples from the n^2 operations of classical procedures to $n \log n$ operations. Not only are there enormous computational savings for large n, but the accumulated round-off errors are diminished so as to give a more accurate transform. With the Fourier transform of the light curve now being so readily available, the use of the frequency domain for the determination of the orbital elements of eclipsing binaries takes on added luster. With modest additional information, such as distance, the masses and other physical parameters of the stars become available with the aid of a pocket calculator. Those physical parameters are of importance to pursue our understanding the formation and structure of stars and aggregates of stars.

Further discussions of the F.F.T. may be found in Chaps. 2 and 3.

Pulsating Variable Stars

Another class of variable stars, the pulsating stars, are of perhaps even more importance to our understanding of stars, galaxies, and the universe. These pulsating stars include Cepheid variables, R R Lyrae stars and long period variables. The Cepheid variables with their characteristic light curves and typically ten day periods took on importance when *Leavitt* [5.12] noticed a clear-cut relation between period and magnitude for those variables in the Small Magellanic cloud. Since all the stars in the Small Magellanic cloud are at roughly the same distance, that made it possible to ascertain the absolute magnitude of a Cepheid variable from its period. Thus it is possible to determine the distances to Cepheid variables elsewhere from the simple knowledge of their periods and apparent magnitudes. That step proved to be a key step in the determination of the distance scale of the universe. Accordingly there is great motivation to measure more and more pulsating variable stars.

Fourier Synthesis with Irregularly Spaced Observations. One of the problems is that astronomical observations are available on an irregular basis. Weather as well as the daily and yearly cycles of the sky combine with the allocation of telescope time to render the observations of any particular star occasional. The goal is to ascertain the period and the light curve from those occasional observations.

The classical, and very accurate, procedure to determine the period requires an initial guess at the period. The observations are then plotted as a function of their time modulo that period. If the guess was adequate a pronounced light curve develops, but that curve starts to drift within the period window. The period is then corrected to compensate for the drift rate. Repeating the procedure with the correct period develops an average light curve. The period and the shape of the light curve are characteristics of the classes of variable stars. The procedure works well for stars that are both conspicuously variable and conspicuously regular. It fails however when the variation is less than obvious.

In that case Fourier transformation sometimes offers a remedy. The nonuniformity of the intervals between observations precludes the use of the fast Fourier transform algorithm. On the other hand the total number of observations will be modest by computer standards. Classical Fourier synthesis is suitable under those circumstances. Two arrays in the computer are assigned to the real and imaginary parts of the frequency spectrum. Each observation then contributes sinusoids (a cosine and a sine, respectively) to the arrays, the frequency of the sinusoid being specified by the observation time and the amplitude proportional to the observed brightness. In that fashion the observations synthesize a spectrum of the time variations.

The observations constitute samples of a continuous curve; in other words we may imagine multiplying the continuous curve by a set of delta functions, one at each observation. The consequence is convolving the genuine spectrum with the Fourier transform of the set of delta functions. If the observations (delta functions) happen to be uniformly spaced, their Fourier transform is again a uniformly spaced set of delta functions. Thus, each frequency of the synthesized spectrum is actually composed of many possible frequencies, called alias frequencies. Usually the alias frequencies are so widely spread that all but the valid one can be ruled out on a priori physical considerations. That is the nature of sampling theory.

With irregularly spaced samples the Fourier transform of the sampling function loses its simplicity. It becomes desirable to ascertain that Fourier transform from calculation, because that serves as the blur function for the frequency spectrum of the observations. A certain amount of judicious tailoring of the blur function, with the aim of expelling any confusing features in the neighborhood of the central peak, may be performed by weighting the observations.

These kinds of procedures are particularly important for studying small amplitude variable stars. A striking example is the identification of astronomical x-ray sources with specific stars. While the x-ray emission is often conspicuously and regularly variable, the optical emission barely changes. If those feeble changes have the identical period as the x-ray variations we can be confident of a correct identification and thus greatly enlarge our understanding of the star. The discoveries resulting from those identifications have been astonishing and fascinating.

5.3.3 High Speed Photometry

The discoveries of flare stars and pulsars have engendered the need for much higher speed photometry than had previously been customary. The pulsars are so remarkably regular that extraordinarily precise timing is necessary to discern small departures from regularity. For almost the first time it is necessary to incorporate the variations of light travel time due to motion of the telescope in space, very much as with Roemer's determination of the velocity of light by careful timing of the eclipses of the Galilean satellites of Jupiter. The achievement of microsecond timing requires compensation for displacements smaller than a kilometer, and it is really only practical to accomplish such compensation with computers.

5.4 Spectroscopic Data Processing

5.4.1 Synthetic Spectra

Ever since the recognition of spectral lines being identified with atomic species, spectroscopy has been a fundamental tool for optical astronomy. The positions, strengths, and shapes of spectral lines depend intricately upon the physical circumstances and chemical composition of the light source. That intricate dependence gives rise to one of the most consuming applications of large-scale computers found in optical astronomy, the characterization of stellar atmospheres. The radiative transfer problem including thousands of spectral lines is utterly immense. Almost all of such programming would be better classified as theoretical astronomy, and outside the scope of this survey. Synthetic spectra derived from the model atmospheres are then generated for comparison with observed optical spectra. These synthetic spectra range from relatively crude, low-resolution spectra to exquisitely detailed, high-resolution spectra that are practically beyond the capabilities of observational techniques.

5.4.2 Automation of Spectrometers

Computers are also playing an increasing role in the purely observational side of obtaining spectra. They are being used increasingly for the largely house-keeping chores of operating a spectrometer, such as controlling the scan in terms of spectral limits and rate, subtracting background due to both dark current and sky, and organizing the data for elegant display. One big gain from the computer control of these chores is that the scan can readily be made rapid and repetitive with signal averaging of the results. This procedure is relatively immune to the perturbing effects of atmospheric scintillation and to sensitivity drifts. It is also particularly adaptable for sources of differing brightness; the fainter stars are simply observed for longer than the brighter ones. The spectra, having the same resolution and signal-to-noise ratio, are much more easily compared for meaningful physical distinctions than if the instrumental parameters had been varied to compensate for the different brightnesses.

5.4.3 Fourier Transform Spectrometry [5.13]

The control of classical dispersing spectrometers takes practically no advantage of the mathematical capabilities of computers, and in that sense the computers are serving only as process controllers. In the early 1950s Fellgett initiated a revolution in infrared spectroscopy by pointing out a multiplex advantage that could be gained through interferometric Fourier transform spectroscopy. At about the same time Jacquinot pointed out that interferometers offer a large throughput advantage compared to classical dispersing spectrometers. Succinctly, these advantages result from elimination of the exit and entrance slits of the classical dispersing spectrometers. Fourier spectroscopy has come to flourish in the infrared and Connes demonstrated a further precision advantage resulting from direct digital comparison of the unknown spectral frequencies with a known monochromatic reference wavelength, now furnished with lasers.

Because the multiplex advantage vanished at visible wavelengths, as a result of photon noise becoming predominant, Fourier spectroscopy has made little impact on optical spectroscopy. There are nevertheless a couple of birefringent polarization interferometers that have been constructed and used in astronomy. Their virtues are large throughput and simplicity. In addition, a couple of high-resolution optical Fourier spectrometers are under constructions. Michelson type interferometers are more difficult in the visible than in the infrared because of the greater mechanical precision required. Experience and progress with infrared spectrometers now permits attaining the requisite mechanical precision, and we may anticipate more accurate measurements of spectrum line profiles soon.

The pertinent aspect for this article is that Fourier spectrometers really require computers. The raw measurements are in the form of an interferogram, which is the Fourier transform of the spectrum. An interferometer can be thought of as a modulator. If one of the mirrors of the interferometer is driven at a constant velocity, monochromatic incident light will be modulated at a chopping frequency proportional to the frequency of that light. If the light is a composite of many optical frequencies, the measured photometric signal will contain a proportional composition of frequencies. It is the computer that decomposes that recorded signal into its component frequencies using the fast Fourier transform algorithm.

Phase Correction

Ideally, the recorded signal is perfectly symmetric about a zero path difference position of the interferometer, so that the real part (cosines) of the calculated Fourier transform serves as the desired spectrum. In real life however the recorded signal is found rarely to be symmetric, so that further clarification of the spectrum is necessary. A simple and occasionally adequate expedient is to use the amplitude (modulus of the real and imaginary parts) of the Fourier transform as the spectrum. That expedient is quite respectable when both sides (around zero path difference) of the interferogram are measured.

On the other hand the computer permits a somewhat more sophisticated correction that preserves linearity (note that amplitude is basically nonlinear), which may be important in relatively weak portions of the spectrum. Furthermore the more sophisticated correction remains legitimate even when the interferogram is grossly off-center so that zero path difference (white light fringes) is practically at one extreme of the measurement interval. The motivation for such off-center operation is to maximize available path difference, since that also maximizes resolving power.

The idea is to select only those sinusoidal components whose phase agrees with what the phase ought to be. What the phase ought to be varies only slowly as a function of wavelength and is determined by a very few samples near zero path difference; those few samples provide the reference for phase-sensitive detection of the sinusoidal fringes composing the interferogram.

Numerically the phase-sensitive detection can be accomplished multiplicatively in the spectral domain or as a convolution that phase shifts the components to create a symmetric interferogram for cosine transformation. The choice is somewhat a matter of taste, convenience, and computer memory. If plenty of core memory is available multiplicative correction is easy and fast; when less memory is available the convolution procedures can be advantageous. In either case care must be taken not to unduly weight the central fringes by inadvertently counting them on both sides of center as compared to distant fringes, which may be counted on only one side.

Dynamic Range

Dynamic range is occasionally restricted by word length in the computer; with Fourier spectroscopy it may be important because the central portion of the interferogram typically exhibits high-contrast fringes, whereas the wings that convey the details of the spectrum are of low contrast. A previously unpublished way to alleviate the word length problem in combination with multiplicative phase correction is as follows.

The multiplicative phase correction is

$$S_{corrected} = |S_{extensive}| \cos \Delta = \frac{S_{extensive} \cdot S_{reference}}{|S_{reference}|},$$

where S are spectra and Δ are the phase differences of the spectral components from the extensive interferogram and the short reference interferogram. Further expressions become

$$\frac{(S_{extensive} - S_{reference} + S_{reference}) \cdot S_{reference}}{|S_{reference}|}$$

$$= \frac{S_{(extensive - reference)} \cdot S_{reference}}{|S_{reference}|} + |S_{reference}|.$$

Note that the central reference fringes have been subtracted off in the parenthetical term of the right-hand side so that less dynamic range or word length is needed.

5.5 Picture Processing

With the growth of memory size in computers it has become possible to cope with the two-dimensional nature of images. One way or another images that are obtained with telescopes are finding themselves sampled, digitized, and placed in computer memory. There, all sorts of numerical massaging treatments are applied so that astronomers can more readily perceive pertinent information relatively uncontaminated by extraneous effects.

5.5.1 Isodensitometry

One of the earliest image treatments was converting conventional black and white pictures to isodensity contours. The reasons for isodensity contours are that it becomes easy to define otherwise vague borders, measure sizes and areas contained, and perform integrated surface photometry. That is precisely the sort of quantitative information needed for comparing and sorting nebulae. For example, studies of the physical conditions in planetary nebulae and ionized hydrogen (H II) regions requires quantitative photometric information concerning size, total brightness, and surface brightness for various of the emitting species wavelengths.

Another example is studies of galaxies that hopefully give clues abut cosmology on a large scale. These studies depend on the photometry and size measurements of individual galaxies. Almost perversely, these studies indicate a power law for the decline of the surface brightness of the galaxies away from their centers, so that no characteristic size can be assigned.

5.5.2 Massaging Images

Rather elaborate picture processing and massaging are available by using various linear and nonlinear filtering procedures. One example of a combination of these procedures has been used by *Arp* and *Lorre* [5.14] to discern faint diffuse nebular structure. Their approach was first to eliminate the stellar images by sensing the steep gradients associated with those images and subsequently interpolating across the background. Following that nonlinear step a linear high-pass (spatial frequency) filtering is applied to the picture. The effect of the high-pass filtering is to overcome the spurious gradients and very low spatial frequency mottling of the photographs. The final step is to augment the contrast so that the appreciable range of output densities corresponds to a very small range of input densities. Discerned nebular structure may be deemed to be real if the resulting pictures are reproducible. The importance is that certain cosmological arguments depend on the reality of those structures.

The ultimate limits of telescope performance have long been the result of atmospheric turbulence. Not only does the resulting blurring severely restrict the resolving power of telescopes but it diminishes the contrast of point sources against the background sky so as to bound the limiting magnitude of telescopes, preventing the detection of very faint objects. As with many fields the frontier areas of resolvability and detection act as the main arena for advancements of knowledge. It is in the anticipation of such an improvement that astronomers are eagerly awaiting the results of space-borne telescopes.

5.5.3 Speckle Interferometry

A separate course of action other than waiting is also underway. Although it had occasionally been noticed previously, in 1969 *Labeyrie* [5.15, 16] recognized the importance of the fact that a star does not really appear as a diffuse blur through a large telescope. The star image appears as a collection of small speckles that wriggle around, the typical size of each speckle being comparable to the diffraction limit of the telscope. Labeyrie's brilliant idea recognized that the presence of such speckles implied that the details of star images were not lost but merely rearranged by atmospheric blurring. Cinema rather than time exposures must be used to preserve the details of the wriggling speckles.

A simple heuristic point of view leading to an understanding of how to disentangle the pictures is based on the Abbé theory of image formation. From this point of view a picture ought not to be considered as an assembly of luminous points but an assembly of spatial frequency components. A spatial frequency component is simply a bar grid pattern. Now the nature of atmospheric turbulence is not to obliterate any pattern, but merely to shift the pattern, differently for each pattern. A simple time average of a pattern, as given by a time exposure, while the pattern shifts back and forth, will obliterate the contrast of the pattern if the shift amounts to more than about half a bar. On the other hand, if we can average the strength (peak brightness) and position of the pattern separately, then no contrast gets lost, and the deleterious effects of the atmospheric turbulence are avoided. Certain difficulties arise concerning averaging the position of a pattern. For centrosymmetric objects, however, all pattern are positioned so that the peak brightness is at the center. The picture then depends only on the relative strengths of the patterns. In other words the spatial-frequency power spectrum (Wiener spectrum) is sufficient, and that power spectrum has not been deteriorated in very short exposures. Thus for centrosymmetric sources, the diffraction-limited image may be obtained as the two-dimensional cosine Fourier transform of the square root of the average spatial-frequency power spectrum of all the short exposures. It is usually not difficult to surmise whether positive or negative square roots should be adopted for the various regions of spatial frequency. Labeyrie's speckle interferometry of centrosymmetric sources is also very useful to resolve double stars, because it almost never makes any difference whether the brighter star is to the left or right.

For the most part the computation of the spatial-frequency power spectra of images have not been accomplished numerically, but with coherent light optical systems. The procedure has proven itself well in the measurements of stellar diameters and close binary stars. An important aspect is that the success of the procedure confirms that pictorial details are not lost, but only rearranged, in the short exposures. The next step is to solve the rearrangement so that the centrosymmetric condition can be lifted.

5.5.4 Speckle Imaging

The problem of determining the average position (phase) of a spatial frequency component is that phase is specified to only a fraction of a cycle (i.e., modulo 2π). It can be drastically erroneous to average a series of numbers when only their fractional parts are known.

The Knox-Thompson Algorithm

The solution by differentiating and integrating has been found by *Knox* and *Thompson* [5.17]. The mean position to be adopted is given by the following average phase:

$$\langle\phi(v)\rangle = \sum_{v=1}^{v} \left\{\frac{1}{T}\sum_{t=1}^{T}[\phi(t,v)-\phi(t,v-1)]\right\}, \quad \phi(t,0)=0,$$

where v is spatial frequency and t time. Note that the phase is differenced with respect to spatial frequency v, and subsequently integrated from zero spatial frequency (by definition having zero phase) to the spatial frequency v in question. It is assumed that each phase difference is really less than one half cycle, that assumption being rather acceptable if the spatial frequencies are taken closer together than they need be. This latter condition is tantamount to assuming a null border around the picture.

Although the assumption that the phase differences are each less than a half cycle is acceptably valid, it is probably not rigorously valid because although both the real and imaginary parts of the spatial-frequency component $Z(v)$ are rigorously band limited, the arctangent of their quotient is not necessarily band limited.

The following approximations for the average phase simplify the data processing:

$$\langle\phi(v)\rangle \approx \sum_{v=1}^{V} \arctan\left[\frac{1}{T}\sum_{t=1}^{T}\frac{\mathrm{Im}\{Z(t,v)\cdot Z^*(t,v-1)\}}{\mathrm{Re}\{Z(t,v)\cdot Z^*(t,v-1)\}}\right]$$

$$\approx \sum_{v=1}^{V}\frac{1}{T}\sum_{t=1}^{T}\frac{\mathrm{Im}\{Z(t,v)\cdot Z^*(t,v-1)\}}{\mathrm{Re}\{Z(t,v)\cdot Z^*(t,v-1)\}},$$

where $Z(t,v)$ is the complex value of a spatial-frequency component v, on frame t of the movie. This procedure given by *Knox* and *Thompson* does involve cumulative errors and is subject to breakdown if the phase becomes indeterminate as the result of negligible amplitude for a spatial-frequency component. Nisenson has taken advantage of the two-dimensional character of spatial frequency v and proposed averaging over several different paths in the spatial-frequency plane to suppress accumulative errors and alleviate some breakdowns.

Since the product $Z(t, v) \cdot Z^*(t, v-1)$ is already available, *Knox* and *Thompson* recommend using its real part for the power of $Z(t, v)$. Thus

$$\langle Z(v) \rangle = \left[\frac{1}{T} \sum_{t=1}^{T} \text{Re}\{Z(t, v) \cdot Z^*(t, v-1)\} \right]^{1/2}$$

$$\cdot \exp\left[i \sum_{v=1}^{V} \frac{1}{T} \sum_{t=1}^{T} \frac{\text{Im}\{Z(t, v) \cdot Z^*(t, v-1)\}}{\text{Re}\{Z(t, v) \cdot Z^*(t, v-1)\}} \right].$$

The fast Fourier transform applied to that specification for each spatial-frequency component reconstructs a picture as would be seen in the absence of atmospheric perturbations.

A summary of the major work involved in doing speckle imaging is then to take movies at the telescope, scan and digitize each movie frame, Fourier transform each frame, compute $Z(t, v) \cdot Z^*(t, v-1)$ to get certain averages for each spatial frequency, and finally to perform a single Fourier transform to reconstruct the picture. Which of those steps is the most arduous depends somewhat on the particular facilities available, and the operational fruition of speckle imaging is imminent.

A Temporal Algorithm for Use at Low Light Levels

At lower and lower light levels some simplifications might be possible [5.18]. When the photon rate count becomes small, only a handful of photons would appear on each movie (or TV) frame. Thus most of the capacity of the detecting and recording system is wastefully used to indicate the absence of photons. A nonpictorial format whereby the detection system writes the coordinates of each photon as it comes in is now more effective, and certain detectors are currently being developed that function in that manner. Not only is this catalog format more efficient than a pictorial format at these low light levels, it is also more informative. For example, the catalog format can always be transformed to pictorial format by simply placing the photons in the appropriate boxes according to their coordinates. However, the transformation is irreversible and therefore entails a loss of information. Some of the extra information may be exploited in the following version of speckle imaging, suitable for photon rates of about 100 to 10,000 photons per second in the picture.

The coordinates from the photon are input one at a time to the computer. Each entry is first placed in a memory stack and then its contribution to the Fourier transform synthesized in a two-dimensional complex array,

$$\text{Re}\{Z(U, V)\} = \sum^{K} \cos(XU + YV)$$

$$\text{Im}\{Z(U, V)\} = \sum^{K} \sin(XU + YV).$$

Since the picture is real, its Fourier transform is Hermitian and so only a half-plane of the transform need be stored. Thus the two arrays of $N^2/2$ words map reversibly to a picture of N^2 pixels. The number of contributing photons K must have originally arrived in the catalog within about $1/50$ s, i.e., while the atmosphere is essentially static. When K is small, Fourier synthesis is much more efficient that a fast Fourier transform. Furthermore there are no multiplications whatever involved in the synthesis; the arguments are generated by successive additions because U and V are sequentially accessed, the sinusoids are obtained from table look-up, and all the coefficients are unity because each photon is one unit.

So far we have the Fourier transform corresponding to a movie frame incorporating the first K photons. Now as with any speckle imaging algorithm the awkward part is to establish a legitimate average phase, based on specimens that are each modulo 2π. With the Knox-Thompson algorithm, differentiation and integration with respect to spatial frequency were used. Differentiation and integration with respect to time may also be used. In this case a scratch pad array is maintained to keep track of the phase so that

$$\Phi(t, U, V) = \Phi(t-1, U, V) + [\phi(t, U, V) - \Phi(t-1, U, V)]_{-\pi}^{+\pi},$$

where $\phi = \arctan(\mathrm{Im}\{Z\}/\mathrm{Re}\{Z\})$, and $\Phi(0, u, v) = 0$. Although ϕ is only known modulo 2π, the bracketed expression is a difference whose absolute value should be specified to be less than π. Φ itself thus keeps track of the phase including full turns and so may be used for obtaining a legitimate average phase.

The amplitude presents no such problems, so that

$$|Z| = (\mathrm{Re}^2\{Z\} + \mathrm{Im}^2\{Z\})^{1/2} = \mathrm{Re}\{Z\} \cos\phi + \mathrm{Im}\{Z\} \sin\phi.$$

The Fourier transform for the next movie frame is obtained from that of the previous frame by adding the cosine and sine terms from the trailing photon. Successive frames overlap substantially; their Fourier transforms are therefore not independent and we can be relatively confident that the Fourier components will have shifted by substantially less than π in phase, thus validating the phase differencing procedure.

When the photon catalog is exhausted the appropriate estimate of the average unperturbed Fourier transform of the picture is

$$\langle Z(U, V) \rangle = \frac{1}{T} \sum_{t=1}^{T} |Z(t, U, V)| \exp\left[i \frac{1}{T} \sum_{t=1}^{T} \Phi(t, U, V)\right]$$

A two-dimensional fast Fourier transform reconstructs that estimate of the picture.

An alternative to this approach was recently taken by *Worden* [5.19].

Logarithmic and Entropy Embellishments

Modified estimates based on different emphasis of the averaging may be obtained with trivial extra effort. For example, Rybicki has suggested that a logarithmic average might be preferable because the atmospheric perturbations are of a multiplicative nature, so that the fluctuating part to be averaged out has a proper zero mean. The logarithmic average has an extra aesthetic appeal because it consolidates amplitude and phase. Although complex logarithms are not commonly used, they behave as ordinary logarithms,

$$Z = a + ib = \exp(\ln Z) = \exp(\alpha + i\beta).$$

The consolidated logarithmic average is then

$$\langle Z(U, V) \rangle = \exp\left[\frac{1}{T} \sum_{t=1}^{T} \ln Z(t, U, V)\right].$$

A further slight embellishment may be made by weighting the average. It is reasonable that when the amplitude $|Z(t, U, V)|$ is strong there will be less uncertainty in the phase $\Phi(t, U, V)$ and so amplitude weighting is justified. Keeping the logarithmic consolidation leads to another estimate

$$\langle Z(U, V) \rangle = \exp\left[\frac{\sum_{t=1}^{T} |Z(t, U, V)| \ln Z(t, U, V)}{\sum_{t=1}^{T} |Z(t, U, V)|}\right].$$

Note that the numerator has the form of entropy. Since entropy is identified with information, this last estimate may give the most probable picture in the Bayesian sense based on the observed photon catalog.

The speed of the calculations, as programmed for a 64×64 picture on a minicomputer without hardware multiply, runs about 400 to 1000 times slower than real time. Such a factor is not at all discouraging for initial trials. If successful, considerable improvements in speed and picture size can readily be anticipated because the procedures are readily adapted to mixed serial and parallel processing. Real time processing for a television size picture is certainly possible.

Reverse Impact on Telescopes

Speckle imaging should have an enormous impact on optical astronomy, whatever procedure eventually proves to be the most satisfactory. How will speckle imaging perform in regard to the basic problem of recognizing a faint point source superimposed on a uniform night sky background? According to the reasoning already presented, speckle imaging simply rearranges the picture to counteract the perturbing effects of the turbulent atmosphere. Rearrangement of a uniform background leaves a uniform background, with no augmentation or attenuation. On the other hand, rearrangement of the structure of a point source so that it becomes concentrated into a much smaller spot will enormously augment the contrast of that spot with respect to the background, thus making the spot relatively more discernable. As mentioned earlier, that contrast enhancement is one of the principal goals of the space telescope, and it now appears that speckle imaging may be competitive in that same goal.

That same contrast enhancement should also vastly increase the motivation towards ever larger telescopes, not only to gather more photons but to improve our acuity. The prospect toward larger telescopes raises a controversial issue concerning the behavior of speckle imaging with respect to telescope aberrations. From the point of view taken above, the positions (phases) of the Fourier components are restored to a mean position, which is the position they would have had in the absence of the atmospherically fluctuating perturbation. Aberrations, on the other hand, present persistent systematic perturbations that are not averaged out. The other side of the controversy holds that as long as the fluctuating perturbations exceed the aberration perturbation, the mean position is the true unaberrated position. In any case the position may be tested by examining a known unresolved star, and, if necessary on the basis of that examination, the systematic aberrational positions can then be subtracted to provide true diffraction-limited imagery rather than aberration-limited imagery.

The reason for the importance of this aberration controversy with respect to future large telescopes is that most candidate designs depend on servo controls to continually maintain the figure of the telescope. With ordinary servo controls that procedure precludes reproducible aberrations. If the aberrations prove a problem, then speckle imaging would require servos that are far more precise and more thorough than any planned. That may prove to be an important argument in favor of a non-servo-controlled Arecibo style telescope, although it is by no means certain whether even that design would have adequate short term reproducibility.

Remarks

No one can pretend to be qualified over the entire field of computers in optical astronomy; the field is just too vast. Therefore, this presentation has been necessarily an individual perspective on the field with due emphasis on the author's specialties.

This work is supplemented by Sect. 1.8 with respect to astronomical picture processing.

Only those references that directly influenced the presentation are included. There is no pretense that it is a thorough or comprehensive bibliography.

References

5.1   F.Hoyle: *From Stonehenge to Modern Cosmology* (Freeman, San Francisco 1972)
5.2   W.J.Eckert: Astron. J. **44**, 177–182 (1935)
5.3   W.J.Eckert, D.Brouwer, G.M.Clemence: Coordinates of the Five Outer Planeters, 1653–2060, Astronomical Papers of the American Ephemeris, Vol. **12**, preface (1951)
5.4   S.P.Wyatt: *Principles of Astronomy*, 2nd ed. (Allyn and Bacon, Boston 1971)
5.5   P.T.Wallace: "Programming the Control Computer of the Anglo-Australian 3.9 Metre Telescope", in *Telescope Automation*, proceedings of conference at MIT (1975) pp. 284–298
5.6   C.Moore, E.Rather, E.Conklin: "Modular Software for On-Line Telescope Control", in *Telescope Automation*, proceedings of conference at MIT (1975) pp. 1–15
5.7   N.M.Pratt: Vistas Astron. **21**, 1–42 (1977)
5.8   J.B.Irwin: "Orbit Determinations of Eclipsing Binaries", in *Astronomical Techniques* ed. by A. Hiltner (University of Chicago Press, Chicago 1962)
5.9   Z.Kopal: Astrophys. Space Sci. **34**, 431–457; **35**, 159–183; **36**, 227–237; **38**, 191–241 (1975)
5.10   M.Kitamura: Adv. Astron. Astrophys. **3**, 27–87 (1965)
5.11   J.W.Cooley, J.W.Tukey: Math. Comput. **19**, 297–301 (1965)
5.12   H.S.Leavitt: "Periods of 25 Variables in the Small Magellanic Cloud"; Harvard College Observatory Circular No. 173 (1912)
5.13   L.Mertz: *Transformations in Optics* (Wiley, New York 1965)
5.14   H.Arp, J.Lorre: Astrophys. J. **210**, 58–64 (1976)
5.15   A.Labeyrie: Astron. Astrophys. **6**, 85–87 (1970)
5.16   For a review see J.C.Dainty (ed.): *Laser Speckle and Related Phenomena*, Topics in Applied Physics, Vol. 9 (Springer, Berlin, Heidelberg, New York 1975) Chap. 7
5.17   K.T.Knox, B.J.Thompson: Astrophys. J. **193**, L45–L48 (1974)
5.18   L.Mertz: Appl. Opt. **18**, 611–614 (1979)
5.19   S.P.Worden: Vistas Astron. **20**, 301–318 (1977)

6. Computer-Generated Holograms

W. J. Dallas

With 25 Figures

In this chapter we describe the computer-generated hologram as one element in an optical display system. Our discussion concentrates on its display potential, and application examples are drawn from this area.

6.1 Background

Image formation by computer-generated hologram (CGH) can be divided into four steps:
1) Choosing the object (desired image).
2) Calculating the object wave front at the hologram.
3) Encoding this wave front into a hologram transmittance.
4) Optically decoding the hologram transmittance or reconstructing the image, the reconstructed image being a somewhat degraded version of the object.

Since the optical decoding configuration, or reconstruction geometry, we are considering is that of Fig. 6.1, a close analogy exists between the CGH and a diffraction grating. In fact, the computer-generated hologram can best be visualized as a distorted diffraction grating [6.1, 2]. When placed in a spherically converging beam of monochromatic light it will, like a diffraction grating, exhibit diffraction orders. Because the hologram grating is distorted, these diffraction orders will not be the sharp points of light expected from a perfect grating. Instead, the diffracted light will spread out into ghost images

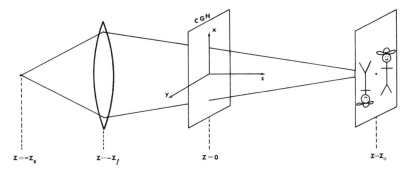

Fig. 6.1. Fourier hologram reconstruction setup

whose shapes depend on the particular distortions of the grating; for example, one might produce a smiling face in the first diffraction order, or the three-dimensional image of a crystal [6.2a]. The ghost image may be three dimensional and, with an appropriate light source, multicolored. To produce a computer-generated hologram one must determine what distortions are necessary in the grating to produce a desired ghost image.

The desired ghost image is the object. Distorting the grating is the calculation and encoding of steps 2 and 3 above. Suitably illuminating the grating plus propagation to the observation plane is optical decoding.

6.1.1 Reconstruction

Choosing the reconstruction geometry illustrated in Fig. 6.1 leads to a Fourier relationship between the complex-amplitude transmittance of the hologram and the reconstructed image [6.3, 4]. The hologram at $z=0$ is illuminated by a spherical wave converging to a point $x=0$, $y=0$, $z=z_0$.

On considering light propagation in the parabolic approximation, ignoring an uninteresting uniform multiplicative factor, and describing points on the hologram in terms of the reduced coordinates

$$\mu = -x/\lambda z_0, v = -y/\lambda z_0, \tag{6.1}$$

the complex amplitude resulting at $z=z_0$ from a CGH with complex-amplitude transmittance $\tilde{v}(\mu, v)$ at $z=0$ is

$$v_1(x, y) = \exp[i\pi(x^2 + y^2)/\lambda z_0] \iint \tilde{v}(\mu, v) \exp[2\pi i(\mu x + vy)] d\mu dv \tag{6.2a}$$

$$= \exp[i\pi(x^2 + y^2)/\lambda z_0] v(x, y). \tag{6.2b}$$

Except for the exponential coefficient, the quadratic phase factor, *the complex amplitude at z_0 is the Fourier transform of the hologram transmittance*. The quadratic phase factor is usually ignored because the intensity $|v_1(x, y)|^2$ is observed. Note that by varying z_0 the scale of the reconstruction is varied.

Generally some compact portion of $v(x, y)$, say of dimensions Δx by Δy, contains the desired image $u(x, y)$,

$$u(x, y) = 0 \quad \text{for} \quad |x| > \Delta x/2 \quad \text{or} \quad |y| > \Delta y/2, \tag{6.3a}$$

$$v(x, y) = u(x - x_0, y - y_0) + \text{rest}(x, y), \tag{6.3b}$$

where $\text{rest}(x, y)$ is a deterministic "noise" arising from the encoding of the object wave at the hologram.

6.1.2 Calculating the Object Wave Front at the Hologram

This wave front is, given the reconstruction geometry described above,

$$\tilde{u}(\mu, v) = \int\int_{-\infty}^{\infty} u(x, y) \exp[-2\pi i(\mu x + vy)]\, dx\, dy. \tag{6.4}$$

For digital computation the transformation must be discretized. This proceeds naturally if we restrict our attention to points in the object $u(x, y)$ separated by distances $(\delta x, \delta y)$ in the x and y directions, respectively. This restriction is motivated by the common practice of periodically repeating holograms thus reconstructing images consisting of points [6.5],

$$u_{mn} = u(m\delta x, n\delta y), \tag{6.5a}$$

$$-(M/2) \leq m \leq (N/2) - 1, \tag{6.5b}$$

$$-(N/2) \leq n \leq (N/2) - 1, \tag{6.5c}$$

the bounds coming from the finite extent of the object. From (6.3),

$$M\delta x = \Delta x, \ N\delta y = \Delta y, \tag{6.6a}$$

$$M \times N = \text{number of points in object.} \tag{6.6b}$$

M and N were chosen to be even only for specificity. Odd M or N would require slight modification of (6.5).

Sampling in the hologram at distances

$$\delta\mu = 1/\Delta x \quad \text{and} \quad \delta v = 1/\Delta y, \tag{6.7}$$

(6.4) is rewritten as the discrete Fourier transform (DFT)

$$\tilde{u}_{jk} = \sum_{m=-M/2}^{(M/2)-1} \sum_{n=-N/2}^{(N/2)-1} u_{mn} \exp[-2\pi i(mj/M) + (nk/N)], \tag{6.8a}$$

$$\tilde{u}_{jk} = \tilde{u}(j/\Delta x, k/\Delta y), \tag{6.8b}$$

$$-M/2 \leq j \leq (M/2) - 1, \tag{6.8c}$$

$$-N/2 \leq k \leq (N/2) - 1. \tag{6.8d}$$

The discrete Fourier transform has two virtues for computer holography. First, "fast" algorithms exist for its computation [6.6, 7, 7a]. Second, many computer holograms are sampled and periodic devices, making the DFT calculation appropriate.

From this point on we shall refer to the object wave at the hologram as the object Fourier spectrum, or simply Fourier spectrum.

6.1.3 Encoding the Fourier Spectrum

Computer holograms can, by their encoding philosophies, be divided into two broad families: cell-oriented holograms and point-oriented holograms.

A cell-oriented hologram has its surface organized into small rectangular units called resolution cells. The transmission of the cell can be, according to the hologram type, binary (clear and opaque), real nonnegative, real bipolar, or truly complex. The transmittance is usually controlled by a single (perhaps complex) number for the whole cell.

A point-oriented hologram can be visualized as the result of a point nonlinearity acting on a continuous object wave front at the hologram. The continuous wave front function is either known in closed form or is obtained from the DFT of (6.8) by interpolation.

Once the desired transmittance has been calculated it is usually outputted to a computer-controlled plotting device. The plot is then photographically processed into a transparency, thus becoming the actual hologram.

The plotter's output is quantized, for example, quantized gray levels from CRT plotters and geometrically quantized patterns from increment pen and ink plotters. The reconstructed images therefore exhibit quantization caused degradations, described in (6.3) as part of rest(x, y).

The degradations can be reduced by increasing the plot size, but increased size leads to increased cost. Quantization effects, together with the number of points in the object, are the strongest factors in determining the relative costs of CGHs.

6.1.4 Choosing the Object

The object consists of $M \times N$ points. This number is termed the space-bandwidth product (SBWP) [6.8, 9],

$$\text{SBWP} = M \times N . \tag{6.9}$$

It is invariant with magnification since from (6.6)

$$\text{SBWP} = (\Delta x/\delta x)(\Delta y/\delta y) . \tag{6.10}$$

The trade between size $(\Delta x, \Delta y)$ and resolution $(\delta x, \delta y)$ in the reconstructed image can be made by changing the lens-to-hologram distance z_0 in Fig. 6.1.

The SBWP of the Fourier spectrum is equal to the SBWP of the object [see (6.8)]. The complexity of the hologram is then directly related to the complexity of the object. A typical SBWP for a computer-generated hologram is 16,384, or

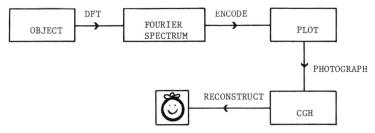

Fig. 6.2. Object to image, sequence of events

128 by 128. Modest SBWPs are a characteristic of CGHs and so should be carefully used. The reconstruction geometry we have chosen, for example, uses a focussing lens. The lens could have been encoded into the hologram by simply multiplying the Fourier spectrum by a quadratic phase factor similar to that in (6.2). The incorporation would, however, have increased the SBWP required of the hologram. Whenever possible one combines conventional optical elements with CGHs to economize on CGH SBWP. SBWP is the first object parameter to be chosen.

The quantization effects mentioned above indirectly affect the choice of the object. Most CGHs can encode only wave fronts which have relatively small variations in modulus (absolute value of the complex amplitude). Because the modulus at the hologram is influenced by both the object modulus and phase, a suitable phase, or diffuser, function must be applied to the object, even though we observe only the image intensity (modulus squared).

Figure 6.2 illustrates the computer hologram generating process we have thus far described. Sections 6.2 through 6.5 concentrate on details of this description. Sections 6.6 and 6.7 expand the description to three-dimensional and color reconstructions. Sections 6.8 and 6.9 discuss selected applications of computer-generated holograms.

6.2 Cell-Oriented Holograms

This family of holograms organizes its surface into small units called resolution cells. The dimensions of one resolution cell, in reduced coordinates [see (6.1)], are $\delta\mu$ by δv. These cell dimensions are related to the reconstructed image size so that,

$$\delta\mu = 1/\Delta x, \ \delta v = 1/\Delta y. \tag{6.11}$$

We consider the hologram to be periodic with period $\Delta\mu$ by Δv. This repetition period is related to the reconstructed image resolution (point separation) by

$$\Delta\mu = 1/\delta x, \ \Delta v = 1/\delta y. \tag{6.12}$$

(Single period, truncated, holograms are discussed in Sect. 6.4.2.) From (6.11, 12) one concludes that there are M by N resolution cells in one period of the hologram,

$$\Delta\mu/\delta\mu = (1/\delta x)/(1/\Delta x) = \Delta x/\delta x = M, \tag{6.13a}$$

$$\Delta v/\delta v = N. \tag{6.13b}$$

This equation is a restatement of the SBWP equality in the object and hologram.

The following manipulation yields an expression for the reconstructed image which closely resembles the discrete Fourier transform. This space-variant DFT provides a convenient framework for discussing cell-oriented holograms.

6.2.1 The Space-Variant Discrete Fourier Transform

The complex-amplitude transmittance of the (j, k)th resolution cell is $\tilde{C}_{jk}(\mu, v)$. The transmittance is not required to be constant over the cell, hence the reduced coordinate arguments. Over one period of the hologram the transmittance is:

$$\tilde{T}(\mu, v) = \sum_{j=-M/2}^{(M/2)-1} \sum_{k=-N/2}^{(N/2)-1} \tilde{C}_{jk}(\mu - j\delta\mu, v - k\delta v). \tag{6.14}$$

The entire hologram transmittance is

$$\tilde{T}_e(\mu, v) = \sum_{p=-\infty}^{\infty} \sum_{q=-\infty}^{\infty} \tilde{T}(\mu - p\Delta\mu, v - q\Delta v). \tag{6.15}$$

Inverse Fourier-transforming this expression gives

$$T_e(x, y) = T(x, y)(\Delta\mu\Delta v)^{-1} \sum_{m=-\infty}^{\infty} \sum_{n=-\infty}^{\infty} \delta(x - m/\Delta\mu)\delta(y - n/\Delta v) \tag{6.16a}$$

$$= \sum_m \sum_n \delta(x - m/\Delta\mu)\delta(y - n/\Delta v) T_{mn}, \tag{6.16b}$$

where the relative complex amplitude at the (m, n)th reconstructed image point is

$$T_{mn} = (\Delta\mu\Delta v)^{-1} T(m/\Delta\mu, n/\Delta v). \tag{6.17}$$

Taking the inverse Fourier transform of (6.14) yields

$$T(x, y) = \sum_j \sum_k C_{jk}(x, y)\exp[2\pi i(j\delta\mu x + k\delta v y)]. \tag{6.18}$$

Substituting from (6.17) gives

$$T_{mn} = (MN)^{-1} \sum_j \sum_k C_{jk}^{mn} \exp\{2\pi i[(jm/M) + (kn/N)]\}, \qquad (6.19a)$$

$$C_{jk}^{mn} = (\delta\mu\,\delta v)^{-1} \int_{-\delta\mu/2}^{\delta\mu/2} \int_{-\delta v/2}^{\delta v/2} \tilde{C}_{jk}(\mu, v) \exp\{-2\pi i[(m\mu/\Delta\mu) + (nv/\Delta v)]\}\, d\mu dv. \qquad (6.19b)$$

Equation (6.19a) is quite similar to the inverse of (6.8)

$$u_{mn} = (MN)^{-1} \sum_j \sum_k \tilde{u}_{jk} \exp\{2\pi i[(jm/M) + (kn/N)]\}. \qquad (6.20)$$

Each resolution cell transmittance $\tilde{C}_{jk}(\mu, v)$ gives rise to pseudo-Fourier coefficients C_{jk}^{mn} which are space variant, i.e., vary with position (m, n) in the reconstructed image. To the extent that this space variance can be ignored, the DFT relates the periodic cell-oriented hologram to the reconstructed image: each hologram resolution cell gives rise to one DFT coefficient.

At this point we turn to particular examples of cell-oriented computer-generated holograms, applying the space-variant discrete Fourier transform to their descriptions.

6.2.2 The ROACH

ROACH is an acronym for referenceless on-axis complex hologram [6.10–12]. The reconstructed image is on the optical axis, or zero diffraction order by the diffraction grating analogy. The complex-amplitude transmittance over one cell of the ROACH is constant and actually complex. The complex transmittance is achieved by using a multi-emulsion photographic film, usually Kodachrome II. One emulsion is used to control transmittance modulus, another to control phase.

Kodachrome II is a color positive film which has three emulsion layers. After processing the layers are red absorbing, green absorbing, and blue absorbing. Besides the color-specific absorption, there is also an exposure-dependent phase shift in each layer. The phase shift is due to index-of-refraction changes within each layer and thickness variations of each layer. By careful attention to exposure, the complex-amplitude transmittance of the film, for monochromatic light, can be controlled.

Consider a processed ROACH inserted in the reconstruction setup of Fig. 6.1. The light source is monochromatic, red for specificity. The incident spherical wave's modulus is altered only by the film's red-absorbing layer. The red-absorbing layer will at the same time contribute a phase shift at each point across the film's surface. This phase shift is usually not that which is desired.

The green-absorbing layer is used to provide an additional shift, bringing the total phase shift to the desired value. The modulus of the red illuminating wave is not affected by the green-absorbing layer. Result: the complex-amplitude transmittance of the ROACH is directly controlled by controlling the exposure pattern of the film in red and green light.

The proper exposure is realized by imaging a computer-generated pattern from the face of a computer display device, usually a CRT, through a color filter onto the film. The film processing after exposure is done by any commercial color-slide film processing company.

Calculation of the CRT-displayed exposing pattern can be divided into two parts. First, analyzing the relation between intensity displayed and final complex-amplitude transmittance of the ROACH. Second, calculating the ROACH complex-amplitude transmittance desired for a specific reconstructed image.

The analysis of CRT plot to ROACH transmittance, though involved, need be done only once for the system used. The results may then be integrated into the computer program for the plot generation. The analysis must consider the nonlinear exposure response of the emulsion layers, including color response. Each layer will respond to a broad band of colors; the response is only peaked at different colors for the different layers. The response of each layer will depend also on the spatial frequency of the exposing pattern. For details the interested reader is referred to [6.11].

To calculate the desired ROACH transmittance for a given object one may use the space-variant DFT approach. We follow the idealization that the transmittance is constant over a ROACH resolution cell of size $\delta\mu$ by δv. The transmittance is arbitrarily adjustable for each of the M by N resolution cells in one period. The transmittance of one ROACH cell will be

$$\tilde{C}_{jk}(\mu, v) = C_{jk} \operatorname{rect}(\mu/\delta\mu) \operatorname{rect}(v/\delta v) \tag{6.21}$$

giving a space-variant DFT coefficient, by (6.19a),

$$C_{jk}^{mn} = (\delta\mu\delta v)^{-1} \iint C_{jk} \exp[2\pi i(m\mu/\Delta\mu) + (nv/\Delta v)] \, d\mu dv \tag{6.22a}$$

$$= C_{jk} \operatorname{sinc}(m/M) \operatorname{sinc}(n/N), \tag{6.22b}$$

where

$$\operatorname{rect}(\xi) = \begin{cases} 1 & \text{for} \quad -0.5 < \xi < 0.5 \\ 0 & \text{elsewhere} \end{cases}$$

$$\operatorname{sinc}(\xi) = \sin(\pi\xi)/\pi\xi. \tag{6.23}$$

The reconstructed image is from (6.19b)

$$T_{mn} = \operatorname{sinc}(m/M) \operatorname{sinc}(n/N)(MN)^{-1} \sum_j \sum_k C_{jk} \exp\{2\pi i[(mj/M) + (nk/N)]\}. \tag{6.24}$$

The leading "sinc" product term dims those parts of the reconstructed image far from the optical axis. It apodizes the image. Setting the reconstructed image equal to the object,

$$T_{mn} = u_{mn}, \qquad (6.25)$$

and defining

$$\varrho_{mn} = u_{mn}/[\mathrm{sinc}(m/M)\,\mathrm{sinc}(n/N)]. \qquad (6.26)$$

(6.23) gives

$$C_{jk} = \tilde{\varrho}_{jk} = \sum_{m=-M/2}^{(M/2)-1} \sum_{n=-N/2}^{(N/2)-1} \varrho_{mn}\exp\{-2\pi\mathrm{i}[(jm/M)+(kn/N)]\}. \qquad (6.27)$$

Calculation of the ROACH cell transmittance is accomplished by a discrete Fourier transform of the apodization compensated image ϱ_{mn}. Alternatively, if the cell transmittances are set equal to the DFT coefficients of the object, i.e., if

$$C_{jk} = \tilde{u}_{jk}, \qquad (6.28)$$

then the reconstructed image is an apodized version of the object

$$T_{mn} = u_{mn}\,\mathrm{sinc}(m/M)\,\mathrm{sinc}(n/N). \qquad (6.29)$$

Note that there will be images other than the one desired. These images are at $|m| > M/2$, $|n| > N/2$ and exist because the ROACH is a cell-oriented CGH.

6.2.3 Computer-Generated Graytone Holograms

The graytone holograms have real, nonnegative transmittances. Such transmittances can be realized using single-emulsion, black and white, photographic films. Fabricating a graytone cell-oriented CGH is much like fabricating a ROACH. The film is exposed to the image of a pattern displayed on a computer-guided plotter, usually a CRT. This exposure controls the modulus of the hologram transmittance. A knowledge of the plotter-film-photoprocessing interaction is necessary, and after being analyzed it is incorporated into the hologram generating computer routines.

There are several methods of coding the Fourier spectrum into the graytone hologram. We restrict our attention to two. The first codes the phase into a spatial carrier wave [6.13] just as with interferometric off-axis holograms [6.14]. The second uses an approximate coding known as detour phase.

Computer-Generated Off-Axis Holograms

Requiring the CGH transmittance to be real implies that the reconstructed image will have Hermetian symmetry

$$T_{mn} = T^*_{-m,-n}. \tag{6.30}$$

That the CGH transmittance is nonnegative implies that T_{00} will have a considerably larger modulus than any image points surrounding it. In terms familiar from interferometric holography: the reconstruction will exhibit a twin image and a dc spike.

The constraint, (6.30), indicates a restriction in assigning desired values to only one-half of the object field, $m > 0$ for instance. With this restriction the description reduces to that used with the ROACH. A difference is that the calculation of the cell transmittance C_{mn} will require an $M \times N$ element DFT while the object consists of only $[(M/2)-1] \times N$ points.

Taking u_{mn} to be an object such that

$$|u_{mn}| = 0 \quad \text{for} \quad m/4 < |m| < M/2, \tag{6.31}$$

the hologram cell transmittance will be [neglecting the image apodization of (6.26, 27)]

$$C_{jk} = K_0 + \operatorname{Re}\left\{\sum_m \sum_n u(m - M/4; n - N/4) \exp\{2\pi i[(mj/M) + (nk/N)]\}\right\}. \tag{6.32}$$

K_0 being an appropriate constant, $\operatorname{Re}\{\ \}$ the operation of taking the real part, and for readability

$$u(m;n) = u_{mn}. \tag{6.33}$$

Rewriting C_{jk} in terms of the object's Fourier spectrum $\tilde{u}_{jk}$, with

$$\tilde{u}_{jk} = \tilde{A}_{jk} \exp(\tilde{\phi}_{jk}), \tag{6.34}$$

$$C_{jk} = K_0 + 2\tilde{A}_{jk} \cos[(\pi j/4) + \tilde{\phi}_{jk}], \tag{6.35}$$

which emphasizes the fact that the off-axis hologram is indeed, in discretized form, a Fourier spectrum coded onto a hologram "carrier wave".

In actual computation one imbeds the desired object in one-half of the object matrix, performs a DFT, takes the *real part* of the result, and then adds a sufficiently large constant to each matrix element to make the minimum value of the resulting matrix zero.

One disadvantage of the off-axis hologram as so far presented is that the desired image is tightly squeezed between the dc spike and the nearest sampling-caused repeated image. Separation from these can be enlarged by

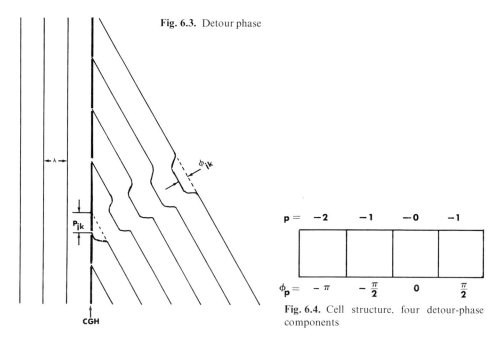

Fig. 6.3. Detour phase

Fig. 6.4. Cell structure, four detour-phase components

surrounding the object with a frame of zeroes, effectively increasing the carrier frequency. This will of course increase the SBWP of the hologram, size of the DFT, and expense.

If one wishes an object of x dimension Δx to have its center at $x = \Delta x$, then the object must be surrounded by a zero frame equal to its own size and the DFT must be 4 times that which would be required by the object alone, a factor of 2 for the zero frame and a factor of 2 for the offset. The cost may be relatively high, but there have been no substantial approximations made. The reconstruction will very closely resemble the object.

Detour-Phase Holograms

Detour phase [6.1] is a cost-saving approximation which allows off-axis reconstruction without increasing the hologram SBWP. If one considers the CGH as a distorted grating, then a wave front diffracted toward the first diffraction order will be advanced or delayed in the vicinity of a grating distortion as illustrated in Fig. 6.3. The amount of phase change will be proportional to the displacement of the grating aperture from its normal location; the farther the wave must "detour" to reach the first diffraction order, the greater the phase delay.

Figure 6.4 represents one resolution cell from a graytone detour-phase CGH [6.15]. The resolution cell is composed of four subcells. The pth subcell has an effective phase shift, at the first diffraction order, of ϕ_p.

The (j, k)th resolution cell transmittance is

$$C_{jk}(\mu, v) = \sum_{p=-2}^{1} a_{jk}(p)\,\mathrm{rect}\,[(4\mu/\delta\mu)p]\,\mathrm{rect}\,(v/\delta v) \qquad (6.36)$$

making the space-variant DFT coefficient

$$C_{jk}^{mn} = (1/4)\,\mathrm{sinc}\,(m/4M)\,\mathrm{sinc}\,(n/N) \sum_{p=-2}^{1} a_{jk}(p)\exp\,[(i\pi p/2)(m/M)]. \qquad (6.37)$$

The expression is simplified if we consider only a region in the image around $m = M$, i.e., at the center of the first diffraction order.

$$C_{jk}^{mn} = (1/4)\,\mathrm{sinc}\,(m/4M)\,\mathrm{sinc}\,(n/N) \sum_{p=-2}^{1} a_{jk}(p)\exp\,[(i\pi p/2)]. \qquad (6.38)$$

The space variance has been approximated away. A more rigorous look at this approximation will be taken in Sect. 6.5.2.

Each of the subapertures contributes according to the modulus of its transmittance, and contributes with a phase proportional to its position in the cell. Setting

$$C_{jk} = \sum_{p=-2}^{1} a_{jk}(p)\exp(i\pi p/2) \qquad (6.39)$$

and substituting (6.38) into the space-variant DFT, (6.19a), gives the reconstructed image,

$$T_{mn} = (1/4)\,\mathrm{sinc}\,(m/4M)\,\mathrm{sinc}\,(n/N)(MN)^{-1} \sum_j \sum_k C_{jk} \exp\{2\pi i[(jm/M)$$
$$+ (kn/N)]\}. \qquad (6.40)$$

This expression is valid near $m = M$. Its similarity to (6.24) suggests a similar method of calculating the hologram transmittance, i.e., set

$$C_{jk} = u_{jk} \qquad (6.41)$$

where u_{jk} is the DFT of the object. The real transmittance of the subcells, $a_{jk}(p)$, is then derived from the $\tilde{C}_{jk}$ by the usual projection method of finding real and imaginary parts of a complex number (see Fig. 6.5a).

A modification of this detour-phase hologram [6.16] takes advantage of the fact that any complex number can be made up of three complex components (see Fig. 6.5b). This leads to a cell structure of three apertures and space-variant DFT coefficients.

$$C_{jk}^{mn} = (1/3)\,\mathrm{sinc}\,(m/3M)\,\mathrm{sinc}\,(n/N) \sum_{p=-1}^{1} b_{jk}(p)\exp\,[2\pi i(pj/3M)]. \qquad (6.42)$$

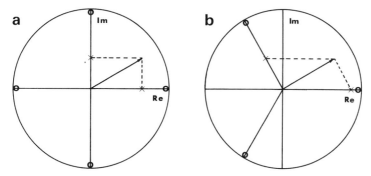

Fig. 6.5a, b. Phase components in complex plane. (**a**) Four components; (**b**) three components

Again restricting our attention to the region around $m=M$, an expression analogous to (6.39) may be written, i.e.,

$$C_{jk}= \sum_{p=-1}^{1} b_{jk}(p)\exp[2\pi i(p/3)].\tag{6.43}$$

Again making use of (6.41) one derives the $b_{jk}(p)$ from the $\tilde{C}_{jk}$ by the vector decomposition illustrated in Fig. 6.5b.

6.2.4 Binary Cell-Oriented Holograms

The binary hologram [6.1] has a transmittance which is, at any point on its surface, either clear or opaque. This simplifies photographic processing since the necessity to obtain precise gray scale values is eliminated. Photographic materials may be used in the saturation regions of their characteristic curves. Film grain noise is minimized [6.17, 18].

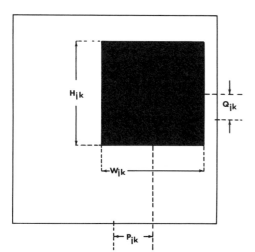

Fig. 6.6. Aperture in resolution cell of binary hologram

A resolution cell containing a single aperture, with width W_{jk} and height H_{jk} (Fig. 6.6), has transmittance

$$\tilde{C}_{jk}(\mu, v) = \text{rect}\left[(\mu - P_{jk}\delta\mu)/(W_{jk}\delta\mu)\right]\text{rect}\left[(v - Q_{jk}\delta v)/(H_{jk}\delta v)\right]. \qquad (6.44)$$

From (6.19) the associated space-variant DFT coefficient is as follows (the integration is carried out over the entire aperture, a necessary constriction because the aperture may "overflow" into an adjacent cell).

$$C_{jk}^{mn} = W_{jk}H_{jk}\,\text{sinc}(W_{jk}m/M)\,\text{sinc}(H_{jk}n/N)\exp\left[2\pi i P_{jk}(m/M)\right]$$
$$\cdot \exp\left[2\pi i Q_{jk}(n/N)\right]. \qquad (6.45)$$

Limiting ourselves to observing the reconstructed image only in the region about the center of the first diffraction order, $m \cong M$, $n \cong 0$, then

$$C_{jk} = (1/\pi)\sin(W_{jk})H_{jk}\exp(2\pi i P_{jk}). \qquad (6.46)$$

The detour phase is determined by the lateral shift P_{jk} of the aperture. The modulus can be controlled by changing either the height or width of the aperture. Choosing to vary the height H_{jk} and fix the width at

$$W_{jk} = 1/2, \qquad (6.47)$$

to maximize C_{jk}, and therefore the hologram diffraction efficiency, gives

$$C_{jk} = (1/\pi)H_{jk}\exp(2\pi i P_{jk}). \qquad (6.48)$$

The cell aperture height and lateral displacement would then be related to the approximately normalized object DFT modulus and phase [from (6.41)] by

$$H_{jk} = \tilde{A}_{jk}, \qquad (6.49a)$$
$$P_{jk} = \tilde{\phi}_{jk}/2\pi. \qquad (6.49b)$$

If the aperture width W_{jk} were varied and the aperture height H_{jk} made a constant then

$$C_{jk} = (1/\pi)\sin(\pi W_{jk})\exp(2\pi i P_{jk}). \qquad (6.50)$$

Equations (6.49a, b) would be changed to

$$W_{jk} = \arcsin(\tilde{A}_{jk}/\pi), \qquad (6.51a)$$
$$P_{jk} = \tilde{\phi}_{jk}/2\pi. \qquad (6.51b)$$

The Gap and Overlap Problem

Both of these binary holograms, (6.49, 51), admit overlapping apertures. The center of the aperture can occupy any lateral position in the cell. Hence, a portion of an aperture can occupy part of an adjacent cell. When two apertures overlap, the transmittance modulus is one, not two as the theory would require. This "gap and overlap" problem [6.19] contributes some noise to the reconstructed image. There exist holograms which correct this problem. These holograms also improve upon the approximations which stemmed from $m \cong M$, $n \cong 0$.

Reconstructions in Higher Diffraction Orders

The binary hologram just discussed reconstructed images in the first diffraction order. We chose to reconstruct the image at $m = M$. Reconstructions can be formed in higher diffraction orders $m = 2M$, $3M$, and so on [6.2] or even at fractional diffraction orders.

Restricting the reconstruction to the neighborhood of the x-axis, i.e., $n \cong 0$, we rewrite (6.45) as

$$C_{jk}^{m0} = W_{jk} \operatorname{sinc}[W_{jk}(m/M)] H_{jk} \exp[2\pi i P_{jk}(m/M)] . \tag{6.52}$$

On choosing the reconstructed image location to be $m = m_0$ and holding W_{jk} constant at

$$W_{jk} = M/2m_0 \tag{6.53}$$

to maximize diffraction efficiency, the space-variant DFT coefficient becomes

$$C_{jk}^{m0} = [(1/\pi)M/m_0 H_{jk}] \exp[2\pi i P_{jk}(m_0/M)] . \tag{6.54}$$

For images reconstructed about $m = m_0$, (6.49), the relation of cell parameters to object DFT coefficient, becomes

$$H_{jk} = \tilde{A}_{jk} , \tag{6.55a}$$

$$P_{jk} = (\tilde{\phi}_{jk}/2\pi)(M/m_0) . \tag{6.55b}$$

The distance of the reconstruction from the optical axis is inversely proportional to the aperture displacement.

For $m_0 \geq (3/2)$ the "gap and overlap" problem does not exist. A $(3/2)$-order binary hologram is then a "corrected" hologram [6.20]. The improvement is at the expense of restricted aperture movement. When the apertures are created by an incremental plotter, the restricted movements lead to coarser phase quantization in the hologram. The Fourier domain phase-quantization contribution to image noise is discussed in Sect. 6.5.2. The advantage of trading overlap for phase quantization depends then on the number of plotter increments per resolution cell.

Resolution Cell Internal Structure

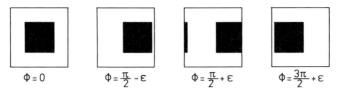

$\Phi = 0$ $\Phi = \frac{\pi}{2} - \epsilon$ $\Phi = \frac{\pi}{2} + \epsilon$ $\Phi = \frac{3\pi}{2} + \epsilon$

Φ = effective phase at first diffraction order

ϵ = a small number

Fig. 6.7. Circular overflow correction to gap and overlap problem

Circular Overflow

Another approach to correcting the "gap and overlap" problem for first-diffraction-order reconstructing CGHs is circular overflow (Fig. 6.7). Displacing any part of an aperture laterally by one resolution cell width results in a detour-phase change of 2π radians. This does not affect the effective complex-amplitude transmittance of the cell. If an aperture is partially outside its respective resolution cell, the protruding piece can be translated by one cell width back into the cell. We term this procedure circular-overflow correction.

The circular-overflow correction is equivalent to repeating the resolution cell transmittance $\tilde{C}_{jk}(\mu, v)$ of (6.44) with repetition period $\delta\mu, \delta v$, and afterwards multiplying by a *rect* function of one resolution cell size [6.21]. The resulting cell transmittance is

$$\tilde{C}'_{jk}(\mu, v) = \mathrm{rect}(\mu/\delta\mu)\,\mathrm{rect}(v/\delta v) \sum_{a=-\infty}^{\infty} \sum_{b=-\infty}^{\infty} \tilde{C}_{jk}(\mu - a\delta\mu, v - b\delta v). \quad (6.56)$$

Fourier transformation gives

$$C'^{mn}_{jk} = \sum_{a} \sum_{b} C^{aM,bN}_{jk} \,\mathrm{sinc}[a-(m/M)]\,\mathrm{sinc}[b-(n/N)] \quad (6.57a)$$

$$= W_{jk} H_{jk} \sum_{a} \mathrm{sinc}[a-(m/M)]\,\mathrm{sinc}(aW_{jk})\exp(2\pi i a P_{jk})$$

$$\cdot \sum_{b} \mathrm{sinc}[b-(n/N)]\,\mathrm{sinc}(bH_{jk})\exp(2\pi i b Q_{jk}). \quad (6.57b)$$

This expression will be useful later in analyzing imperfections in the reconstructed image. It can be simplified by carefully applying the Fourier expansion [6.22]

$$\exp[i\alpha\,\mathrm{p.v.}(\beta)] = \sum_{a=-\infty}^{\infty} \mathrm{sinc}(\alpha - a)\exp(ia\beta), \quad (6.58a)$$

$$\mathrm{p.v.}(x) = (x+\pi)_{\mathrm{MOD}\,2\pi} - \pi, \quad (6.58b)$$

$$-\pi \leq \mathrm{p.v.}(x) < \pi. \quad (6.58c)$$

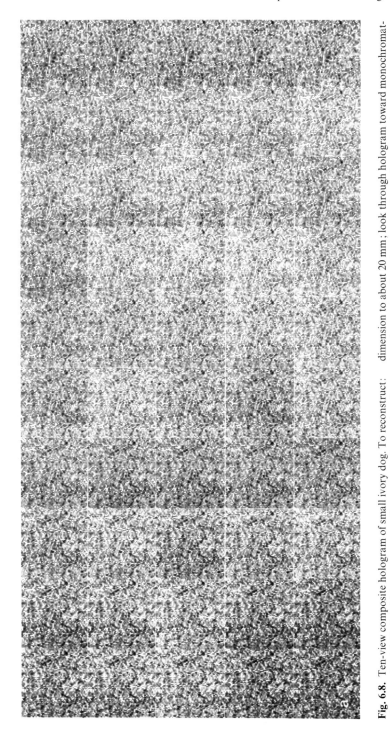

Fig. 6.8. Ten-view composite hologram of small ivory dog. To reconstruct: photograph with Kodak high-contrast copy film or equivalent; reduce long dimension to about 20 mm; look through hologram toward monochromatic point source, observing appropriate safety precautions

The principal value (p.v.) operator is necessary to give the resulting function a period 2π in x, as is required by the Fourier series representation. Writing

$$f[P, W, (m/M)] = \sum_{a=-\infty}^{\infty} \bar{A}_a \bar{B}_a \exp(2\pi iaP), \tag{6.59a}$$

$$\bar{A}_a = \text{sinc}[(m/M) - a], \tag{6.59b}$$

$$\bar{B}_a = W \text{sinc}(aW). \tag{6.59c}$$

The $\bar{A}_a$ are Fourier series coefficients of (6.57), while the $\bar{B}_a$ are coefficients of the square wave of relative width W. "f" is the convolution of these two functions.

$$f[P, W, (m/M)] = \int_{P-(W/2)}^{P+(W/2)} \exp\{i(m/M)[\text{p.v.}(P')]\} dP'. \tag{6.60}$$

This equation expresses the fact that each element in the hologram resolution cell contributes a complex amplitude whose modulus is the area and whose phase is the detour phase given by the element's location and the observation point in the image.

The space-variant DFT coefficient for circular-overflow binary holograms is

$$C'^{mn}_{jk} = f[P_{jk}, W_{jk}, (m/M)] \, f[Q_{jk}, H_{jk}, (n/N)]. \tag{6.61}$$

As a particular example consider a CGH where the aperture is vertically centered ($Q_{jk} = 0$), and has constant width ($W_{jk} = 0.5$). Modulus is varied by changing the height, H_{jk}, and the phase is controlled by the lateral displacement P_{jk}. For $(-1/4) \leq P_{jk} \leq 1/4$ there is no overflow. For $P_{jk} > 1/2$,

$$C'^{mn}_{jk} = H_{jk} \text{sinc}[(n/N)H_{jk}] \{\text{sinc}(m/M) - (1/2)$$
$$\cdot \exp[2\pi i(m/M)(P_{jk} - (1/2)] \text{sinc}(m/2M)\}, \tag{6.62}$$

similarly for $P_{jk} < -1/2$.

Near the first diffraction order $m \cong M$, $n \cong 0$, (6.62) reduces to the expected

$$C'^{mn}_{jk} \cong (1/\pi)H_{jk} \exp(2\pi i \, P_{jk}). \tag{6.63}$$

Bleached Binary Holograms

We have discussed the binary hologram as a device with transmittance zero or one. It is not necessary that the transmittance have these values, only that it take on distinguishable values. If one is restricted to real positive values then the two transmittances might be a_1 and a_2. The transmittance of a resolution cell would become

$$\tilde{C}''_{jk}(\mu, v) = a_2 \tilde{C}_{jk}(\mu, v) + a_1 [1 - \tilde{C}_{jk}(\mu, v)] \tag{6.64a}$$

$$= (a_2 - a_1)\tilde{C}_{jk}(\mu, v) + a_1, \tag{6.64b}$$

where $\tilde{C}_{jk}$ takes the values zero and one, as in (6.44). Thanks to the Fourier transform's linearity, a_1 will contribute only to the "dc spike" in the reconstruction while the space-variant DFT coefficients will be multiplied by $(a_2 - a_1)$. The intensity of the reconstructed image will be proportional to $|a_2 - a_1|^2$. For real transmittances $a_2 = 1$, $a_1 = 0$ (or vice versa) maximizes the desired image brightness. The transmittance values should be assigned so the hologram area with the higher transmittance are minimized; the dc spike will thus be minimized.

The transmittances a_1 and a_2 need not be restricted to real values. If the photographic processing includes bleaching [19, 23, 24] the transmittance may take the form

$$a_1 = \exp(i\phi_1) = \exp(i\phi_0)\exp(i\theta_0/2), \tag{6.65a}$$

$$a_2 = \exp(i\phi_2) = \exp(i\phi_0)\exp(-i\theta_0/2). \tag{6.65b}$$

Ignoring a constant phase factor, (6.64) becomes

$$\tilde{C}''_{jk}(\mu, v) = 2\sin(\theta_0/2)\tilde{C}_{jk}(\mu, v) - i\exp(i\theta_0/2). \tag{6.66}$$

The strength of the reconstructed image is seen to be maximized when the phase excursion in the bleached material is just $\theta_0 = \pi$. The image intensity is then four times that obtainable with positive transmittances.

6.2.5 Controlling the Modulus by Detour-Phase Effects

If two apertures are placed in the resolution cell, say two slits of width $W\delta\mu$ and height δv [6.1, 25, 25a], the CGH cell transmittance becomes

$$\tilde{C}_{jk}(\mu, v) = \{\text{rect}[(\mu - P_{jk}^{(1)}\delta\mu)/W\delta\mu] + \text{rect}[(\mu - P_{jk}^{(2)}\delta\mu)/W\delta\mu]\} \text{rect}(v/\delta v), \tag{6.67}$$

giving the space-variant DFT coefficient

$$C_{jk}^{mn} = W\text{sinc}[W(m/M)]\,\text{sinc}(n/N)\,\{\exp[2\pi i\,P_{jk}^{(1)}(m/M)]$$
$$+ \exp[2\pi i P_{jk}^{(2)}(m/M)]\} \tag{6.68}$$

or, upon setting

$$P_{jk} = [P_{jk}^{(1)} + P_{jk}^{(2)}]/2, \tag{6.69a}$$

$$\Delta P_{jk} = [P_{jk}^{(1)} - P_{jk}^{(2)}]/2, \tag{6.69b}$$

the space-variant DFT coefficient becomes

$$C_{jk}^{mn} = W\text{sinc}[W(m/M)]\,\text{sinc}(n/N)\cos[\pi\Delta P_{jk}(m/M)]\exp[2\pi i P_{jk}(m/M)]. \tag{6.70}$$

Observing the reconstructed image only near the first diffraction order $m \cong M$, $n \cong 0$ allows the approximation

$$C_{jk}^{mn} \cong C_{jk} = (1/\pi)\sin(\pi W)\cos(\pi\Delta P_{jk})\exp(2\pi i P_{jk}). \tag{6.71}$$

The effective modulus is a function of the slit separation. This variation is effected because the two slits exhibit different detour phases. The phase is the average detour phase of the two (equal width) slits.

A somewhat different hologram [6.25] also controls modulus by aperture separation, but relies on detour-phase effects in two directions. The two apertures might be small rectangles of constant width W and height H.

$$\tilde{C}_{jk}(\mu, v) = \text{rect}[(\mu - P_{jk}\delta\mu)/W\delta\mu]$$
$$\cdot \{\text{rect}[(v - Q_{jk}\delta v)/H\delta v] + \text{rect}[(v + Q_{jk}\delta v)/H\delta v]\}, \tag{6.72}$$

giving

$$C_{jk}^{mn} = WH\,\text{sinc}[W(m/M)]\,\text{sinc}[H(n/N)]\exp[2\pi i P_{jk}(m/M)]$$
$$\cdot \{\exp[2\pi i Q_{jk}(n/N)] + \exp[2\pi i Q_{jk}(n/N)]\}. \tag{6.73}$$

The image is observed in the vicinity of the (1,1) diffraction order $m \cong M$, $n \cong N$ where

$$C_{jk}^{mn} \cong C_{jk} = (2/\pi^2)\sin(\pi W)\sin(\pi H)\exp[2\pi i P_{jk}(m/M)]\cos(2\pi Q_{jk}). \tag{6.74}$$

Another approach which attempts to minimize the phase quantization breaks each resolution cell into several subcells [6.26]. Each subcell can then assume a transmittance of zero or one. For M_s by N_s subcells per resolution cell the subcell dimensions are

$$\delta\mu_s = \delta\mu/M_s, \tag{6.75a}$$

$$\delta v_s = \delta v/N_s. \tag{6.75b}$$

The resolution cell transmittance is

$$\tilde{C}_{jk}(\mu, v) = \sum_{r=-M_s/2}^{(M_s/2)-1} \sum_{s=-N_s/2}^{(N_s/2)-1} a_{jk}^{rs} \operatorname{rect}[(\mu - r\delta\mu_s)/\delta\mu_s]$$
$$\cdot \operatorname{rect}[(v - s\delta v_s)/\delta v_s], \tag{6.76}$$

where a_{jk}^{rs} can assume the values zero and one. The space-variant DFT coefficient is

$$C_{jk}^{mn} = (1/M_s N_s) \operatorname{sinc}[m/(M_s M)] \operatorname{sinc}[n/(N_s N)]$$
$$\cdot \sum_r \sum_s a_{jk}^{rs} \exp\{2\pi i[(rm/M_s M) + (sn/N_s N)]\}. \tag{6.77}$$

Observing near the first (1,0) diffraction order this expression becomes approximately

$$C_{jk} = [1/(\pi N_s)] \sin(\pi/M_s) \sum_r \sum_s a_{jk}^{rs} \exp[2\pi i(r/M_s)]. \tag{6.78}$$

The double sum can take on many values according to the subcell configuration, i.e., which of the subcells are transparent and which are opaque. There are $2^{M_s N_s}$ such subcell configurations, though not all of the resulting complex amplitudes are necessarily distinct. In plotting such a hologram one generally stores a table relating a selection of subcell configurations and cell transmittances. One calculates the C_{jk} by discrete Fourier-transforming the object; the corresponding a_{jk}^{rs} are determined from the table.

6.3 Point-Oriented Holograms

For this type of CGH the complex amplitude to be coded into the hologram is assumed known at each point. The mapping of complex amplitude to CGH transmittance is done point by point in contrast to the one-sample-per-cell mapping with cell-oriented CGHs.

In this section we first analyze three point-oriented holograms. Next, a formalism connecting point-oriented and cell-oriented holograms is described. This formalism is then applied to several CGHs.

6.3.1 The Square Wave

The square wave

$$\operatorname{Sq}(\xi; \alpha) = \sum_{n=-\infty}^{\infty} \operatorname{rect}[(\xi - n)/\alpha] = \sum_{m=-\infty}^{\infty} \alpha \operatorname{sinc}(m\alpha) \exp(2\pi i m\xi) \tag{6.79}$$

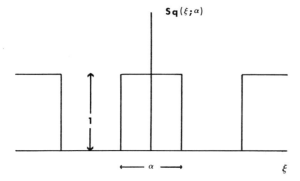

Fig. 6.9. Square wave

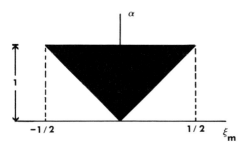

Fig. 6.10. Two-dimensional representation of square wave using modular arithmetic. Binarization diagram for single modulation square wave hologram

represents a binary grating whose stripe width is α times the grating period. By suitably distorting this ruling one generates a hologram [6.27–29].

Figure 6.9 shows the square wave as a function of the single variable ξ, with the parameter α being the relative width of the transparent stripes. Figure 6.10 is also a representation of the square wave, but as a function of the two variables ξ_M and α. Modular arithmetic is used to suppress the square wave's periodicity

$$\xi_M = (\xi + 0.5)_{\text{MOD } 1} - 0.5, \tag{6.80a}$$

$$-0.5 \leq \xi_M < 0.5. \tag{6.80b}$$

An appropriate integer is added to (or subtracted from) ξ to yield ξ_M in the given range. This representation is useful for hologram-generating routines [6.29].

6.3.2 Modulated Square Wave Holograms

Single Modulated Square Wave

The (continuous) Fourier spectrum to be coded into the square wave grating is noted by

$$\tilde{u}(\mu, v) = \tilde{A}(\mu, v) \exp[i\tilde{\phi}(\mu, v)]. \tag{6.81}$$

The coding is accomplished by setting

$$\xi = x_0 \mu + (\tilde{\phi}/2\pi),$$ (6.82a)

$$\alpha = (1/\pi) \arcsin(\tilde{A}).$$ (6.82b)

Equation (6.79) becomes

$$Sq(\xi; \alpha) = (1/\pi) \sum_{m=-\infty}^{\infty} (1/n) \sin[m \arcsin(\tilde{A})] \exp(im\tilde{\phi}) \exp(2\pi i m x_0 \mu).$$ (6.83)

The $m=1$ term of the sum is

$$(1/\pi) \tilde{A} \exp(i\tilde{\phi}) \exp(2\pi i x_0 \mu).$$ (6.84)

This is the desired Fourier spectrum, but on a carrier wave. The carrier causes a displacement of the reconstructed image away from the optical axis a distance x_0.

The total reconstruction from the distorted square wave grating of (6.83) is a sum of images

$$u_{TOT}(x, y) = (1/\pi) \sum_{m=-\infty}^{\infty} (1/m) u_m(x - m x_0, y),$$ (6.85)

where each component image of the sum is given by

$$u_m(x, y) = \iint \sin\{m \arcsin[\tilde{A}(\mu, v)]\}$$
$$\cdot \exp[im\tilde{\phi}(\mu, v)] \exp[-2\pi i(\mu x + vy)] d\mu dv.$$ (6.86)

Since the component images are reconstructed at different positions a careful choice of x_0 will, essentially, separate the desired reconstruction $u_1(x, y)$ from the other images [6.30].

The position $x = m x_0$ is the location of the mth diffraction order of the undistorted grating. For this example the desired image was reconstructed in the first diffraction order. Proper choices of ξ and α will allow reconstruction in any nonzero order.

$$\xi = x_0 \mu + (\tilde{\phi}/2m\pi),$$ (6.87a)

$$\alpha = (1/\pi) \arcsin(\tilde{A}/m)$$ (6.87b)

put the desired image in the mth diffraction order.

To plot this hologram one first obtains the proper Fourier spectrum $\tilde{u}(\mu, v)$. This function may be available in closed form, or may be calculated by interpolation of sampled data as described in Sect. 6.3.3. The variables ξ_M and α are then calculated from (6.82) and (6.80). A test is then made to see if the (ξ_M, α) pair falls within the dark triangle of Fig. 6.10. If yes, the point (μ, v) is plotted. In practice, edges of the plotted stripes are so hunted and entire stripes then drawn.

Phase-Only Square Wave Hologram

If the Fourier spectrum to be encoded has constant modulus then the relative width, α, becomes a constant [6.29]

$$\alpha = \alpha_0 . \tag{6.88}$$

The diagram of Fig. 6.11 becomes appropriate. If α_0 is very small the plot consists only of narrow lines, single pen strokes. The hologram then becomes very easily and rapidly plottable. Disadvantages of the narrow stripes are low diffraction efficiency and sensitivity to plotter inconsistencies.

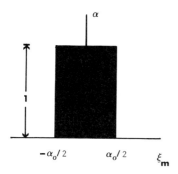

Fig. 6.11. Binarization diagram for phase-only square wave hologram

The phase-only hologram is appropriate if the Fourier spectrum has uniform modulus, or if the modulus information has been destroyed. In Sect. 6.5 we shall discuss the effects of destroying modulus information.

The component images of (6.86) become, for this phase-only hologram, multiple autoconvolutions of the desired image. This is because the various Fourier spectra are powers (and powers of conjugates) of the desired image Fourier spectrum.

Narrow-Line Hologram with Modulus Control

There is a simple method of combining the simplicity of single-stroke plotting with modulus control. The method is analogous to the cell-oriented hologram which controlled modulus by aperture separation [see (6.67)].

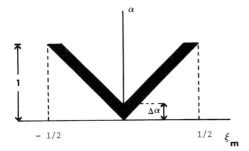

Figure 6.12 shows a ξ_M versus α diagram for this narrow-line modulus-controlled hologram. As before, a point would be plotted only if it fell in the shaded area of the diagram. The diagram represents a function (for $\alpha \leqq 1$)

$$G(\xi, \alpha; \Delta\alpha) = \mathrm{Sq}(\xi; \alpha) - \mathrm{Sq}(\xi; \alpha - \Delta\alpha) \tag{6.89a}$$

$$= \sum_{m=-\infty}^{\infty} [\alpha \operatorname{sinc}(m\alpha) - (\alpha - \Delta\alpha)\operatorname{sinc}(\alpha - \Delta\alpha)] \exp(2\pi i m\xi). \tag{6.89b}$$

The bracketed term can be manipulated into the form

$$m\pi[\ ] = \sin(\pi m\alpha) - \sin(\pi m\alpha)\cos(\pi m\Delta\alpha) + \sin(\pi m\Delta\alpha)\cos(\pi m\alpha) \tag{6.90}$$

which for $\Delta\alpha$ small reduces (6.89) to

$$G(\xi, \alpha; \Delta\alpha) = (1/\pi) \sum_{m=-\infty}^{\infty} (1/m)\sin(m\pi\Delta\alpha)\cos(m\pi\alpha)\exp(2\pi i m\xi). \tag{6.91}$$

A reconstructed image can be obtained in the first diffraction order by setting

$$\xi = x_0 \mu + (\tilde{\phi}/2\pi), \tag{6.92a}$$

$$\alpha = (1/\pi)\arccos(\tilde{A}). \tag{6.92b}$$

Crossed Modulated Square Waves

Consider two crossed square wave gratings [6.31]

$$\mathrm{Sq}(\xi_1; \alpha_1)\,\mathrm{Sq}(\xi_2; \alpha_2) = \sum_m \sum_n \alpha_1\alpha_2 \operatorname{sinc}(m\alpha_1)\operatorname{sinc}(n\alpha_2)$$

$$\cdot \exp[2\pi i(m\xi_1 + n\xi_2)], \tag{6.93}$$

where

$$\xi_1 = x_0\mu + \tilde{\phi} \qquad \alpha_1 = 1/2, \tag{6.94a}$$

$$\xi_2 = y_0\nu \qquad \alpha_2 = (1/\pi)\arcsin(\tilde{A}). \tag{6.94b}$$

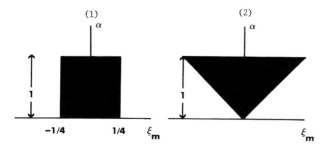

Fig. 6.13. Binarization diagram for crossed-square wave hologram

This hologram corresponds to the (ξ_M, α) diagram of Fig. 6.13. One grating carries modulus information, the other, phase. In the (1.0) diffraction order, $m=1$, $n=0$, the desired image is again reconstructed.

Close analogies exist between the point-oriented holograms discussed and corresponding cell-oriented holograms. The single modulated square wave CGH controls modulus by stripe width much as the first binary cell-oriented hologram discussed [(6.46)]. The crossed modulated square wave CGH controls modulus by the heights of broken stripe segments as did the cell-oriented hologram of (6.48). The narrow-line CGH which controlled the modulus by varying the separation of two narrow lines is quite similar to the cell-oriented hologram described by (6.67).

In the next subsection we look at a formalism for processing discrete Fourier spectral data into continuous point-oriented holograms. The above-mentioned analogies will be described by this formalism.

6.3.3 From Discrete Information to Point-Oriented Holograms

As noted, the point-oriented hologram requires a continuous Fourier spectrum. This requirement presents no difficulty if the function is known in closed form, as for some holograms used in interferometry [6.29, 32, 33]. Most often, however, the Fourier spectrum is obtained by the discrete Fourier transform. It is then a sampled version of the desired spectrum.

One method of converting sampled information to continuous is by interpolation of the complex amplitude. If the sampled Fourier spectrum is

$$\tilde{u}_s(\mu, v) = \sum_j \sum_k \tilde{u}_{jk}\delta(\mu - j\delta\mu)\,\delta(v - k\delta v),\tag{6.95}$$

then interpolation by a function $\tilde{S}(\mu, v)$ takes the form of the convolution

$$(\tilde{u}_s * \tilde{S})(\mu, v) = \sum_j \sum_k \tilde{u}_{jk}\tilde{S}(\mu - j\delta\mu, v - k\delta v).\tag{6.96}$$

The image reconstructed from this interpolated Fourier spectrum is

$$u(x, y) = u_s(x, y)\, S(x, y); \tag{6.97}$$

$u_s(x, y)$ and $S(x, y)$ are inverse Fourier transforms of $\tilde{u}(\mu, v)$ and $\tilde{S}(\mu, v)$.
One easily visualized interpolation function choice is

$$\tilde{S}(\mu, v) = \operatorname{sinc}(\mu/\delta\mu)\operatorname{sinc}(v/\delta v), \tag{6.98a}$$

$$S(x, y) = \delta\mu\,\delta v\,\operatorname{rect}(x\delta\mu)\operatorname{rect}(y\delta v). \tag{6.98b}$$

For this interpolation function only one period of $u_s(x, y)$ survives. Because the period survives unaltered this "sinc interpolation" may be considered an ideal interpolation [6.30].

A binary hologram could now be formed from the continuous Fourier spectrum $\tilde{u}(\mu, v)$ by the methods described in the previous subsection. The "sinc" function is however relatively costly to implement: every point in one period of the sampled Fourier spectrum must be used in calculating each point of the post-interpolation spectrum. By choosing a narrower function $\tilde{S}(\mu, v)$ one involves fewer sample points in the interpolation, thereby decreasing the computational costs. In fact, a family of holograms may be developed which offer diverse cost-fidelity trades.

Following this argument, the most economical hologram would issue from an interpolation function which involved only one sample point. Discussion of image fidelity will be left till Sect. 6.5. The following one-sample-interpolation example not only illustrates the described procedure, it also demonstrates the relationship between cell-oriented and point-oriented CGHs. Picking the interpolation function

$$\tilde{S}(\mu, v) = \operatorname{rect}(\mu/\delta\mu)\operatorname{rect}(v/\delta v) \tag{6.99}$$

together with various forms of point-oriented holograms results in previously detailed cell-oriented CGHs. This choice of $\tilde{S}(\mu, v)$ together with the sampled spectrum of (6.95) gives

$$\tilde{u}(\mu, v) = \sum_j \sum_k \tilde{u}_{jk}\operatorname{rect}\left[(\mu - j\delta\mu)/\delta\mu\right]\operatorname{rect}\left[(v - k\delta v)/\delta v\right], \tag{6.100}$$

where it is useful to express

$$\tilde{u}_{jk} = \tilde{A}_{jk}\exp(i\tilde{\phi}_{jk}), \tag{6.101a}$$

$$\tilde{u}(\mu, v) = \tilde{A}(\mu, v)\exp[i\tilde{\phi}(\mu, v)]. \tag{6.101b}$$

Combining the interpolated Fourier spectrum of (6.100, 101) with the single modulated square wave of (6.82, 83) gives

$$\mathrm{Sq}(\xi;\alpha) = \sum_j \sum_k \mathrm{Sq}[(\mu/\delta\mu) + P_{jk};(1/\pi)\arcsin(\tilde{A}_{jk})]\,\mathrm{rect}[(\mu - j\delta\mu)/\delta\mu]$$
$$\cdot \mathrm{rect}[(v - k\delta v)/\delta v],\tag{6.102a}$$

$$P_{jk} = \tilde{\phi}_{jk}/2\pi,\tag{6.102b}$$

$$W_{jk} = (1/\pi)\arcsin(\tilde{A}_{jk}),\tag{6.102c}$$

$$\delta\mu = 1/x_0.\tag{6.102d}$$

Expanding the square wave under the double sum into its Fourier series representation gives

$$\mathrm{Sq}(\xi;\alpha) = \sum_j \sum_k \sum_a W_{jk}\,\mathrm{sinc}(aW_{jk})\exp(2\pi i a P_{jk})\,\mathrm{rect}[(\mu - j\delta\mu)/\delta\mu]$$
$$\cdot \mathrm{rect}[(v - k\delta v)/\delta v]\exp(2\pi i a\mu/\delta\mu).\tag{6.103}$$

Fourier transformation yields a reconstruction which, because of W_{jk} and P_{jk}'s periodicity, is nonzero only at the points $x = m/(M\delta\mu)$, $y = n/(N\delta v)$. This reconstruction is

$$T_{mn} = \sum_j \sum_k \sum_a W_{jk}\,\mathrm{sinc}(aW_{jk})\exp(2\pi i a P_{jk})\,\mathrm{sinc}[(m/M) - a]\,\mathrm{sinc}(n/N)$$
$$\cdot \exp\{2\pi i[(jm/M) + (kn/N)]\},\tag{6.104}$$

rewritten as

$$T_{mn} = \sum_j \sum_k C_{jk}^{mn}\exp\{2\pi i[(jm/M) + (kn/N)]\},\tag{6.105a}$$

$$C_{jk}^{mn} = \sum_a W_{jk}\,\mathrm{sinc}(aW_{jk})\,\mathrm{sinc}[(m/M - a]\,\mathrm{sinc}(n/N),\tag{6.105b}$$

is recognized as (6.57) with $H_{jk} = 1$ and $Q_{jk} = 0$. Modulus is controlled by aperture width, phase by lateral displacement.

Other cell-oriented binary CGHs can be similarly described. Picking the crossed-modulated-square-wave point-oriented CGH will give (6.57) but with $W_{jk} = 1/2$ and $Q_{jk} = 0$, modulus being controlled here by height and phase by lateral displacement. If the narrow-line hologram with modulus control encoding scheme had been chosen, the resulting cell-oriented hologram would have been the detour-phase controlled modulus CGH of (6.71).

A recently introduced hologram [6.4, 30, 30a, 34] uses a modified form of interpolation. The hologram is similar in structure to the three subcell detour-phase CGH of (6.42) with binary apertures of varying size replacing the earlier continuously variable graytone transmittance. Though the structure is similar, calculation is quite different. Conceptually, the sampled Fourier spectrum is "sinc" interpolated, not to a continuum of points but only to a sampling grid with one-third the original sample spacing in the "x" direction. The function is then placed on a carrier whose period equals the original sampling distance. The real part is then taken and a bias is added, yielding the real, nonnegative transmittance to be implemented at each of the new sampling sites. The bias need not be a constant, though its Fourier transform must not intrude into the desired reconstruction image. An appropriate choice of a variable bias can lead to enhanced (simulated) fringe contrast [6.35, 36] and thereby an increased diffraction efficiency [6.37].

One calculational technique used in this CGH is a "fast" interpolation. Three DFTs are performed on the object u_{mn}. We distinguish between the three resulting matrices using the superscript "l".

$$\tilde{u}^{l}_{jk} = \sum_{m}\sum_{n} u_{mn}\exp[2\pi i lm/(3M)]\exp[2\pi i(jm/M)+(kn/N)], \qquad (6.106a)$$

$$l = -1, 0, +1. \qquad (6.106b)$$

The linear phase factor

$$\exp[2\pi i lm/(3M)] \qquad (6.107)$$

shifts the points at which the Fourier spectrum is sampled by ($+$) one-third of the original distance, thereby sampling "between" the original points. The time taken by this fast interpolation is three times that for a single DFT since one processes three times as many points. The alternative, surrounding the object matrix by a frame of zeroes and then transforming the three-times wider matrix, does take somewhat more computing time. The time taken by the DFT is proportional to [6.6]

$$t_c = N_p \log_2 N_p, \qquad (6.108a)$$

$$N_p = \text{number of points in transform}. \qquad (6.108b)$$

A three-times larger transform would take

$$(3N_p\log_2 3N_p)/(N_p\log_2 N_p) = 3\{1+[(\log_2 3)/(\log_2 N_p)]\} \qquad (6.109)$$

times that for the single DFT. Typically $N_p = 4096$, giving the value 3.4 for (6.109).

Up to this point we have used interpolation of the complex amplitude, which is equivalent to interpolation of the real and imaginary parts. Another possibility is the interpolation of modulus and phase. One CGH combines a cubic polynomial fit of the phase with a rect function interpolation of the modulus. The resulting function is then encoded into a crossed-square-wave point-oriented CGH [6.19]. The combination results in simple location of the binary apertures.

Four adjacent phase samples $\tilde{\phi}_{jk}$ are picked. The subscript k remains constant for any group of four. A cubic polynomial in "μ" is then fit to these samples. Once the fit is made, one searches for edges of the phase-modulated square wave, [see (6.93, 94)]. If $\Phi(\mu, v)$ is the interpolated phase function then one wishes to find

$$\xi_M = 0.5 \tag{6.110a}$$

and

$$\xi_M = -0.5, \tag{6.110b}$$

where

$$\xi = x_0\mu + \Phi/2\pi. \tag{6.110c}$$

These edges, or zero crossings of the square wave can be found from

$$\Phi = a\mu^3 + b\mu^2 + c\mu + d \tag{6.111a}$$

$$\tilde{\phi}_{(j-l),k} = a(j-l)^3 + b(j-l)^2 + c(j-l) + d, \tag{6.111b}$$

$$-2 \leqq l \leqq 1. \tag{6.111c}$$

Equation (6.111b) is invertible to give the polynomial coefficients as a function of the phase sample values. The modular arithmetic causes no difficulties as long as "μ" is measured from the center of the resolution cell being considered. The relations

$$-0.5 \leqq x_0\mu < 0.5, \tag{6.112a}$$

$$-0.5 \leqq \Phi/2\pi < 0.5 \tag{6.112b}$$

will then be simplified.

For an analysis of the reconstructed image errors one may refer to [6.30, 30b, 30c, 30d].

6.4 Diffusers for Computer Holograms

6.4.1 Diffraction Efficiency, Dynamic Range, and Clipping

For display purposes the image intensity is usually of interest; the phase is not observed. Yet, the object phase influences the structure of the computer hologram. The most strongly felt of these influences is in the Fourier power spectrum peak-to-average-value ratio "R_I". This ratio determines the relation between CGH diffraction efficiency and what information will be lost in plotting.

As an example consider the cell-oriented circular-overflow-corrected binary hologram of Fig. 6.7. Let us call the two possible apertures the principal aperture and the overflow aperture. The diffracted modulus is controlled by the height of the aperture(s) and the phase by the position of the left edge of the principal aperture. When an incremented plotter is used to draw this hologram only a finite combination of aperture heights and positions can be drawn. For a square cell containing an even number of incremental steps, N_i in each direction, the number of effective modulus values N_M and phase values N_P is

$$N_P = N_i, \tag{6.113a}$$

$$N_M = (N_i/2) + 1, \tag{6.113b}$$

where zero is included in the counted attainable modulus values. Because of symmetrical plotting the aperture height can change only by an even number of increments. This number, N_i, depends on the number of resolution cells across the CGH, M, the size of the plot, L_P, and the incremental step size, L_i.

$$N_i = L_P/ML_i. \tag{6.114}$$

Clearly N_i (the number of incremental steps across the cell) can be increased by increasing L_P (the size of the plot). The number of modulus- and phase-quantization levels is thus increased, and quantization errors are decreased. To reduce plotting costs (and the labor of taping standard-sized plots together) L_P is usually chosen to have the minimum value consistent with acceptable reconstruction quality. If the plot is too small, reconstruction quality suffers. An empirical result is that usually

$$N_i = 16 \tag{6.115}$$

(see Sect. 6.5.2, Fourier domain phase quantization). This value makes the number of attainable phase and modulus values

$$N_P = 16, \tag{6.116a}$$

$$N_M = 9. \tag{6.116b}$$

The dynamic range for the modulus in terms of the step size L_i is

$$D_M = L_i N_M / L_i \Delta N_M = 9/2 = 4.5 \,. \tag{6.117}$$

This dynamic range is important since it determines how a Fourier spectrum will actually "fit" into the CGH. For example, consider the square root of the Fourier power spectrum peak-to-average ratio to be significantly greater than the dynamic range, i.e.,

$$D_M < \sqrt{R_I} \,. \tag{6.118}$$

If the Fourier spectrum modulus is simply scaled so that the maximum modulus is one, then most of the hologram will be quantized to zero. Even if the results are not so severe, the diffraction efficiency will be very low. Diffraction efficiency depends inversely on R_I through Parseval's theorem.

There are two alternatives for increasing the diffraction efficiency. First, to perform top-clipping: multiply the Fourier spectrum by a positive constant so that the maximum modulus is greater than one, then set all modulus values greater than one equal to one. Second, to provide the desired image with a phase function, or diffuser, which will bring $\sqrt{R_I}$ and D_M closer together.

The first alternative, top-clipping, decreases $\sqrt{R_I}$ but affects the image. Edge enlargement is the usual result. A desired image with slowly varying modulus and constant phase will have a Fourier spectrum which is sharply peaked at $\mu = 0$, $v = 0$. Top-clipping results in diminishing the low spatial frequencies relative to the high.

In the following subsections we shall discuss the application of diffuser functions. For ideal, untruncated CGHs the diffuser functions have no effect on the image intensity. In the following subsection we consider truncation briefly.

6.4.2 Truncation and Speckle

Up to this point we have considered computer holograms as infinite periodic objects, the periodicity giving rise to images which consist of points. CGHs of only a few periods (say four in each direction) follow the description given so far very well. Images obtained from computer-generated holograms which contain only one period do conform to our discrete Fourier analysis, but only at the sample points. Between the sample points the image intensity exhibits speckle: spatial intensity fluctuations giving an impression of graininess. The speckle arises from weighted sums of the image sample value complex amplitude. The weights are different at each point in the image. Ideally,

$$u(x, y) = \sum_m \sum_n u_{mn} \operatorname{sinc}(\Delta \mu x - m) \operatorname{sinc}(\Delta v y - n) \,, \tag{6.119}$$

where the u_{mn} are the sample value complex amplitudes

$$u_{mn} = u(m/\Delta\mu, n/\Delta v). \tag{6.120}$$

For an image phase of zero this sum consists of positive numbers and $u(x, y)$ is a smooth function. However, when phases are assigned to the u_{mn}, the sum is a sum of complex numbers and fluctuations occur between the sample points. Even though the u_{mn} may have nonzero modulus, the intermediate points can have zeroes. The pattern formed by the fluctuations is speckle. The speckle structure is also influenced by an aliasing error [6.30e]. This graininess can be quite disturbing in a displayed image. The nature of the pattern is dependent on the diffuser used and so consideration must be given to speckle in the design of diffusers for computer holography.

Decoupling Diffuser Design and Speckle

The ideal diffuser fulfills three important functions: equalizing the Fourier spectrum modulus (power spectrum leveling), distributing object information over the CGH, and minimizing attendant speckle. The last function generally conflicts with the first two. Whenever possible it is well to remove the minimum speckle restriction, optimize the diffuser for spectrum leveling, and counteract speckle by some other means.

The simplest way to avoid speckle is to reconstruct only the sample points u_{mn} in (6.119). This can be accomplished by periodically repeating the hologram. The image point size for a finite number of hologram repetition periods, $M_{RP} \times N_{RP}$ periods in the "x" and "y" directions, respectively, arises from the point-spread function

$$\text{sinc}(M_{RP}\Delta\mu x)\,\text{sinc}(N_{RP}\Delta vy) \tag{6.121}$$

which generalizes (6.119) to the following:

$$u(x, y) = \sum_m \sum_n u_{mn} \text{sinc}(M_{RP}\Delta\mu x - m)\,\text{sinc}(N_{RP}\Delta vy - n). \tag{6.122}$$

A binary hologram could be repeated four times in each direction making each "point" of the image approximately one-quarter resolution cell wide. The effect is to separate the image points and eliminate the interaction between them. The more repetition periods of the hologram, the better the separation.

Although the speckle noise is eliminated by periodic continuation of the CGH, the resulting punctated image is sometimes not as desirable as a smoothed one. An easy way to obtain a smooth image from the periodic CGH is incoherent interpolation. If an incoherent source is used in the reconstruction setup of Fig. 6.1, an incoherent interpolation of the image is performed [6.38].

If the source image has the proper scale and intensity profile, the image will appear smooth. An ideal source image intensity is

$$I_s(x, y) = \text{sinc}^2(\Delta \mu x) \, \text{sinc}^2(\Delta v y). \tag{6.123}$$

Another method of obtaining an incoherent interpolation [6.39] makes use of an observation concerning (6.119). If the sample values u_{mn} are fairly uniform, then only the nearest neighboring sample points significantly affect the complex amplitude at any point. The nearest neighbors are then reconstructed in-coherently, making the sum of (6.119) somewhat incoherent.

Another method of speckle reduction makes use of some properties of the random diffusers discussed next. We shall therefore defer its description till the end of that subsection.

6.4.3 Random Diffusers

The simplest way to pick a diffuser phase function for the object is to use a random number generator, a computer routine which assigns pseudo-random phases distributed uniformly between zero and two pi radians. These phases may be quantized, i.e., restricted to take on only a finite number of values. It has been shown [6.40] that as few as three randomly chosen phases, equally spaced about the unit circle, are sufficient to closely approximate behavior of the continuous-phase random diffuser.

This "random diffuser" has the desired effect of decreasing the peak to mean intensity ratio R_1. It also gives rise, in the single period CGH, to a random looking speckle pattern resembling black spaghetti strewn between sample points.

To reduce the speckle effects a modified form of the random diffuser was introduced [6.19]. Only every second point in the object is assigned a phase. Intermediate sample-point phases are then assigned the average value of their nearest neighbors. The basis for this reduction is that the sample points adjacent to the point at which the intensity is being measured have the strongest effect on the speckling. The averaged random diffuser brings the phases of adjacent points as close together, on the average, as possible under the constraint that every second point be uncorrelated (random). This tech-nique trades Fourier spectrum leveling for speckle reduction.

Speckle Suppression by Multiple Holograms

For this method of speckle suppression [6.41] two or more CGHs are prepared. The CGHs are of objects with identical moduli, but different random phases. Each hologram will reconstruct an image with a different speckle pattern. We label the objects

$$u_1 = A \exp(i\phi_1), \tag{6.124a}$$

$$u_2 = A \exp(i\phi_2), \tag{6.124b}$$

and the speckle patterns S_1 and S_2. If the hologram centers are separated by μ_0, the reconstructed intensity will be,

$$I = |A \exp(i\phi_1)S_1 + A \exp(i\phi_2) \exp(2\pi i \mu_0 x)|^2 \tag{6.125a}$$

$$= A^2 [|S_1|^2 + |S_2|^2 + 2S_1 S_2 \cos(2\pi \mu_0 x + \phi_2 - \phi_1)]. \tag{6.125b}$$

Assuming a reasonably large separation μ_0 between the two CGHs, the last term will be rapidly varying compared to the image sample spacing; the observed intensity will be

$$I \cong A^2 [|S_1|^2 + |S_2|^2], \tag{6.126}$$

thus resulting in some speckle reduction through "incoherent" averaging of the speckle patterns.

6.4.4 Deterministic Diffusers

Deterministic diffusers can be divided into the general-purpose diffusers and image-specific diffusers. General-purpose diffusers are designed to work reasonably well with a large class of objects; the diffuser functions are independent of the desired image moduli. Image-specific diffusers are designed for one image; the generating algorithm takes image modulus values into account. Because of the close mathematical relation the diffuser design problem bears to radar pulse spectrum flattening, many of the deterministic computer holographic diffusers are closely related to radar "codes".

One of the simplest general purpose diffusers has a quadratic phase [6.41]

$$\phi_{mn} = 2\pi[(m^2/c_x) + (n^2/c_y)], \tag{6.127a}$$

$$-M/2 \leq m \leq (M/2) - 1, \tag{6.127b}$$

$$-N/2 \leq n \leq (N/2) - 1, \tag{6.127c}$$

analogous to a lens placed on the desired image. The focal lengths of this "lens" along the x and y axes are given by

$$f_x = c_x(\delta x)^2/\lambda, \tag{6.128a}$$

$$f_y = c_y(\delta y)^2/\lambda. \tag{6.128b}$$

This lens defocuses the Fourier spectrum leading to better uniformity. A difficulty with this diffuser is that it causes small regions of the desired image to be mapped more or less into small regions of the Fourier spectrum. Shadow casting occurs, so areas on the image with small modulus are lost. This tendency is termed burst error sensitivity.

If the parameters in (6.127) are adjusted so that

$$\phi_{mn} = \pi[(m^2/M) + (n^2/N)] \tag{6.129}$$

then a uniform Schroeder code [6.42] is obtained which, for an object with uniform modulus, has an absolutely uniform discrete Fourier transform. When used as a general-purpose diffuser it is unfortunately burst error sensitive. The Schroeder code generating algorithm does however provide image-specific diffusers. These diffusers give good Fourier spectral uniformity and are quite burst error insensitive. For one-dimensional binary objects the diffuser-generating algorithm is [6.43]

$$\phi_m = \begin{cases} 0 & \text{for} \quad m = -M/2 \\ \\ -2\pi \displaystyle\sum_{\alpha=-M/2}^{m} [(M/2) - \alpha] p_m + [(\pi/M)m], \end{cases} \tag{6.130a}$$

$$p_m = |u_m|^2 \Big/ \sum_{\alpha=-M/2}^{(M/2)-1} |u_\alpha|^2. \tag{6.130b}$$

For objects containing an odd number of points the term $(\pi/M)m$ is dropped.

The Frank-Heimiller [6.44, 45, 45a, 45b] radar codes provide another family of general-purpose diffusers. Although in unmodified form they exhibit burst error sensitivity, there exist modifications which reduce this sensitivity. The unmodified form is

$$\phi_{mn} = 2\pi[(\alpha_m \sigma_m/M) + (\beta_n \tau_n/N)], \tag{6.131a}$$

$$\alpha_m = m - \sigma_m, \tag{6.131b}$$

$$\sigma_m = m(\text{MOD } M^{1/2}), \tag{6.131c}$$

$$\beta_n = n - \tau_n, \tag{6.131d}$$

$$\tau_n = n(\text{MOD } N^{1/2}). \tag{6.131e}$$

One modified version (a particularly burst error insensitive choice) is

$$\phi_{mn} = 2\pi[(\alpha_m \sigma_m/M) + (\beta_n \tau_n/N)] + \pi[(m^2/M^{1/2}) + (n^2/N^{1/2})], \tag{6.132}$$

where α_m, σ_m, β_n, τ_n are as defined in (6.131).

This modified Frank-Heimiller code diffuser is one of a family which results from application of the following algorithm [6.46]. Let $D(m, n)$ be the diffuser complex amplitude,

$$D(\gamma M^{1/2} + \zeta, \delta N^{1/2} + \eta) = \sum_{r = -M^{1/2}/2}^{(M^{1/2}/2) - 1} \sum_{s = -N^{1/2}/2}^{(N^{1/2}/2) - 1} T_{rs}^{\zeta\eta}$$

$$\cdot \exp\{2\pi i[(\gamma r/M^{1/2}) + (\zeta s/N^{1/2})]\}, \qquad (6.133)$$

where $T_{rs}^{\zeta\eta}$ is such that for each subscript pair (r, s) there is one and only one superscript pair (ζ, η) for which $|T_{rs}^{\zeta\eta}| = 1$, and it is otherwise zero. Each subscript and superscript pair has $M^{1/2} \times N^{1/2}$ values. This motivates the interpretation that "T" occupies a "square root domain" in some sense midway between the object and Fourier domains.

$$T_{rs}^{\zeta\eta} = \begin{cases} 1 & \text{if } (\zeta, \eta) = (r, s) \\ 0 & \text{otherwise} \end{cases} \qquad (6.134)$$

together with the above algorithm, (6.133), gives the unmodified Frank-Heimiller code diffuser of (6.131).

Diffusers obtained in this manner, by manipulating the DFT, are most useful when the CGH consists of many periods. Additionally the object should be reasonably extended. Under these conditions the diffuser of (6.132) will give a high diffraction efficiency and pleasing reconstruction. When used with single period holograms this diffuser exhibits a very regular speckle pattern which is extremely displeasing to the eye.

Another family of diffusers are the unmodified [6.47] and modified hyperbolic codes [6.12]. The algorithm which generates them makes use of a "transition domain" between the x and y stages of the DFT.

$$S_{jn} = \sum_m u_{mn} \exp[-2\pi i(mj/M)], \qquad (6.135a)$$

$$\tilde{u}_{jk} = \sum_n S_{jn} \exp[-2\pi i(nk/N)]. \qquad (6.135b)$$

One chooses S_{jn} such that for each j there is one and only one n for which $|S_{jn}| = 1$ and it is zero otherwise.

The hyperbolic code general-purpose deterministic diffusers are used for spectrum preleveling in a work concerning a third approach to spectrum leveling [6.43]. The approach involves interlacing the sample points in an object with a second set of points termed a "parity sequence". By proper choice of a parity sequence the Fourier spectrum modulus can be made perfectly uniform. The parity sequence is then discarded on readout, by using, for example, an appropriate grating in the image plane.

6.5 Reconstructed Image Degradation

In this section we deal with five sources of image distortion: phase quantization noise, phase clipping, phase matching, the linear phase error in detour-phase holograms, and the constant modulus error in kinoforms. Each of these distortions is conveniently described as a Fourier domain point nonlinearity. Limiting the discussion to cell-oriented holograms, we have the desired image u_{jk} and its discrete Fourier transform $\tilde{u}_{jk}$ related by

$$u_{mn} = \sum_{j=-M/2}^{(M/2)-1} \sum_{k=-N/2}^{(N/2)-1} \tilde{u}_{jk} \exp\{2\pi i[(jm/M)+(kn/N)]\}, \qquad (6.136a)$$

$$\tilde{u}_{jk} = \tilde{A}_{jk} \exp(i\tilde{\phi}_{jk}). \qquad (6.136b)$$

We consider a nonlinearity acting on the Fourier spectrum $\tilde{u}_{jk}$ to produce the actual post-nonlinearity reconstructed image

$$\hat{u}_{mn} = \sum_{j}\sum_{k} \hat{C}_{jk}^{mn} \exp\{2\pi i[(jm/M)+(kn/N)]\}, \qquad (6.137)$$

where we have used the circumflex to emphasize the fact that a nonlinear operation has been performed. We have included a dependence of the nonlinearity on the observed image point. Note that the post-nonlinearity coefficients are functions of the pre-nonlinearity coefficients, i.e.,

$$\hat{C}_{jk}^{mn} = \hat{C}_{jk}^{mn}(\tilde{A}_{jk}, \tilde{\phi}_{jk}, m, n). \qquad (6.138)$$

Expressing this functional relation as a mixed Fourier-Taylor series gives

$$\hat{C}_{jk}^{mn} = \sum_{p=0}^{\infty} \sum_{\alpha=-\infty}^{\infty} G_{p\alpha}^{mn}(\tilde{A}_{jk})^{p} \exp(i\alpha\tilde{\phi}_{jk}), \qquad (6.139a)$$

$$G_{p\alpha}^{mn} = 1/2\pi p! \int_{0}^{2\pi} [\partial^{p}\hat{C}_{jk}^{mn}/\partial\tilde{A}^{p}]_{A=0} \exp(-i\alpha\tilde{\phi}_{jk})d\tilde{\phi}_{jk}. \qquad (6.139b)$$

The interpretation of this somewhat formidable looking series is simplified by considering the post-nonlinearity image as composed of several component images [6.48, 57]. The (p,α)th component image is

$$v_{mn}^{p\alpha} = \sum_{j}\sum_{k} \tilde{v}_{jk}^{p\alpha} \exp\{2\pi i[(jm/M)+(kn/N)]\}, \qquad (6.140a)$$

where

$$\tilde{v}_{jk}^{p\alpha} = (\tilde{A}_{jk})^{p} \exp(i\alpha\tilde{\phi}_{jk}). \qquad (6.140b)$$

The component images are combined with the weighting functions $G_{p\alpha}^{mn}$ to yield the final reconstructed image

$$\hat{u}_{mn} = \sum_p \sum_\alpha G_{p\alpha}^{mn} v_{mn}^{p\alpha}. \tag{6.141}$$

The component image for $p=1$, $\alpha=1$ is the object, or the primary image [6.48],

$$v_{mn}^{11} = u_{mn}. \tag{6.142}$$

The remaining component images are false images contributing to noise in the reconstruction.

The decomposition, (6.141), of the post-nonlinearity image is a decomposition in complex amplitude. The intensity is observed, so that the component images may become mixed in a complicated fashion. The post-nonlinearity image intensity is

$$I_{mn} = |\hat{u}_{mn}|^2 = \sum_p \sum_\alpha \sum_q \sum_\beta G_{p\alpha}^{mn}(G_{q\beta}^{mn})^* v_{mn}^{p\alpha}(v_{mn}^{q\beta})^*. \tag{6.143}$$

To reduce this equation to a tractable form we follow the approach of [6.49–52]. It is convenient to work with the DFT of the intensity $\tilde{I}_{jk}$. This matrix is the circular autocorrelation of the post-nonlinearity Fourier spectrum

$$\tilde{I}_{jk}^{mn} = \sum_p \sum_q \sum_\alpha \sum_\beta G_{p\alpha}^{mn}(G_{q\beta}^{mn})^* \tilde{K}_{jk}(p,\alpha;q,\beta). \tag{6.144}$$

Note that the space invariance is contained in the "G". The space variance and this particular description mean that I_{mn} is the DFT over indices (j,k) of $\tilde{I}_{jk}^{mn}$, but the inverse DFT relation does not hold. The $\tilde{K}_{jk}$ are circular cross correlations between the (p,α)th and (q,β)th component image Fourier spectra

$$\tilde{K}_{jk}(p,\alpha;q,\beta) = \sum_{\varrho=-M/2}^{(M/2)-1} \sum_{\sigma=-N/2}^{(N/2)-1} \tilde{v}_{\varrho\sigma}^{p\alpha}(\tilde{v}_{(\varrho-j),(\sigma-k)}^{q\beta})^*. \tag{6.145}$$

For a DFT this cross correlation may also be expressed, exactly, as

$$\tilde{K}_{jk}(p,\alpha;q,\beta) = \langle \tilde{A}_1^p \exp(i\alpha\tilde{\phi}_1)\tilde{A}_2^q \exp(-i\beta\tilde{\phi}_2)\rangle_{jk}, \tag{6.146}$$

where $\langle\ \rangle$ signifies an ensemble average over all possible circular shifts of the discrete Fourier spectrum. The subscripts refer to two points separated by a vector displacement $(j\delta\mu, k\delta\nu)$. For the primary image $p=q=\alpha=\beta=1$,

$$\tilde{K}_{jk}(1,1;1,1) = \sum_m \sum_n |u_{mn}|^2 \exp\{2\pi i[(jm/M)+(kn/N)]\} \tag{6.147a}$$

$$= \langle A_1 \exp(i\phi_1)A_2 \exp(-i\phi_2)\rangle_{jk}. \tag{6.147b}$$

If the object had a random diffuser applied and was reasonably large, then the real and imaginary parts of the Fourier spectrum can be considered Gaussian processes [6.53]. The DFT is very amenable to such a description [6.54]. The $\tilde{K}_{jk}(p, \alpha; q, \beta)$ can then be expressed in terms of $\tilde{K}_{jk}(1,1; 1,1)$. To compress the following expressions in this section we define

$$\tilde{K}_{jk}(1,1; 1,1) = B_{jk} \tag{6.148}$$

giving

$$\tilde{K}_{jk}(p, \alpha; q, \beta) = (B_{jk}/B_{00})^\alpha B_{00}^{(p+q)/2} \left[\frac{\Gamma\left(\frac{p+|\alpha|}{2} + 1\right)\Gamma\left(\frac{q+|\alpha|}{2} + 1\right)}{|\alpha|!} \right]$$

$$\cdot {}_2F_1\{[\Gamma(|\alpha|-p)/2], [(|\alpha|-q)/2]; (|\alpha|+1); |B_{jk}/B_{00}|^2\}\delta_{\alpha\beta} \tag{6.149}$$

where ${}_2F_1$ is the Gaussian hypergeometric function and is simply a power series in $|B_{jk}/B_{00}|^2$

$${}_2F_1[a,b; c; |B_{jk}/B_{00}|^2] = \sum_{l=0}^{\infty} g_l(|B_{jk}/B_{00}|^2)^l, \tag{6.150a}$$

$$g_l = [\Gamma(c)/\Gamma(a)\Gamma(b)][\Gamma(a+l)\Gamma(b+l)/\Gamma(c+l)l!]. \tag{6.150b}$$

Note that on inverse discrete Fourier-transforming, the $(B_{jk})^\alpha$ will become $(\alpha-1)$-fold convolutions of the primary image intensity while the $(|B_{jk}|^2)^l$ will become $(l-1)$-fold convolutions of the primary image intensity autocorrelation. We interpret a zerofold convolution as the function itself and a minus onefold convolution as a delta function.

We note in passing that an object which has a fine intensity structure, i.e., whose intensity autocorrelation is approximately a delta function, will suffer very little degradation on reconstruction from the hypergeometric function.

The summary result is that the post-nonlinearity image Fourier spectral autocorrelation is

$$I_{jk}^{mn} = \sum_p \sum_q \sum_\alpha G_{p\alpha}^{mn}(G_{p\alpha}^{mn})^*(B_{jk}/B_{00})_2^\alpha F_1\{[(|\alpha|-p)/2], [(|\alpha|-q)/2]; (|\alpha|+1);$$

$$\cdot |B_{jk}/B_{00}|^2\} B_{00}^{(p+q)/2} \left\{\left[\Gamma\left(\frac{p+|\alpha|}{2} + 1\right)\Gamma\left(\frac{q+|\alpha|}{2} + 1\right)\right]/|\alpha|!\right\}. \tag{6.151}$$

One can experimentally observe separate component images in this sum. One first picks a compound object, one consisting of some recognizable object together with a strong point. Forming the CGH with some known nonlinear degradation then gives rise to false images whose strength can be calculated

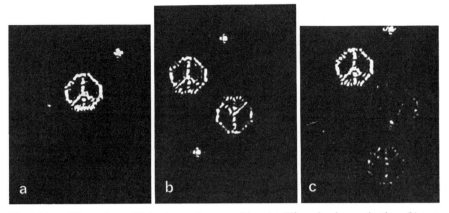

Fig. 6.14a–c. Illustrations of false image decomposition. (**a**) Fifteen-level quantization; (**b**) two-level quantization; (**c**) three-level quantization

from (6.151). The various convolutions and correlations then reproduce the recognizable figure through interaction of the point and figure. These reproductions will however have varying orientations and displacements from the viewing field center, depending on where they originate in the sum of (6.151) [6.55]. Figure 6.14 [6.56] shows an application of this technique to studying Fourier domain phase quantization.

Phase Nonlinearities

For most objects, distorting the Fourier spectrum phase has stronger effects than distorting the modulus. This has been shown for objects with random diffusers [6.58] and demonstrated for other objects [6.59]. Because of the Fourier spectrum phase's importance, we concentrate first on phase nonlinearities. For phase nonlinearities (6.139) reduces to

$$\hat{C}_{jk}^{mn} = \tilde{A}_{jk} \sum_{\alpha=-\infty}^{\infty} G_{1\alpha}^{mn} \exp(i\alpha\tilde{\phi}_{jk}). \tag{6.152}$$

Space-invariant phase nonlinearities have the simpler form

$$\hat{C}_{jk} = \tilde{A}_{jk} \sum_{\alpha=-\infty}^{\infty} G_{\alpha} \exp(i\alpha\tilde{\phi}_{jk}), \tag{6.153a}$$

$$G_{\alpha} = 1/2\pi \int_{0}^{2\pi} \hat{C}_{jk} \exp(-i\alpha\tilde{\phi}_{jk}) d\tilde{\phi}_{jk}, \tag{6.153b}$$

where unused superscripts and subscripts have been suppressed.

6.5.1 Phase Quantization

Computer-controlled plotters cause quantization effects. Section 6.4.1 described the relation between incremented plotter pen movement and the geometrical quantization which leads to the quantization of modulus and phase. The finite number of levels in the CRT plotter and its discrete addressing also give rise to modulus and phase quantization in graytone holograms. Concentrating on space-invariant phase quantization [6.60–62a], the nonlinearity mapping the pre-quantization phase ϕ into a post-quantization phase $\hat{\phi}$ is illustrated in Fig. 6.15.

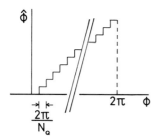

Fig. 6.15. N_Q-level quantization

Letting N_Q be the number of equally spaced quantization levels, (6.153b) gives

$$G_\alpha = \begin{cases} \text{sinc}(\alpha/N_Q) & \text{for} \quad \alpha = lN_Q + 1 \quad l = \text{integer} \\ 0 & \text{otherwise}. \end{cases} \tag{6.154}$$

One sees, as expected, that as the number of quantization levels N_Q gets very large, the only significant component image is $\alpha = 1$. So for $N_Q \to \infty$

$$\hat{C}_{jk} = A_{mn} \exp(i\phi_{mn}) \tag{6.155}$$

so that an ideal reconstruction would occur. This is not a surprise since we assumed no errors except phase quantization and of course $N_Q \to \infty$ means no phase quantization.

Equation (6.151) can be used to obtain the circular autocorrelation function of the post-quantization Fourier spectrum and thereby the reconstructed image intensity.

$$\tilde{I}_{jk}^{mn} = B_{00} \sum_{\substack{l=-\infty \\ \alpha = lN_Q + 1}}^{\infty} \text{sinc}^2(\alpha/N_Q)(B_{jk}/B_{00})_2^{\alpha} F_1 \{[(|\alpha|-1)/2], [(|\alpha|-1)/2];$$

$$\cdot (|\alpha|+1); |B_{jk}/B_{00}|^2\} \, \Gamma^2 [(|\alpha|/2)+(3/2)]/|\alpha|!. \tag{6.156}$$

The primary image is contributed by the $\alpha=1$ ($l=0$) term in this sum. This primary image we know to be undegraded which is confirmed by the fact that

$$_2F_1(0,0;2;|B_{jk}/B_{00}|^2)=1.\tag{6.157}$$

This gives the $\alpha=1$ *contribution* to the sum as

$$\tilde{I}_{jk}^{mn}=\text{sinc}^2(1/N_Q)B_{jk}.\tag{6.158}$$

Performing a DFT on the (j,k) indices of $\tilde{I}_{jk}^{mn}$ gives

$$I_{mn}=\text{sinc}^2(1/N_Q)|u_{mn}|^2.\tag{6.159}$$

The primary image is undegraded but is diminished in strength by $\text{sinc}^2(\alpha/N_Q)$ by the phase quantization.

A signal-to-noise ratio can be determined by noting that the integrated intensity of the post-nonlinearity intensity is, from (6.151),

$$\sum_m\sum_n\tilde{I}_{00}^{mn}=\sum_m\sum_n\sum_p\sum_q\sum_\alpha G_{p\alpha}^{mn}(G_{q\alpha}^{mn})^*B_{00}^{(p+q)/2}.\tag{6.160}$$

We have made use of the fact that [6.63]

$$_2F_1[a,b;c;1]=[\Gamma(c)\Gamma(c-a-b)]/[\Gamma(c-a)\Gamma(c-b)]\tag{6.161}$$

and that

$$\Gamma(a+1)=a\Gamma(a)=a!,\tag{6.162}$$

implying that

$$_2F_1[a,a;2a+2;1]=[\Gamma(2a+1)\Gamma(2)]/[\Gamma^2(a+2)]=(|\alpha|!)/\{\Gamma^2[(|\alpha|+3)/2]\}.\tag{6.163}$$

For space-invariant phase quantization the integrated intensities of (6.160) become

$$B_{00}\sum_{\substack{l=-\infty\\\alpha=lN_Q+1}}^{\infty}\text{sinc}^2(\alpha/N_Q)=B_{00}\sum_{l=-\infty}^{\infty}\text{sinc}^2[l+(1/N_Q)].\tag{6.164}$$

The handy relation

$$\sum_{m=-\infty}^{\infty}\text{sinc}(m-a)\,\text{sinc}(m-b)=\text{sinc}(a-b)\tag{6.165}$$

shows the sum in (6.164) to be one.

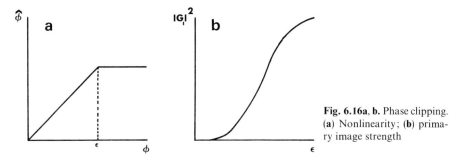

Fig. 6.16a, b. Phase clipping. (a) Nonlinearity; (b) primary image strength

The N_Q level phase quantization signal-to-noise ratio is then

$$S/N=[\text{sinc}^2(1/N_Q)]/[1-\text{sinc}^2(1/N_Q)]. \tag{6.166}$$

The signal-to-noise ratio for any phase nonlinearity is

$$S/N=(G_1)^2/[1-(G_1)^2]. \tag{6.167}$$

6.5.2 Phase Clipping

This phase nonlinearity arises when a full 2π phase variation is not attainable in the recording medium [6.64, 65]. The post-nonlinearity phases are equal to the pre-nonlinearity phases up to a clipping level. Above this level the phases are equal to the threshold value ε (see Fig. 6.16).

One can calculate the primary image strength as a function of the phase clipping level using (6.153b) as follows:

$$|G_1|^2 =[1/(2\pi)^2]\,[(\varepsilon-\sin\varepsilon)^2 +(1-\cos\varepsilon)^2]. \tag{6.168}$$

Figure 6.16b is a plot of $|G_1(\varepsilon)|^2$ versus ε.

6.5.3 Phase Matching

If one chooses to scale the plotted phase to the reduced phase range instead of clipping, a phase mismatch occurs [6.50, 52, 66]. This phase nonlinearity is important when a dielectric phase delay is implemented as with the ROACH or kinoform. The phase matching is very sensitive to the photographic processing. The phase matching error is described by

$$\hat{\phi}=k_m\phi, \tag{6.169}$$

where k_m is a constant which would ideally be one. For the phase matching error the relative primary image strength is

$$|G_\alpha|^2 =\text{sinc}^2(k_m-\alpha). \tag{6.170}$$

6.5.4 Linear Phase Error in Detour-Phase Holograms

Detour-phase holograms, for instance that described by (6.37), effect a phase which is space variant. If $\hat{\phi}_{jk}$ is the desired phase of the hologram and we consider only the linear phase error, then [6.2, 66]

$$\exp[i\hat{\phi}_{jk}] = \exp[\tilde{\phi}_{jk}(m/M)] = \sum_{\alpha=-\infty}^{\infty} \text{sinc}[\alpha - (m/M)] \exp(i\alpha\tilde{\phi}_{jk}). \qquad (6.171)$$

From this form it is clear that

$$G_{1\alpha}^{mn} = \text{sinc}[\alpha - (m/M)]. \qquad (6.172)$$

The signal-to-noise ratio is space variant and is

$$S/N = \text{sinc}^2[1 - (m/M)]/\{1 - \text{sinc}^2[1 - (m/M)]\}. \qquad (6.173)$$

At the edges of the first diffraction, $(m/M) = 1 \pm (1/2)$, the average signal-to-noise ratio is $S/N = 0.68$. A bit closer to the center of the first diffraction order, at $(m/M) = 1 \pm (1/4)$, this ratio has increased to 4.2. The restriction that detour-phase holograms reconstruct images only near the chosen diffraction order is seen to be a very mild restriction. Also recall that this is an average signal-to-noise ratio. The image structure has not been included. Since the false images will tend to be more diffusely distributed than the primary image, this restriction is even further relaxed.

6.5.5 The Constant Modulus Error for Kinoforms and Phase-Only Holograms

A phase-only hologram is one where the Fourier spectral modulus is constant. Either the modulus is originally constant, as is true for many applications of CGHs to interferometry and interferometric optical component testing, or the modulus is forced to be constant. Forcing the modulus to be constant results in degradation of the reconstructed image, but this degradation is surprisingly mild. The greater importance of the Fourier spectral phase than modulus accounts for this mildness.

The kinoform [6.66, 67] is a phase-only hologram where the phase is implemented by dielectric phase shifting. The device is generally fabricated using a CRT plotter and a bleaching step in the photographic processing. The photographic film is exposed to an intensity pattern. After developing, the film is placed in a bleaching bath which converts the metallic silver to a silver salt, thereby creating index changes in the emulsion and surface relief [6.24]. An alternate method of fabrication is identical to forming the ROACH (Sect. 6.2.1), except that the modulus controlling layer is exposed to uniform illumination

[6.10]. Other fabrication methods include use of a pen-and-ink plotter plus coherent low-pass spatial filtering [6.68] and use of a Fabry-Perot etalon (for kinoform lenses) [6.69].

The kinoform transmittance is obtained through a nonlinearity which destroys the modulus information (sets the modulus to one). From (6.139) this nonlinearity is expressed as

$$G^{mn}_{p\alpha} = \delta_{p0} \text{ (the Kronecker delta)}. \tag{6.174}$$

Calculation of the signal-to-noise ratio does *not* proceed from (6.167) since we are now considering a modulus nonlinearity. Returning to (6.151), the post-nonlinearity circular autocorrelation can be written as

$$\tilde{I}_{jk} = B_{jk} \, {}_2F_1(\tfrac{1}{2},\tfrac{1}{2};2;|B_{jk}/B_{00}|^2)\,[\Gamma^2(3/2)/B_{00}], \tag{6.175}$$

where the superscript (m, n) has been suppressed since there is no space variance. Writing the hypergeometric function in the series form

$$\tilde{I}_{jk} = B_{jk} \sum_l \{[\Gamma^2(\tfrac{1}{2}+l)]/[(l+1)!\,l!]\}|B_{jk}/B_{00}|^{2l}[9/(4B_{00})]. \tag{6.176}$$

The primary image is associated with the $l=0$ term in the sum which has a strength

$$\Gamma^2(\tfrac{1}{2})\,[9/(4B_{00})]. \tag{6.177}$$

Since the integrated intensity of the post-nonlinearity will just be $\tilde{I}_{00}$, from (6.175) the relative strength of the primary image is [6.50, 52]

$$\Gamma^2(3/2) = 0.785, \tag{6.178}$$

where (6.161) has been used in taking the quotient of (6.177) and $\tilde{I}_{00}$ [from (6.176)]. About 79% of the intensity goes into the primary image.

These calculations depend on the object having a superimposed random diffuser. The rather high image fidelity expressed by (6.178) can be further improved by computer tailoring of the object diffuser. One such procedure [6.70] uses the computer to first calculate the Fourier spectrum. The modulus is then set to a constant and the inverse DFT taken. The degraded object has its correct modulus values restored, but the new phases are kept. This procedure is repeated until the merit function (rms difference between object modulus and retransformed modulus) increase per iteration becomes small. A modified algorithm which allows constrained floating of the object and spectrum moduli has also been described [6.11].

6.6 Three-Dimensional Display

One potential advantage of computer-generated holograms for display purposes is that they can reconstruct three-dimensional images. This potential was recognized early in the CGH's development and three-dimensional computer holograms were fabricated [6.5, 19, 71]. It was realized from the outset that computer holograms specifying all depth information would be expensive and so some cost reducing techniques were investigated.

To gain some perspective, let us describe a calculational method which results in a hologram containing all three-dimensional information. Next, we mention some of the economies which are available because of the way the human observer perceives depth.

The "exact" method we label the ping-pong algorithm for reasons which should become clear shortly. First consider the reconstruction of a Fourier geometry computer-generated hologram in Fig. 6.1. The image is planar, but as a first intuitive step let us move the image a distance Δz out of the image plane z_0 (Δz is positive away from the lens). We can of course implement this movement by building an auxiliary lens of the proper focal length into the hologram and so move the reconstruction plane. To reconstruct an image in the plane $z = z_0 + \Delta z$, an effective lens of focal length

$$f_e = \{[1/(z_0 + \Delta z)] - (1/z_0)\}^{-1} = [z_0(z_0 + \Delta z)]/\Delta z \tag{6.179}$$

must be built into the CGH. The effective lens is realized by multiplying the object Fourier spectrum by the quadratic phase factor

$$\exp[i\pi(x^2 + y^2)/\lambda f_e]. \tag{6.180}$$

Written in terms of the new reduced coordinates

$$\mu = x/[\lambda(z_0 + \Delta z)], v = y/[\lambda(z_0 + \Delta z)] \tag{6.181}$$

the quadratic phase factor becomes

$$\exp\{i\pi\lambda\Delta z[(z_0 + \Delta z)/z_0](\mu^2 + v^2)\}. \tag{6.182}$$

If $\Delta z \ll z_0$ we can ignore the slight scale change resulting from the change from old to new reduced coordinates. The Fourier spectrum for the displaced object is

$$\tilde{u}_d(\mu, v) = \tilde{u}(\mu, v)\exp[i\pi\lambda\Delta z(\mu^2 + v^2)]. \tag{6.183}$$

Equation (6.183) expresses translation of an image by Δz along the optical axis.

6.6.1 Ping-Pong Propagation

The ping-pong propagation algorithm uses this translation as follows. The object is first expressed as a collection of planes. The first plane is translated to the second by a DFT, multiplied by the appropriate quadratic phase factor, and then an inverse DFT is performed on it. The resulting complex-amplitide at the second plane, due to the first plane, is then multiplied by the complex-amplitude transmittance of the second plane. Any self-luminous sources in the second plane are then added. This total complex amplitude is then translated to the third plane through a DFT, multiplied by a quadratic phase factor, and then inverse DFT-ed [6.41]. This algorithm produces a fully realistic image since the later planes have the ability to block light transmitted or scattered by previous planes. One has the ability to simulate hidden lines, parts of an object which are visible from one viewing angle but not another.

Because the multiplication of the incident wave by the plane's transmittance is performed in the object domain and the propagating takes place in the Fourier domain, one is constantly transforming from one domain to the other; hence the term ping-pong propagation. If there are N_{PL} planes in the object then $2N_{PL} - 1$ DFTs are performed and $N_{PL} - 1$ transmittance multiplications. One must be very careful that the space-bandwidth product of the hologram, number of resolution cells, is large enough. The image space in the last plane must be surrounded by a zero frame which is large enough to essentially capture waves expanding from previous planes. A good rule of thumb is to multiply the reciprocal of the CGH's f-number at the first plane by the distance from the plane of interest to the final plane. Dividing by the sampling distance in the final plane gives the number of samples in the zero frame.

6.6.2 Direct Convolution

An alternate method, similar to ping-pong propagation, may be used when the interplanar distance divided by the hologram f-number on the order of one sampling cell, and the phase variations in the object are not rapid. The point-spread function of the propagation is then somewhat limited in spatial extent. One may then use a propagation convolution involving only a few elements at a time. The direct convolution can then be comparatively economical, especially if the object field is sparsely occupied. Some experiments along these lines have met with moderate success [6.72].

6.6.3 Born Approximation

It is even more economical, but less realistic, to ignore the interaction between planes of the image. One can calculate the Fourier spectra of the various image planes, multiply each function by the appropriate quadratic phase factor for the plane on which you wish it to reside, then add all resulting Fourier spectra together. One need perform only one Fourier transform per depth plane. Since a sum has been formed, none of these image planes will interact. If an image in one plane happens to be behind an image in another plane, the former will shine through the latter. One has formed an image of transparent self-luminous objects. This method of computation is sometimes referred to as the Born approximation as there is no secondary scattering of the optical field.

6.6.4 Multiple Perspectives

One parameter we have neglected in this discussion so far is the acceptability of three-dimensional information to the human observer. Is all the information which can conceivably be coded into the computer hologram needed? The answer is no. Taking advantage of this fact, one can fabricate holograms which are much less complicated than the ones discussed so far, and yet more pleasing to the eye.

The first extra information to be eliminated should be vertical parallax [6.73], since most depth perception comes from horizontal parallax. Thus instead of one large hologram one might just as well have a hologram which consists of identical horizontal strips. Since each strip is identical, the vertical parallax is lost, and one does not peer through a narrow slit.

The next possible information reduction would come from noting that a computer hologram large enough to allow sufficient parallax for a three-dimensional impression would supply far too many views. The angular increment would be unnecessarily fine. Therefore some horizontal parallax can be eliminated. The technique then is to construct a compound hologram consisting of horizontal strips, each strip being composed of individual holograms. Each individual hologram supplies only one flat perspective of the image. Several adjacent holograms might be identical. The duplicate holograms, both the different horizontal strips and the identical adjacent holograms, represent only photographic replication, reducing costs considerably.

Multiple perspective holograms may be generated by

1) digitizing several perspectives of an existing object;
2) computer-generating perspective drawings of a stored three-dimensional object matrix, then recording interferometric holograms of each view;
3) computing perspectives of a stored three-dimensional object matrix, calculating a CGH for each view, then outputting the finished computer holograms.

The first alternative is useful when an actual object exists, but is not suitable for interferometric holography (e.g., has coherent noise problems or is subject to movement). The CGH of Fig. 6.8 illustrates this technique. The object, a small ivory dog, was placed on a pedestal and a television camera was moved in a circle around it. The television camera was interfaced to a PDP-11/40 minicomputer through a Colorado Video model 260 video bandwidth compressor (digitizer). The binary CGHs were then replicated by an offset printing press and taped together. Such a composite hologram can also be formed from several digitized frames from a still or movie camera [6.5]. Alternative two [6.74] is useful when the object is known in mathematical form only. Interferometric holography is combined with inexpensive computer image projection techniques to provide a three-dimensional display with minimum computing time, but more complicated recording techniques. Alternative three uses the same image projection philosophy (as alternative two), but trades optical recording complexity for computing cost [6.75, 75a, 75b]. The object is approximated by several intersecting planes; these planes are then appropriately projected into the various views. Easily fabricated binary detour-phase CGHs are then made of the projected views. An alternative is to produce the impression of three dimensionality in the object by simulated diffuse reflecting surface properties [6.75b, 75d].

6.7 Color Reconstructions

Besides producing pleasant visual sensations, color displays can also convey a great deal of simultaneous information. It is therefore appropriate to discuss some methods by which computer-generated holograms can be made to give color reconstructions.

As in color photography, CGH color reconstructions are obtained by combining three (or more) monochrome images. The images are known as color-separation images and are most often in the three (additive) primary colors: red, green, blue.

Because multiple images are involved, the CGH forming these reconstructions must be in some form multiplexed (meaning that it carries more than one image). The additional degree of freedom, time, has also been used to produce CGH movies [6.75c, 75d].

6.7.1 Multiplexing

There are three common multiplexing varieties used in producing CGH color reconstructing holograms: space division, carrier frequency, and theta modulation multiplexing. We apply these labels to the hologram (in contrast to the reconstructed image).

Space Division Multiplexing

Space division multiplexing means that the color separation images are produced by different holograms. The holograms may be placed side by side in the same plane, or they may be in quite different locations and combined

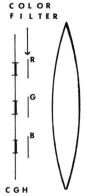

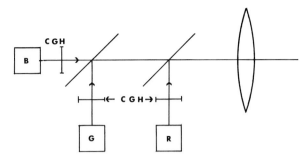

Fig. 6.17. Two color-reconstruction geometries [6.76]

optically (see Fig. 6.17) [6.76]. The holograms may even be interlaced [6.76a]. The separate holograms are illuminated by the appropriate colors and the reconstructed images caused to overlap and be scaled appropriately. Scaling is necessary because hologram reconstructed images vary in size and position with wavelength. One advantage of using space division multiplexing is that the color separation holograms can be separately scaled by photographic reduction to suit the reconstruction.

To visualize the effects of differing wavelengths on the hologram reconstruction, one observes that the reduced coordinates μ, v used in specifying a position in the Fourier plane are themselves functions of wavelength [see (6.1)]. This wavelength dependence is reflected in the DFT used to describe cell-oriented holograms

$$u_{mn} = \sum_j \sum_k \tilde{u}_{jk} \exp\{2\pi i[(mj/M)+(nk/N)]\}, \tag{6.184}$$

where the subscripts (m, n) referred to the point in the output plane

$$x_m = m/(M\delta\mu) = (m\lambda z_0)/(M\delta x_h), \tag{6.185a}$$

$$y_n = n/(N\delta\mu) = (n\lambda z_0)/(N\delta y_h), \tag{6.185b}$$

where δx_h, δy_h are the real coordinate dimensions of the resolution cells on the hologram. Either the CGH dimensions $M\delta x_h$ and $N\delta x_h$ can be adjusted or the object can be prescaled to compensate for wavelength-dependent size differences in the reconstruction.

Carrier Frequency Multiplexing

Another type of multiplexing, carrier frequency multiplexing, makes use of the ability of the hologram to store images on separate carrier frequencies, which means that the reconstructed color separation images will occur at different places in the reconstruction plane. In the computer hologram we can divide the first-order reconstructed image into three vertical or three horizontal strips.

Three point sources of light (red, green, blue) are then used to illuminate the hologram. Each source reconstructs all three color separation images. We can express this by writing u_{mn}^{RG}, where the first superscript designates the color separation image and the second the color it is reconstructed in. All of the images

$$u_{mn}^{RR}, u_{mn}^{RG}, u_{mn}^{RB}$$
$$u_{mn}^{GR}, u_{mn}^{GG}, u_{mn}^{GB} \qquad (6.186)$$
$$u_{mn}^{BR}, u_{mn}^{BG}, u_{mn}^{BB}$$

are reconstructed simultaneously but in locations which depend on the light source locations. The sources can be positioned such that u^{RR}, u^{GG}, and u^{BB} overlap in some region of the reconstruction plane. The other images will fall outside this region of overlap. The result is a multicolor reconstruction [6.77].

The color separation images u^{RR}, u^{GG}, and u^{BB} must have the correct relative sizes. Since no hologram is being used to record all images, the scale differences cannot be provided for by photographic reduction. The scale differences can however be precompensated when the object is input to the computer hologram generating program.

Theta Modulation

A third multiplexing alternative is theta modulation [6.78]. Here the two-dimensional nature of optical spatial frequencies is exploited so that different images are carried on spatial frequencies of the same modulus, but different angular orientations. The reconstructed images occur at the same distance from the optical axis, but at different angular positions. The binary CGH of (6.44) is easily multiplexed using theta modulation. The space-variant DFT coefficient of (6.45) in the neighborhood of the (1,0) diffraction order ($m = M, n = 0$) has the approximate value

$$C_{jk}^{M0} = (1/\pi) \sin(\pi W_{jk}) H_{jk} \exp[2\pi i P_{jk}]. \qquad (6.187)$$

However, in the neighborhood of the (0,1) diffraction order ($m = 0, n = N$) the same space-variant DFT coefficient has the value

$$C_{jk}^{0N} = (1/\pi) W_{jk} \sin(\pi H_{jk}) \exp(2\pi i Q_{jk}). \qquad (6.188)$$

It is possible to reconstruct two different images $u_{mn}^{(1)}$ and $u_{mn}^{(2)}$ whose DFTs are $\tilde{u}_{mn}^{(1)}$ and $\tilde{u}_{mn}^{(2)}$, respectively. To reconstruct $u_{mn}^{(1)}$ in the (1,0) diffraction order and $u_{mn}^{(2)}$ in the (0,1) diffraction order, the cell parameters in the CGH are adjusted so that

$$C_{jk}^{M0} \propto \tilde{u}_{jk}^{(1)}, \qquad (6.189a)$$

$$C_{jk}^{0N} \propto \tilde{u}_{jk}^{(2)}, \qquad (6.189b)$$

Setting the proper displacement is accomplished by making the horizontal displacement P_{jk} of the aperture proportional to the phase of $\tilde{u}_{jk}^{(1)}$ and the vertical displacement proportional to the phase of $\tilde{u}_{jk}^{(2)}$. The modulus adjustment is slightly more complicated since the equations

$$\sin(\pi W_{jk}) H_{jk} = |\tilde{u}_{jk}^{(1)}|, \tag{6.190a}$$

$$W_{jk} \sin(\pi H_{jk}) = |\tilde{u}_{jk}^{(2)}|, \tag{6.190b}$$

must be solved simultaneously. For each value of the sine function there are two possible values for the argument. For instance,

$$W_{jk} = 1.0, H_{jk} = 0.5 \quad |C_{jk}^{\mathrm{MO}}| = 0.0$$
$$|C_{jk}^{\mathrm{ON}}| = 0.5 \tag{6.191}$$

while

$$W_{jk} = 0.5, H_{jk} = 1.0 \quad |C_{jk}^{\mathrm{MO}}| = 0.5$$
$$|C_{jk}^{\mathrm{ON}}| = 0.0. \tag{6.192}$$

Zeroes in the Fourier spectra of one image do not force zeroes for the other image. Scaling each of the Fourier spectra so that the maximum modulus is 0.5 guarantees that (6.190a, b) are soluable. For generating the hologram a table of the cell parameters W_{jk} and H_{jk} is stored in the computer. This table is keyed to desired values of C_{jk}^{MO} and C_{jk}^{ON}. For example, with nine levels of modulus quantization [see (6.113)] the table has only 81 elements.

The CGH just described is a two-image multiplex hologram. As with the carrier frequency multiplexed hologram, the theta modulation multiplexed hologram is reconstructed with several light sources, the various images being caused to overlap by proper positioning of the sources.

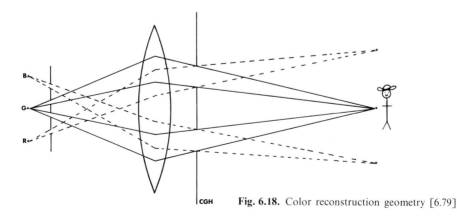

CGH   **Fig. 6.18.** Color reconstruction geometry [6.79]

A particular combination of the space division multiplexed and the theta modulation multiplexed holograms provides a good example of the consideration necessary in producing color reconstructions [6.79]. Two theta modulated two-image holograms are fabricated. One hologram reconstructs the red and a green color separation images, while the other reconstructs the blue and a green color separation images. Two green images are used because the eye has greater resolution at green than at blue and red. The two images in green have different random-phase diffuser functions effecting a speckle reduction as in (6.125). The reconstruction setup is drawn in Fig. 6.18.

Suppose we consider one hologram, that containing the red and green images, illuminated by a red light source whose image falls at x_r, y_r in the reconstruction plane, and a green source whose image falls at x_g, y_g. From (6.175) the reconstruction of the red color separation image in red light, u_{mn}^{RR}, will be centered at

$$x = x_r + (\lambda_r z_0)/(\delta x), \tag{6.193a}$$

$$y = y_r, \tag{6.193b}$$

while u_{mn}^{GG} will be centered at

$$x = x_g, \tag{6.194a}$$

$$y = y_g + (\lambda_g z_0)/(\delta y), \tag{6.194b}$$

where λ_r and λ_g are the wavelengths of the red and green illuminations, respectively. Since we wish to cause color separations R_r and G_g to overlap, we can set the coordinate pairs (x, y) equal in (6.193, 194), giving

$$x_r = x_g - (\lambda_r z_0)/(\delta x), \tag{6.195a}$$

$$y_r = y_g + (\lambda_g z_0)/(\delta y), \tag{6.195b}$$

for the relative image positions of the green and red sources.

6.8 Display of Radio Telescope Gathered Data

Consider a quasi-monochromatic incoherent radio source distribution. To describe the source we use a right-handed coordinate system with the $x - y$ plane on the earth's surface and the z axis pointing normally outward. We define (α, β) as the direction cosines of the angles from the x and y axes, respectively. A point source at (α_0, β_0) with radio complex amplitude "S" would give rise to a plane wave at the earth's surface of

$$S(\mu_0, \nu_0) \exp[-2\pi i(\mu_0 x + \nu_0 y)], \tag{6.196a}$$

$$\mu_0 = \alpha_0/\lambda; \nu_0 = \beta_0/\lambda, \lambda \text{ being the radio wavelengths}. \tag{6.196b}$$

A continuous incoherent source would be described by an incoherent sum of such plane waves. The result is a signal with uniform intensity whose autocorrelation is [6.80, 81]

$$\tilde{R}(x, y) = \overline{(\tilde{S} \circledast \tilde{S})(x, y)} = \iint |S(\mu, \nu)|^2 \exp[-2\pi i(\mu x + \nu y)] \, d\mu d\nu . \tag{6.197a}$$

This autocorrelation represents both an ensemble average and a time average. The ensemble average is from the usual definition of the instantaneous spatial autocorrelation, i.e.,

$$\tilde{R}_i(x, y) = \int \tilde{S}(x', y') S^*(x + x', y + y') \, dx' = \langle S_1 S_2^* \rangle , \tag{6.197b}$$

where (x, y) is a vector from point one to point two. The time average is from the consideration of source coherence

$$R(x, y) = \overline{R_i(x, y)} = \overline{\langle S_1 S_2^* \rangle} = \overline{S_1 S_2^*} . \tag{6.197c}$$

The last equation indicates assumed space invariance of the process. Equations (6.197a) and (6.197c) together imply that the source intensity distribution is obtainable by measuring the time correlation between single receiving antennas whose vector separation is (x, y), i.e.,

$$|S(\mu, \nu)|^2 = \iint \overline{S_1 S_2^*} \exp[2\pi i(\mu x + \nu y)] \, dxdy \tag{6.198a}$$

or equivalently

$$R(\mu, \nu) = \iint \tilde{R}(x, y) \exp[2\pi i(\mu x + \nu y)] \, dxdy . \tag{6.198b}$$

In discrete form

$$R_{mn} \propto \sum_j \sum_k \tilde{R}_{jk} \exp\{2\pi i[(mj)/M] + [(nk)/N]\} , \tag{6.199a}$$

$$\tilde{R}_{jk} = \tilde{R}(jx_a, ky_a) , \tag{6.199b}$$

where (x_a, y_a) is the separation between elements in the effective antenna array. The instantaneous effective antenna is given by the support of the actual antenna array position autocorrelation. This relation stems from considering pairs of actual antennas in determining $\overline{S_1 S_2^*}$. If (x_p, y_p) are the actual antenna positions, then the effective antenna element "positions" are given by the

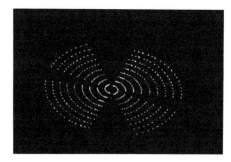

Fig. 6.19. Sampling grid in spatial frequency domain: the effective antenna [6.82]

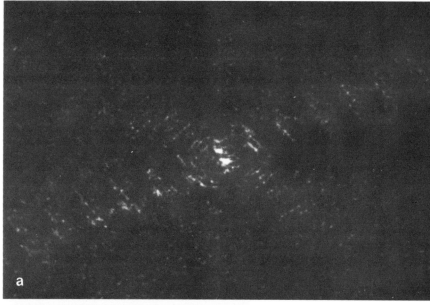

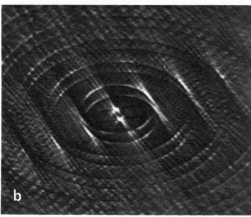

Fig. 6.20. (a) Computer holographic reconstruction of Cygnus-A; (b) digital reconstruction of Cygnus-A [6.82]

support of

$$\iint \sum_p \sum_q \delta(x'-x_p)\,\delta(x'-x_q+x)\,\delta(y'-y_p)\,\delta(y'-y_q+y)\,dx'dy'$$

$$= \sum_p \sum_q \delta[x-(x_q-x_p)]\,\delta[y-(y_q-y_p)]. \tag{6.200}$$

Since the earth is rotating, these instantaneous effective antenna elements will move, tracing out curves on the earth's surface. $\tilde{R}_{jk}$ in (6.199) are measurements from this rotationally synthesized effective antenna.

The DFT of (6.199) can be done on a digital computer, and the image can then be displayed. Alternatively, $\tilde{R}_{jk}$ can be encoded into a CGH. Reconstructing the hologram using the setup of Fig. 6.1 will produce an optical image of the radio sources. Note that no DFT is digitally computed, the measured data already being in that form. Figures 6.19 and 6.20 show a CGH reconstruction of a radio source brightness distribution and a digital reconstruction [6.82].

6.9 Spatial Filtering

When making a decision on the presence or absence of a 51-pointed star in a displayed image, it would be a poorly designed system which forced the observer to distinguish the difference between a 50-pointed star and a 51-pointed star. It would be easier to distinguish between the presence or absence of a bright point. This complexity reduction of displayed information is especially valuable when a simple machine, say a robot, must interpret the displayed data. Such image format conversion can be accomplished through spatial filtering. Computer holograms, like interferometric holograms, can be used to perform filtering in both coherent and incoherent light.

6.9.1 Coherent Matched Filtering

The image reconstruction setup of Fig. 6.1 can be converted to a coherent matched filtering setup by replacing the light source at $z = -z_s$ with a photographic transparency. This "input transparency" is illuminated by a spherical wave which, in the absence of the input transparency, would come to a focus at the plane of the CGH, i.e., at $z=0$. The result is that the Fourier transform $\tilde{u}_i(\mu, v)$ of the input transparency complex amplitude $u_i(x, y)$ (which we scale to the image plane $z=z_0$) will illuminate the CGH. System geometry determines that $\tilde{u}_i(\mu, v)$ will be multiplied by a quadratic phase factor. If $\tilde{T}(\mu, v)$ is the transmittance of the CGH, the complex amplitude just after the hologram is

$$\tilde{T}(\mu, v)\,\tilde{u}_i(\mu, v)\exp[-i\pi\lambda z_0(\mu^2+v^2)]. \tag{6.201}$$

One picks the object for the CGH to be

$$u_s^*(-x, -y). \tag{6.202}$$

This $u_s(x, y)$ is an appropriately sampled version of the object to be recognized. If a point source were placed in the center of the plane at $z = -z_s$, the CGH would reconstruct, among other images,

$$u_s^*[-(x-x_0), -(y-y_0)], \tag{6.203}$$

where (x_0, y_0) is depends on the type of CGH used. For a ROACH $x_0 = 0$, $y = 0$. For first-order reconstructing circular overflow corrected binary hologram $x_0 = 1/\delta\mu$ and $y_0 = 1/\delta v$, where $(\delta\mu, \delta v)$ are the reduced coordinate resolution cell sizes in the CGH.

Considering only the part of the hologram transmittance which reconstructs u_s^*, (6.201) becomes

$$\tilde{u}_s^*(\mu, v)\tilde{u}_i(\mu, v)\exp[-2\pi i(x_0\mu + y_0 v)]\exp[-i\pi\lambda z_0(\mu^2 + v^2)]. \tag{6.204}$$

Inverse Fourier-transforming, one has the cross correlation [6.83]. The observed intensity of this cross correlation is

$$|(u_s \circledast u_i)(x, y)|^2 = |\int\int u_i(x', y')u_s^*(x+x', y+y')dx'dy'|^2. \tag{6.205}$$

The cross-correlation function will be centered at (x_0, y_0) in the output plane $z = z_0$. There is also the quadratic phase factor of (6.2) multiplying the output, but because one observes intensity this phase is unimportant. The cross correlation is a measure of the similarity between the CGH-stored image u_s and the input image u_i. This measure is especially valuable if

$$(u_s \circledast u_s)(x, y) \cong \delta(x)\delta(y). \tag{6.206}$$

An output which matches u_s will then give a sharp strong recognition peak in the plane $z = z_0$.

6.9.2 Incoherent Matched Filtering

For incoherent matched filtering the same setup is used (Fig. 6.1) as for coherent matched filtering. The input transparency is located in the plane $-z_s$. The illumination is however quasi-monochromatic incoherent. Either a moving ground glass is placed just before the coherently illuminated input, or an incoherent source such as a color-filtered incandescent lamp is used, or the incident angle of illumination is varied with time [6.84].

Although the above sources of incoherent illumination are equivalent, the most easily visualized is the rotating ground glass. The input transparency complex amplitude $u_i(x, y)$ now has a time-varying phase function applied, becoming

$$u_i(x, y) \exp[i\phi_d(x, y, t)] . \tag{6.207}$$

The time-varying diffuser is assumed to be strong enough to at least scatter light to the edges of the hologram. To maximize the light efficiency of the process, the diffuser should uniformly fill the hologram aperture and scatter no light outside. An approximation to this ideally scattering diffuser may be implemented by fabricating a kinoform with a specially distributed random-phase transmittance [6.85]. Another diffuser for this purpose is produced by low-pass spatial filtering a strong diffuser and bleaching a photograph of the resulting speckle pattern [6.86]. Finally, one may use a kinoform fabrication method which involves low-pass filtering [6.68] and input random or deterministic diffuser functions. Some computer simulations have shown that typically 65% to 70% of the light can be directed through the hologram while retaining good coverage.

This input diffuser design problem is closely related to the kinoform image-reconstruction quality calculation of Sect. 6.5.5. The kinoform is in the input plane and its reconstructed image is in the CGH plane. We are trying to reconstruct a uniform rectangle with random phases. Equation (6.178) implies that about 80% of the light will fall within the rectangle. This number of course neglects truncation and sampling effects.

The time variation of the input diffuser is such that the time correlation is

$$\overline{\exp[i\phi_d(x, y, t)] \exp[-i\phi_d(x'', y'', t)]} = \delta(x - x'')\delta(y - y''), \tag{6.208}$$

where the bar indicates a time average. The cross correlation of (6.205) becomes

$$\int\int\int\int u_i(x', y')u_i^*(x'', y'')u_s^*(x + x', y + y')u_s(x + x'', y + y'')$$

$$\cdot \{\overline{\exp[i\phi_d(x', y', t)] \exp[-i\phi_d(x'', y'', t)]}\} dx' dy' dx'' dy'' . \tag{6.209}$$

Making use of (6.208) reduces this to

$$(|u_s|^2 \circledast |u_i|^2)(x, y) = \int\int |u_i(x', y')|^2 |u_s(x + x', y + y')|^2 dx' dy' \tag{6.210}$$

again a correlation function, but this time, in intensity, (6.210) is a measure of the similarity between the input intensity and the reconstructed image intensity of the hologram.

The phase of $u_s(x, y)$, the image reconstructed by the CGH, is unimportant to incoherent matched filtering. The diffusers described in Sect. 6.4 can therefore be applied to $|u_s(x, y)|$ in making the CGH. This freedom suits CGHs

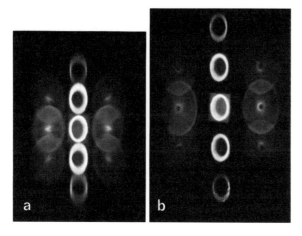

Fig. 6.21a, b. Multi spectral magnification compensation in incoherent spatial filtering. (a) Filter is "matched" to output for blue light, as evidenced by correlation points; (b) Illumination with red light causes magnification change and thereby a mismatch; thus correlation points vanish. Zirconium arc and Kodak gelatine color filters provided effective magnification change of approximately 25%

very well to incoherent matched filtering. The considerably detailed descriptions of CGH properties important for image display are directly transplantable to incoherent matched filtering.

One advantage of incoherent spatial filtering is that a displacement of the CGH transverse to the optical axis does not affect the filtering process, thus greatly reducing the critical tolerance. A movement along the optical axis changes the magnification of $u_s(x, y)$ thus allowing different magnifications of the $u_i(x, y)$ to be matched. Figure 6.21 shows the results of a simple incoherent matched filtering experiment.

6.9.3 Translation Invariant Incoherent Spatial Filtering

Another form of incoherent spatial filtering is illustrated in Fig. 6.22 [6.87]. An input transparency is illuminated by coherent light. Its Fourier transform falls on a moving ground glass. An incoherent matched filtering is then performed on the Fourier power spectrum of the input transparency. The Fourier power spectrum is invariant to transverse translation of the input transparency.

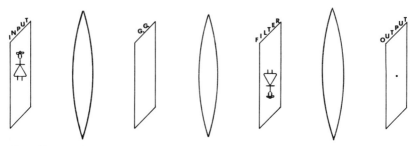

Fig. 6.22. Translation invariant incoherent spatial filtering

Furthermore, the incoherent recognition is invariant with respect to transverse CGH movement. No matter what lateral positions the input and CGH filter occupy, the output correlation pattern is in the same position.

Again using $u_i(x, y)$ for the input transparency complex-amplitude transmittance, the input to the system is $|\tilde{u}_i|^2$. The matched CGH would reconstruct

$$u_s \approx |\tilde{u}_i| \exp(i\tilde{\phi}_R), \tag{6.211}$$

where the phase function $\tilde{\phi}_R$ is arbitrary. If $\tilde{\phi}_R$ is chosen to be the phase of the input transparency's Fourier spectrum, then the CGH is the original object,

$$\tilde{u}_s = u_i. \tag{6.212}$$

6.9.4 Increasing the Usable Input Transparency Size

Whether the matched filtering is coherent or incoherent, the resulting cross-correlation function width will be the sum of the widths of $|u_s|$ and $|u_i|$. The area the correlation function may occupy is governed by the fact that computer holograms are sampled devices and so the reconstructed image occupies a space

$$\Delta x = (\lambda z_0)/\delta\mu, \tag{6.213a}$$

$$\Delta y = (\lambda z_0)/\delta v. \tag{6.213b}$$

This is true whether ROACH or binary hologram is used. The reconstruction $u_s(x, y)$ of the CGH must therefore be surrounded by a large zero frame so that the entire image, plus reconstructed width, will fit in the area. The conceptually simplest way this can be done is by CGH oversampling, i.e., surround the original object by a frame of zeroes before DFT is applied. This approach may be quite costly. Suppose a zero frame four times the linear dimension of the hologram is desired. This frame will require approximately $25 \log_2 25 \cong 117$ times as much computing time to perform the DFT, plus about 25 times the auxiliary computing and plotting times. Alternatives are therefore desirable.

We shall describe two alternatives to this costly zero frame. The first combines computer and interferometric holography. The second combines photographic preprocessing with a special variety of CGH.

The first method [6.88, 89] uses the reconstructed image from a CGH as an input to an interferometric hologram recording system. All parts of the CGH reconstruction except the desired image are blocked. The reference wave for the interferometric recording is then brought in at an arbitrarily large angle to the object wave. The resulting interferometric hologram produces a reconstruction of the computer hologram image surrounded by an arbitrarily great dark area. This interferometric hologram can then be used as the matched filter for a large input transparency.

The second method uses a special binary computer hologram together with some photographic processing [6.90, 90a]. Using the format illustrated in Fig. 6.7, the reconstruction can be obtained in any diffraction order simply by changing the maximum amount by which the rectangle is laterally displaced [see (6.53)]. Moving the cell aperture one cell width for a 2π phase shift places the reconstruction in the first diffraction order, while moving $\frac{1}{2}$ cell width for a 2π phase shift causes a reconstruction in the second diffraction order. To maximize diffraction efficiency the rectangle width is set at $1/(2N_d)$ where N_d is the diffraction order in which the reconstruction is to take place. For $N_d > 2$ this results in a hologram whose surface is only sparsely occupied by apertures. The hologram is now photographically interlace replicated. The CGH is copied N_d times with displacement $\delta\mu_c$ of a fraction of one resolution cell width $\delta\mu$,

$$\delta\mu_c = (1/N_d)\,\delta\mu, \tag{6.214}$$

between each copy.

The resulting, interlace replicated CGH reconstructs the desired image in the N_dth diffraction order. It also suppresses all neighboring orders, thereby providing the input zero frame necessary to large input-format matched filtering. The suppression can be understood as follows. The replication can be described by

$$\tilde{H}_2(\mu,v) = \sum_{\alpha=0}^{M_d-1} \sum_{\beta=0}^{N_d-1} \tilde{H}_1[\mu-(\alpha\delta\mu/M_d), v-(\alpha\delta v/N_d)], \tag{6.215}$$

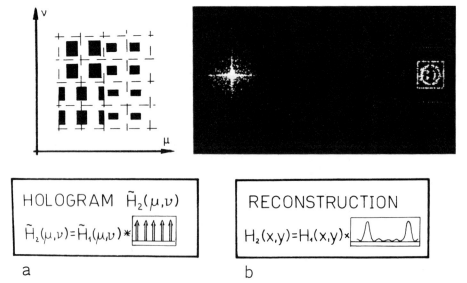

Fig. 6.23. (a) Interlace replicated hologram; (b) envelope function and reconstruction in fourth diffraction order [6.91]

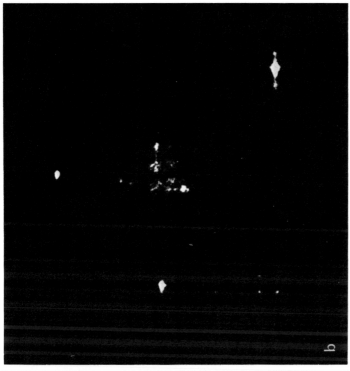

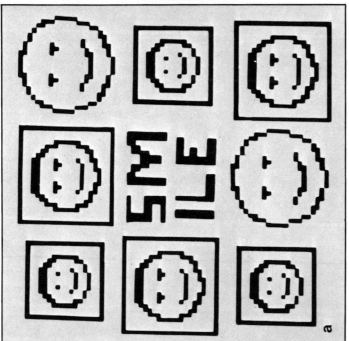

Fig. 6.24a, b. Incoherent matched filtering [6.91]. (**a**) Input; (**b**) result using hologram of Fig. 6.23

where $\tilde{H}(\mu, v)$ is the pre-replication CGH transmittance. Fourier transformation gives

$$H_2 = H_1(x, y) \sum_{\alpha=0}^{M_d-1} \sum_{\beta=0}^{N_d-1} \exp\{2\pi i[(\alpha x \delta\mu/M_d) + (\beta y \delta v/N_d)]\} . \tag{6.216}$$

Summing the geometric series gives

$$H_2 = H_1(x, y) \sin(\pi x \delta\mu) \sin(\pi y \delta v)/[\sin(\pi x \delta\mu/M_d) \sin(\pi y \delta v/N_d)]$$

$$= E(x, y) H_1(x, y) , \tag{6.217}$$

where an uninteresting constant phase factor has been dropped. The envelope function $E(x, 0)$ pictured in Fig. 6.23 suppresses all orders between 0 and N_d and all orders between M_d and $2M_d$ in the x direction and similarly in the y direction. Figure 6.24 shows some results using this method [6.91].

6.9.5 Character Recognition by Principal Components

The present application example uses the flexibility of computer-generated holograms to detect quite artificially constructed objects. This artificial, "principal component", set arises as follows.

Recognizing characters can be done straightforwardly by matched filtering. Given a 32-character alphabet, one can construct 32 matched filters to do the recognition. However, from information theory one knows that it is possible to do the detection with five yes-no decisions. In fact, given 2^{N_f} characters in the alphabet, one needs only N_f filters. Intuitively one might imagine lining the characters in a row from left to right. The first measurement should decide whether the input character is in the left or right half of the row. The next measurement decides which quarter of the row, and so on. One eliminates half the remaining choices with each decision. The problem comes in arranging the characters.

One approach is to break each character in an alphabet into "principal components", functions which are added together in different combinations to form each of the characters [6.92, 93]. For instance, a 32-character alphabet can be made up of sums of 5 principal components. Recognition filters are then matched to each of these principal components. The principal components are found by first digitizing the character set and then applying an algorithm to be described shortly.

The character recognition is done by incoherent matched filtering. We label the intensity spatial distribution for the rth character as $I_r(m, n)$. Noting the sth principal component as $P_s(m, n)$, it is assumed to be composed of a linear combination of characters, i.e.,

$$P_s(m, n) = \sum_r a_{rs} I_r(m, n) \tag{6.218a}$$

$$r = 1, \ldots, N_f \tag{6.218b}$$

$$s = 1, \ldots, \log_2 N_f. \tag{6.218c}$$

The combining weights a_{rs} are defined such that

$$\sum_m \sum_n I_r(m, n) P_s(m, n) = D_{rs}, \tag{6.219}$$

where each D_{rs} is either zero or one. D_{rs} is the cross correlation, at $m=0$, $n=0$, between I_r and P_s. Incoherent matched filters are made of the objects $P_s(m, n)$. Each of the $\log_2(N_f)$ filters is applied to the input character $I_r(m, n)$ resulting in that number of values for the D_{rs}. The ordered values of the D_{rs} then form a binary word associated with one of the characters in the alphabet. The recognition is then completed.

To calculate the principal components P_s, (6.219) is inserted into (6.218), giving

$$D_{rs} = \sum_q a_{qs} \sum_m \sum_n I_r(m, n) I_q(m, n) = \sum_q a_{qs} X_{rq}, \tag{6.220}$$

where the X_{rq} are the values of the correlation function (evaluated at $m=0, n=0$) between the rth and qth characters. If the determinant of the correlation coefficients X_{rq} is nonzero the system of simultaneous linear equations, (6.220), can be inverted to give a_{rs} in terms of the correlations X_{rq} and the code words D_{rs}. The correlations are determined by the character set I_r and the code words can be assigned arbitrarily.

On solving for the a_{qs} and using (6.218) to generate the $P_s(m, n)$, one finds this "intensity" point-spread function to be real but bipolar. To implement this bipolar function using nonnegative physical intensities, the reconstruction system is split into two channels, one corresponding to the negative part $P_s^-(m, n)$ of the principal component $P_s(m, n)$, and one channel corresponding to the positive part $P_s^+(m, n)$,

$$P_s(m, n) = P_s^+(m, n) - P_s^-(m, n). \tag{6.221}$$

This splitting of each of the principal components into two parts also splits each of the code words into two parts so that

$$D_{rs} = D_{rs}^+ - D_{rs}^-, \tag{6.222a}$$

$$D_{rs}^+ = \sum_m \sum_n I_r(m, n) P_s^+(m, n), \tag{6.222b}$$

$$D_{rs}^- = \sum_m \sum_n I_r(m, n) P_s^-(m, n). \tag{6.222c}$$

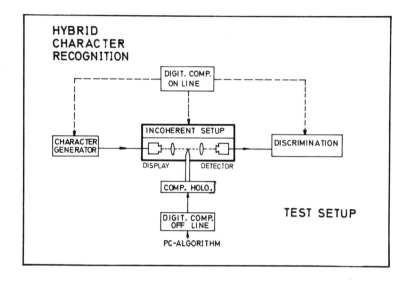

Fig. 6.25a

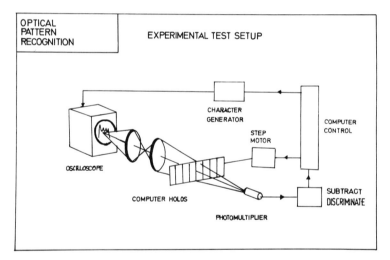

Fig. 6.25b

Fig. 6.25c

Fig. 6.25a–f. Principal character recognition.
(a) Hybrid optical-digital character recognition; (b) incoherent matched filtering using oscilloscope input; (c) input character set; (d) principal components of characters; (e) filter intensity point spread function; (f) intensity correlation output

Fig. 6.25d

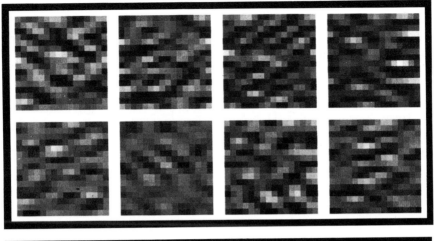

Fig. 6.25e

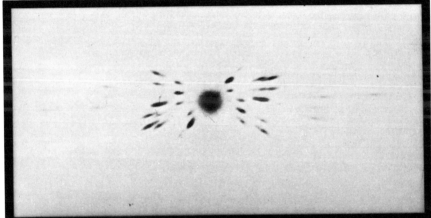

Fig. 6.25f

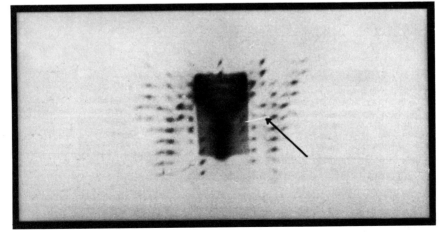

Fig. 6.25d–f. Figure captions see opposite page

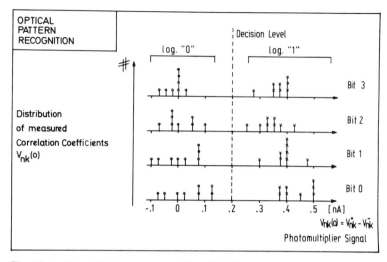

Fig. 6.25g. Principal character recognition. Distribution of the correlation coefficients about the decision level. [6.94]

Table 6.1. Relative advantage of principal component character recognition for alphabets of various sizes

N	2	4	8	16	32	64	128	256
$2\log_2 N$	2	4	6	8	10	12	14	16
$(2\log_2 N)/N$	1	1	0.75	0.5	0.31	0.19	0.11	0.06

Table 6.1 shows a few values of this expression. As the table shows, the advantage in number of measurements for principal component measurements increases.

This principal component recognition system has been built [6.94, 94a]. Some results are shown in Fig. 6.25.

6.10 High Space-Bandwidth Product Holograms

In this section we discuss hardware limitations on the attainable SBWP of computer-generated holograms. We begin by describing a very simple holo-gram generating system. After discussing the limitations of this system we describe first commonly available, then state of the art, generating systems.

We mentioned in Sect. 6.1 that computer-generated holograms generally have a modest SBWP with 128×128 resolution cells given as a typical value. The actual number is determined by two factors: available computing facilities and plotting facilities. The factors can be further divided into hardware, software, and time. The basic limitations are set by the hardware. It is true that, to a certain extent, hardware limits can be extended by the intelligent or even clever use of software techniques, by elimination of unnecessary information as in Sect. 6.6, or by dedicating additional time to each task. Eventually, however, one begins to approach an asymptotic limit which is determined by the given hardware configuration.

As a simple but illustrative example consider the computer hologram generating system to consist of

1) Computer = person + pencil + paper + trig-table.
2) Plotter = person + pen + graph-paper.

Given such a system, one can generally produce a binary cell-oriented "CGH" with a SBWP of 256 (= 16 × 16 resolution cells). A simple object with a closed-form solution for the DFT helps but is not necessary; patience is necessary. Clever "software design" such as making a table of the relatively few sine and cosine values which occur in (6.8) for this small SBWP hologram speeds calculation, though eventually tiredness, boredom, and time pressure lead to error proneness in the "computer". The "plotter" suffers similar difficulties in maintaining positional accuracies of slightly better than 1% (assuming eight-level phase quantization).

These same difficulties are experienced by digital computer systems, though admittedly a bit differently. A commonly available configuration is a small mainframe computer coupled to a pen-and-ink drum plotter. The computer suffers mainly under time pressures: it is time consuming to perform the necessary DFT and to generate the detailed plotting instructions. Again clever software design can minimize the time consumption. For instance, the plotting instructions can be issued by table lookup: the table containing complete resolution-cell structures for all allowed, quantized, cell configurations. This particular "trick" can save up to a factor of 50 in plot instruction generating time on some installations. In this instance table storage capacity is traded for processor time. Where this trade can be effected, the Fourier transform is the limiting time factor. For installations where this is not possible, the Fourier transform and plot-instruction generation times are similar.

With some simple consideration we can now define a somewhat fuzzy boundary a which large SBWP holograms begin to be large. Most small mainframe computers can perform a 128 × 128 Fourier transform reasonably quickly. A 1024 × 1024 transform is generally not reasonably quick and additionally necessitates much manipulation of externally stored data (e.g., on magnetic disk). Plotting a 128 × 128 hologram with 16 levels of phase quantization requires one part in two thousand plotting accuracy. This accuracy is generally obtainable at installations with large modern plotters. The many times much greater number of addressable points of the plotter is generally not reproducibly usable. Paper stretching is one ground (dimensionally stable plotting surfaces are available, but not everywhere), absolute positioning inaccuracy is another. A CGH of 128 × 128 resolution cells is easy to plot, one of 256 × 256 cells is not. From these two, admittedly very rough, considerations of generally available Fourier transform capacity and plotting ability we see that the lower SBWP bound where a CGH becomes large is around 256×256.

Present trends indicate that this largeness boundary will be shifted upward in the near future as it already has been for a few installations. The increasing popularity of the combination minicomputer with array processor [6.95] in picture processing laboratories and elsewhere together with the general increases in computing power, in memory, and mass storage capacity of minicomputers is moving the computing limitations into the background. Plotting limitations are being overcome by several techniques.

The pen-and-ink drum plotter has improved in the past few years to a distortion-free addressable area of 1500×1500 points [6.96], though for the aforementioned reasons it is not well adapted to producing large holograms. An alternative which is designed for rastered graytone picture production rather than line drawing is the light emitting diode (LED) and film drum plotter [6.97]. In this device a film-carrying drum rotates at constant speed in a dark environment. The image of a stationary LED-illuminated aperture is pulsed with variable intensity onto the film so that a line of small aperture images (squares) is recorded. After the line exposure is complete, the LED is moved by a stepping motor parallel to the rotating drum's axis into a position from which it exposes another line along the film. After processing the film one obtains a two-dimensional grid of varying transmittance squares. The square spacing is commonly $25 \mu m$. The exposed area varies between 100×100 mm and 300×300 mm, i.e., 4000 to 12,000 points linearly. Both binary and graytone hologram types can be plotted, though graytone CGHs more effectively utilize the information transfer capacity of the plotter. For many applications the plot may be directly used as the hologram transparency without photographic reduction, though the angular size of a reconstructed image is small. Such a hologram was used in producing the results shown in Sect. 6.9.3. SBWPs of up to 1024×1024 have been reported using this type of plotting device [6.98, 99]. Related flatbed plotters can also be used in the plotting [6.100]. They are generally slower but can address film position with micron accuracy. One device has been reported which can potentially address $125,000 \times 125,000$ points on $0.633 \mu m$ centers [6.101]. It is a relatively fast, flatbed laser scanning device where the focussing optics executes an X scan and the substrate holder executes the Y displacement. The plotting is done in photoresist; no photoreduction is necessary. Holograms generated for a feasibility study utilized $16,000 \times 16,000$ of the distortion-free addressable points. Though this type of device will not be generally available to computer holographers in the foreseeable future, it does demonstrate the realizability of very large computer-generated holograms.

Another possibility for plotting large format CGHs is suggested by electron beam writing devices such as have been described for integrated circuit manufacture or are installed in scanning electron microscopes. Computer holograms of modest SBWP generated by electron beam writing have been reported [6.102–104].

6.11 Computer-Generated Volume Holograms

Volume holograms can reconstruct either monochrome or polychrome images when illuminated by simple white-light sources [6.105]. A computer-generated volume hologram (CGVH) combines flexibility in wave front production with the capability of white-light operation. Since the structures present in a volume hologram are three dimensional and very fine, straightforward calculation and plotting of CGVHs is not practiced. Hybrid methods combining CGH mask production and interferometric recording are applied.

Two methods for producing CGVHs have been published. The first uses three on-axis real-transmittance graytone holograms (see Sect. 6.2.2) to multiply expose an interferometric hologram. The second method used a single off-axis CGH (see Sect. 6.2.4) as the exposing mask.

The first method [6.106] is based on the fact that any complex number lying within the unit circle can be composed of three positive real numbers less than one. These three numbers are shifted by constant phases, then added (see Sect. 6.2.3). If the desired CGVH complex transmittance is $u(x, y)$, this may be written as

$$u(x, y) = \sum_{n=0}^{2} u_n(x, y) \exp(2\pi n i/3), \tag{6.223}$$

where the $u_n(x, y)$ are real and positive.

Consider a multiple-exposure interferometric hologram where a CGH of amplitude transmission $u_n(x, y)$ is placed in contact with the photographic plate for the nth exposure. Consider also that for each exposure a reference wave of unit magnitude but a different constant phase for each exposure is used. The resulting exposure will be

$$\sum_{n=0}^{2} |u_n(x, y) + \exp(-2\pi n i/3)\exp(-2\pi i \mu_0 x)|^2$$

$$= \sum [|u_n(x, y)|^2 + 1 + \exp(-2\pi n i/3)\exp(-2\pi i \mu_0 x)u_n^*(x, y)]$$

$$+ \exp(2\pi i \mu_0 x) \sum u_n(x, y) \exp(2\pi i n/3). \tag{6.224}$$

The last, desired, term in the sum is separated angularly from the others by the carrier frequency coefficient in front of the sum. Since thick holograms can be designed to have only one diffraction order, i.e., to select a small angular band of exiting directions, the remaining terms can be suppressed, leaving only the desired image. The desired color can also be selected from an illumination white-light source.

The second method [6.107] trades simplicity of fabrication against the presence of spurious images produced by the CGVH. Here a single binary mask is placed in contact with the photographic plate. This binary mask is a CGH whose transmittance $b(x, y)$ is a superposition of terms (see Sect. 6.2.4)

$$b(x, y) = \sum_m b_m(x, y). \tag{6.225}$$

Using a plane reference wave gives an exposure

$$|b(x, y) + \exp(-2\pi i \mu_0 x)|^2$$
$$= |b(x, y)|^2 + \exp(-2\pi i \mu_0 x) b^*(x, y) + \exp(2\pi i \mu_0 x) b(x, y). \tag{6.226}$$

Again the influence of the first two terms would be eliminated from a volume hologram since the Bragg condition would not be satisfied. The last term contains all orders of the binary CGH which each represent an isolated image. All of these orders will be reconstructed; the volume nature of the hologram acts mainly as a color filter. Using a ROACH (see Sect. 6.2.2) as a mask instead would result in only the desired image being reconstructed from the illuminating simple white-light source.

6.12 Computer-Generated Polarization Holograms

The term polarization hologram is unfortunately ambiguous. There are holograms which reconstruct the polarization of an object; these we shall call polarization-reconstructing holograms. There are also holograms which are recorded on materials which are sensitive to the polarization of incident illumination and which influence the polarization of transmitted light; these we term polarization-recorded holograms.

Polarization-reconstructing holograms have been proposed [6.108] and implemented as interferometric holograms [6.109, 110]. The principle is easily extendable to computer holograms. A twofold multiplex hologram (see Sect. 6.7.2) is created which reconstructs two-image intensity distributions corresponding to the two polarization components (linear or circular) in the image. The hologram is then illuminated by two reconstruction beams of the corresponding polarizations so that the proper multiplexed images of the proper polarization overlap in register. The method is similar to that described for color reconstructions in Sect. 6.7. In fact, for a mathematical description of the process, (6.193–195) can be applied by simply changing the color subscripts (r, g) to the polarization subscripts (π, σ) and noting that the wavelengths λ_π and λ_σ will be the same for monochrome reconstructions. Polychrome reconstructions are also possible.

The polarization-recorded holograms use the interaction of polarized light and some materials in order to create real-time, erasable CGHs [6.111, 112]. Since a polarized beam is used for readout, the reconstructed image is a scalar, rather than a vector. Polarization-recorded holograms are therefore not polarization-reconstructing holograms. To construct polarization-recorded holograms one needs a material whose polarization properties can be locally influenced. One such family of materials is the M-center supplemented alkali-halide crystals. These materials, when illuminated by a spot of polarized ultraviolet radiation, change their transmission selectively for orthogonal linear polarization directions. Before illumination, the M-center orientations are distributed equally between two directions. At the illuminated spot this equilibrium is disturbed and M-centers align preferentially in the polarization direction of the irradiating beam. The transmission of this area then becomes greater for incident light oriented parallel to the recording direction. Because the equilibrium of orientation has been changed, the orthogonal direction exhibits increased dichroic absorbtion. Illuminating the crystal with randomly polarized light shows, on the average no effect; an analyzer must be used to select one of the preferred directions.

The polarization-recorded hologram offers the possibility of real-time creation of CGHs and the possibility of dynamically varying the CGHs complex transmission.

References

6.1   B.R.Brown, A.W.Lohmann: Appl. Opt. **5**, 967 (1966)
6.2   A.W.Lohmann, D.P.Paris: Appl. Opt. **6**, 1739 (1967)
6.2a   T.Sakurai, M.Karibe, T.Yatagai: J. Appl. Cryst. **7**, 399 (1974)
6.3   J.W.Goodman: *Introduction to Fourier Optics* (McGraw-Hill, New York 1968) pp. 83–89
6.4   T.C.Lee, D.Gossen: Appl. Opt. **10**, 961 (1971)
6.5   L.B.Lesem, P.M.Hirsch, J.A.Jordan, Jr.: Commun. ACM **11**, 661 (1968)
6.6   J.W.Cooley, J.W.Tukey: Math. Comp. **19**, 297 (1965)
6.7   R.C.Singleton: IEEE Trans. AU-**17**, 93 (1969)
6.7a   L.P.Jaroslavski: Radiotechnic **32**, 15 (1977) (in Russian)
6.8   A.W.Lohmann: "The Space-Bandwidth Product Applied to Spatial Filtering and Holography"; Tech. Rept. IBM RJ 438, IBM Research Laboratories, San Jose (1967)
6.9   D.Slepian, H.O.Pollack: Bell Syst. Tech. J. **40**, 43 (1961)
6.10   D.C.Chu, J.R.Fienup, J.W.Goodman: Appl. Opt. **12**, 1386 (1973)
6.11   J.R.Fienup: "Improved Synthesis and Computational Methods for Computer-Generated Holograms"; Ph. D. Dissertation, Dept. of Appl. Physics, Stanford Univ. (1975)
6.12   D.C.Chu: "Spectrum Shaping for Computer-Generated Holograms"; Ph. D. Dissertation, Dept. of Elec. Eng., Stanford Univ. (1973)
6.13   L.B.Lesem, P.M.Hirsch, J.A.Jordan, Jr.: Proc. Symp. Mod. Opt. (Polytechnic Inst. of Brooklyn) **17**, 681 (1967)
6.14   E.N.Leith, J.Upatnieks: J. Opt. Soc. Am. **51**, 1469 (1961)
6.15   W.H.Lee: Appl. Opt. **9**, 639 (1970)
6.16   C.B.Burckhardt: Appl. Opt. **9**, 1949 (1970)
6.17   T.C.Strand: Opt. Eng. **13**, 219 (1974)
6.18   W.H.Lee: Opt. Soc. Am. **62**, 797 (1972)
6.19   B.R.Brown, A.W.Lohmann: IBM J. Res. Dev. **13**, 160 (1969)
6.20   H.Becker, W.J.Dallas: Opt. Commun. **15**, 50 (1975)
6.21   W.J.Dallas: Appl. Opt. **13**, 2274 (1974)
6.22   K.Miyamoto: J. Opt. Soc. Am. **51**, 17 (1961)

6.23   G.L.Rogers: Proc. Roy. Soc. Edinburgh A**63**, 193 (1952)

6.24   R.L.Lamberts: Appl. Opt. **11**, 33 (1972)

6.25   R.E.Haskell, B.C.Culver: Appl. Opt. **11**, 2712 (1972)

6.25a   C.K.Hsueh, A.A.Sawchuk: Appl. Opt. **17**, 3874 (1978)

6.26   R.E.Haskell: J. Opt. Soc. Am. **63**, 504 (1973)

6.27   G.L.Rogers: Nature **166**, 1027 (1950)

6.28   A.Kozma, D.L.Kelly: Appl. Opt. **4**, 387 (1965)

6.29   W.H.Lee: Appl. Opt. **13**, 1677 (1974)

6.30   J.P.Hugonin, P.Chavel: Opt. Commun. **16**, 342 (1976)

6.30a   H.O.Bartelt, K.-D.Föster: Opt. Commun. **26**, 12 (1978)

6.30b   J.Bucklew, N.C.Gallagher, Jr.: Appl. Opt. **18**, 575 (1979)

6.30c   M.J.Bastiaans: J. Opt. Soc. Am. **67**, 1666 (1977)

6.30d   R.A.Gabel: Appl. Opt. **14**, 2252 (1975)

6.30e   J.P.Allebach, N.C.Gallagher, Jr., B.Liu: Appl. Opt. **15**, 2183 (1976)

6.31   W.J.Dallas: "Computer Holograms – Improving the Breed"; Ph. D. Dissertation (Univ. Microfilms Ann Arbor 1973), Appendix E

6.32   A.J.MacGovern, J.C.Wyant: Appl. Opt. **10**, 619 (1971)

6.33   A.F.Fercher, M.Kriese: Optik **35**, 168 (1972)

6.34   P.Chavel, J.P.Hugonin: J. Opt. Soc. Am. **66**, 989 (1976)

6.35   T.S.Huang, B.Prasada: MIT/RLE Quar. Prog. Rep. **81**, 199 (1966)

6.36   T.S.Huang: Proc. IEEE **59**, 1335 (1971)

6.37   H.Kogelnik: Proc. Symp. Mod. Opt. (Polytechnic Inst. of Brooklyn) **17**, 605 (1967)

6.38   M.Kato, Y.Nakayama, T.Suzuki: Appl. Opt. **14**, 1093 (1975)

6.39   A.Ioka, K.Kurahashi: Appl. Opt. **15**, 1787 (1976)

6.40   C.B.Burckhardt: Appl. Opt. **9**, 695 (1970)

6.41   Y.Ichioka, M.Izumi, T.Suzuki: Appl. Opt. **10**, 403 (1971)

6.42   D.C.Chu: IEEE Trans. IT-**18**, 531 (1972)

6.43   D.C.Chu, J.W.Goodman: Appl. Opt. **11**, 1716 (1972)

6.44   R.L.Frank, S.A.Zadoff: IRE Trans. IT-**8**, 381 (1962)

6.45   R.C.Heimiller: IRE Trans. IT-**7**, 254 (1961)

6.45a   N.Nagashima, T.Asakura: Optik **50**, 53 (1978)

6.45b   Y.Torii: Opt. Commun. **24**, 175 (1978)

6.46   W.J.Dallas: Appl. Opt. **12**, 1179 (1973)

6.47   D.Calabro, J.K.Wolf: Inf. Control **11**, 537 (1968)

6.48   J.W.Goodman, A.M.Silvestri: IBM J. Res. Dev. **14**, 478 (1970)

6.49   J.W.Goodman, G.R.Knight: J. Opt. Soc. Am. **58**, 1276 (1968)

6.50   D.Kermisch: J. Opt. Soc. Am. **60**, 15 (1970)

6.51   H.Dammann: J. Opt. Soc. Am. **60**, 1635 (1970)

6.52   T.Yatagai, M.Takeda: Optik **43**, 337 (1975)

6.53   D.Middleton: *Introduction to Statistical Communication Theory* (McGraw-Hill, New York 1960) Sect. 7.7

6.54   N.C.Gallagher, B.Liu: Optik **42**, 65 (1975)

6.55   O.Bryngdahl, A.W.Lohmann: J. Opt. Soc. Am. **58**, 1325 (1968)

6.56   W.J.Dallas: Appl. Opt. **10**, 674 (1971)

6.57   N.M.Blachman: IEEE Trans. IT-**10**, 162 (1964)

6.58   W.A.Pearlman: "Quantization Error Bounds on Computer-Generated Holograms"; Tech. Rpt. No. 6503-1, Information Systems Laboratory, Stanford Univ. (1974)

6.59   A.W.Lohmann: "Comments About Phase-Only Holograms", in *Acoustical Holography*, Vol. 2, ed. by A.F.Metherell, L.Larmore (Plenum Press, New York, London 1970) Chap. 14, pp. 203–210

6.60   R.A.Gabel, B.Liu: Appl. Opt. **9**, 1180 (1970)

6.61   H.Dammann: Phys. Lett. **29**A, 301 (1969)

6.62   J.W.Goodman, R.S.Powers: Appl. Opt. **14**, 1690 (1975)

6.62a   N.C.Gallagher, Jr.: Appl. Opt. **17**, 109 (1978)

6.63   M. Abramowitz, I. A. Stegun (eds.): *Handbook of Mathematical Functions*, 7th printing (Dover, New York 1970) p. 556

6.64   C. S. Vikram, R. S. Sirohi: Appl. Opt. **10**, 2790 (1971)

6.65   W. J. Dallas: IEEE Cat. No. 74CH0862-3C, Digest of Papers, Intern. Opt. Comp. Conf. (1974)

6.66   L. B. Lesem, P. M. Hirsch, J. A. Jordan, Jr.: IBM J. Res. Dev. **13**, 150 (1969)

6.67   L. B. Lesem, P. M. Hirsch, J. A. Jordan, Jr.: Opt. Spectra **4**, 18 (1970)

6.68   W. J. Dallas: Opt. Commun. **8**, 340 (1973)

6.69   J. J. Clair: Opt. Commun. **6**, 135 (1972)

6.70   N. C. Gallagher, B. Liu: Appl. Opt. **12**, 2328 (1973)

6.71   J. P. Waters: Appl. Phys. Lett. **9**, 405 (1966)

6.72   H. Becker: "Synthetisieren von Computer-Hologrammen zur Rekonstruktion dreidimensionaler Bilder"; Diplomarbeit, Inst. Angewandte Optik der Universität Erlangen-Nürnberg (1975)

6.73   R. J. Collier, C. B. Burckhardt, L. H. Lin: *Optical Holography* (Academic Press, New York 1971) pp. 523–541

6.74   M. C. King, A. M. Noll, D. H. Berry: Appl. Opt. **9**, 471 (1970)

6.75   T. Yatagai: Appl. Opt. **15**, 2722 (1976)

6.75a L. P. Jaroslavski, N. S. Merzlyakov: Appl. Opt. **16**, 2034 (1977)

6.75b N. S. Merzlyakov, L. P. Jaroslavski: Sov. J. Phys.; J. Tech. Phys. **47**, 1263 (1977)

6.75c L. P. Jaroslavski, V. N. Karnaukhor, N. S. Merzlyakov: Sov. Phys.; Lett. J. Tech. Phys. **2**, 169 (1976) (in Russian)

6.75d Ref. 6.98, p. 105

6.76   J. R. Fienup: Proc. SPIE **48**, 101 (1974)

6.76a H. Bartelt: Opt. Commun. **23**, 203 (1977)

6.77   E. N. Leith, J. Upatneiks: J. Opt. Soc. Am. **54**, 1295 (1964)

6.78   A. W. Lohmann, B. Morgenstern: Optik **20**, 450 (1963)

6.79   W. J. Dallas, Y. Ichioka, A. W. Lohmann: J. Opt. Soc. Am. **62**, 739 (1972)

6.80   J. D. Kraus: *Radio Astronomy* (McGraw-Hill, New York 1966) pp. 172–198

6.81   G. L. Verschuur, K. I. Kellermann (eds.): *Galactic and Extra-Galactic Radio Astronomy* (Springer, Berlin, New York, Heidelberg 1974) pp. 256–290

6.82   P. Kellman, S. Leonard, E. Barrett: Appl. Opt. **16**, 1113 (1977)

6.83   A. B. Vander Lugt: IEEE Trans. IT-**10**, 2 (1964)

6.84   J. D. Armitage, A. W. Lohmann: Appl. Opt. **4**, 461 (1965)

6.85   C. N. Kurtz, H. O. Hoadley, J. J. De Palma: J. Opt. Soc. Am. **63**, 1080 (1973)

6.86   F. Bestenreiner, W. Weiershausen: Optik **32**, 446 (1971)

6.87   A. W. Lohmann: IEEE Cat. No. 75EH0941-5C, Intern. Opt. Comp. Conf. (1975)

6.88   S. Lowenthal, P. Chavel: Appl. Opt. **13**, 718 (1974)

6.89   W. H. Lee, M. O. Greer: Appl. Opt. **13**, 929 (1974)

6.90   H. Bartelt: "Erweiterung des Orts-Bandbreite-Produkts von digitalen Filtern"; Diplomarbeit, Inst. Angewandte Optik der Universität Erlangen-Nürnberg (1976)

6.90a T. Yatagai: Opt. Commun. **23**, 347 (1977)

6.91   H. Bartelt, W. J. Dallas, A. W. Lohmann: Opt. Commun. **20**, 50 (1977)

6.92   D. Gabor: Nature **208**, 422 (1967)

6.93   B. Braunecker, A. W. Lohmann: Opt. Commun. **11**, 141 (1974)

6.94   B. Braunecker, R. Hauck, A. W. Lohmann: Proc. SPSE Conf. on Image Analysis and Evaluation, Toronto (1976)

6.94a B. Braunecker, R. Hauck: Opt. Commun. **20**, 234 (1977)

6.95   M. Tasto: Opt. Acta **24**, 391 (1977)

6.96   J. C. Wyant, V. P. Bennett: Appl. Opt. **11**, 2833 (1972)

6.97   T. Sandor, G. Cagliusio: Rev. Sci. Instrum. **45**, 506 (1974)

6.98   L. P. Jaroslavski, N. S. Merzlyakov: *Methods of Digital Holography* (in Russian) (Nauka, Moscow 1977) p. 81

6.99   L. P. Jaroslavski, N. S. Merzlyakov: Comp. Graph. Inf. Proc. **10**, 1 (1979)

6.100 K.Campbell, G.W.Wecksung, C.R.Mansfield: Opt. Eng. **13**, 175 (1974)
6.101 K.Biedermann, O.Holmgren: Appl. Opt. **16**, 2014 (1977)
6.102 S.Yonezawa, Y.Kando, S.Kasai, A.Maekawa: Jpn. J. Appl. Phys. **10**, 1279 (1971)
6.103 A.Maekawa, N.Saitou, Y.Honda, Y.Miura: Jpn. J. Appl. Phys. **10**, 1658 (1971)
6.104 O.Ersoy: Optik **46**, 61 (1976)
6.105 H.Kogelnik: Bell Syst. Tech. J. **48**, 2909 (1969)
6.106 D.R.MacQuigg: Appl. Opt. **16**, 1380 (1977)
6.107 S.K.Case, W.J.Dallas: Appl. Opt. **17**, 2537 (1978)
6.108 A.W.Lohmann: Appl. Opt. **4**, 1667 (1965)
6.109 O.Bryngdahl: J. Opt. Soc. Am. **57**, 545 (1967)
6.110 G.L.Rogers: J. Opt. Soc. Am. **56**, 831 (1966)
6.111 M.Nakajima, H.Komatsu, Y.Mitsuhashi, T.Morikawa: Appl. Opt. **15**, 1030 (1976)
6.112 M.Nakajima, M.Sahara, T.Morikawa, Y.Mitsuhashi: Appl. Opt. **17**, 922 (1978)

Subject Index

Digital Picture Analysis

Editor: A. Rosenfeld
1976. 114 figures, 47 tables. XIII, 351 pages
(Topics in Applied Pysics, Volume 11)
ISBN 3-540-07579-8

Contents: *A. Rosenfeld:* Introduction. –
R. M. Haralick: Automatic Remote Sensor Image
Processing. – *C. A. A. Harlow, S. J. Dwyer III,
G. Lodwick:* On Radiographic Image Analysis. –
R. L. McIlwain, Jr.: Image Processing in High
Energy Physics. – *K. Preston, Jr.:* Digital Picture
Analysis in Cytology. – *J. R. Ullmann:* Picture
Analysis in Character Recognition. – Subject
Index.

Laser Beam Propagation in the Athmosphere

Editor: J. W. Strohbehn
1978. 78 figures, 1 table. XII, 325 pages
(Topics in Applied Physics, Volume 25)
ISBN 3-540-08812-1

Contents: *J. W. Strohbehn:* Introduction. Laser
Beam Propagation in the Atmosphere. –
S. F. Clifford: The Classical Theory of Wave Pro-
pagation in a Turbulent Medium. – *J. W.
Strohbehn:* Modern Theories in the Propagation
of Optical Waves in a Turbulent Medium. – *M. E.
Gracheva, A. S. Gurvich, S. S. Kashkarov, V. V.
Pokasov:* Similarity Relations and Their Experi-
mental Verification for Strong Intensity Fluctua-
tions of Laser Radiation. – *A. Ishimaru:* The Beam
Wave Case and Remotes Sensing. – *J. H. Shapiro:*
Imaging and Optical Communication Through
Atmospheric Turbulence. – *J.L.Walsh, P.B.Ulrich:*
Thermal Blooming in the Atmosphere. – Subject
Index.

Laser Speckle and Related Phenomena

Editor: J. C. Dainty
1975. 133 figures. XIII, 286 pages
(Topics in Applied Physics, Volume 9)
ISBN 3-540-07498-8

Contents: *J. C. Dainty:* Introduction. - *J. W.
Goodman:* Statistical Properties of Laser Speckle
Patterns. - *G. Parry:* Speckle Patterns in Partially
Coherent Light. - *T. S. McKechnie:* Speckle
Reduction. - *M. Françon:* Information Processing
Using Speckle Patterns. - *A. E. Ennos:* Speckle
Interferometry. - *J. C. Dainty:* Stellar Speckle Int-
erferometry. - Additional References with Titles.
- Subject Index.

Optical Data Processing

Applications

Editor: D. Casasent
1978. 170 figures, 2 tables. XIII, 286 pages
(Topics in Applied Physics, Volume 23)
ISBN 3-540-08453-3

Contents: *D. Casasent, H. J. Caulfield:* Basic Con-
cepts. – *B. J. Thompson:* Optical Transforms and
Coherent Processing Systems.– With Insights From
Cristallography. – *P. S. Considine, R. A. Gonsalves:*
Optical Image Enhancement and Image Restoration. – *E. N. Leith:* Synthetic Aperature Radar. –
N. Balasubramanian: Optical Processing in Photo-
grammetry. – *N. Abramson:* Nondestructive Testing
and Metrology. – *H. J. Caulfield:* Biomedical Applications of Coherent Optics. – *D. Casasent:* Optical
Signal Processing. – Subject Index.

Picture Processing and Digital Filtering

Editor: T. S. Huang
2nd corrected and updated edition. 1979. 113 figures, 7 tables. XIII, 297 pages
(Topics in Applied Physics, Volume 6)
ISBN 3-540-09339-7

Contents: *T. S. Huang:* Introduction. – *H. C. Andrews:*
Two-Dimensional Transforms. – *J. G. Fiasconaro:*
Two-Dimensional Nonrecursive Filters. –
R. R. Read, J. L. Shanks, S. Treitel: Two-Dimensio-
nal Recursive Filtering. – *B. R. Frieden:* Image
Enhancement and Restoration. – *F. C. Billingsley:*
Noise Considerations in Digital Image Processing
Hardware. – *T. S. Huang:* Recent Advances in Pic-
ture Processing and Digital Filtering. – Subject
Index.

Springer-Verlag
Berlin
Heidelberg
New York

The Monte Carlo Methods in Atmospheric Optics

By G. I. Marchuk, G. A. Mikhailov, M. A. Nazaraliev,
R. A. Darbinjan, B. A. Kargin, B. S. Elepov
1980. 44 figures, 40 tables. VIII, 208 pages
(Springer Series in Optical Sciences, Volume 12)
ISBN 3-540-09402-4

Contents: Introduction. – Elements of Radiative-Transfer Theory Used in Monte Carlo Methods. – General Questions About the Monte Carlo Technique for Solving Integral Equations of Transfer. – Monte Carlo Methods for Solving Direct and Inverse Problems of the Theory of Radiative Transfer in a Spherical Atmosphere. – Monte Carlo Algorithms for Solving Nonstationary Problems of the Theory of Narrow-Beam Propagation in the Atmosphere and Ocean. – Monte Carlo Algorithms for Estimating the Correlation Function of Strong Light Fluctuations in a Turbulent Medium. – References. – Subject Index.

T. Pavlidis

Structural Pattern Recognition

1977. 173 figures, 13 tables. XII, 302 pages
(Springer Series in Electrophysics, Volume 1)
ISBN 3-540-08463-0

Contents: Introduction. Mathematical Techniques for Curve Fitting. – Graphs and Grids. – Fundamentals of Picture Segmentation. – Advanced Segmentation Techniques. – – Scene Analysis. – Analytical Description of Region Boundaries. – Syntactic Analysis of Region Boundaries and Other Curves. – Shape Description by Region Analysis. – Classification, Description and Syntactic Analysis. – References. – Subject Index.

B. Saleh

Photoelectron Statistics

With Applications to Spectroscopy and Optical Communication

1978. 85 figures, 8 tables. XV, 441 pages
(Springer Series in Optical Sciences, Volume 6)
ISBN 3-540-08295-6

Contents: Introduction. – Tools From Mathematical Statistics: Statistical Description of Random Variables and Stochastic Processes. Point Processes. – Theory: The Optical Field: A Stochastic Vector Field or, Classical Theory of Optical Coherence. Photoelectron Events: A Doubly Stochastic Poisson Process or Theory of Photoelectron Statistics. – Applications: Applications to Optical Communication. Applications to Spectroscopy. – References. – Subject Index.

Springer-Verlag
Berlin
Heidelberg
New York